KU-515-220

Budapest

timeout.com/budapest

Ràdlơ

Penguin Books

dús (go⁻)

PENGUIN BOOKS

Published by the Penguin Group
Penguin Books Ltd, 80 Strand, London WC2R ORL, England
Penguin Books USA Inc., 375 Hudson Street, New York, New York 10014, USA
Penguin Books Australia Ltd, 250 Camberwell Road, Camberwell, Victoria 3124, Australia
Penguin Books Canada Ltd, 10 Alcorn Avenue, Toronto, Ontario, Canada M4V 3B2
Penguin Books (NZ) Ltd, cnr Rosedale and Airborne Roads, Albany, Auckland, New Zealand

Penguin Books Ltd, Registered Offices: Harmondsworth, Middlesex, England

First published 1996
Second edition 1998
Third edition 1999

Fourth edition 2003
10 9 8 7 6 5 4 3 2 1

Copyright © Time Out Group Ltd 1996, 1998, 1999, 2003
All rights reserved

Colour reprographics by Icon, Crowne House, 56-58 Southwark Street, London SE1 1UN
Printed and bound by Cayfosa-Quebecor, Ctra. de Caldes, Km 3 08 130 Sta, Perpètua de Mogoda, Barcelona, Spain

Except in the United States of America, this book is sold subject to the condition that it shall not, by way of trade or
otherwise, be lent, re-sold, hired out, or otherwise circulated without the publisher's prior consent in any form of binding
or cover other than that in which it is published and without a similar condition including this condition being imposed
on the subsequent purchaser.

Edited and designed by
Time Out Guides Limited
Universal House
251 Tottenham Court Road
London W1T 7AB
Tel + 44 (0)20 7813 3000
Fax + 44 (0)20 7813 6001
Email guides@timeout.com
www.timeout.com

Editorial

Editor Peterjon Cresswell
Deputy Editors Dominic Earle, Tom Popper, Jonathan Cox
Listings Editor Ildikó Lázár
Proofreader Tamsin Shelton
Indexer Julie Hurrell

Editorial/Managing Director Peter Fiennes
Series Editor Ruth Jarvis
Deputy Series Editor Lesley McCave
Guides Co-ordinator Anna Norman
Accountant Sarah Bostock

Design

Art Director Mandy Martin
Art Editor Scott Moore
Senior Designer Tracey Ridgewell
Designers Astrid Kogler, Sam Lands
Digital Imaging Dan Conway
Ad Make-up Charlotte Blythe
Picture Editor Kerri Littlefield
Acting Picture Editor Kit Burnet
Acting Deputy Picture Editor Martha Houghton
Picture Desk Trainee Bella Wood
Picture Researcher Alex Ortiz

Advertising

Sales Director Mark Phillips
International Sales Manager Ross Canadé
International Sales Executive James Tuson
Advertising Sales (Budapest) In Your Pocket
Advertising Assistant Sabrina Ancilleri

Marketing

Marketing Manager Mandy Martinez
US Publicity & Marketing Associate Rosella Albanese

Production

Guides Production Director Mark Lamond
Production Controller Samantha Furniss

Time Out Group

Chairman Tony Elliott
Managing Director Mike Hardwick
Group Financial Director Richard Waterlow
Group Commercial Director Lesley Gill
Group Marketing Director Christine Cort
Group General Manager Nichola Coulthard
Group Art Director John Oakey
Online Managing Director David Pepper

Features in this guide were written, updated and researched by:

Introduction Peterjon Cresswell. **History** Desmond McGrath, Bob Cohen, Tom Popper. **Budapest Today** Chris Condon.
Accommodation Tibor Sáringer, Peterjon Cresswell. **Sightseeing** Tom Popper, Dave Rimmer, Desmond McGrath, Bob Cohen,
Reuben Fowkes, Gabriella Bartha. **Restaurants** Eileen Brown, Malcolm Carruthers, Tom Popper, Steve Carlson. **Cafés & Bars**
Matthew Higginson, Lucy Mallows, Peterjon Cresswell, Oran Maccuirc. **Shops & Services** Tibor Sáringer, Bob Cohen. **Festivals
& Events** Tom Popper, Bob Cohen. **Baths** Chris Condon. **Children** Ildikó Lázár. **Film** Natalia Jánossy, Peterjon Cresswell.
Galleries Reuben Fowkes, Gabriella Bartha. **Gay & Lesbian** Nathan Sukkar, Judit Hatfaludi. **Music: Classical & Opera** Kevin
Shopland, Lucy Mallows. **Music: Rock, Roots & Jazz** Ágnes Molnár, Bob Cohen. **Nightlife** Matthew Higginson, Tom Popper.
Sport & Fitness Matthew Higginson, Bob Cohen. **Theatre & Dance** Mike Kelly, Reuben Fowkes, Natalia Jánossy. **Trips Out of
Town** Tom Popper, Dave Rimmer, Tibor Sáringer, Reuben Fowkes, Peterjon Cresswell. **Directory** Ágnes Molnár, Chris Condon,
Desmond McGrath, Bob Cohen, Steve Carlson, Kate Carlisle.

The Editor would like to thank: DJ Zózó, Popper úr.

Maps by Mapworld: 71 Blandy Road, Henley-on-Thames, Oxon RG9 1QB.

Photography by Hadley Kincade except: pages 68, 69 A Kertész, Ministere de la Culture – France; 16 Hungarian Military
Museum; 191 Péter Hapák; 155 Ronald Grant Archive.

The following image was provided by the featured establishment: page 113.

© Copyright Time Out Group Ltd
All rights reserved

Contents

Introduction

Aw, you haven't changed a bit...

They can dress you up as an EU capital, throw euros at you, cast you promises of hard-earned fortune, and underneath you'll still be the same old Budapest – shabby, spectacular old Budapest.

The Hungarian capital was created in grand style from 19th-century nationalist endeavour, and rebuilt from conflict and Holocaust before its olive-and-marzipan Habsburg stucco façades were left to crumble in Communist decay. For the last decade, it has been in limbo, trapped in the time freeze of the previous regime while building shiny malls for the new millennium. And not just malls, but bridges, five-star hotels and airport terminals.

And somewhere alongside – certainly in Pest – will still be a third-generation umbrella repair shop with wireless-era signage, offset by 1960s neon, run by an old guy indifferent to ringing up a sale once in a blue moon.

He'll have time for you. Budapest always has time for you. As your umbrella is repaired, three floors up a cellist might be practising, or an old lady beating her carpet as it hangs from the purpose-built frame in the welcome cool of the communal courtyard. Time passes satisfyingly. Only recently have a few locals begun to make hesitant steps down the metro escalator instead of blocking it two-by-two, because catching this train matters more than waiting two minutes. The hangover from the old days means a superb, cheap transport system and little street crime – but awkward shop staff and the smell of cheap meat, of making ends meet in a society of scarcity.

By nature of its geography (Germanic? Balkan?), history and downright singularity, Hungary is like a revolving door through which many cultures pass. Budapest can seem like some bizarre hotel with Turkish baths, Socialist plumbing, Slavic death-wish drinking habits, Balkan coffee customs and Habsburg upholstery, where the bellhops only speak the bastardised slang of Volga fur trappers and the piped music is pentatonic folk with its roots in remote northern China. Still, you could be somewhere bland and brand-named, where no one plays grand piano in the main station bar or repairs other people's umbrellas.

Few cities have a backdrop as spectacular as the Danube, panoramically dividing inescapably bourgeois Buda from busy Pest, moving traffic between the Black Forest, Belgrade and the Black Sea. Budapest is not only a river city, it's a port city, lascivious when required and, thanks to its bathhouses, a resort city. Strolling towards the Danube, quiet, dusty downtown streets offer shards of riverscape before the waterfront throws open a burst of cityscape so dramatic, the tingle of the moment will transmit a secret promise of return. Nothing at all can touch it, not even remotely, not even in Brussels.

ABOUT THE TIME OUT CITY GUIDES

The *Time Out Budapest Guide* is one of an expanding series of Time Out City Guides produced by the people behind London and New York's successful listings magazines. Our guides are all written and updated by resident experts who have striven to provide you with the most up-to-date information to explore the city, whether you're a local or first-time visitor.

THE LOWDOWN ON THE LISTINGS

Above all, we've tried to make this book as useful as possible. Addresses, telephone numbers, websites, transport information, opening times, admission prices and credit card details are all included in our listings, all checked and correct at the time we went to press. However, in a city like Budapest, opening hours – of small shops and major tourist attractions – are subject to change. We would advise you whenever possible to phone ahead. While every effort has been made to ensure the accuracy of the information contained here, the publishers cannot accept responsibility for any errors it may contain.

PRICES AND PAYMENT

Prices throughout this guide are given in euros (€) or Hungarian forints (Ft). The prices we've supplied should be treated as guidelines, not

Advertisers

We would like to stress that no establishment has been included in this guide because it has advertised in any of our publications and no payment of any kind has influenced any review. The opinions given in this book are those of Time Out writers and entirely independent.

gospel. If they vary wildly from those quoted, please let us know. We aim to give the best and most up-to-date advice, so we always want to know if you've been badly treated or overcharged. We have noted whether venues take credit cards, but have listed only the major ones – American Express (**AmEx**), Diners Club (**DC**), MasterCard (**MC**) and Visa (**V**).

THE LIE OF THE LAND
Budapest is divided into 23 different districts, *kerületek*, indicated by a Roman numeral before the street name. Postcodes are written in four figures, the middle two indicating the district: 1051 is District V. In listings we've used the Roman numeral because it's easier for finding your way around town. For an overview of the city districts, *see p44*. Wherever possible, a map reference is provided for every venue listed, indicating the page and grid reference at which it can be found on the street maps.

TELEPHONE NUMBERS
To call other places in Hungary from Budapest, or to call Budapest from the rest of the country, you have to dial 06 first, wait for the second tone, and then follow with code and number. You also have to dial 06 for mobile phones. To

call Hungary from abroad, you must dial 36 and then 1 for Budapest, followed by the number given. For more information on telephones and codes, *see p230*.

ESSENTIAL INFORMATION
For all the practical information you'll need for visiting the city – including emergency phone numbers, visa and customs information, advice on facilities for the disabled, a list of useful websites and the full lowdown on the local transport network in and around Budapest – turn to the **Directory** chapter. You'll find it at the back of this guide, starting on p212.

LET US KNOW WHAT YOU THINK
We hope you enjoy the *Time Out Budapest Guide*, and we'd like to know what you think of it. We welcome tips for places that you consider we should include in future editions of the guide and take notice of your criticism of our choices. There's a reader's reply card at the back of this book – or you can email us at guides@timeout.com.

There is an online version of this guide at **www.timeout.com**.

Money matters
Hungary will accede to the European Union in May 2004 – but is unlikely to adopt the euro until 2007, at the very earliest. Until then, forints will be the currency in use.

WE ADD A NEW DIMENSION TO INTERNATIONAL HOTEL STANDARDS IN BUDAPEST

STYLE AND HISTORY EQUALS THE ROYAL ART OF TRAVEL.

With a grand investment the Royal has been brought back to life. Now it is time to experience Budapest's newest 5-star Luxory Hotel:

€ 180

per night including Executive Club Service:

– Royal Breakfast
– Coffee, Tea, Refreshments
– Cocktail hour

excluding tax.

Valid upon availability!
Please refer to this advertisement.

CORINTHIA
GRAND HOTEL ROYAL
★★★★★
BUDAPEST

A legend reborn

FOR FURTHER INFORMATION PLEASE CONTACT ANDREA KOLTAI, royalres@corinthia.hu,
TEL.: (+36-1) 479 4813, FAX: (+36-1) 479 4333

In Context

History

Location, location, location – strategic Budapest has been attracting foreign developers for 2,000 years.

Buda and Pest are considered two distinct settlements by those who live on either side of the Danube. Buda's leafy hills are a retreat from the dusty bustle across the river. Pest is the stage for the city's commercial, political and cultural life, where careers are made, strangers become friends and the future takes shape. Set on a vast plain, it seems open to all possibilities.

The fault line is something more than a psychological one. Budapest sits on an ancient geological rift, a line of least resistance that attracted the waters of the Danube south in their search for a resting place. It's too deep to disturb the city today, but that fault line determined the whole character of Budapest millennia ago, ensuring that the hills stayed on one side and the level plain on the other. When the first humans arrived here, some half a million years ago, those hills were seen as prime real estate, a defensible settlement with a fabulous view. Later still, the plain of Pest proved the ideal greenfield site for the rapid urban expansion which took place in the 19th and 20th centuries.

EARLY HISTORY

The earliest human history in what is now Hungary consisted of agricultural communities around the River Tisza, where large neolithic sites have been discovered. During the first millennium BC, Illyrian populations shared the plains with groups of Celtic peoples, known as the Eravi. They settled by the natural springs of Buda; excavations have unearthed a Celtic site on Gellért Hill, and remains at Óbuda, an area conquered by the Romans in 35 BC.

The region now enters written history, and was officially incorporated into the Roman Empire in 14 BC under the name Pannonia. Known to the Romans as Aquincum, Buda was a modest trading town on the far edge of the empire. Today, you can see Roman ruins at the Aquincum Museum *(pictured, see also p65)*, including an old amphitheatre. More Roman ruins can also be seen across the Danube in Pest, at Március 15 tér.

Meanwhile, political and cyclical climatic changes in Central Asia were inducing the first of a series of westward migrations in what is known as either the 'Age of Barbarians' or the

'Age of Migrations'. In 430 the Huns, a Central Asian confederacy of Turkic-speaking nomads, burst into Europe. Under Attila, they defeated the Romans and vassals alike. Attila returned to Pannonia in 453 without sacking Rome, but died mysteriously on the night of his wedding to Princess Ildikó. Legend has it that he's buried near the River Tisza, in eastern Hungary.

The Huns returned to their homelands. Next came the Avars, then the Bulgars, Turkic peoples from the Volga steppes. Meanwhile, the lands west of the Danube were being populated by more sedentary, agricultural Slavs, closely related to today's Slovenians.

ENTER THE MAGYARS

The exact origin of the Hungarian people is unknown (*see below* **Who do they think they are?**). We do know that Magyar is a branch of the Finno-Ugric language group, a subgroup of the Altaic language family of Finns, Turks, Mongolians and many Siberian peoples. The earliest Hungarian homeland was in the dense forests between the River Volga and the Urals.

These proto-Hungarians moved south into the central Volga region around 500 BC. In the first centuries AD, the Hungarians came into contact with Turkic cultures pushing west, but historically speaking, the Magyars first became known in the seventh and eighth centuries as vassals of the Turkic-speaking Khazar Empire between the Black and Caspian Seas.

By the 800s the Hungarians were based in today's Ukraine and had begun raiding deep into Frankish Europe. St Cyril described the horde of Magyars he met in 860 as *luporum more ululantes*, 'howling in the manner of wolves'. Faced with a howling gang from Asia pillaging the Holy Roman Empire, Western Christendom amended the Catholic mass with: 'Lord save us from sin and the Hungarians'.

While the main Magyar armies spent the spring of 895 raiding Europe, their villages were devastated by Bulgars and Pechenegs.

Who do they think they are?

Alone in a sea of Slavs, the Magyars are a breed apart. Why? Where on earth could Árpád's ancestors have possibly come from?

The Byzantines mislabelled them 'Turks' or 'Ungeri' after the Ten Arrows confederation of Central Asian tribes. Medieval Hungarian chroniclers recorded that Hungarians came from 'Magna Hungaria' in the east, so King Béla IV sent the monk Julianus to the Volga to search for those lost Magyars. Hungarians have been researching their origins ever since.

Hungarians were fascinated by the myth of Hun origins. Poet János Arany's epic poem about the Huns, written in the 19th century, influenced generations into believing a literary device to be the explanation of their national origins (Attila is still a common first name).

In the 1820s scholar Sándor Körösi Csoma (*see p9* **One-offs Csoma**) travelled to Tibet in search of lost Hungarians. The fact that he didn't find any was more due to his sojourn in a remote Himalayan refuge; malaria found Csoma before he could find traces of Magyar origins across the forbidden territory of Tibet. At the time, his failure was considered proof that Asian soil held no secrets of Hungary's ancient past. This was encouraged by the ruling Habsburgs, keen to play up ties closer to Europe – in particular Finland, whose language shares certain similarities with Hungarian. A century later, the Soviets found it expedient to link Hungary's past to lands found within the USSR. Hungarians, of course, saw this as a Communist plot, but linguistic ties do link Magyar, Vogul and Ostyak, spoken by 35,000 fur trappers and fishermen on the left bank of the Ob river in the northern Ural region of Siberia. You can still buy 'three fish' using Hungarian if you ever find yourself on the Ob in need of lunch.

Meanwhile, others were looking further east. Csoma himself believed that Uigur people of Central Asia held the key. Chinese annexation in 1915 of the Uigur homelands beyond the Gobi Desert closed its borders to foreigners for 70 years. A thaw between Moscow and Beijing in the 1980s allowed in a handful of scientific visits from 'friendly' states. From 1986, a research team under anthropologist István Kiszely nosed around Xinjiang province in north-west China. In 1995, 50 kilometres east of Urumchi, they excavated 1,200 graves and found objects similar to ones in Hungarian cemeteries of the ninth and tenth centuries. 'The methods of burial and writing systems have definite similarities,' declared Kiszely, proudly. He even heard an Uigur folk ballad, telling of one tribe venturing west, never to be seen again. According to Kiszely, Magyar and Finnish ancestors then spent three generations camped near each other in the Urals, hence the linguistic similarities, before they separated. The jury, however, is still out.

A 3 8   S H I P

THE COOLEST PLACE IN THE CITY

OPEN EVERY DAY
ALL YEAR AROUND
11:00 — 04:00

3 FLOORS- 2000M2 RESTAURANT,
GREAT VIEWS, CONCERT HALL,
BARS, TERRACES, DANUBE

JAZZ, WORLD MUSIC,
ROCK, DJs
WWW.A38.HU

VÉGE A SZOKÁS
HATALMÁNAK

A38

eatdrink.timeout.com

Subscribe now
for a taste of over
2,500 London bars
& restaurants

eatdrink.timeout.com Time Out's
online bar and restaurant guide

The surviving tribes of Magyars, led by their king, Árpád, fled across the Verecke pass in the northern Carpathians and on to the Hungarian plain. Meeting little resistance from the local Slavs, Goths and Avars, the Hungarians pushed their competitors, the Bulgars, south of the Danube, and began raiding as far west as France, Germany and northern Spain. They continued to plunder Western Europe until they were defeated by German King Otto I at the Battle of Augsburg in 955. Retiring to Pannonia, the Hungarians realised that an alliance with a major power might be a good idea. This meant dealing with the Christian church.

THE ROAD TO FEUDALISM

Hungary was poised between the Byzantine Orthodox and Roman churches, when King Géza, Árpád's grandson, requested missionaries be sent from Rome to convert the Magyars to the Western church, still trumpeted as a decision to be 'linked with the West'. Géza was baptised along with his son, Vajk, who took the name István (Stephen) upon his accession to the Hungarian throne on Christmas Day 1000.

King Stephen didn't have an easy time convincing his countrymen. Tribes loyal to the older, shamanic religion led a revolt in 1006. One consequence was the death of Venetian missionary St Gellért, put into a spiked barrel and rolled down Gellért Hill by miffed Magyar traditionalists. Stephen crushed the revolt and set about destroying the power of the chieftains by appropriating their land and setting up a new class of nobles. He minted coins, forged

alliances, built castles and put Hungary on the road to feudalism. He was canonised in 1083.

Stephen's son, Imre, died young, and the next 200 years saw many struggles for the throne of the House of Árpád, a preferred tactic being to blind potential rivals. Despite this, Stephen's successors consolidated and expanded the kingdom, conquering as far as Dalmatia. At home, tribal revolts were common.

The tensions between the landowning nobility and the office of the king were eventually settled by the signing of the 'Golden Bull' under King András in 1222. It recognised the nobility as the 'Hungarian Nation', granted them an exemption from taxation and laid the framework for an annual assembly of nobles, the Diet. This was to be held in Rákos meadow in Pest; the annual gathering of the nation's high and mighty provided a push that helped Pest grow into a central market town.

In 1241 the Mongol invasion devastated Hungary. Towns were sacked, crops burned and regions depopulated. The invaders chased King Béla IV to Dalmatia, only to return east a year later after the death of the Great Khan. Béla built a series of castles, including Buda, that came to dominate the Magyar realm.

HUNGARIAN RENAISSANCE

When Béla's son, András III, died without leaving an heir, the House of Árpád came to its end. The Hungarian crown eventually settled on the head of Charles Robert of Anjou in 1310, inaugurating 200 years of stability. Charles Robert and his son, Louis the Great, made Hungary into one of the great powers of

One-offs Sándor Körösi Csoma

Of all the unique Magyars, surely linguist and scholar Sándor Körösi Csoma was the most bizarre. Born to peasant stock in a remote Transylvanian village in 1784, Csoma spent his life in extreme penury and hardship, desperate to find the key to the origins of the Magyar race and tongue. In vain.

In the end, he trekked thousands of miles on foot from Transylvania to Tibet – and spent entire Himalayan winters hunched over rare Tibetan texts in tiny unheated cells of fortress monasteries 3,000 metres up, living off yak blood soup and sleeping on stone floors – which only compounds the extent of his quite magnificent, ultimately miserable failure.

Although Csoma eventually produced the world's first English-Tibetan dictionary, opening up this closed culture to the West,

this task set by William Moorcroft of the East India Company waylaid Csoma for the worst part of a decade. Csoma found nothing pertaining to Hungarians.

Still convinced that their roots roots lay with the Uigurs of north-west China (*see p7* **Who do they think they are?**), after his life-wasting sidetrack, poor Csoma lay on his malarial deathbed babbling away to any baffled westerner who would care to listen about a long-lost tribe.

Csoma died with a legacy of an obscure dictionary the size of a doorstep – and a plaque raised to him 200 years after his birth in Aleppo, Syria, where he slipped by unnoticed en route to Tibet in 1820.

Only the odd passing Magyar would be able to read the plaque today.

Rebel leader Rákóczi II.
See p12.

medieval Europe, a position financed by the output of gold and silver mines in Slovakia and Transylvania. Their successor was Sigismund of Luxembourg, convenor of the Council of Constance and eventual Holy Roman Emperor.

The threat lay to the south, where the remorseless expansion of the Ottoman Empire in the Balkans was eventually stemmed by János Hunyadi, a Transylvanian prince who finally regained control of Belgrade in 1456. Church bells rang all over Europe. Hunyadi's death then led to a bloody struggle for the throne, until in 1458 one of his sons, Mátyás, found himself king by default at the age of 16.

With Mátyás, known to Western historians as Matthias Corvinus, Buda became the focus of Hungarian life. He undertook building within Buda Castle and constructed a palace at Visegrád. Among his achievements was the Royal Library, one of the world's largest. It's said that Mátyás roamed the countryside, disguised as a peasant, seeking out injustices in the feudal system. Even today, his name symbolises good governance. 'Mátyás is dead,' goes the saying, 'and justice died with him.'

Further afield, Mátyás halted the Ottoman advance in Bosnia while expanding his empire to the north. His chief instrument of war, a highly efficient one, was the multi-ethnic Black Army of mercenaries. With his own standing army, a rarity for the time, Mátyás didn't have to depend on the nobles for recruits.

When Mátyás died heirless in 1490, the legacy of culture and order he'd built collapsed. The nobles resented him as a strong leader who could dispense with their services, and chose a weak successor. They appropriated land and taxes, sold his library and dismissed the Black Army. Hungary has never won a war since.

> **'The nobles sold off the Royal Library and dismissed the Black Army. Hungary has never won a war since.'**

In 1514 the Pope ordered a new crusade against the Turks. Hungary's peasantry, under the leadership of György Dózsa, rallied near Pest and turned against the nobles. They were quickly defeated. Dózsa was burned on a hot iron throne and his followers were made to bite into his roasting flesh. The nobility also voted in the Tripartum Law, reducing the peasantry to serfdom and forbidding them to bear arms. Their timing could not have been worse.

A TURKISH PROVINCIAL CAPITAL
When the young Hungarian King Lajos II, with 10,000 armoured knights, met the Turkish cavalry on the swampy plains of Mohács on 29 August 1526, some 80,000 Ottoman spahis routed the Hungarians in under two hours. Lajos drowned in a muddy stream, trapped in heavy

from Bohemia and Galicia, settling in Pest, just beyond the dismantled city walls in what is today District VII. This neighbourhood became the centre of Hungarian Jewry, and is still the most complete Jewish quarter remaining in Eastern Europe (*see p76-7* **Jewish Budapest***)*.

NATIONAL REVIVAL

Repercussions of the French Revolution were felt all across Europe, even in Hungary. A conspiracy of Hungarian Jacobins was nipped in the bud, and its leaders executed near Déli station on land still known as the 'field of blood' (Vérmező). Their ideas gained an audience through the Hungarian-language writings of Ferenc Kazinczy. As the 19th century dawned, Hungarians eagerly embraced their own tongue as a revolutionary and literary language, even if it was only spoken by peasants, and by nobles in the Calvinist east. Hungarian now began to unite people as 'Hungarian' and not 'Habsburg'.

This period is known as the Reform. Buda and Pest perked up under the Embellishment Act, an 1808 law which began to plan the city on modern development ideas. After the floods in 1838, Pest was redesigned along a pattern of concentric ringed boulevards. The man of the day was Count István Széchenyi, who sought to bring Hungary out of its semi-feudal state and into the world of industrialisation, credit financing and middle-class gentility (*see p11* **One-offs Széchenyi***)*. While he championed the ideal of development within the Habsburg Empire, other members of the Diet were less accommodating. Lajos Kossuth, a minor noble of Slovak origin, was the eloquent voice of nationalist sentiment against Austrian rule. His popular appeal to the powerful middle gentry saw Széchenyi overshadowed.

Pressure on Habsburg internal affairs elsewhere led to a lessening of repression in 1839, and a reform-oriented liberal Diet was convened, led by Ferenc Deák. Kossuth lambasted the Austrian administration. The debate grew until civil nationalist uprisings spread across Europe in 1848, threatening the old monarchical order. On 3 March Kossuth delivered a parliamentary speech demanding a separate Hungarian ministry and an end to tax privileges for land-owning nobles.

HEADY DAYS OF REBELLION

On 15 March Kossuth met with the cream of Hungarian dissident liberals in the Pilvax coffeehouse (*see p35*) to develop a revolutionary strategy. Among the rebels was the poet Sándor Petőfi who, later that day, famously read his newly penned poem *Nemzeti dal* ('National Song') on the steps of the National Museum – an event still commemorated annually.

A proposal for a liberalised constitution, giving Hungary far-reaching autonomy, was dispatched to Vienna that day and consented to by the frightened Imperial government. On 7 April the Emperor sanctioned a Hungarian Ministry headed by Count Lajos Batthyány, and including Kossuth, Széchenyi and Deák. Hungarian was made the language of state; freedom of the press, assembly and religion were granted; noble privileges were curtailed; and peasants were emancipated from serfdom.

This might have satisfied some, but Kossuth wanted a separate fiscal and army structure. The new Diet went against the Emperor and voted in funding for the creation of a 200,000-man army. Kossuth's tactic was short-sighted. Hungary's minorities comprised over 50 per cent of the population, but they essentially lost all rights under the new constitution. This made it easy for Vienna to encourage a Croatian invasion of Hungary to induce a compromise, and soon the entire region was at war. Buda and Pest fell early to the Austrian army and the Hungarian government moved to Debrecen while fighting continued. By the spring of 1849, the Hungarian troops had the upper hand.

Emperor Franz Joseph appealed to the Tsar of Russia for help. With Russian troops, the rebellion was quickly, and brutally, crushed, and Kossuth fled to Turkey. Petőfi was killed on a battlefield in Transylvania. The Hungarian generals were executed, celebrated by Austrian officers clinking beer glasses, a custom socially taboo in Hungary until recent times.

THE GOLDEN AGE

With the crushing of the rebellion, Hungarian prisoners were made to construct an Austrian military redoubt, the Citadella, atop Gellért Hill (*see p57*). Its guns were intended as a deterrent to any future Hungarian attempts to dislodge Habsburg power.

The Austrians' military defeat in Italy in 1859, however, made accommodation with the Magyars a political necessity. In Pest, the remnants of the Liberal Party coalesced around Ferenc Deák, who published a basis for reconciliation with the Austrians in 1865.

The *Ausgleich*, or Compromise, of 1867 made Hungary more like an equal partner in the Habsburg Empire. Austria-Hungary was to be a single entity with two governments and two parliaments, although ruled by Habsburg royalty, who would recognise the legitimacy of the crown of St Stephen. For the first time since 1526, Hungarians were again rulers of modern-day Slovakia, Transylvania, northern Serbia, and northern Croatia as far as the Adriatic.

The year 1867 also saw a law guaranteeing civic and legal equality to Jews, whose status

was unique in the region. Many arrived from Poland and Russia, their know-how developing industry and construction (*see p76-7* **Jewish Budapest**). This half-century until World War I is known as the Golden Years. Buda, Óbuda and Pest were officially united as Budapest in 1873. Pest boomed with urban development projects, such as Andrássy út and the Nagykörút, which linked once separate districts. Pest became the hub of a rail system bringing many in from the country. Even today, Hungarians refer to Budapest as simply 'Pest'.

Landowners deserted the countryside to man the vast bureaucracy needed to administer the state-run railway, schools, hospitals and post service. The city's population rose from 280,000 in 1867 to almost a million on the eve of war. By 1900 Budapest was the sixth largest city in Europe. The language of administration was Hungarian. The boom came with the Magyarisation policies of Prime Minister Kálmán Tisza (1875-90). He feared the Austrians could endanger Hungary's newly strengthened position by leverage among the non-Hungarian minorities of the empire, just as in 1848. His response was a programme to assimilate the assorted Croats, Slovaks and Romanians of the Hungarian realm. He declared all schools would have to teach in Hungarian, and attempts were made to make Magyar the language of churches. The policy laid the groundwork for the minority unrest that would cost Hungary dear in 1918 and still festers among Hungary's neighbours.

Hungarian became the linguistic ticket to success in Budapest. A lively cultural life began to flourish, as artists, writers and politicians exchanged ideas in the coffeehouses of Pest.

HŐSEINK EMLÉKÉRE

NATIONAL CONFIDENCE

Emperor Franz Joseph, on the 25th anniversary of the 1867 agreement, issued a decree that Budapest was to be a capital equal to that of Vienna. The city became the focus of a new sense of national confidence and, in anticipation of the millennial anniversary of Árpád's invasion, a huge exposition was planned.

The celebration in the City Park incorporated continental Europe's first underground railway, leading to a gargantuan memorial to Árpád and his chieftains. An exhibition hall was built and today houses the Agriculture Museum. Nearby, the Wampetics Gardens, home to celebrity chef Károly Gundel (*see p103*), served traditional cuisine with a touch of French flair. Hungarian food was the culinary fad of the new century.

It was also the golden age of Hungarian literature and arts. Mór Jókai was one of the most widely translated novelists in the world. Endre Ady's volume of new poetry, *Új versek*, sparked a veritable literary explosion. Béla Bartók and Zoltán Kodály created the study of ethnomusicology, composing masterpieces of modern music based on Magyar folk traditions, while architects such as Ödön Lechner drew on Magyar motifs for the art nouveau buildings sprouting up around the city (*see p72-3* **Art nouveau Budapest**). The city was also at the forefront of cinema and photography (*see p68-9* **Black-and-white Budapest**), and became the in-spot for the vacationing aristocracy of Europe.

The new Parliament building, opened in 1902, was the largest in the world, naively anticipating a long and prosperous rule. Politics, however, began to take an ominous turn. Working-class unrest first asserted itself on the great May Day demonstration in 1890 and its influence grew over the next decade. Ageing Liberals were challenged by newer right-wing elements who introduced Austrian-influenced anti-Semitism, previously alien to Hungarian political and social life, into political dialogue. Meanwhile, Hungary's high-handed administration of non-Magyars fuelled resentment and nationalism. Slavs and Romanians headed in droves for Paris or America, where a modest political voice could be heard. To the south, an idea of a South Slav ('Yugoslav') nation gained credence. The vast edifice of the revived Hungarian kingdom rested on rotten foundations.

POLITICAL INCONGRUITY

As World War I came to an end, so did the Austro-Hungarian Empire. When Hungary declared its independence as a republic on 16 November 1918, the country was faced with food shortages and unsympathetic neighbours aligned with France. No clear lines existed at the border, while Serbian troops occupied Pécs and the French camped in Szeged. At the post-war negotiations in Paris, the peacemakers were resolved to uphold promises made to bring Romania into the war. In America, Czech leader Masaryk found favour with Woodrow Wilson on issues of national self-determination. In late 1918 British forces had bombarded Austrian lines with leaflets promising independence for subject nationalities. The die was cast.

Hungarian diplomatic efforts at Versailles fell on deaf ears. Their own sorry treatment of minorities proved as good an advert as any for ethnic self-determination, the guiding principle behind the redrawing of Europe. The French were keen to take strategic rail lines out of Hungarian hands – Romania would be granted not only Transylvania, but also the Magyar towns of Szatmár (Satu Mare), Nagyvárad (Oradea) and Temesvár (Timisoara), all on a

The Romanian army enter Budapest on 3 August 1919.

major line. When the Allies showed their determination to give over two-thirds of Hungary's territory to neighbouring states, the government of Mihály Károlyi resigned and handed over power to the Social Democrats. They in turn made a coalition with the new Hungarian Communist Party.

On 21 March the Hungarian Soviet Republic was declared by Béla Kun, who formed a Red Army, nationalised Budapest's banks and institutes, and sent emissaries to the new Soviet Union. Moscow did nothing in response. Czech and Romanian armed forces entered a Hungary in chaos. As severe food shortages swept the nation, Kun's new currency wasn't even valid in most shops. The Romanian army occupied Budapest on 3 August 1919. Kun and his ministers fled to Vienna, most never to return.

Admiral Miklós Horthy entered Budapest from Szeged mounted on a white horse at the head of 25,000 Hungarian troops. The weeks that followed were known as the 'White Terror', as Communists and Jews were killed for their collaboration, real or otherwise, with the Kun regime. On 25 January 1920, Hungarian national elections brought in a Christian-right coalition parliament, with Admiral Horthy as regent. Hungary was now a monarchy without a king, led by an admiral without a navy.

> **'Refugees clogged the city, unemployment raged and the economy virtually came to a standstill.'**

On 4 June 1920 the Treaty of Trianon was signed in Versailles. Overnight, Hungary had lost two-thirds of its territory and a third of its Hungarian population. Budapest was now the only major city in Hungary, a city of one million in a country of seven million. Refugees clogged the city, unemployment raged and the economy virtually came to a standstill.

THE SILVER AGE

A new political coalition came to power under Count Gábor Bethlen, a skilful conservative. He kept left and right in check and worked abroad to gain international credit and sympathy. Budapest continued to be the focus of national development. Financial stability returned,

prison and 200,000 fled Hungary. Nagy was executed in secret in 1958. Slowly, some made surreptitious visits to his secret grave at Plot 301 of Újköztemető. His official reburial there in 1989 relit public dissent months before the fall of the Wall.

Kossuth tér is also a major memorial site. The eternal flame of 1956 burns faintly in a marble block; the Ministry of Agriculture is dotted with bronze spheres in memory of demonstrators shot by the ÁVH. A statue of Nagy (*pictured*) stands on a bridge, implying his dilemma. Significantly, Nagy is turned away from the Soviet liberators' monument on Szabadság tér, and faces Parliament, the seat of Hungarian sovereignty.

and appeasing the population. Abroad Hungary maintained a strong Cold War stance and toed the Moscow line; at home Hungarians enjoyed a higher standard of living than most of Soviet Eastern Europe. Life under Kádár meant food in the shops but censorship and 'psychological hospital' prisons for dissenters. By the 1960s, the rubble from World War II and the aftermath of the 1956 revolution were cleared away. Historic buildings were restored, museums replacing ministerial buildings in Buda. Tourism began to grow, although Western visitors were still followed around by government spies after dinner.

Kádár's balancing act reached giddy heights in 1968. When Czechoslovakia irked the Soviets with the reforms of the Prague Spring, Hungarian troops loyally participated in the invasion. At the same time, Kádár introduced

his 'New Economic Mechanism', a radical new economic reform that broke with previous hard-line Communist theory and laid the ground for modest entrepreneurship.

By the 1980s flaws in 'Goulash Communism' grew harder to ignore. Hungary became more dependent on foreign trade and inflation rose. Hungary's relations with its Warsaw Pact neighbours was beginning to show signs of strain. A number of writers started to test the limits of open criticism, and Hungary became the centre of Eastern Europe's boom in banned *samizdat* literature.

Younger party members began to take positions of power. Known as the 'Miskolc Mafia', after the city where they'd begun their political careers, many, such as Prime Minister Károly Grósz and his successor Miklós Németh, openly tolerated debate and 'market socialism'.

INTOXICATING POSSIBILITIES

In 1989 the bubble burst. In July people took to the streets to rebury the remains of Imre Nagy. It was a hero's funeral attended by thousands. The 'reform Communists' who controlled power declared that political parties could form to discuss the possibility of free elections.

Most damaging to the Iron Curtain was the mass exodus of East Germans to the West through Hungary. When Hungary ceremonially cut the barbed wire fence on its Austrian border, thousands of East Germans poured into Hungary 'on vacation'. East Germany's faltering Communist government was incensed when trainloads of refugees were taken by the Hungarian government on 'tours' that dropped them conveniently by the Austrian border.

Hungary had tipped over the first domino, bringing about the collapse of Communism in Eastern Europe. Hungarians breathed a sigh of collective relief, then got down to the business of politics. The Communist Party changed its name to the Hungarian Socialist Party and declared that it was running in the elections.

All talk was focused on new-found freedoms, democracy and market capitalism. Many were quick to position themselves in the emerging economic picture. Others found themselves confused and frustrated by yet another upheaval in history. The elections of March 1990 brought in a coalition led by the Hungarian Democratic Forum, a mixed bag of nationalist and conservative views. The 'change of system' (*rendszerváltás*) brought more than just democratic government. The face of Budapest changed as new businesses opened and fast-food restaurants began replacing the city's classy old neon. Street names were changed, so that Lenin Boulevard and Marx Square were no longer, and their respective statues and monuments were removed to the Statue Park (*see p86-7* **Socialist Budapest**). A law forbade public use of 'symbols of tyranny', such as red stars or swastikas.

A new class arose, the *menedzser*. Many found opportunities working in Western businesses. But the boom didn't materialise. Unemployment rose as state industries were privatised or shut down, high inflation ruined pensioners' savings and incomes, and homeless people appeared. For many, the standard of living dropped below pre-1989 levels, when prices were fixed and services subsidised by the state.

A MATURING DEMOCRACY

Nostalgia for more stable and affordable times contributed to the 1994 election triumph of the Socialist Party, led by Gyula Horn, the man who, as Communist foreign minister, opened the borders in 1989. The Socialists, along with

their coalition partners the Free Democrats, prescribed austerity and belt-tightening. This meant more privatisation, forint devaluations, slashes in social funding and high energy prices to set Hungary towards EU membership.

Foreign investors loved it, and the revived Budapest stock exchange enjoyed two years as the world's fastest growing stock market. As the currency and the banks were stabilised, many companies made Budapest their regional centre. Shiny office blocks and business centres, rendered less obnoxious by height restrictions, settled among their crusty brick-and-plaster elders. New malls finished off the corner shop.

Hungarians, particularly those in the countryside, baulked. The winners were foreign or old Communists, the losers were ordinary folk and their traditional ways and values. In 1998, voters turned to a third party, the Young Democrats (FIDESZ), founded and led by the charismatic Viktor Orbán. Born out of a late-1980s student activist group, this party initially adopted a liberal stance, then swung right as the Democratic Forum splintered. The change was marked by the addition of 'Hungarian Middle Class Party' to the official moniker.

Orbán began promoting pre-war Christian-national values, most conspicuously by taking the crown of St Stephen out of the National Museum, floating it up the Danube for a consecration ceremony in Esztergom Cathedral, then installing it in Parliament. Relations between state and city reached a nadir, as cosmopolitan Budapest was viewed as 'non-Magyar', just as it had been a century earlier.

FIDESZ re-ordered the political landscape in stark left-right terms, bringing a new level of bitterness to debate ahead of the 2002 elections. FIDESZ MPs called the opposition traitors for failing to support nationalist initiatives, and the party attempted to monopolise patriotism on the national holiday of 15 March.

Ultimately, it was too much. Hungarians shocked FIDESZ by voting in the Socialists again, albeit by a narrow margin. The new Prime Minister was Péter Medgyessy, a former banker and finance minister in the old regime.

For Budapest, led by liberal mayor Gábor Demszky, the return of the Socialist-Free Democrat alliance was good news. Financing for a fourth metro line, thwarted by FIDESZ in 1998, looks likely to be approved. Having joined NATO in 1999, Hungarians voted in favour of entering the European Union in a 2003 referendum, and will become EU citizens on 1 May 2004. Again, nobody is expecting utopia. But the new pragmatists in power have figured out one thing better than their predecessors – how to tap into EU funding.

Key events

c1000 BC Celtic tribes inhabit Danube Basin.
c500 BC Proto-Hungarians begin migration.
35 BC Romans conquer Basin, or Pannonia.
6 AD Pannonians rebel against Romans.
430-52 Huns make Hungary their base for European excursion.
700-850 Hungarians serve as vassals of the Khazar Empire in southern Russia.
895 King Árpád leads Hungarians across Carpathians into the Danube Basin.
955 King Otto of Bavaria defeats Hungarians at Augsburg, ending period of Hungarian raids.
972 King Géza and his son Vajk convert to Christianity.
1000 Vajk enthroned as King István (Stephen) with a crown donated by Pope in Rome.
1006 Revolt of pagan Hungarian leaders.
1066 First written example of Hungarian.
1222 'Golden Bull' signed by nobles at Rákos meadow, defining the Hungarian nation.
1241 Mongol Invasion.
1243 King Béla IV decrees the building of fortified towns. Buda gains in importance.
1301 House of Árpád ends.
1396 Hungarians defeated by Ottoman Turks at Nicopolis.
1456 János Hunyadi defeats Turks at Belgrade.
1458 Hunyadi's son Mátyás crowned King of Hungary. Buda's first 'Golden Age'.
1490 King Mátyás dies, leading to chaos between nobles and peasants.
1514 Peasants revolt, unsuccessfully. Peasantry reduced to serfdom.
1526 Turks led by Suliman the Magnificent defeat Hungarians at Mohács, then burn Buda.
1541 Buda occupied by Turks.
1683 Turks defeated at Siege of Vienna.
1686 Habsburgs defeat Turks at Siege of Buda. Buda destroyed.
1699 Turks relinquish claims to Hungary.
1703 Hungarians led by Ferenc Rákóczi rebel unsuccessfully against Austrians.
1723 Habsburgs claim right to rule under the Hungarian crown.
1808 The Embellishment Act sets guidelines for the urban development of Buda and Pest.
1839-49 Construction of the Chain Bridge.
1848 Hungarians rebel unsuccessfully against the Austrians.
1867 *Ausgleich* signed, uniting Austria and Hungary as Imperial equals.
1873 Pest, Buda and Óbuda united as Budapest.
1896 Budapest hosts Millennial Exhibition.
1914 Austria-Hungary enters World War I.
1918 Austria-Hungary loses World War I. Hungary declares independence from Austria.

1919 Shortlived Soviet Republic under Béla Kun. Romanian army occupies Budapest. Return of Admiral Horthy.
1920 Treaty of Trianon is signed. Hungary loses two-thirds of its territory to neighbouring states.
1938 Hungary, allied with Nazi Germany, receives a part of Slovakia under the second Vienna Awards.
1940 Hungary is awarded most of Transylvania. Hungarian troops assist Nazi invasion of Yugoslavia.
1943 Hungarian army defeated by Russians.
1944 Horthy kidnapped by Nazis, Arrow Cross Party begins murders and mass deportations of Jews to concentration camps.
1945 Red Army captures Budapest.
1946 Hungarian monarchy abolished and a Hungarian People's Republic declared.
1948 Land ownership collectivised.
1949 Mátyás Rákosi, Communist chief, executes traditional Hungarian Communist Party leaders.
1953 Stalin dies. Rákosi replaced by Imre Nagy, then by Ernő Gerő.
1956 Hungarians revolt against Russian occupation. Hungarian Socialist State proclaimed by Imre Nagy, but Russian tanks soon move in. Budapest in ruins. János Kádár placed in power by Russians.
1963 Kádár declares a partial amnesty for those jailed for their role in the 1956 revolt.
1968 Hungary aids Russia in crushing the Prague Spring. Kádár institutes his 'New Economic Mechanism' allowing restricted private enterprise.
1978 The crown of St Stephen is returned to Hungary.
1989 Kádár dies. Mass protests. Reform Communists promise free elections. East Germans flee via Hungary. Communist Party defunct.
1990 Hungarian elections elect conservative government headed by Hungarian Democratic Forum (MDF). Hungary declared a Republic.
1994 Socialist Party trounces MDF in the second democratic election. Gyula Horn is named Prime Minister.
1998 Elections replace Socialists with a FIDESZ-led coalition. Vicktor Orbán is new Prime Minister.
1999 Hungary joins NATO.
2002 Bitter election run-offs see the Socialists return to power under Péter Medgyessy.
2003 Overwhelming 'Yes' vote in EU referendum.

The new face of Millenáris Park.

Budapest Today

Brussels beckons as the Hungarian capital papers over the cracks of history.

Budapest is pinching itself. On 1 May 2004, barring any last-minute shenanigans in Brussels, Hungary will join the European Union, along with nine other lucky winners. Budapest will, at last, become an EU capital.

It's hard to overstate the meaning this has to many locals. Some still remember the whistle of bombs falling from Allied planes in World War II and the boom of Soviet tank fire in 1956. Many more recall the fear of snitches and secret police that persisted well into the 1970s. The latter days of Goulash Communism, Hungary's ever-softening brand of Soviet despotism, were pleasant enough. Food, fags and booze were cheap. Satellite television brought a window to the West. Foreign travel was possible. Yet life was still filled with lies. The Party still jailed dissidents, and the economy ran on borrowed cash. The city, once grand and imperial, had grown shabby where it hadn't been destroyed, bland where it had been rebuilt. The pace of life was slow. Budapest was caught on the wrong side of history, watching life charge past from the other side of Europe's great fence.

The Changes changed everything. Suddenly, the fence was gone and the world came charging into Budapest. The ground grew thick with managers over from London, Amsterdam and Chicago. The bars were even thicker with freelance journalists and itinerant English teachers. Budapest itself began hurrying to get somewhere and, in the process, become something different. The next 13 years were a blur, a rush to leave one great dark century and head for some other splendid destination. In that quest, EU membership took on great symbolic power. For starters, it represented economic prosperity and the great conviction that Budapest – and Hungary – would no longer be left behind. It also meant restoration to Budapest's rightful place geopolitically and culturally, so it was said over and over again, in the heart of Europe. This is, after all, a city that hates to be told it lies in Eastern Europe. No, no, this is Central Europe, you will hear. For Hungarians, it seems, part of the indignity of living in the Soviet bloc was in being lumped with countries like Romania and Bulgaria.

Now they've made it, Hungarians may not know what to make of their arrival. Expectations can be dangerous things. Looking back some day, they'll surely realise the excitement lay in the getting there. It's also certain, and already apparent, that Budapest has erupted into something very different from the droopy Socialist flower of 1989.

HUNGARY FOR CHANGE

It was never possible to completely manage the frenetic pace of change that's transformed this city. But Budapest does have a plan. It's had one, in fact, since Gábor Demszky became mayor. First elected in 1990 at the age of 38, Demszky is now in his fourth term. He's a former dissident who made his name leading pro-democracy demonstrations and handing out banned literature in the 1980s. Some of the police he employed when he first took office were the same who'd beat him in jail cells only a few years before. His moral authority propelled him to office, but his vision and his skills as a dynamic manager have kept him there. Under Demszky, fiscal discipline, long-term planning and intelligent financing have delivered a steady stream of public works projects that, together, have made for spectacular renewal. New water mains, tram tracks and road reconstruction projects are constantly under way. A new bridge gracefully spans the Danube. Several downtown areas have been pedestrianised, adding energy and commerce to sleepy neighbourhoods (see *p80* **Pedestrianised Budapest**). Once-shabby Ráday utca is now lined with the kind of modern cafés and gastrobars that would grace any capital in the West (see *pp108-123*). Pavements, once monopolised by parked cars and dog mess, look cleaner and wider every year. Two more bridges over the Danube are planned, as is a fourth metro line.

Not everything is under the good mayor's control, of course. The plan to build the new metro line was blocked for four years after political foes on the centre-right won national elections in 1998. That same government halted construction of a new **National Theatre** (see *p191*) in the heart of the city at Erzsébet tér. They sited it a few miles further south, by the river, rewarding contracts to a set of politically connected architects and construction companies, and leaving a giant hole in the ground outside the city's main bus station at Erzsébet tér – explaining the ugly plaza that sits there now.

But something else has proven even more difficult to corral than politics: the raw energy of capitalism. To a limited extent, Budapest has become Everycity. Postmodern commercial uniformity, just like Tokyo, London, New York and LA, paints the city centre. Aggressive glass office blocks lurch over busy intersections across from more gentle turn-of-the-century houses and churches. Brash multistorey malls have risen from vacant lots and railyards, packed with Benetton, Marks & Spencer, bowling alleys and cineplexes. Billboards for *Shape* magazine and Deejay Rádió compete for space with a barrage of multinational corporate logos: Citibank, Volkswagen, KPMG, Sony, Coca-Cola, Philips. On and on it goes. Ten years ago it was almost impossible to find a lime in this city. Now you can dine on internationalised versions of dishes from Vietnam, Argentina, India, Iran and Mexico, not to mention every imaginable form of fast food. Waiters are even helpful. Hunglish is today's lingua franca for restaurant etiquette, not GCSE German.

No less than the infrastructure, architecture, shopping and restaurants, the people have been transformed too. Already by the late 1980s you could find the *menedzser*, something of a chancer with good connections. He stalked the street in a purple shellsuit, white short-sleeved shirt and white socks peeking out of his worn black loafers. He's already a museum piece, replaced by an army of twenty- and thirty-something modern-day capitalists who look and act the part. They trade stocks and currencies, arrange credit and merge companies. They lease fleets of cars, design software, create advertising campaigns, produce reality TV shows, launch glossy magazines and web portals. And don't think they had to relearn the world around them. The 30-year-old Hungarian has no adult memory of Communism. It makes the generation gap – driven wide by pop culture and technology – positively gape from the quantum leap in the range of professional and personal possibilities brought by political and economic change.

Thus the Budapest of only 15 years ago – a place that had actually changed very little in the previous 75 years despite wars and revolutions – is slipping away. It sometimes seems that the old face of the city, along with the city's own memory, is being built over and replaced at breakneck speed. To some, that's disturbing. An English teacher, having spent some time in Budapest in the 1980s, recently wrote in the *Spectator* his lament for the simpler, less materialistic Eastern Europe that was vanishing. Too many McDonald's, too much capitalist money-grubbing, no more poetry and classical music on state TV, he moaned. True, perhaps. But it couldn't have been more patronising. Some visitors seem to regret that Eastern Europe's cities can't be preserved in their dreary yet charming

Fun and games at the Budapest Parade.

pre-capitalist form, like giant theme parks for Westerners eager to imagine travelling (but not living) behind the Iron Curtain. And wouldn't the noble savages be happier that way, carrying on in dignity without the venality of HBO, credit cards and three-ply tissue paper? Thankfully, Budapesters can make their own choices. And when they can afford (and they can afford more and more), they've chosen the same trash and treasure the rest of the post-industrial world has chosen.

HIDDEN PAST

But let's not get carried away. The Everycity crust, though very real and ever thickening, goes only so deep. Much of what lies beneath the new surface – physical and psychological – remains distinctly Budapest. Some of it is greyscale Soviet bloc at its finest. Other layers carry the scars of war or reflect lost Habsburg grandeur. And still deeper are echoes of a more distant, foggy past that whispers of the East.

Budapest is filled with niches and hideaways, time capsules of scenery and people touched in many ways but not fundamentally changed by the Changes. On the fringes of town, in Csepel, Békásmegye or Kelenföld, a great mass of the city's inhabitants live in faceless post-war tower blocks, around which local butchers, bakers and greengrocers run a brisk trade. After all, taking advantage of Tesco means you need a car and a big fridge. Small basement wine bars, choked with smoke, still pack in the early-morning crowd starting at 6am.

Back near the centre, much of turn-of-the-century Budapest actually remains neglected by the renovation boom. For every sparkling building on the main boulevards, dozens of sooty façades line the quiet side streets, flaking bricks and masonry. Plenty of bullet holes remain too. The ones in Pest date mostly from 1956, those in Buda from World War II. Venturing into any dilapidated old house can

yield surprises. If once an elegant residence, most of the details of wealth will be gone. Small clips often dot the recess of each stair, where brass rods once held carpets neatly in place. Hollow niches speak of stolen statuary. Maybe a few panes of stained glass remain. And there's always the courtyard. Some are paved over and draped with laundry. Others are overgrown oases of ivy, great trees and crumbling fountains. It's said that during the Soviet siege of Budapest in 1944-45, the dead, including many hundreds of soldiers, were buried in courtyards, it being too dangerous to venture out in some quarters. The old buildings always have old residents watching carefully over these little open spaces. Shocking events were played across their very eyes, decade after decade. Depressions, occupations, deportations, bombardments, dictatorships and knocks at the door late in the night. And like the silent, leafy courtyards, the old witnesses are unnoticed and forgotten by the bustle outside.

Deeper layers are harder to find. Some, strangely, are revealed only by visitors. Watch for plump middle-aged women in black skirts and vests, kerchiefs tightly fastened over their hair. These are rural Transylvanian Hungarians who've come to sell fresh vegetables at outdoor markets or embroidered linens and clothing to tourists along Váci utca. They travel to Budapest from villages in Romania that have preserved the least spoiled (or most isolated) versions of Hungarian culture, dating back hundreds of years. To 21st-century Budapesters, they're like annoying or amusing time travellers, carrying hints of the foggy Magyar past.

Here and there, traces of Ottoman occupation remain, most strikingly in the still-working Turkish baths (*see p54* **Turkish Budapest**). The Rudas and Király baths date from the 16th century. And atop a hill overlooking Margaret Island from Buda lies another 16th-century Turkish remnant, the now-restored tomb of Gül Baba, a noted poet and bektashi dervish sent to Hungary by Suleiman the Magnificent. Not far from the site are Roman ruins dating from the third century. Wave after wave of new conquerors have swept through here, each bringing their own new era.

The galloping onslaught of global capitalism hasn't really destroyed its predecessors. They may end up hidden more and more as the years go by, but here they'll remain, waiting to be rediscovered by someone willing to look for them. Perhaps that's why many of those old folks quietly watching over Budapest's silent courtyards don't ever let events excite them one way or the other.

Hungary in the European Union? History is simply adding another layer.

Accommodation

Accommodation 26

Features

Accommodation

From neo-baroque to modern, the building boom has given Budapest five-star
quality – and visitors the odd bargain.

The millennial building mania has re-mapped
the boundaries of Budapest for the urban
traveller. That makes accommodation the least
of your worries – so long as you know your
criteria. If you're looking for location, the
dilemma is: how central do you want to be?
Even in the more residential and green Buda
side of the city, you might be only a bridge
away from the heart of town in Pest. Also, bear
in mind that you might just end up counting
one star too many for the rate you're paying –
especially if you bargain or look on the net.
Given the renovation and refurbishment rush,
another criterion should be style: will it be neo-
baroque, neo-classical, Jugendstil or modern?
Also be aware that the quality of the rooms will
improve tremendously if the hotel has recently
been refurbished, which might override
financial concerns.

Most of the good news is happening at the
upper end of the market, in the four- and five-,
even five plus-star category. Still, prices will be
lower than at comparable hotels elsewhere in
the world, so they're worth a try. Also, the
three-star segment has been developing at a
slower, but nonetheless promising pace, and
many three-stars now offer four-star services.

Competition has improved service as well,
with a trickle-down effect at budget hotels,
although don't be surprised if you're being
served in the middle of someone's conversation
with another staff member or friend. Also,
Hunglish can come off as rude, which probably
has more to do with a lack of communicative
English than ill manners. Still, English is now
more widely spoken than German.

There's now a comprehensive catalogue of
accommodation online at www.hotelinfo.hu,
www.hotels.hu, www.travelport.hu,
www.ohb.hu (complete with a booking tool) or
the Hungarian National Tourist Office's own
official site www.hungarytourism.hu, where
there's a thematic search function.

It's possible to book your room upon arriving
at Ferihegy airport. Both terminals have an
airport minibus service desk, with a select list
of hotels, from expensive to budget, on offer at
rates generally under walk-in prices. You will
be required to pay 10-20 per cent of the rate at
the desk, and the rest at the hotel. There have
no commission charge. At Keleti main train

station, **Wasteels** books primarily modest
three-star hotels and apartments, mostly in the
vicinity of the station itself.

In town, for a full list of accommodation,
pick up a catalogue at the Hungarian National
Tourist Office's **Tourinform** offices, now
conveniently located at central locations, as
well as Nyugati station. The one just off Váci
utca is open round the clock. **INKA Travel**
operates a 24-hour booking office, Hotel Service
(previously run by IBUSZ), where practically
any type of accommodation is available – from
hotel rooms to private rooms and apartments.
INKA's partners offer a discount here, but the
staff will also book any specific room you want.
There's no booking fee. **Expressz** and **IBUSZ**,
two of the die-hard full-service travel agencies,
offer discounts at their partner hotels, but will
book any specific location with no booking fee.

High season runs from late spring to early
autumn with prices hiked accordingly. Seasonal
specials lift or lower prices: around Christmas
rates can hit rock-bottom, with the New Year
suddenly shooting them back up. Similarly, the
Spring Festival (in March) is a rate-raiser, and
the Grand Prix (the third weekend of August)
simply runs riot on rates and availability.

WHAT'S ON OFFER?

Many hotels have been rebuilt, renovated or
refurbished, and many in the industry speculate
on whether or not Budapest is big enough to
sustain the oversaturation of investment at the
top end of the hospitality industry. The classic
five-stars lining the Danube on the Pest
embankment have all upgraded their services:
the **Inter-Continental Budapest** has
refurbished all its floors and built one of the
city's biggest convention centres. The **Hyatt
Regency** is to boast the Sofitel brand as of July
2003, and the **Marriott Hotel** is gradually
renovating its rooms. Boldly facing the Chain
Bridge stands the landmark **Gresham Palace**,
a new addition to the Four Seasons family –
lavish, luxurious and laden with history,
scheduled to open late 2003. Away from the
Danube, the **Kempinski** is a reminder of the
city's transition into the free market in the early
1990s, outshone in architectural serenity by the
new **Le Meridien**. The körút is being dragged
into the future of urban regeneration by the

The best Hotels

For sightseeing
The **Hilton** (see p31) is built into the very walls of the Castle District, adjacent to Matthias Church and the Fisherman's Bastion, and offers superb views over Pest and the Danube.

For history
The **Astoria** (see p37) is steeped in historical significance, not all of it cheery. Used by both the Nazis and the Soviets as headquarters in 1944 and 1956, the Astoria was also the meeting place for the first Hungarian government of 1918. Nearby stands the National Museum, where poet Sándor Petőfi urged patriots to revolution in 1848. Earlier that day, the revolutionaries had met at the **Pilvax** coffeehouse (see p35), converted into a chain hotel in the 1990s.

For the coolest lobby
Nothing can be more chic than the domino-patterned rugs of New York designer Donald Sultan, as displayed in the lobby of the boutique **art'otel** (see p40 **The postmodern delights of Sultan's boutique palace**).

For sheer class, the reconstructed **Corinthia Grand Hotel Royal** (see p36 **The empire strikes back**) has the original fittings from the empire days of the late 19th century.

For spa therapy
The classic **Gellért** may have all the trappings and lashings of tradition, but requires interior renovation. Set on Margaret Island, the **Danubius Grand** combines fin-de-siècle style with superb spa facilities and treatments. See p39 **Taking the waters**.

For backpackers
The **Caterina** (see p42) is set in a lovely building in a handy downtown location; the **Citadella** (see p42) is no-frills but is panoramically perched on top of Gellért Hill.

For leafy surroundings
The **UhU Villa** (see p35) is nestled among fir trees, an easy tram ride from the bustle of Moszkva tér; the more remote **Petneházy Club Hotel** (see p35) has horse-riding and hiking opportunities on its doorstep.

massive reconstruction of the luxury **Corinthia Grand Hotel Royal** (see p36 **The empire strikes back**) and the ongoing renovation of the **New York Café** (see p111 **So good they built it twice**) on the same ring road. Across the river, the **Hilton** has been renovating its rooms, while the opening of the **art'otel** (see p40 **The postmodern delights of Sultan's boutique palace**) marked the millennium on the Buda side of the Danube.

Down the pyramid, the Hilton chain opened a four-star branch, the very modern **Westend Hilton**, as part of one of the grandest construction projects of Pest. The former **Palace Hotel** has been restored to its Jugendstil glory, pushing the limits of downtown out to Blaha Lujza tér. And Király utca now has a new three-star hotel, the **Fiesta**, located in one of the hottest spots in Pest.

Another option native to Budapest is the spa hotel – the city's healing waters have been attracting tourists for over a century (see p39 **Taking the waters**). Along with the famous if faded **Gellért**, there are modern alternatives on Margaret Island, outer Pest and in Óbuda, and by late 2003 the **Corinthia Grand Hotel Royal** will be the first to offer spa facilities downtown.

In between, various older hotels are scattered. Commie kitsch or pure period, all offer a novel insight into the history of taste – or history of Budapest. The **Pilvax** and **Astoria** ooze the air of old times, while the **Taverna** and the **Erzsébet** offer a conveniently central but soulless atmosphere. Alternatively, try smaller privately run hotels or *panziók*, where service might be more personal, although the overall environment will be simple and standardised.

Non-smoking rooms, a slew of international TV stations, internet access, lifts, fax, currency exchange and air-conditioning are now basic services at the upper end of the industry. At the lower end, make sure you specify your needs when you make your reservation.

ROOMS AND APARTMENTS
Private rooms (*fizetővendég szolgálat*) are the least expensive choice in the city outside of the youth hostel scene (singles range from Ft1,000 to Ft2,000, doubles Ft3,000 to Ft5,000). Expressz and IBUSZ book private rooms, although fewer people are offering rooms to let in their homes; safety concerns have brought that line of business into recession.

If your budget dictates that you must rent a room in someone else's private house, always make sure to book it through a reputable

Radisson SAS
Béke Hotel
Budapest

Hospitality is the science of care & comfort

A friendly oldtimer with all modern amenities one can need, located in the heart of the city.

239 air-conditioned rooms, 8 suites, all with private bathroom, direct dial telephone, minibar, colour TV with satellite programs, pay movie, personal safe, Internet access. Non-smoking and business class rooms.

Szondi Lugas Restaurant is member of the Chaine des Rotisseurs, Zsolnay Café offers excellent home made cakes. Drinkbar, swimming pool with sauna, indoor garage, 24-hours room service, same day laundry.

6 function rooms for 2 x 300 persons on two levels.

Please contact us for further information.

Radisson SAS Béke Hotel
H-1067 Budapest, Teréz krt. 43.
Tel.: (+361) 889 3900 · Fax: (+361) 889 3915
E-mail: Sales.Budapest@RadissonSAS.com
www.radissonsas.com

Radisson SAS
HOTELS & RESORTS

agency, which at least means that the rooms – and their owners – have gone through some kind of inspection process.

For a longer-term stay, apartment hotels now take a significant slice of the local hospitality industry. The Marriott's own residences occupy a separate building around the corner from the main hotel. **Hotel Charles** (formerly the Charles Apartments) is an old and nondescript favourite in Buda. Smaller private hotels also offer apartments at very reasonable rates. *See also p227* **Flat hunting**.

CAMPING

Budapest boasts several campsites, the better ones in leafy Buda. Most are clean and well kept – some even have a swimming pool. Prices vary from around Ft1,500 to pitch a tent to Ft2,000 for caravans and Ft2,500 for bungalows. If you're planning on camping here in the summer months, book ahead. If you're planning to camp illegally, don't – the city parks and green spaces are regularly inspected for that very reason. Tourinform can provide a full list of available campsites; the following is the largest in town and open all year round.

Római Camping

III. Szentendre út 189 (368 6260/ romai@matavnet.hu). HÉV to Római fürdő. **Open** all year round. **No credit cards.** Room for more than 2,000 campers at this huge site on the main road to Szentendre. Facilities include laundry and the use of a swimming pool.

PRICES

Prices are usually quoted in Hungarian forints, euros or US dollars, but payments can be made in all of them. (*See p3* **Money Matters**) The smaller the hotel, the further its flexibility. Prices here are listed in euros, which in 2003 trade at around Ft250. Rates include breakfast and 15 per cent tax (12 per cent VAT and three per cent tourist tax), unless otherwise noted. It's always worth haggling, even in five-star hotels.

The prices given are for a double room at low and high season. Allowing for the occasional discrepancy for bargain weekend rates, we have classified hotels into four categories: deluxe (above ¤270); expensive (¤170-¤270); moderate (¤70-¤170); and budget (below ¤70). Such is the range of rooms on offer at the larger hotels that some may straddle two or three categories.

Booking

American Express

V. Deák Ferenc utca 10 (235 4330/fax 235 4339). M1, M2, M3 Deák tér/tram 47, 49. **Open** 9am-5.30pm Mon-Fri; 9am-2pm Sat. **Credit** AmEx, DC, MC, V. **Map** p249 C4.

Hotel reservations are provided free for AmEx Platinum cardholders, $20 for anyone else. Make sure to ask about discounts.

IBUSZ

V. Ferenciek tere 10 (Hotels & panziók: 485 2716/fax 342 2594. Rooms & apartments: 485 2767, 485 2769/fax 337 1205/www.ibusz.hu). M3 Ferenciek tere/bus 7. **Open** 8am-4pm Mon-Thur; 8am-3pm Fri. **Credit** MC, V. **Map** p249 C4.

Room and apartment bookings are separate from hotels and *panziók*. Both offer comprehensive lists at better than walk-in hotel rates. No booking fee.

INKA Travel

V. Apáczai Csere János utca 1 (266 8042/fax 483 1685). M1 Vörösmarty tér/tram 2. **Open** 24hrs daily. **No credit cards. Map** p249 C4.

Books for any of Budapest's hotels, private rooms, *panziók* or apartments free of charge, and will often offer you a better rate than you would get by going directly to the hotel yourself.

Expressz

V. Semmelweis utca 4 (266 3277/fax 266 6191/ www.expressztravel.hu). M2 Astoria/bus 7. **Open** 9am-5.30pm Mon-Fri. **Credit** AmEx, DC, MC, V. **Map** p249 D4.

Reserves rooms in any of Budapest's hotels, private rooms, *panziók* or apartments with no commission charge – often giving you a better rate than you would get if approaching the hotel directly.

Tourinform

V. Sütő utca 2, V. Vigadó utca 6, Nyugati station by platform 10 (438 8080/fax 488 8661/ www.hungarytourism.hu). M1, M2, M3 Deák tér/tram 47, 49. **Open** Sütő utca & railway station outlets 8am-8pm daily; Vigadó utca outlet 24hrs daily. **No credit cards. Map** p249 C4.

No room bookings, but stop by any time to pick up a comprehensive list of hotels in Hungary, or collect brochures, train schedules and other information.

Wasteels

VII. Keleti station, Kerepesi utca 2-6 (210 2802/343 3492/fax 210 2806/www.wasteels.hu). M2 Keleti pu.. **Open** 8am-7pm Mon-Fri; 8am-1pm Sat. **Credit** AmEx, DC, MC, V. **Map** p247 F3.

Budget hotels and smaller apartment hotels offered.

Deluxe

Pest

Corinthia Grand Hotel Royal

VII. Erzsébet körút 43-49 (479 4000/fax 479 4333/ www.corinthiahotels.com). M2 Blaha Lujza tér/tram 4, 6/bus 7. **Rates** single ¤140-¤250; double ¤160-¤350; suite ¤460-¤1,150. **Credit** AmEx, DC, MC, V. **Map** p250 E4.

Maverick luxury hotel fabulously reconstructed in the style of the famous 1896 original (*see p36* **The empire strikes back**).

Arresting development – the former police HQ now houses **Le Meridien Budapest**.

Hotel services *Beauty salon. Bus park. Business centre. Car park (€18 per day). Conference facilities. Disabled: adapted rooms (2 junior suites). Exhibition centre. Fitness & sauna centre. Non-smoking rooms (2 floors). Restaurants (5). Shopping arcade.* **Room services** *Hairdryer. Minibar. Radio. Room service (24hrs). Safe. Telephone. TV.*

Hotel Inter-Continental Budapest

V. Apáczai Csere János utca 12-14 (327 6333/ fax 327 6357/www.budapest.interconti.com). M1 Vörösmarty tér/tram 2. **Rates** *single/double €270; suite €570-€1,600; triple €30 surcharge; Danube view €40 surcharge; breakfast (not incl) €21.* **Credit** *AmEx, DC, MC, V.* **Map** *p249 C4.*

The forerunner of the renovation rush, the Inter-Continental now boasts brand new rooms and one of the town's biggest conference facilities. Don't let the lugubrious brown façade discourage you: it hides a lobby buzzing with live music at the bar, and offers dramatic views from the Danube-facing rooms, well worth the extra surcharge. Excellent service spoils guests, coupled with what the Inter-Continental calls 'icons': massage, jetlag recovery kit, instant money pack for tipping and various international newspapers.

Hotel services *Air-conditioning. Babysitting. Bar. Beauty salon. Business centre. Cake shop. Car parking (€24 per day). Conference facilities. Disabled:* adapted rooms (2). Executive floor. Laundry facilities. Massage. Non-smoking rooms (3 floors). Restaurant. Sauna. Solarium. Swimming pool.* **Room services** *Hairdryer. High-speed internet. Minibar. Radio. Room service (24hrs). Safe. Telephone. TV.*

Le Meridien Budapest

V. Erzsébet tér 9-10 (429 5500/fax 429 5500/ www.lemeridien-budapest.com). M1, M2, M3 Deák tér/tram 47, 49. **Rates** *single €150-€360; double €180-€400; suite €360-€1,600; extra bed €49; breakfast (not incl) €19.* **Credit** *AmEx, DC, MC, V.* **Map** *p249 C4.*

Morphed from a police headquarters in 2000, the Meridien meticulously adopted clear millennial minimalism. The white austerity of the exterior is ornamented with wrought-iron balconies and statuettes, while the rooms feature shades of beige and blue and are adorned with high ceilings, French windows and oriental rugs. The top-floor health club features a pool bathed in natural light. Le Bourbon restaurant (*see p99*) sparkles under a stained-glass dome.

Hotel services *Babysitting. Bar. Beauty salon. Business centre. Car park (€24 per day). Conference facilities. Disabled: adapted rooms (2 deluxe suites). Gym. Laundry. Massage. Non-smoking rooms (59). Restaurants (2). Safe. Sauna. Swimming pool.* **Room services** *Internet. Minibar. Radio. Room service (24hrs). Telephone. TV.*

Expensive

Buda

art'otel

I. Bem rakpart 16-19 (487 9487/fax 487 9488/ www.artotel.hu). M2 Batthyány tér/bus 86. **Rates** single €160; double €180; suite €260-€280; extra bed €20. **Credit** AmEx, DC, MC, V. **Map** p245 B2.

Floating between the four- and five-star category, the unique boutique art'otel is in limbo between time and space, incorporating original baroque fishermen's houses and abstract modern interiors by designer Donald Sultan (*see p40* **The postmodern delights of Sultan's boutique palace**).

Hotel services *Bar. Beauty salon. Business centre. Car park (€13 per day). Conference facilities. Disabled: adapted room (1). Fitness centre. Nonsmoking rooms (2 floors). Restaurant. Safe. Sauna.* **Room services** *Hairdryer. High-speed internet. Minibar. Radio. Room service (7am-10pm). Safe. Telephone. TV.*

Danubius Grand Hotel

XIII. Margitsziget (452 6200/fax 452 6264/ www.danubiusgroup.com/grandhotel). Bus 26. **Rates** single €118-€156; double €146-€188; suite €230; studio apartment €180; extra bed €42. **Credit** AmEx, DC, MC, V.

Sister spa hotel of the Thermal Margitsziget (*see p32*) with old-world charm and superb facilities (*see p39* **Taking the waters**).

Hotel services *Babysitting. Bar. Beauty salon. Business centre. Car park (€13, free outside). Coffee shop. Conference facilities. Disabled: adapted rooms (4). Fitness centre. Laundry. Medical services. Nonsmoking rooms (40). Restaurant. Safe. Sauna. Solarium. Swimming pool.* **Room services** *Hairdryer. Minibar. Radio. Room service (24hrs). Telephone. TV.*

Hilton Budapest Hotel

I. Hess András tér 1-3 (488 6600/fax 488 6644/ www.hilton.com). Várbusz from M2 Moszkva tér/ bus 16. **Rates** single €170-€350; double €190-€370; suite €450-€2,000; extra bed €25. **Credit** AmEx, DC, MC, V. **Map** p245 A3.

With spectacular views over the Danube and the old quarter, the Hilton is located in the heart of the romantic Castle District. One of the first of Budapest's high-end hotels, it's designed around a 17th-century façade (once part of a Jesuit cloister) and the remains of a 13th-century Gothic church, with a small, open-air concert hall between the two wings often used for summer opera performances. The medieval time travel more than compensates for the relative distance from the city centre. All rooms have undergone extensive refurbishment; the quieter ones have courtyard views.

One-offs Ernő Goldfinger

Utopian residency was the goal of Hungary's controversial architect, Ernő Goldfinger. A life-long anglophile, Goldfinger is famous for building dreamhomes in the sky – in London.

Born in Budapest in 1902, he spent his early years around the sawmills in the forests of Transylvania, and his formative ones at the School for Fine Arts in Paris. There he met Le Courbusier and other progressive architects, and married ideas of social housing to the use of reinforced concrete; he then met Ursula Blackwell, the Crosse & Blackwell millionairess, and married into baked beans.

After a short spell in Horthy's right-wing Hungary, leftist Goldfinger fled his homeland for the second and last time, settling in London with financial security but rather few commissions. Despite local opposition, he built a terraced house at 2 Willow Road in Hampstead, an avant-garde example of pre-war modernism, and filled it with pieces by Henry Moore and Max Ernst. This became the Goldfingers' family home.

Socialist contacts managed to provide him with a little work designing the headquarters of the British Communist Party and the offices

of the *Daily Worker*, but his big chance didn't come until introduction of the Housing Act of 1956. This new law placed a premium on buildings over five floors, and Goldfinger was well positioned to offer his blueprint for a high-rise future. His three most famous buildings, Alexander Fleming House, Balfron and Trellick Towers, shot up as other tower blocks of the era were being pulled down. Revered and reviled in equal measure, Goldfinger even lived at the top of Balfron in Poplar to mute the criticism by his peers.

But it's the Trellick, overlooking the Westway, that Goldfinger is best remembered for. This 31-storey block became a modern icon, dubbed the 'tower of terror' and inspiring JG Ballard's doom-laden novel *High Rise*. Once synonymous for crime and suicide, the Trellick is now the last word in urban cool. With a $6-million refurbishment due, one-bedroom flats are selling for $300,000. Two-and three-bed flats have long been sold.

Goldfinger died at his Willow Road home in 1987. After being acquired by the National Trust (www.nationaltrust.org.uk), the family house is now open to the public.

Hotel services *Bar. Beauty salon. Business centre.*
Car park (€25 per day). Coffee shop. Conference
facilities. Disabled: adapted rooms (3). Executive
floor. Fitness & sauna centre. Non-smoking
rooms (68). Restaurants (2). Safe. Solarium.
Room services *Hairdryer. Internet. Minibar. Radio.*
Room service (24hrs). Safe. Telephone. TV.

Thermal Hotel Margitsziget
XIII. Margitsziget (452 6200/fax 452 6261/
www.danubiusgroup.com/thermalhotel). Bus 26.
Rates single €136-€176; double €168-€208; suite
€230; studio apartment €180; extra bed €42.
Credit AmEx, DC, MC, V.
More modern than the Grand (*see p31*), with high-
quality comprehensive medical and spa services
available (*see p39* **Taking the waters**).
Hotel services *Air-conditioning. Babysitting.*
Bars (2). Beauty salon. Business centre. Car park
(€13 per day; free outside). Conference facilities.
Disabled: adapted rooms (4). Hairdryers. Laundry.
Non-smoking rooms (2 floors). Restaurant.
Safe. Sauna. Solarium. Swimming pool. **Room**
services *Minibar. Radio. Room service (24hrs).*
Telephone. TV.

Óbuda

Corinthia Aquincum Hotel
III. Árpád fejedelem útja 94 (436 4100/fax 436
4156/www.corinthiahotels.com). M2 Batthyány
tér/HÉV to Árpád híd. **Rates** single €175; double
€205; suite €300; extra bed €30. **Credit** DC, MC, V.
The Aphrodite Spa and Wellness Centre salvages
this five-star aspirant of a red-brick relic from the
1980s, plopped in between old Buda's remains and
housing project central. Aquincum's attractions
spring from the nearby healing waters of Margaret
Island and the medicinal mud of Hévíz (*see p39*
Taking the waters).
Hotel services *Babysitting. Bar. Beauty salon.*
Business centre. Car park (€16 per day). Conference
facilities. Disabled: adapted rooms (2). Health
services. Gym. Laundry. Massage. Non-smoking
rooms (2 floors). Restaurant. Safe. Sauna. Spa.
Swimming pool. **Room services** *Internet (executive*
rooms only). Minibar. Radio. Room service (24hrs).
Telephone. TV.

Pest

Hotel Andrássy
VI. Munkácsy Mihály utca 5-7 (462 2100/fax 322
9445/www.andrassyhotel.com). M1 Bajza utca.
Rates single €130; double €180; suite €270-€360;
extra bed €25; breakfast (not incl) €15. **Credit**
AmEx, DC, MC, V. **Map** p247 E2.
This yellow eyesore is the black sheep of embassy
central – the leafy land of old villas now housing
diplomatic missions just off Heroes' Square – but it
still offers five star-ish services in the small luxury
hotel category. The small rooms are graced with
warm tones of beige and blue, but reflect little of the
lobby's grandly serene and chic elegance.

Hotel services *Babysitting. Bar. Car park (€11 per*
day). Conference facilities. Fitness room. Non-smoking
rooms (2 floors). Gym. Laundry. Massage. Restaurant.
Safe. Sauna. **Room services** *Internet. Minibar.*
Radio. Room service (7am-10pm). Telephone. TV.

K+K Hotel Opera
VI. Révay utca 24 (269 0222/fax 269 0230/
www.kkhotels.com). M1 Opera. **Rates** single €153;
double €190; suite €310; extra bed €43. **Credit**
AmEx, DC, MC, V. **Map** p246 C3.
Around the corner from the Opera House and within easy reach of the theatre district, the location can't
be beat for cultural and dining options. The ultra-
modern interior radiates Austrian efficiency and
calm ('Kaiserlich und Königlich', as the chain name
royally suggests), while the rooms feature bright yellow walls and light wooden furniture – although
don't expect much of a view. Internet is free in the
rooms. Service remains attentive and friendly and
there's a big buffet breakfast. Underground parking
space a boon in this part of town.
Hotel services *Air-conditioning. Babysitting. Bar.*
Car park (€10 per day). Conference facilities.
Disabled: access. Fitness centre. Internet corner (free).
Laundry. Massage. Sauna. Snack bar. **Room**
services *Hairdryer. Internet (free). Minibar. Radio.*
Room service (7am-11pm). Safe. Telephone. TV.

Kempinski Hotel Corvinus Budapest
V. Erzsébet tér 7-8 (429 3777/fax 429 4777/
www.kempinski-budapest.com). M1, M2, M3 Deák
tér/tram 47, 49. **Rates** single €150-€350; double
€170-€420; suite €600-€4,000; extra bed €50;
breakfast (not incl) €25. **Credit** AmEx, DC, MC, V.
Map p249 C4.
Built in 1992, the glass-laden Kempinski offers the
biggest rooms in the very heart of Budapest.
Madonna stayed here while filming *Evita*, to name
but one of the many celebrities in need of luxury.
The rooms feature 70 different shapes and some
have views over a small courtyard. Recognition of
the decor is such that some of the smaller decorative
statues were stolen even after being nailed to their
stands. The spacious but somewhat cold lobby is
one of the most popular in town.
Hotel services *Babysitting. Bars (3). Beauty salon.*
Business centre. Car park (€25 per day). Coffee shop.
Conference facilities. Disabled: adapted rooms (3).
Fitness centre. Laundry. Non-smoking rooms (180).
Restaurants (3). Sauna. Shopping arcade. Solarium.
Swimming pool. **Room services** *Hairdryer.*
Internet. Minibar. Radio. Room service (24hrs). Safe.
Telephone. TV.

Radisson SAS Béke Hotel Budapest
VI. Teréz körút 43 (301 1600/fax 301 1615/
www.radissonsas.com). M3 Nyugati pu./tram 4, 6.
Rates single/double €170; suite €300; extra bed €30;
breakfast (not incl) €16. **Credit** AmEx, DC, MC, V.
Map p246 D2.
Don't trust appearances. While the Béke boldly
oozes a Vienna-esque air on the outside, its recent
refurbishment has dragged the interior into the standard light wood world of four-star hotels. Although

Accommodation

Thermal Hotel Margitsziget – the perfect end to a hard day's sightseeing. *See p32.*

the rooms have also lost the old communist decor, in truth the Béke ('Peace') has been refurbished so many times, there's little to show for its eventful 80-year history. Built with all the trappings as the Hotel Britannia in 1912, the Béke also housed a famous jazz club in the 1950s. Footballer Ferenc Puskás was among the many Magyar personalities to live here for a while. These days non-guests come here for afternoon tea and gooey cakes at the old-world Zsolnay Café – and for guests, *béke* is best found in the quieter rooms away from busy ring-road traffic. **Hotel services** *Babysitting. Bars (2). Business centre. Car park (€21 per day). Coffee shop. Conference facilities. Disabled: adapted room (1). Pharmacy. Laundry facilities. Massage. Non-smoking rooms (80). Restaurant. Safe. Sauna. Swimming pool.* **Room services** *Hairdryer. Internet. Minibar. Radio. Room service (24hrs). Safe. Telephone. TV.*

Moderate

Buda

Danubius Hotel Gellért

XI. Szent Gellért tér 1 (385 2200/fax 466 6631/ www.danubiusgroup.com/gellert). Tram 18, 19, 47, *49/bus 7.* **Rates** single €65-€125; double €120-€240; suite €270-€300; extra bed €50. **Credit** AmEx, DC, MC, V. **Map** p249 C5.

Historic art nouveau gem, basking in misleadingly luxurious illumination at night, as many of its rooms are in urgent need of refurbishment. Amazing architecture, spa, outdoor pool and terrace perched halfway up Gellért Hill compensate (*see p39* **Taking the waters**).
Hotel services *Air-conditioning (some rooms). Babysitting. Bar. Beauty salon. Business centre. Car park (€5 per day). Coffee shop. Conference facilities. Laundry. Massage. Non-smoking rooms (49). Restaurant. Safe. Sauna. Solarium. Swimming pool.* **Room services** *Hairdryer. Minibar. Radio. Room service (24hrs). Telephone. TV (most rooms).*

Gold Hotel Buda

I. Hegyalja út 14 (209 4775/fax 209 5431/ www.goldhotel.hu). Bus 8, 112. **Rates** single €84; double €94. **Credit** MC, V. **Map** p248 B5.
The overkill signature Austro-Hungarian yellow is impossible to miss, and is indicative of the airs this small establishment cultivates. But the location is hard to beat; two bus stops from the city, and in between Gellért and Castle Hills, Gold offers one of Buda's most centrally located hotels, its back tucked

heavenly hotels, devilish deals...

With up to 50% off hotels' standard rates in budapest!

We offer a superb range of quality hotels in over 85 European cities & resorts. Booking is extremely easy and offered through both our call centre and online.

2★	from	**£19**
3★	from	**£22**
5★	from	**£59**

prices are per person per night based on 2 people sharing a twin/double room, breakfast & taxes inc.

book now on:

0845 230 8888
www.hotelconnect.co.uk

hotelconnect
the hotel specialist

Maria & István
Private rooms and apartments

IX. Ferenc körút 39.
Tel/fax:
+36-1-216-0768
E-mail:
mariaistvan@axelero.hu

- 1-,2-, and 3 bedrooms with shower, toilet, fridge
- 2- bedroom aparments, including bathroom, fully equipped kitchen, cable TV
- garage
- centrally located, close to public transport

- pickup from Airport can be arranged
- € 11-25/night/person (depending on the lenght of stay and number of guests)
- Tourist tax included

into the greens of Gellért. Insist on a room facing the hill and garden, away from the busy road channelling city traffic on to the westbound motorways. **Hotel services** *Bar. Business centre. Car park (free). Conference facilities. Laundry. Non-smoking rooms (request upon reservation). Restaurant. Safe.* **Room services** *Minibar. Radio. Room service (8am-10pm). Telephone. TV.*

Hotel Victoria

I. Bem rakpart 11 (457 8080/fax 457 8088/ www.victoria.hu). M2 Batthyány tér/bus 60, 86. **Rates** single €74-€97; double €79-€102. **Credit** AmEx, DC, V. **Map** p245 B3.

One of Budapest's first private hotels occupies a townhouse below the castle, facing the Danube and within easy reach of the main sights. Rooms are comfortable in a simple way, commanding a view of the river, and the garden rooms offer nice patios at no extra charge. Excellent value for the location, size of rooms and services offered.
Hotel services *Air-conditioning. Babysitting. Bar. Car park (€9 per day). High-speed internet. Laundry. Sauna.* **Room services** *Hairdryer. Minibar. Radio. Room service (24hrs). Safe. Telephone. TV.*

Petneházy Club Hotel

II. Feketefej utca 2-4 (391 8010/fax 376 5738/ www.petnehazy.hu). Bus 56 (red). **Rates** small bungalow (2-4 people) €130; large bungalow (4-6 people) €160; extra bed €30; breakfast (not incl) €7. **Credit** AmEx, MC, V.

Doubling as a country club, this hotel is actually 45 private bungalows – four with disabled access – with a central building housing the reception, pool and restaurant. Every room has its own sauna, adding a tremendous plus to this peaceful, albeit remote location. There are loads of sports and leisure facilities here (*see p186*), including horse-riding next door, as well as organised bus and boat excursions.
Hotel services *Babysitting. Bar. Bicycles. Car park (free). Conference facilities. Disabled: adapted bungalows (4). Fax. Laundry. Restaurant. Safe. Sauna. Solarium. Swimming pool.* **Room services** *Kitchen. Minibar. Radio. Room service (8am-9pm). Safe. Sauna. Telephone. TV.*

UhU Villa

II. Keselyű út 1A (275 1002/fax 398 0571/ www.uhuvilla.hu). Tram 56. **Rates** single €85; double €100-€200; extra bed €20. **Credit** AmEx, DC, MC, V.

Excellent *panzió* nestled among fir trees in a quiet valley a ten-minute tram ride from Moszkva tér, the perfect getaway from downtown bustle. This turn-of-the-century villa, done out in monarchical white and yellow, has small but cosy rooms and a quaint charm pervades the common areas. The American breakfast overlooking the lovely flower garden is the perfect prelude to a short walk down the hill to the tram and the heart of Budapest.
Hotel services *Air-conditioning. Car park (free; six spaces). Fax. Safe. Solarium.* **Room services** *Minibar. Telephone. TV.*

Pest

Budapest Marriott Hotel

V. Apáczai Csere János utca 4 (266 7000/fax 266 5000/www.marriotthotels.com/budhu). M1 Vörösmarty tér/tram 2. **Rates** single/double €115-€145; suite €355; breakfast (not incl) €18. **Credit** AmEx, DC, MC, V. **Map** p249 C4.

Celeb-spotting? The surprisingly low-cost Marriott is your hunting ground. Brad Pitt, Robert Redford and Glenn Close lead the list of recent guests at this burgundy brass old-timer – almost all visiting film crews stay here. Cosy and welcoming despite the constant come and go, the lobby is always buzzing. Every room has a river view, and refurbishment will upgrade drab utilitarian to glam utilitarian.
Hotel services *Babysitting. Bar. Business centre. Car park (€25 per day). Coffee shop. Conference facilities. Disabled: adapted rooms (2). Fitness club. Laundry. Non-smoking rooms (180). Restaurants (3). Sauna. Solarium.* **Room services** *Hairdryer. Minibar. Radio. Room service (24hrs). Safe. Telephone. TV.*

City Hotel Pilvax

V. Pilvax köz 1-3 (266 7660/fax 317 6396/ www.taverna.hu). M3 Ferenciek tere. **Rates** single €52-€70; double €72-€95; extra bed €20-€25. **Credit** AmEx, DC, MC, V. **Map** p249 C4.

Laden with history, the Pilvax café played host to the revolutionaries of 1848 – although its existence as a hotel only goes back five years. The small street provides one of the best and quietest central digs, while the restaurant comes alive with Gypsy music – well, popular tunes on the violin.
Hotel services *Bar. Car park (€25 per day). Conference facilities. Laundry. Non-smoking rooms (4). Restaurant. Safe.* **Room services** *Air-conditioning. Minibar. Radio. Telephone. TV.*

City Panzió Mátyás

V. Március 15 tér 7-8 (338 4711/fax 317 9086/ www.taverna.hu/matyas). M3 Ferenciek tere/ tram 2. **Rates** single €52-€70; double €70-€95; suite €95-€130; extra bed €20-€25. **Credit** AmEx, MC, V. **Map** p249 C4.

Few beat the Mátyás for its spectacular building, great rates and perfect location. Rooms offer no excitement, but the river makes this a secondary consideration. Press for a view higher up. Breakfast is served in the folksy Mátyás Pince restaurant.
Hotel services *Car park (nearby). Internet. Laundry. Non-smoking rooms (12). Safe.* **Room services** *Minibar. Room service (limited; noon-11pm). Telephone. TV.*

Danubius Thermal & Conference Hotel Helia

XIII. Kárpát utca 62-64 (452 5800/fax 452 5801/ www.danubiusgroup.com/helia). Trolleybus 79. **Rates** single €137; double €160; suite €258; suite with sauna €275. Rates incl parking and access to certain fitness & health services. **Credit** AmEx, DC, MC, V.

The empire strikes back

For once the PR motto rings true: 'A legend reborn'. Calligraphed in fountain-pen curlicue underneath sepia images of its glory days, the legend reborn is Budapest's landmark **Grand Hotel Royal** (*see p29*). Faithfully reconstructed after a decade of neglect and, bizarrely, semi-official DJ parties, the Royal, as it was christened when first built for the 1896 millennial celebrations, is indeed reborn. It's like the Austro-Hungarian empire has never gone away.

The hotel has been at the cutting edge of two centuries of culture and design. From the late 1890s, the Royal was the Queen of the Grand Boulevard. Its façade featured cast-iron statues imported from Paris, its interior a tropical garden, concert and banqueting halls, and plush restaurants and cafés. Some of the most famous names in Hollywood would meet here and at the **New York Café** nearby (*see p111* **So good they built it twice**), continuing a silver-screen tradition that began with an early presentation of moving pictures here just after the Lumière Brothers first showed films in Paris. A favourite of the literary elite, and where Bartók often played in the grand ballroom, the Royal ruled in Budapest's pre-war silver age.

Almost completely destroyed in the war, this huge hotel was twice reconstructed, to the contemporary tastes of the 1960s and 1980s, before being closed in the early 1990s. Revived later that decade by the new wave of DJ culture, the Royal proved a very popular setting for local clubbers desperate to find downtown venues with a difference. Sixties retro decor juxtaposed a grand marble staircase and a bar converted from the classic reception desk, with clocks overhead showing the time in New York, Amsterdam, Kingston, Bangkok and Goa.

After the entertainment lease ran out in 2001, the Malta-based Corinthia Hotel Group and local architects dragged the Royal – Corinthia Grand Hotel Royal, if you please – from the club culture of the late 20th century back into the quiet elegance of the late 19th.

Reopened in December 2002, modern twists now embellish a majestic icon of Hungarian hospitality. The exquisite lobby features original fittings, set under a glassed-in triple atrium. The rooms combine historic grandeur with tasteful contemporary furniture – marble bathrooms, South African carpets, cherrywood headboards and modern artwork. The Grand Ballroom is beautifully restored and lined with portraits of Hungary's cultural giants. Five restaurants – two sitting under glass atriums – include the French-influenced Brasserie Royale.

To top it off, in late 2003 a spa is to be opened next door, the only one of its kind in a downtown location. Once the New York Café reopens with modern design in 2004, this busy location will again be the finest address on this side of the river.

Modern spa hotel with the cleanest and most comprehensive facilities in town, albeit surrounded by a drab housing estate (*see p39* **Taking the waters**). **Hotel services** *Babysitting. Bar. Beauty salon. Business centre. Car park (free). Conference facilities. Non-smoking rooms (2 floors). Disabled: adapted rooms (5). Gym. Laundry. Massage. Medical clinic. Restaurant. Safe. Sauna. Solarium. Swimming pool.* **Room services** *Minibar. Radio. Room service (6am-10pm). Telephone. TV.*

Hilton Budapest Westend

VI. Váci út 1-3 (288 5500/fax 288 5552/ www.hiltonbudapestwestend.com). M3 Nyugati pu./ tram 4, 6. **Rates** single €129; double €149; extra bed €50. **Credit** AmEx, DC, MC, V. **Map** p246 D2.
Wedged in between various shops in the Westend City Center mall, this Hilton is overshadowed by the lugubrious building project, ambitiously aiming at becoming the 'new downtown'. Purpose-built, the hotel offers tastefully furnished, spacious rooms, a warm colour scheme with a stroke of yellow and purple, and a good diving board into the city – if you manage to avoid the maddening mall.
Hotel services *Bar. Business centre. Car park (€16 per day). Conference facilities. Disabled: adapted rooms (2). Non-smoking rooms (96). Gym. Laundry. Massage. Restaurants (2). Safe. Sauna.* **Room services** *Internet. Minibar. Radio. Room service (24hrs). Telephone. TV.*

Hotel Astoria

V. Kossuth Lajos utca 19-21 (484 3200/fax 318 6798/www.danubiusgroup.com/astoria). M2 Astoria/ tram 47, 49/bus 7. **Rates** single €90-€115; double €110-€140; suite €152-€190; extra bed €30. **Credit** AmEx, DC, MC, V. **Map** p249 D4.
Built between 1912 and 1914 on the site of the old National Theatre, and lending its name to the busy central intersection on which it stands, the historic landmark Hotel Astoria reeks of old *Mitteleuropa*. The first Hungarian government was formed here in 1918 (*see p15*), declaring independence from Austria; a year later the Communist directorate used it as a meeting place. The hotel went on to become the hangout of Nazi officials during World War II (the hotel looked over the Jewish Ghetto), before housing the infamous post-war Pengő jazz club. It even became the Soviet headquarters during the 1956 Revolution. The elegant chandeliered art nouveau coffee lounge (*see p115*) at street level recalls the atmosphere of pre-war Budapest. Windows are now soundproofed and rooms 609 and 610 have superb views of the Central Synagogue.
Hotel services *Café. Car park (free). Conference facilities. Disabled: adapted. Fax. Hypo-allergenic room (1). Internet. Laundry. Non-smoking floor. Restaurant. Safe. Shop.* **Room services** *Hairdryer. Internet. Minibar. Room service (7am-11pm). Telephone. TV.*

Hotel Benczúr

VI. Benczúr utca 35 (479 5650/fax 342 1558/ www.hotelbenczur.hu). M1 Hősök tere. **Rates** single €67-€87; double €84-€107; suite €98-€124; extra bed €15. **Credit** AmEx, MC, V. **Map** p247 E2.

This once-stuffy hotel is now post-renovation: lighter colours in the rooms, a cleaner feel and a good leafy location in the diplomatic quarter off Andrássy utca, near the City Park. Internet use is free for guests. Over 150 rooms, but austere common areas.
Hotel services *Air-conditioning. Bar. Car park (€8 per day). Conference facilities. Dentist. Internet. Laundry. Non-smoking rooms (22). Restaurant.* **Room services** *Minibar. Telephone. TV.*

Hotel Erzsébet

V. Károlyi Mihály utca 11-15 (328 5700/fax 328 5763/www.danubiusgroup.com). M3 Ferenciek tere/ tram 2/bus 7. **Rates** single €95-€120; double €110-€140; extra bed €30. **Credit** AmEx, DC, MC, V. **Map** p249 C4.
Gone is the staple dark wood, giving way to a lighter shade. The Erzsébet had a facelift in 2002, giving it a fresher feel, although the main draw is still the downtown location, although the street is one-way and congested. The János Pince restaurant features scenes from the Hungarian folk tale *János Vitéz*.
Hotel services *Air-conditioning. Bar. Car park (free). Conference facilities. Hairdryers. Laundry. Non-smoking rooms (32). Restaurant. Safe.* **Room services** *Minibar. Radio. Room service (7am-11pm). Telephone. TV.*

Hotel Fiesta

VI. Király utca 20 (328 3000/fax 266 6024/ www.hotelfiesta.hu). M1, M2, M3 Deák tér/tram 47, 49. **Rates** single €112; double €132; extra bed €46. **Credit** AmEx, MC, V. **Map** p246 D3.
This new three-star has emerged from a neo-classicist block, shedding period character to give way to a light, modern hotspot. The preserved façade hides 112 IKEA-esque rooms, spacious and sun-soaked on the higher floors. Ideally located in up-and-coming Király utca, the Hotel Fiesta is a testament to the slow gentrification of the area between the city centre, the theatre district and the nightlife of Liszt Ferenc tér. Superb access, in fact, to all city spots that matter.
Hotel services *Bar. Conference facilities. Dentist. Disabled: adapted rooms (4). Internet. Laundry. Non-smoking rooms (1 floor). Restaurant. Safe.* **Room services** *Air-conditioning. Hairdryer. Minibar. Room service (7am-11pm). Telephone. TV.*

Hotel Liget

VI. Dózsa György út 106 (269 5300/fax 269 5329/ www.liget.hu). M1 Hősök tere. **Rates** single €96; double €112; extra bed €32. **Credit** AmEx, DC, MC, V. **Map** p247 E1.
Conveniently situated for guests to take advantage of the City Park – you can even rent out bicycles here – on a busy street, the Liget ('Park') is also close to the tourist attractions of Heroes' Square. The Finta-designed building is 1980s time travel, but the rooms are spacious. Attractive winter rates.
Hotel services *Air-conditioning. Bar. Business centre. Car park (€12 per day). Coffee shop. Conference facilities. Laundry. Massage. Non-smoking rooms (24). Safe. Sauna. Solarium.* **Room services** *Minibar. Radio. Room service (7am-11pm). Safe. Telephone. TV.*

Hotel Taverna

V. Váci utca 20 (485 3100/fax 485 3111/ www.hoteltaverna.hu). M3 Ferenciek tere/tram 2/ bus 7. **Rates** single €124; double €166; suite €344. **Credit** AmEx, DC, MC, V. **Map** p249 C4.

Despite the most central location in Budapest, the Taverna is very pricey. Located in the heart of the pedestrianised zone, the standard, no-frills rooms in this typically 1980s hotel offer a convenient option and easy access to downtown.
Hotel services *Babysitting. Bar. Café. Car park (€22 per day). Conference facilities. Disabled: adapted rooms (2). Internet. Laundry. Non-smoking rooms (80). Restaurant. Sauna.* **Room services** *Hairdryer. Minibar. Radio. Room service (7am-10pm). Safe. Telephone. TV.*

Ibis Budapest Centrum

IX. Ráday utca 6 (456 4100/fax 456 4186/www.ibis-centrum.hu). M3 Kálvin tér/tram 47, 49. **Rates** single/double €69-€79; breakfast (not incl) €8. **Credit** AmEx, DC, MC, V. **Map** p249 D5.

Plenty of night-time entertainment around this plain Ibis hotel built in 1998. The location is excellent and the 126 rooms are air-conditioned and soundproofed, all dressed in uniform green. Spacious bar area; friendly, efficient reception staff.
Hotel services *Car park (€13 per day). Bar (24hrs). Disabled: adapted rooms (4). Internet.* **Room services** *Air-conditioning. Telephone. TV.*

Inn-Side Hotel Kálvin Ház

IX. Gönczy Pál utca 6 (216 4365/fax 216 4161/ www.hotels.hu/kalvinőhaz). M3 Kálvin tér/tram 47, 49. **Rates** single €62; double €82; extra bed €20; apartment €102. **Credit** AmEx, DC, MC, V. **Map** p249 D5.

In the central end of the IX District, at the gateway to Ráday utca's bar crawl, the Kálvin not only attracts with location; its rooms are all different and feature parquet flooring and antique furniture. Buffet breakfast included in the price. Also handy for landmark market hall, the Nagyvásárcsarnok.
Hotel services *Babysitting. Car park (in Baross Parkolóház). Laundry. Non-smoking rooms (5). Pets. Photocopying. Safe.* **Room services** *Room service (24hrs). Telephone. TV.*

Marriott Executive Apartments

V. Pesti Barnabás utca 4 (235 1800/fax 235 1900/ www.executiveresidences.com). M3 Ferenciek tere/tram 2/bus 7. **Rates** 1-bedroom €100-€130; 2-bedroom €150-€180. **Credit** AmEx, DC, MC, V. **Map** p249 C4.

The concept is five-star luxury services for travellers spending more than a few weeks in Budapest. The historic Vasudvar was redesigned to become the first short-term residential apartment hotel service in the city, with a high-end shopping centre. The hotel is clean and bright, matched with comfortable, friendly yet top-quality facilities. There's a housekeeping and secretarial service, and guests have access to all the facilities at the nearby Marriott.
Hotel services *Air-conditioning. Babysitting. Bar. Beauty salon. Business centre. Car park €25 per day. Conference room. Disabled: access. Fitness centre.*

Kitchen with dishwasher. Offices to rent. Shopping centre. TV/VCR. **Room services** *Clock radio. Fully equipped kitchen. Office with double phone & fax lines. TV.*

Mercure Budapest Metropole

VII. Rákóczi út 58 (462 8100/fax 462 8181/ www.mercure-metropole.hu). M2 Blaha Lujza tér/ tram 4, 6. **Rates** single €100; double €105; extra bed €30; breakfast (not incl) €12. **Credit** AmEx, DC, MC, V. **Map** p249 D4.

Renovated in 2000 in monarchical Budapest's ghastly yellow, but hidden from view by the busy arcades at the entrance, the Metropole is admittedly torn between three and four stars. The neighbourhood has a promising future with at least four newly restored hotels reviving their buildings' history and amenities, with the Metropole providing a less expensive choice to delve into the körút's own version of boulevard culture. The clean rooms, in warm shades of red, also put sister hotel Nemzeti, just around the corner and painted undie blue, in perspective.
Hotel services *Bar. Business centre. Car park (€15 per day). Conference facilities. Disabled: adapted rooms (4). Internet. Laundry. Non-smoking rooms (71). Restaurant. Safe.* **Room services** *Air-conditioning. Hairdryer. Internet. Minibar. Radio. Room service (7am-10pm). Telephone. TV.*

Novotel Budapest Centrum

VIII. Rákóczi út 43-45 (477 5400/fax 477 5454/ www.novotel-bud-centrum.hu). M2 Blaha Lujza tér/ tram 4, 6/bus 7. **Rates** single/double €130; extra bed €30; breakfast (not incl) €15. **Credit** AmEx, DC, MC, V. **Map** p250 E4.

Built as the Palace Hotel in 1911 and closed since 1989, this neglected Jugendstil treasure was at last restored in 2002, becoming a 227-room Novotel hotel. Unfortunately, the rooms reflect standard industry decor rather than period, but represent good value in the vicinity of the gentrifying körút. Rákóczi út views from the balconies can be Vienna-esque, but come with traffic noise – the Csokonai utca rooms are quieter and some have balconies too.
Hotel services *Babysitting. Bar. Car park (€12 per day). Children's corner. Disabled: adapted rooms (3). Fitness centre. Jacuzzi. Laundry. Non-smoking rooms (4 floors). Restaurant.* **Room services** *Air-conditioning. Internet (on request). Minibar. Room service (24hrs). Safe. Telephone. TV.*

Residence Izabella

VI. Izabella utca 61 (475 5900/fax 475 5902/ www.orcogroup.com). M1 Vörösmarty utca. **Rates** single €65-€300; double €110-€400; triple €145-€550; breakfast (not incl) €8. **Credit** AmEx, DC, MC. **Map** p246 D2.

Halfway between the city and Heroes' Square, Izabella offers the longer-term traveller 38 non-smoking apartments in this entirely smoke-free recent development (although you can smoke on the balconies). All apartments feature a very modern open kitchen, and subdued beiges and bright reds for a modern, dynamic look. A three-month stay grants you access to lower fares.

Taking the waters

Few European destinations can provide a spa break of the quality offered by a handful of the city's top-class hotels. Thanks to a tradition stretching back for the best part of a century, today ten per cent of Budapest's visitors come purely for the good of their health.

The oldest and most famous of the genre, the **Gellért** (pictured; *see p33*) was built on the site of an old Turkish mud-bathing facility, pulled down to make way for the construction of the Szabadság Bridge. It took seven years for an opulent spa hotel to be constructed here, completed in 1918 in art nouveau style at the foot of the hill of the same name: Gellért. Overlooking the Danube, it featured a dome-topped hall, music hall, marble-columned indoor swimming pool and labyrinth of thermal pools. In the rooms, the taps ran thermal and mineral waters as well as plain hot and cold. With the finest chef in the land, János Gundel, running a hotel restaurant of impeccable taste, the Gellért was an essential stop for any visiting dignitary or touring member of high society. It was the closest Magyarország ever got to Monte Carlo.

It's a little different now. True, the grande dame still has a wonderful façade and fabulous outdoor and indoor pools. But only a third of the rooms have been renovated since post-war reconstruction, the rest left to time's devices. Room inspection before registration is the key to splashing out on a stay here. Damaged in the war, repaired in the 1950s and gradually renovated from the 1960s, the most famous hotel in Budapest has long been living on its golden laurels.

Today access to the spa is included in the room rate, guests going down by separate lift; the extensive medical services are run by the Ministry for Baths (*see pp146-8*).

While part of the Gellért was left to decay, a new wave of spa hotels were built in the 1970s and 1980s. Making use of the hot springs on Margaret Island, the **Danubius Grand** (*see p31*) and its sister **Thermal Hotel Margitsziget** (*see p32*) offer a range of spa facilities and supervised health services such as spine treatments and balneotherapy. Extensively renovated in 2000, the Grand features fin-de-siècle furniture, whereas the Thermal, also recently renovated, comprises more standard decor. A tunnel between the two gives indoor access to facilities in both.

The modern **Danubius Thermal & Conference Hotel Helia** (*see p35*) offers diagnostic and curative reflexology, along with hydromassage, electrotherapy, mud body wraps and rheumatic treatments. In Óbuda, the **Corinthia Aquincum** (*see p32*) is set in a thermal complex, making use of the healing waters of Margaret Island and the medicinal mud of Hévíz.

The postmodern delights of Sultan's boutique palace

The boutique **art'otel** (*see p31*), the first of its kind in Budapest, glides effortlessly between the 18th and 21st centuries. Set in the poetic disorder of the atmospheric Víziváros, where fishermen once sold their catch, the location allows superb views of the Danube below and Castle Hill above.

The hotel makes full use of both space and time, ultra-urban at the front, baroque at the back. The rear side is made up of four original 18th-century fishermen's houses, where the tastefully furnished rooms are graced with period fixtures and fittings – authentic down to the door handles – arches and actual passageways. The huge rooms open on to the tiny romantic streets of the Víziváros, which curve all the way up to the top of Castle Hill.

The Danube-facing modern wing is blessed with the abstract expressionist work of maverick New Yorker Donald Sultan. His minimalist artwork and postmodern rugs (thread and needle pattern in the rooms, domino pattern in the lobby and bar, buttons in the corridor), tableware and fountain design all give a surreptitiously sweet touch to the determining detail.

Each room – superbly equipped with an ISDN internet link, voicemail and distinctive fire-red dressing gowns – features a little decorative bird watching over the well-being of each guest. Those staying three floors up enjoy a castle vista as well as a riverside one. Übermodern with a medieval view – what could be better?

Hotel services *Babysitting. Bar. Business centre. Car park (€18 per day). Conference facilities. Disabled apartment (1). Gym. Laundry. Massage. Non-smoking rooms (all). Sauna.* **Room services** *DVD. Internet. Minibar. Radio. Room service (24hrs). Telephone. TV.*

Sissi Hotel

IX. Angyal utca 33 (215 0082/fax 216 6063/ www.hotelsissi.hu). M3 Ferenc körút. **Rates** single €100; double €110; suite €360-€1,600; extra bed €30. **Credit** DC, MC, V. **Map** p250 E6.

Nestled in the up-and-coming IX District, Sissi opens a little gateway to the various neighbouring regeneration projects in the area – from the busy barland of Ráday utca to the colourful residential revival of the hotel's surroundings. The simplicity of the 44 rooms is smartly unalluded to by the terraced

façade, and the tacky influence of Habsburg legend Sissi only surfaces in modest attempts at liberal antique decoration and an unassuming Sissi room.
Hotel services *Bar. Car park (€9 per day). Disabled: adapted room (1). Laundry. Massage. Non-smoking rooms (2 floors). Safe.* **Room services** *Internet. Minibar. Radio. Telephone. TV.*

Starlight Hotel

V. Mérleg utca 6 (484 3700/fax 484 3711/ www.starlighthotels.com). M1, M2, M3 Deák tér/ tram 2. **Rates** single suite €135; double suite €165; extra bed €30. **Credit** AmEx, DC, V. **Map** p246 C3.

With 54 suites each featuring a living room and separate bedroom (plus make-up table and desk), this apartment/hotel is in an excellent downtown location. Check for internet specials.

Hotel services *Breakfast. Car park (€16 per day). Coffee shop. Disabled: access. Fitness facilities. Non-smoking rooms (33). Sauna. Steam bath.* **Room services** *Microwave. Minibar. Telephone (2). TV (2).*

Budget

Buda

Ábel Panzió

XI. Ábel Jenő utca 9 (tel/fax 209 2537/fax 381 0553). Tram 61. **Rates** single €65; double €70; extra bed €15 (free for under-10s). Cash payment €10 discount per night. **Credit** AmEx, MC, V. **Map** p248 A6.
Probably the most beautiful *panzió* in Budapest, set in an ivy-covered turn-of-the-century villa on a quiet side street, and fitted with period furniture in the common areas. The ten rooms are all sunny and clean with antique furniture, although those on the ground level are slightly bigger and with a bathtub. No television in the rooms. Breakfast takes place around a pleasant common dining table overlooking a terrace and well-kept garden. A summer favourite, so make sure to reserve well in advance.
Hotel services *Bar. Car park (free; 3 spaces). Hairdryer. TV.* **Room services** *Safe. Telephone.*

Hotel Charles

I. Hegyalja út 23 (212 9169/fax 202 2984/ www.charleshotel.hu). Bus 8, 112. **Rates** single €44-€48; double €52-€64; triple €64-€80; extra bed €10. **Credit** AmEx, DC, MC, V. **Map** p248 B5.
Formerly known as the Charles Apartments, this converted apartment block has elevated itself to hotel status. Half the rooms are now executive, with new furniture and open-plan kitchens, giving them a spacious and modern feel. The rest are studios with a separate kitchen. Breakfast is included in the rates. Perfect location in Buda, five minutes from the city, but make sure your room doesn't overlook noisy Hegyalja út.
Hotel services *Business centre. Car park (€8 per day). Hairdryer. High-speed internet. Laundry. Non-smoking rooms (1 floor). Photocopying. Safe.* **Room services** *Internet (6 rooms). Minibar. Telephone. TV.*

Hotel Villa Korda

II. Szikla utca 9 (325 9123/fax 325 9127/ www.geocities.com/hotelvillakorda). Bus 29, 65. **Rates** single €54; double €49; triple €59; suite €69. **Credit** MC, V.
The owners are an evergreen couple of former stage singers, and their hotel brings another era to life too. Recreated yellow and white dominate this purpose-built villa, with rustic antique furniture testifying to a higher style. Gorgeous views can be enjoyed from this quiet location in the rich heartland of the Buda hills. Half the rooms command a city vista, the other half overlook the forests.
Hotel services *Bar. Car park (€5 per day). Hairdryer. Non-smoking rooms (8). Safe. Sauna.* **Room services** *Air-conditioning. Telephone. TV.*

Kulturinnov Hotel

I. Szentháromság tér 6 (355 0122/06 20 320 5726/fax 375 1886). Várbusz from M2 Moszkva tér/ bus 16. **Rates** single €49; double €69; extra bed €15. **Credit** DC, MC, V. **Map** p245 A3.
What a bargain! Sixteen big rooms in a palace built in 1904 make up this gem of a budget hotel. The entrance is across from Matthias Church, and while only three rooms have a street view (of the older wing of the Hilton, the rest overlook a courtyard), the bustle of the Castle District will compensate. Don't let the lack of air-conditioning deter – the old walls are thick enough to protect from the heat. Buffet breakfast is included in the rates.
Hotel services *Babysitting. Bar. Car park (€9 per day). Conference facilities. Disabled: access. Fax. Laundry. Non-smoking rooms (8). Safe. TV.* **Room service** *Minibar. Telephone.*

Óbuda

Alfa Hotel

III. Kossuth Lajos üdülőpart 102 (240 7125/fax 439 0563/www.hotels.hu/alfa). HÉV to Árpád híd/bus 34. **Rates** double €36; triple €48; extra bed €14. **No credit cards**.
The two-star quality shows at the newly renovated Alfa – but then it's the Danube you come here for. The four-storey block (box, in reality), once a resort for the workers, is conveniently located on the Római embankment with plenty of outdoor activities close by: tennis, cycling, and the Pünkösdő swimming pool and canoeing. Unfortunately, none of the activities is directly offered by the hotel, but everything is within easy reach.
Hotel services *Bar. Bus park. Car park (free). Non-smoking rooms (20).* **Room services** *TV.*

Pest

Amadeus Apartments

V. Váci utca & neighbourhood (tel/fax 302 8268/ www.amadeus.hu). M3 Ferenciek tere/bus 7. **Rates** double €40-€60; triple €56-€70. **No credit cards**. **Map** p249 C4/5.
Amadeus maintains central two-room apartments, each with two beds, bathroom and kitchen with cooking facilities. You're pretty much on your own here, but you can always reach the representative on mobile phone. Parking available in the vicinity of the apartments. Free transfer from wherever you arrive. One disabled apartment.

Fortuna Hotel Boat

XIII. Szent István Park, lower quay (288 8100/ fax 270 0351/www.fortunahajo.hu). Trolleybus 76, 79. **Rates** single €50-€65; double €60-€80; suite €75-€100; extra bed €15. **Credit** AmEx, MC, V. **Map** p249 C1.
The wooden rooms in this moored boat are small and spartan, to say the least, but if you want to match aquaphilia with a good location in a quasi-

novel milieu, this is the place. Just off Margaret Bridge, it provides good access to Margaret Island (on foot), Buda (trams 4 and 6) and downtown Pest (tram 2). Parking is free for guests and 41 of the 60 rooms have their own showers.

Hotel services *Car park (free). Conference facility. Non-smoking rooms (5). Pub. Restaurant.* **Room services** *Air-conditioning. Minibar. Room service (8am-10pm). Telephone. TV.*

Medosz Hotel

VI. Jókai tér 9 (374 3000/fax 332 4316/ www.medoszhotel.hu). M1 Oktogon/tram 4, 6. **Rates** single €42; double €55; triple €65; apartment €84. **No credit cards. Map** p246 D3.

Not the most luxurious hotel in the city centre, but one of the least expensive, and certainly one of the best located – and a slow but hopeful renovation of this former party workers' hostel is indeed going on. Rooms are simple, stuffy and spartan, and beds can be lumpy. But being right next to Liszt Ferenc tér, transport hub Oktogon and the Opera House, you'll perhaps not mind the drab hotel itself.

Hotel services *Breakfast. Café. Car park (free). Conference facilities. Safe.* **Room services** *Telephone. TV.*

Panzió Leo

V. Kossuth Lajos utca 2A (266 9041/fax 266 9042/ www.ohb.hu/cgi-bin/list.pl) M3 Ferenciek tere/bus 7. **Rates** single €45-€66; double €69-€82; extra bed €19-€26. **Credit** AmEx, DC, MC, V. **Map** p249 D4.

Budget meets excellent location in this new hotel – as well as most of the city traffic. But the rooms are tastefully furnished, even if the interior lays on thick blue and yellow. One of the most central budget options.

Hotel services *Car park (€12 per day). Laundry. Non-smoking rooms (14). Translation services.* **Room services** *Air-conditioning. Minibar. Radio. Telephone. TV.*

Victor Apartment Hotel

XIII. Victor Hugo utca 25-27 (239 7928/fax 452 0575/www.victor.hu). M3 Lehel tér/trolleybus 76. **Rates** single €34-€49; double €44-€59; extra bed €15. **Credit** AmEx, MC, V. **Map** p246 C1.

As if in a reality show, in the middle of residential Újlipótváros, the Victor offers its visitors a sneak view of how the Budapest middle classes live. The hotel is worth every penny – it's clean, it's cheap, it's in a pleasant neighbourhood, and it has access to Szent István park, Nyugati station and the Danube. **Hotel services** *Breakfast. Car park (€8 per day). Car rental. Laundry. Pets. Safe. Sightseeing.* **Room services** *Air-conditioning. Cable TV. Hairdryer. Internet. Kitchen. Microwave. Minibar. Telephone.*

Youth hostels

Access to hostels is just a click away. Three websites – www.backpackers.hu, www.reservation.hu, www.hungaryhostels.hu – centralise the budget end of the industry online. Their agents offer a face-to-face booking service on the trains, and at Keleti station three tourist information desks are available (343 0748/303 9818/travellers@hostels.hu; open 7am-10pm daily) to help you find a place in one of their 15 hostels. Rates are about €10-€18 per person. International Youth Hostel cards are recognised and earn a ten per cent discount. There's no booking fee and you're entitled to free transfer on arrival.

Caterina Hostel

VI. Eötvös utca 20 I/8 (291 9538/fax 297 3830/ www.extra.hu/caterinahostel). M1 Oktogon/tram 4, 6. **Rates** single €20; double €24; triple €30; dorm €8; apartment €25-€40. **No credit cards. Map** p246 D3.

Once graced by an architectural gem, Caterina had to move house to a more modest, but still historical building on a smaller, more intimate scale. This small, unaffiliated, personally run hostel offers very clean rooms and free transfer from wherever you arrive. Only the apartment has a separate bathroom. **Hotel services** *Kitchen. Laundry. TV.*

Citadella Hotel

XI. Citadella sétány (466 5794/fax 386 0505/ citadella@hotmail.com). Bus 27. **Rates** double with shower €56; extra bed €10; dorm €10 per person; breakfast €5. **No credit cards. Map** p249 D5.

In a fortress built by the Habsburgs to intimidate Budapesters, this no-frills hotel boasts spectacular views from the top of Gellért Hill over the Danube. Book in advance, as the 12 double and four-bed rooms go fast – or there's one 14-person dorm room. The lot also features the very touristy Citadella restaurant, beer terrace and dance club (see *p178*). **Hotel services** *Bars (2). Café. Car park (free). Museum. Nightclub. Restaurant. Safe. Shops.*

Hotel Fortuna

IX. Gyáli út 3B (215 0660/fax 217 0666/ www.fortunahostel.hu). M3 Nagyvárad tér. **Rates** single €25-€50; double €42-€70; suite €67-€92; extra bed €17-€23. **Credit** AmEx, MC, V. **Map** p250 F4.

This simple hotel/hostel is a good launch pad into the speedily regenerated IX District, with its colourful buildings, pedestrianised streets and nightlife. The two suites feature their own kitchenette and air-conditioning. HI card yields a ten per cent discount. **Hotel services** *Bar. Breakfast. Car park (€5 per day). Internet. Non-smoking rooms (22).* **Room services** *Air-conditioning (in the suites). Minibar. Telephone. TV.*

Hostel Marco Polo

VII. Nyár utca 6 (413 2555/fax 413 6058/ www.marcopolohostel.com). M2 Blaha Lujza tér/tram 4, 6/bus 7. **Rates** single (€43-€50); double (€58-€68); dorm (€15-€18). **No credit cards. Map** p249 D4.

True to its name, Marco Polo ventures into new realms of hosteldom, matching budget facilities with hotel-like services. Clean and conveniently located near downtown, this hostel has great access to the barland of the VII District. **Hotel services** *Bar. Crib. Garden. Highchair. Internet. Kitchen. Laundry. Luggage room. Non-smoking rooms (all). Restaurant. Safe. 24hr reception.* **Room services** *Bathroom. Telephone. TV.*

Sightseeing

Feature boxes

Budapest

Districts - Kerületek

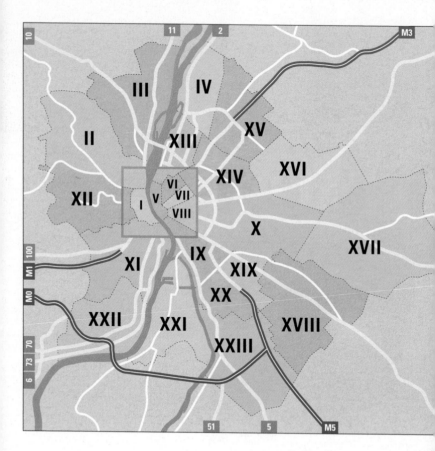

▶For more details on Budapest's 23 postal districts, *see p47*. For detailed street maps, *see pp243-251*.

Introduction

The Hungarian capital is far more than the sum of its three unequal parts:
Buda, Óbuda and Pest.

Few sights in Europe are as breathtaking as the panoramic one of Budapest straddling the Danube. Of all the spots on the river's long course between the Black Forest and the Black Sea, Budapest is the one to make full aesthetic use of the river. Necklaced by a series of pretty bridges, it is almost as if the Danube has been invented to lend the city its stunning beauty.

The metropolis spread out on either bank is a city constructed out of the economic boom of the late 19th century, Hungary's Golden Age. Most of the major sights and features – **Parliament**, the **Basilica**, the neo-medieval confectionery of **Castle Hill**, the classic attractions of **City Park**, the grandiose, ponderous municipal edifices of Pest – derive from Dual Monarchy dynamism.

The iconic **Chain Bridge**, built on the eve of the revolution that would eventually grant Hungarians the political and economic freedom to assemble their superb capital, was the first permanent span to connect Buda and Pest.

Before 1848 each developed independently. Early settlers, rulers and royalty – Celtic, Roman, Magyar, Mongol and Turk – were drawn to the controlling vantage over the river of hilly Buda. Set behind then German-speaking Buda, the rigid order of Vienna. The wide plain

St Stephen stands guard over **Fishermen's Bastion**. *See p57.*

Sightseeing

The best Transport connections

Bus 7: Runs the north-south Pest axis from Keleti station, down Rákóczi út, past Blaha Lujza tér, Astoria and Ferenciek tere, over Elizabeth Bridge and then down to Buda, running past the Gellért Hotel.

Bus 16: From Erzsébet tér up to Castle Hill.

Bus 26: From Nyugati station down to Margaret Island and along to Árpád Bridge.

Bus 86: From southern Buda past Gellért tér and right through the Víziváros towards Óbuda.

Várbusz: Regular minibus service from Moszkva tér to the Castle District.

Night bus 6É: Transports giggly drunks along the Nagykörút all night.

Tram 2: Takes a picturesque route along the pretty Pest embankment.

Trams 4/6: Run the length of the Nagykörút between Moszkva tér and back into Buda. Every two minutes in rush hour.

Tram 19: Bisects Víziváros between Batthyány tér and Kelenföld station.

Trams 47/49: Trundle along the Kiskörút from Deák tér, past Kálvin tér, over Szabadság Bridge, past the Gellért Hotel and on to Buda.

Travel the Nagykörút on the **No 4 tram**. *See p45.*

Sightseeing

Top ten Sights

Basilica
The city's cathedral, famous for containing the mummified right hand of Hungary's patron saint Stephen (*see p75*).

Central Synagogue
Newly restored, the world's second biggest synagogue offers a moving tribute to those lost in the Holocaust (*see p76* **Jewish Budapest**).

Chain Bridge
City icon spanning the Danube (*see p50*).

Gellért Baths
An art nouveau masterpiece set in the complex of the city's most famous hotel (*see p39* **Taking the waters**).

Margaret Island
An oasis of green amid a metropolis of choking traffic (*see p60* **Green Budapest**).

Matthias Church/ Fishermen's Bastion
Neo-Gothic revamping of the medieval temple where Good King Mátyás was twice married stands next to a neo-romantic confectionery with a perfect view over the river to Pest (*see p57*).

National Gallery
Vast collection of Hungarian art occupying three wings of the Royal Palace (*see p57*).

National Museum
Fascinating artefacts from Hungary's turbulent history (*see p79*).

Opera House
Sumptuous edifice, home of Liszt, Mahler and Erkel (*see p81*).

Parliament
Modelled on Westminster, the Magyar version is only accessible by taking a guided tour (*see p75*).

other business-like, sprawling and smog-bound. Wearing the scars of conflict, holocaust and uprising rises a city of quite extraordinary architecture, some of it pleasingly tatty, some swishly renovated as it heads towards a bright future as an EU capital by mid-2004.

Today's Budapest boasts two opera houses, 40 theatres, 60 museums, 90 galleries and countless cinemas. Entry to most costs little and travel between each is easily achieved with a superb transport system of three – soon to be four – colour-coded metro lines, buses, trams and trolleybuses. Even the furthest flung Roman ruins of Óbuda are 20 minutes from Parliament by the fast suburban train, the HÉV. Until 2004, though, don't expect much by way of English-language documentation in all but the most major museums.

Unlike Prague or Kraków, Budapest has no impenetrable old town of dark, narrow streets. Its main tourist treasures stand amid the rebuilt remains of what was Buda, the baroque city that emerged from lackadaisical Turkish occupation and the bitter conflict which ended it. Buda's remodelled **Royal Palace**, galleries, **bastion**, museums and churches of its Castle District can be reached from the river by a two-minute funicular and covered in an afternoon.

For the grimy, grid-patterned districts of Pest, let a strong pair of shoes do the walking, and a strong eye wander on its detail. Signs, shopfronts, secret courtyards, so soon devoured by global progress, preserve a pre-war past. Even as they go the way of most of the city's bright neon, the sounds and smells remain: a cello rehearsal, a scratch game of football in the yard, a barking dog following the wafts of meat stewing from kitchen windows. It seems as if someone has bottled up your childhood and tipped its contents out gently in front of you. The reality is that it's all backdropped by the occasional snatches of Hungarian's bizarre speech pattern, a sound made all the more alien by the warm familiarity of the tatty streets. Pest is a living, dying city.

Budapest is divided into 23 districts. The main areas of Buda are Districts I and II. Óbuda is District III. Pest is also divided according to its old Habsburg quarters, linked by ring roads as part of 19th-century planning. Downtown is the Belváros, or District V, the main shopping and business quarter. Districts VI and VII, bisected by the main ring road, the körút, and the grand avenue of Andrássy út, feature the bulk of the city's theatres, clubs, bars and cinemas. An average weekend's tourism will not go beyond VI and VII, apart from the City Park at the northern edge of each. Districts VIII, IX and XIII, though, also merit a wander.

of Pest would remain unfettered until the rapid invention of urbanisation and gradual cultural intervention of Hungarian after 1848. Beyond Pest lay the Byzantine chaos of the Balkans.

Once linked, Buda and Pest would be joined by the bygone village of Óbuda, in north Buda, to create the one city of Budapest in 1873.

Altitude and attitude still mark Buda from Pest, the one quiet, leafy and comfortable, the

Go green on **Margaret Island**.
See p60.

In this chapter we take you around Budapest area by area, single out the most important sights, and round up an assortment of other things to see and do. Places marked in **bold**, if they're not listed below, will be found with full listings in the appropriate chapters elsewhere in the book. Museums (www.museum.hu) range from those of national importance to the most unusual (*see p59* **Obscure Budapest**). Some of their buildings surpass their collections, Ödön Lechner's **Museum of Applied Arts** being a prime example (*see pp72-3* **Art nouveau Budapest**). Most open Tuesday to Sunday, 10am to 6pm, some closing earlier in winter. Most have one day a week free for visitors. Ticket offices close an hour before the museum does. Booklets (EB) and guided tours in English are available where indicated below.

Budapest Card

If you're sightseeing in a hurry, you should buy a Budapest Card, available from main metro stations, tourist offices, travel agencies and some hotels. It allows free travel on public transport, entry to 55 sights and museums, and discounts around town. A card for one adult plus one under-14 costs Ft4,000 for two days, Ft5,000 for three.

Tours

Budatours

VI. Andrássy út 2 (353 0558). M1 Bajcsy-Zsilinszky út. **Tours** every hr, 10.30am-3.30pm daily. **Tickets** Ft4,800; Ft2,400 children. **No credit cards**. Two-hour tours leave from outside the main office. Some buses in summer are open-top.

Ibusz

V. Ferenciek tere 10 (485 2700/www.ibusz.hu). **Tours** Parliament 10am daily. City tours 11am, 2pm daily. **Tickets** Parliament Ft8,800; city tour Ft6,000; Ft3,000 concessions. **Credit** MC, V. **Map** p249 C4. Buses leave from outside the Kempinski Hotel Corvinus (*see p32*) on Erzsébet tér. Tours last three hours, those with a Parliament visit four-and-a-half hours. One child under 12 allowed free.

Queenybus

XI. Törökbálinti út 28 (247 7159). **Tours** *Parliament* Mon, Wed-Sun 9am. *City tours* 10am, 1pm, 2.40pm daily. **Tickets** Parliament Ft8,200; city tour Ft6,000; Ft4,000 concessions. **No credit cards**. The first of the daily three-hour city tours includes a Parliament visit and sets off from the Museum of Ethnography (*see p75*). City tours without the visit leave from the main entrance of the Basilica (*see p75*). Reduced price for Budapest Card holders (*see above*); one child up to 12 allowed free. Open-top buses run from 1 June.

The Danube & Bridges

Panoramic backdrop for Europe's most beautiful capital.

The Danube river is integral to Budapest's history, economy and soul – as well as being a major contributor to some of the city's most beautiful scenery. Always present in the panorama from the Buda Hills, the Danube asserts itself even when out of sight. Stroll along one of the Pest streets leading down to the embankment and the light changes as you begin to approach the river, the result of refraction and sudden space.

When there are heavy rains or thaws upstream, the river can swell to twice its normal volume, flooding the roadways alongside the Danube. The city's history has been marked by more severe floods, and a particularly devastating one hit in 1838. Afterwards, flood control measures were implemented and Pest's streets were redesigned to incorporate the concentric ringed boulevards in place today.

Even when the water is at normal height, the Danube isn't blue, but rather a dull, muddy brown. Although people swim in the river north of the city, by the time the Danube passes through Budapest it is heavily polluted, even though old men still fish here.

The Danube is at its narrowest in Budapest, which makes it easier to span, and all of the seven bridges that carry traffic over the river here are short enough to stroll across in a matter of minutes. Stopping in the middle of any bridge (*híd*) affords excellent views of the city.

The northernmost span, the Újpesti Train Bridge, only carries rail, pedestrian and bicycle traffic over the river. The next one along, Árpád, is the longest. It connects the districts of Óbuda and Újpest, and also passes over **Margaret Island** (*see p60* **Green Budapest**). In theory, it's possible to get off in the middle of

Parliament – beautifully positioned on the brown Danube. *See p75.*

Árpád Bridge to access Margaret Island, but vehicle traffic is restricted here.

The Y-shaped French-built Margaret Bridge (Margit-híd), which carries the körút over the Danube, offers access to the downtown entrance of Margaret Island. From the fork in the middle of the bridge – a major tram stop – the city's pleasure gardens spread out below.

The next bridge down the Danube is the **Chain Bridge** (Lánchíd), constructed by diehard Anglophile Count István Széchenyi,

whose foresight would create much of general civic benefit throughout the 19th century (*see p11* **One-offs Széchenyi**). Guarded by stone lions and lit up at night, Széchenyi's bridge is one of the city's great icons. Plans are afoot to pedestrianise it.

South of this is Elizabeth Bridge (Erzsébet-híd), a modern, prosaic suspension bridge, replacing the ornate single-span chain version built in 1903. All of Budapest's downtown bridges were blown up by retreating Nazis at

Margaret Bridge gives access to the greenery of Margaret Island. *See p49.*

the end of the war; this one was the last to be rebuilt, in the 1960s. Szábádság Bridge, which connects the kiskörút with Gellért tér, has an appealing criss-cross of green girders, and is topped with golden-coloured mythical turul birds.

Further south, on the lower stretch of the Nagykörút, is the rather ordinary-looking Petőfi Bridge, on the Buda side of which are outdoor bars that open through the night in summer (*see p178* **Summer night city**).

Like Lágymányosi Bridge, south of it, Petőfi is long, full of fast-moving traffic and less inviting to strollers than the more central bridges. The southernmost bridge for traffic, Lágymányosi is the city's newest, opened in 1995. The high-tech, low-energy lighting on this bridge comes from mirrors overhead that reflect bright beams shooting up from pinpoint spotlights at road level.

Just ten metres south of Lágymányosi is the rail bridge that was once the only crossing here.

Buda

Sleepy, hilly and historic, blessed with healing waters, former royal Buda is now the city's main tourist draw.

Sightseeing

The strategic hill town of Buda grew up around its two main features, the castle (today's **Royal Palace**) and **Matthias Church**. King Béla IV established Buda as his capital by building the castle here in the 13th century; he founded the church at the same time, although it would take 200 years to complete. Each would be destroyed and rebuilt, most recently after 1945.

When its most prestigious sights were being built or rebuilt at the end of the 19th century, Buda consisted of pretty houses decked out in uniform Habsburg marzipan yellow stucco, set on cobbled streets, below vineyards and garden restaurants stretched out over the Buda Hills.

Although the vineyards and restaurants have now gone, locals still live here, an older, conservative generation who creep about while tourists gawp at the Gothic arches, plaques and fancy façades.

Castle and **Gellért Hills** carve up central Buda into a patchwork of separate parts. Below lie the old quarters of the Tabán and the Víziváros. Behind them, the area loses its definition around the two main transport hubs this side of the river, seedy Moszkva tér and Móricz Zsigmond körtér. To the north and west, smart residential districts amble up into still higher hills – leafy, spotted with villas and laced with excellent hiking trails. *See p60* **Green Budapest**.

Castle District

Castle Hill, Várhegy, is the city's leading tourist attraction, and no visit to Budapest is complete without at least one afternoon spent here.

Officially, the Castle District (Várnegyed) is the enclosed area of old residences north of the Royal Palace, but the terms 'District' and 'Hill' have become interchangeable.

Aside from the obvious major landmarks – the Royal Palace complex, Matthias Church and the **Fishermen's Bastion** – the narrow streets and open squares that top this 60-metre hill also contain museums from appealing oddities (*see p59* **Obscure Budapest**) to national institutions such as the **Széchényi Library** and the **National Gallery**, as well as assorted other churches, mansions and statues. Practically every building, as the ubiquitous stone plaques with their Hungarian-only

inscriptions indicate, seems to have been declared a *műemlék* ('historic monument').

The air of unreality is abetted by the quiet. You have to hold a permit, or else be staying at the **Hilton Hotel** (*see p31*), to bring a car into the Castle District (*see p80* **Pedestrianised Budapest**). Because this UNESCO-protected area is neatly contained on the top of a hill, the tourists have their own playground isolated from the rest of the city. They arrive by coach, by the regular diminutive Várbusz that pootles up from Moszkva tér, or by clip-clopping horse and carriage steered by traditionally costumed coachmen ready for hire at Szentháromság tér. The more adventurous can climb breathlessly up the twisting walkway that leads from Clark Ádám tér, or ride the elevator that leads from Dózsa György tér by the stop for the Nos.5 or 78 buses or No.18 tram.

A more romantic way to ascend the hill is the **sikló** (funicular) that crawls up the side of the Castle Hill in two minutes, offering a superb view of the Danube and Pest on the way up. Originally built in 1870 to provide cheap transport for clerks working in the Castle District – in the days when it was a centre of municipal offices and not museums – the first funicular was powered by a steam engine. It was restored and electrified in 1986.

Its lower entrance stands on Clark Ádám tér, named after the Scottish engineer who both supervised the construction of the nearby Chain Bridge and thwarted the Austrian army's attempt to destroy it shortly before its grand opening in 1849. Later, adjacent to it, Clark also built the Tunnel (Alagút) running under Castle Hill, allowing easy passage from Chain Bridge into Buda. On this same square stands the Zero Kilometre Stone, the point from which all distances to Budapest are measured.

Above towers the flat, rocky promontory of Castle Hill, whose strategic setting over the Danube has seen it fought over for centuries. Evidence of the most recent attack on the castle, the last desperate battles between the Nazis and Soviets, can be seen in the wrecked stump of the former **Ministry of Defence**, parts of which remain unrestored and bullet-pocked from the fighting in 1945. **Buda Castle** has been destroyed and rebuilt so many times that virtually nothing historically authentic remains.

Still, the past peeks through the architecture of the reconstruction: the baroque façades on Úri utca often include Gothic windows and doorframes; reconstructed merchants' houses can be found at Tárnok utca 14 and 16, and distinctive *sedilias*, seats for servants inside gateways, are located at Országház utca 9 and Szentháromság tér 5 and 7.

The centrepiece of Castle Hill, though, is the huge Royal Palace, a post-war reconstruction of an architectural hotch-potch from the 18th, 19th and 20th centuries. It was under the reign of King Mátyás (1458-90) that the Royal Palace reached its apogee. Mátyás's renaissance-style court featured hot and cold running water and fountains that spouted wine. Partially wrecked during the Turkish siege of 1541, the area was completely laid waste when recaptured from the Turks in 1686. Empress Maria Theresa caused a new 203-room palace to be built in the late 18th century. This was badly damaged in the 1848-49 War of Independence, then rebuilt and expanded in neo-baroque style by Miklós Ybl and Alajos Hauszmann at the same time as Frigyes Schulek's reconstruction of Matthias Church and erection of Fishermen's Bastion at the end of the century.

Destroyed in the war, it took 30 years to rebuild Buda Castle to the simpler state you find it in today, a large complex housing the Hungarian National Gallery, the National Széchényi Library, the **Budapest History Museum** and the **Ludwig Contemporary Art Museum** (*see p161*).

Occupying central wings B, C and D of the palace, the Hungarian National Gallery is a vast museum that attempts to chronicle Magyar art since the birth of the nation. Seeing all six permanent exhibits of paintings, sculptures, ecclesiastical art, medallions and graphics would require more than one visit. The two collections considered the most important are its 15th- and 16th-century winged altarpieces and its mid 19th- to early 20th-century art. Most of the work here derives from major European art movements of classicism, impressionism, Fauvism and art nouveau. There are depictions of Hungarian history by Viktor Madarász and lively sculptures of Hungarian peasants by Miklós Izsó. Mihály Munkácsy's paintings are considered an important contribution to Hungarian art, especially his *Yawning Journeyman* (1868).

Also noteworthy are the many works of impressionist József Rippl-Rónai, Hungary's Whistler (he even painted his mother), and great early 20th-century painters, such as the symbolists Lajos Guláscy and János Vaszary, the mad, self-taught genius Tivadar Koszta Csontváry and the sad figure of István Farkas,

a Jew murdered at the end of the war. For a small fee, a guide can take you round the Palatine Crypt under the museum, built in 1715 as part of the Habsburg palace reconstruction.

The National Széchényi Library in wing F contains seven storeys, housing more than five million books, manuscripts, papers, newspapers and journals – anything, in fact, related to Hungary or in Hungarian published anywhere in the world. To browse or research, bring a passport and ask for English-speaking staff. The building is named after Count Ferenc Széchényi (father of 19th-century reformer István), who donated his library to the state in 1802. The institution has volumes (*Corviniani*) that belonged to King Mátyás, who owned one of the largest collections in renaissance Europe. Sadly, these are rarely displayed.

Not surprisingly, the Budapest History Museum presents the city in an attractive historical light. Beginning with the earliest tribal settlements, artefacts, illustrations and excavation photos, all described in English, trace Budapest's development up to the present day. Displays focus on key symbols: Charles of Lothringen's Triumphal Arch to celebrate the defeat of the Ottomans, the Danube which both divides and unites Budapest, the May Day 1919 red drapes which represent the Socialist ideal

Socialist style at **Moszkva tér**.
See p62.

Sightseeing

Turkish Budapest

Sightseeing

Although Budapest is often described as standing between east and west, locals prefer to stress the occident and denigrate the orient. 'What did the Turks ever do for us?' might be the cry. While sipping coffee in garden cafés near the baths of Buda, they can hardly imagine that both the coffee and the baths share their origins in the days when Buda was the centre of the Ottoman Empire's final, and fatal, drive to conquer Christian Europe in the 16th century.

When Béla Bartók collected songs among the folk bards of Turkish Anatolia, they were still singing about the beauties of the great city along the Danube. Even today, every dining table in the restaurants and kitchens of Hungary has a three-piece condiment set of salt, pepper and paprika, the latter an essential ingredient of Magyar cuisine brought here, circuitously, from Turkey.

Hungarian historians tended to revile Turkish rule – understandably since most historians tended to be clerics, unlikely to remember Muslim rule favourably.

Buda Castle fell to the Turkish armies in 1541, yet Ottoman rule provided 150 years of relative peace and stability until the castle fell to Habsburg siege in 1686. Under Turkish rule, Buda Castle was declared a Muslim city, and Matthias Church and other churches were converted into mosques. When they were converted back, some still contained *mihrabs*, small prayer niches pointing towards Mecca.

The Ottomans repopulated Buda with trustworthy subjects in various *mahalle*, or residence districts. Turks settled in the castle itself as well as in today's Víziváros district; Sephardic Jews, fleeing the Spanish Inquisition, settled on Fortuna utca; Coptic Gypsy swordsmiths set up shop near Buda Gate by Moszkva tér; and Italian merchants had the run of Szentháromság tér. Allied Bosnian Muslims and loyal Serbs both manufactured gunpowder just south of the castle in the Tabán (named after the Turkish *tabahane*, 'armoury'). A stroll through the park along Buda Castle's southern slope in

Tabán still reveals turban-topped Turkish gravestones hidden among the bushes.

The Turks were quick to take advantage of Buda's limestone hot springs, and the construction of hamams, or traditional bathhouses, were among the first public works projects. Originally a bath, social centre and teetotaler's pub, today the best-preserved examples of classic Turkish baths include the **Rudas**, **Rác** and **Király** baths, all on the Buda side (*see pp146-148*). On the cliff above the Rudas, over the road from the No.7 bus stop, plaques note the springs emerging from the hill here: among the names are Sokoli Mustapha, Pasha from 1566-1578, who built the Rudas, and **Gül Baba**. Also known as the 'Father of the Roses', the tomb (*see p63*) of this Dervish saint and personal companion of Sultan Suliman the Magnificent stands further north near Margaret Bridge, on Mecset utca ('Mosque Street'), a quaint, cobbled alleyway. It remains the northernmost active centre of pilgrimage for Bektashi Muslims. It is thought that Gül Baba introduced the rose to Hungary, and gave his name to the now-glitzy hill behind his tomb: Rózsadomb, or Rose Hill.

At the northern end of the Castle District is a memorial to the last Pasha of Buda. Vizir Abdurrahman Abdi Arnaut Pasha was killed and buried here in 1686. 'A valient foe,' reads the inscription, 'may he rest in peace.' People still leave fresh flowers. The Vienna Gate nearby marks the 1686 reconquest.

While most of their monuments later fell into ruins, Turks left their mark on Hungarian cuisine and language. Paprika, kukorica ('corn') and dohány ('tobacco') owe their names to the people that first introduced them. Fig trees still adorn Ménesi utca on Gellért Hill, first planted there 400 years ago.

When the Turks abandoned their failed siege of Vienna in 1683, they left behind sacks of nearly inedible beans to be found by the starving Habsburg defenders. Roasted and sweetened into a kind of palatable black soup, coffee had arrived in the Austro-Hungarian world.

and contemporary urban sites including József Finta's hotels and bank centres contrasted with Imre Makovecz's organic villas and yurt houses. A dark room is full of ghoulish Gothic statues unearthed at the castle, pre-dating King Mátyás. The lower levels are partially

reconstructed remains of Mátyás's palace, with a vaulted chapel and music room. The upper floor houses temporary exhibits.

The Ludwig is one of the few museums here that doesn't concentrate solely on Hungarian themes. Its standing collection features pieces

Castle Hill – fought over for centuries and now under tourist control. *See p52.*

by Picasso, Warhol, Oldenburg and other big names, its rotating exhibitions showcasing the best contemporary European artists and attracting non-tourists up to Castle Hill.

Outside the palace, at Szent György tér, you come across the Turul Statue, a huge mythical bird portrayed in bronze by Gyula Donáth in 1905. According to legend, this protector of the Hungarian nation raped the grandmother of Árpád, legendary conqueror of the Carpathian Basin, and sired the first dynasty of Hungarian kings. Later he flew with the invading tribes, carrying the sword of Attila the Hun. In Siberian mythology, the eagle is the creator of the world, lord of the sun. Ancient Magyars believed they were descended from this god. By 1896, Austrian conquerors claimed their share of this Hungarian blue blood. The Turul myth, co-opted to serve this new master, was positioned here by the palace. The turul eagle is a common motif on turn-of-the-century Budapest structures, including the main gates of the Parliament and Szabadság Bridge.

Strolling from the palace towards Szentháromság tér, you'll pass the **Golden Eagle Pharmacy Museum**, located in a 15th-century house that is one of the oldest in the Castle District. It offers an attractive collection from Hungarian and pharmaceutical history, including a reconstruction of an alchemist's laboratory, mummy powder from Transylvania (believed to cure epilepsy) and a painting of a nun performing, as they did in the Middle Ages, the duties of a chemist. On the parallel street of Úri utca is the **Buda Castle Labyrinth** (Budavári Labirintus), Castle Hill's ten-kilometre network of caves and man-made

passageways, used as an air-raid shelter in the war before being converted into a poor waxworks museum, and today illustrating the history of shamanism and cave painting. Along the same street is the appealingly antiquated **Telephone Museum** (*see p59* **Obscure Budapest**).

At the heart of the Castle District stands Szentháromság tér. Centrepieced by a decorated column celebrating the ending of the plague epidemic of 1713, 'Holy Trinity Square' is dominated by the neo-Gothic mish-mash of Matthias Church (Mátyás templom). Named after Good King Mátyás, who was twice married here, parts of the structure date from the 13th century, but most was reconstructed in the 19th century. Converted into the Great Mosque by Buda's Turkish rulers in 1541, the building suffered terribly during the six-week siege in 1686 when Vienna took it back from Istanbul. Some 200 years later, architect Frigyes Schulek returned to the original 13th-century plan but also added his own decorative details, such as the gargoyle-bedecked stone spire. The interior is brightly coloured, almost playful, as is the gingerbread house roofing on the exterior. There's a Museum of Ecclesiastical Art in the crypt. In the evenings, the church hosts classical concerts (*see p168*).

Harmonising his romanticised reconstruction of Matthias Church, Schulek built the crenellated Fishermen's Bastion (Halászbástya) next door. Proudly guarded by a statue of St Stephen, this neo-Romanesque vantage point offers several fantastic views across the Danube and Pest. It has seven turrets, one for each of the original Hungarian tribes.

Várkert Casino – from pumphouse to gambling house. *See p58*.

Less ostentatious sights abound. Where Úri utca and Szentháromság utca meet stands the equestrian statue of the hussar András Hadik, a favourite of Maria Theresa and later governor of Transylvania. Pre-exam engineering students still consider it good luck to rub the testicles of Hadik's horse. Just around the corner, on Hess András tér – named after the man who printed the first Hungarian book on the same square – is the Red Hedgehog House (Vörös Sün-ház), which dates back at least as far as 1390. Once apparently owned by a nobleman whose coat of arms was the hedgehog, it was converted to an inn after the Turks were driven from Buda and is now a private residence with several flats. Nearby is the **Ruszwurm** (*see p114*), the city's oldest pastry shop, *cukrászda*, and a tourist haven. Famous confectioners are also celebrated at the **Museum of Commerce and Catering** (*see p59* **Obscure Budapest**), round the corner at Fortuna utca.

The streets of the Castle District still follow the lines of their medieval ones, protected by a series of gates. At the northern end, between the Vienna Gate, the Memorial to the last Pasha of Buda (*see p54* **Turkish Budapest**) and the Anjou Bastion, stands the **Museum of Military History**, set in a former 18th-century barracks, with displays on hand weapons and the street fighting of the 1956 Uprising. Beside it is the site of the Mária Magdolna templom (Church of St Mary Magdelene), where Magyar Christians worshipped when Matthias Church was ruled by Buda's German population. All but the tower and gate were pulled down after the destruction of World War II.

Running along the western ramparts is Tóth Árpád sétány, the promenade overlooking Vérmező, a pretty park first used by King Mátyás for jousting tournaments, but named after a mass execution of Hungarian rebel leaders by the Habsburgs in 1795. Beyond stand the houses of Krisztinaváros and ugly **Déli station**, the main departure point for trains to former Yugoslavia and the Adriatic. The view, beautiful at sunset under the chestnut trees, extends westwards over the rolling Buda Hills. Relatively tourist-free, this is where the old folk of the Castle District come to stroll.

Buda Castle Labyrinth

Budavári Labirintus
I. Úri utca 9 (212 0287 ext 34). Várbusz from M2 Moszkva tér/bus 16. **Open** 9.30am-7pm daily. **Admission** Ft1,000; Ft800 concessions; call to arrange tours in English. **No credit cards. Map** p245 B3.

Budapest History Museum

Budapesti Történeti Múzeum
I. Buda Palace, Wing E (225 7816/www.btm.hu).

Várbusz from M2 Moszkva tér/bus 16. **Open** *16 May-15 Sept* 10am-6pm daily; *16 Sept-15 May* 10am-6pm Mon, Wed-Sun. **Admission** Ft700; Ft350 concessions. Call to arrange a guided tour in English prior to visit. EB Ft1,000-Ft2,570. **No credit cards. Map** p248 B4.

Fishermen's Bastion

Halászbástya
I. Várhegy. Várbusz/bus 16. **Open** 24hrs daily. **Admission** (9am-11pm) Ft300; Ft150 children. **No credit cards. Map** p245 A3.

Funicular

Sikló
I. Clark Ádám tér (201 9128). Tram 19/bus 16, 86, 105. **Open** 7.30am-10pm daily. Closed every other Mon 7.30am-3pm. **Tickets** Ft500 up; Ft400 down; Ft300 children. **Map** p248 B4.

Golden Eagle Pharmaceutical Museum

Arany Sas Patikamúzeum
I. Tárnok utca 18 (375 9772). Várbusz from M2 Moszkva tér/bus 16. **Open** *Nov-Feb* 10.30am-4pm Tue-Sun; *Mar-Oct* 10.30am-6pm Tue-Sun. **Admission** Ft150; Ft100 concessions; guided tour in English Ft800. EB Ft600. **No credit cards. Map** p245 A3.

Hungarian National Gallery

Magyar Nemzeti Galéria
I. Buda Palace, Wings B, C, E (375 7533 ext 423/ www.mng.hu). Várbusz from M2 Moszkva tér/ bus 16. **Open** 10am-6pm Tue-Sun. **Admission** Ft700; Ft350 concessions; guided tour in English for up to 5 people Ft1,300. EB Ft300. **No credit cards. Map** p248 B4.

Matthias Church

Mátyás templom
I. Szentháromság tér 2 (355 5657/www.matyas-templom.hu). Várbusz from M2 Moszkva tér/ bus 16. **Open** 9am-5pm daily. **Admission** *to treasury* Ft400; Ft200 concessions. **No credit cards. Map** p245 A3.

Museum of Military History

Hadtörténeti Múzeum
I. Tóth Árpád sétány 40 (356 9522/ www.militaria.hu). Várbusz from M2 Moszkva tér. **Open** *Oct-Mar* 10am-4pm Tue-Sun; *June-Sept* 10am-6pm Tue-Sun. **Admission** Ft400; Ft200 concessions. Call to arrange a guided tour in English a week prior to visit. **No credit cards. Map** p245 A3.

National Széchényi Library

Országos Széchényi Könyvtár
I. Buda Palace, Wing F (224 3848/www.oszk.hu). Várbusz from M2 Moszkva tér/bus 16. **Open** *Exhibits* 1-5pm Mon, 9am-5pm Tue-Fri, 9am-1pm Sat; *Library* 1-9pm Mon, 9am-9pm Tue-Fri, 9am-5pm Sat. **Admission** most exhibits free, others cost Ft200-Ft300. Full passport required to enter library – ask for English-speaking member of staff. **No credit cards. Map** p248 B4.

Sightseeing

Sightseeing

The Tabán & Gellért Hill

South of Castle Hill is a quiet, shady park that dominates the neighbourhood known as Tabán. The area was once a disreputable quarter, inhabited by Serbs, Greeks and Gypsies, most of whom made their living on the river – until the Horthy government levelled it in the 1930s.

Appropriately enough for an area once renowned for its gambling dens, one of the sites that wasn't levelled now houses the Várkert Casino. The building was originally a pumphouse that furnished water for the Royal Palace. It was designed in neo-renaissance style by Miklós Ybl, who also designed the 19th-century exterior of the **Rác baths** (*see p148 and p54* **Turkish Budapest***), on the other side of the park below Gellért Hill. The Rác's original domed Turkish pool survives within.

Across the street from the Várkert is the **Semmelweis Museum of Medical History**, named after Dr Ignác Semmelweis, the Hungarian surgeon who discovered how to prevent puerperal fever – blood poisoning contracted during childbirth. Semmelweis, who was born in this building, became known as the 'mothers' saviour', because he realised that doctors who'd just performed an autopsy should wash their hands before delivering babies. The museum shows his belongings, as well as a general medical exhibition. Another room contains the 1786 Holy Ghost Pharmacy, transported whole from Király utca.

Further south, past Elizabeth Bridge are the **Rudas baths** (*see p148 and p54* **Turkish Budapest***), soon to be renovated. In summer, there's usually a small terrace bar operating next door, and offering a view of the river.

The intimidating Gellért Hill is easy to climb via a network of paths and steps that are cut into the cliff and begin at the stairs below the **Gellért Statue**, across from the entry to Elizabeth Bridge. The short, steep hike may leave you panting by the time you reach the **Citadella**, but you'll be rewarded with fine views of Budapest on the way up, as well as a close-up look at the 11-metre tall sculpture of Bishop Gellért (Gerard) raising his cross towards Pest, as if admonishing the sinners there. The statue and the artificial waterfall underneath were erected in 1904 to mark the country's first Christian martyr. Gellért, an Italian missionary, was caught up in a ninth-century pagan revolt against St Stephen's efforts to make Hungary Catholic. According to legend, the heathens put the bishop inside a barrel lined with spikes and rolled him down this hill into the Danube.

The grim Citadella on the 230-metre summit was built by the Habsburgs to assert their authority after they put down Hungary's 1848-49 War of Independence. The site's commanding view put the city within easy range should the Magyars choose to get uppity again. The Dual Monarchy meant that its guns were never fired in anger against the city – although the Hungarian army set off a blaze of fireworks from the hilltop for the celebrations on **St Stephen's Day** every 20 August (*see p144*). The site now houses a **youth hostel** (*see p42*), restaurant and **nightclub** (*see p178*), plus an exhibition of the area's history since its settlement by the Celts.

Perched above it, and visible from points all around the city, is the 14-metre **Liberty Statue** (Felszabadulási Emlékmű), depicting Lady Liberty hoisting a palm frond over her head. The statue was built to mark liberation from Fascist rule by Soviet soldiers in 1945. Stories abound of sculptor Zsigmond Kisfaludy-Stróbl being originally commissioned to create the statue as a memorial to the son of Admiral Horthy, the ultra right-wing leader of the inter-war years, and that the palm branch was meant to be a propeller blade (Horthy junior was a pilot). But this is a myth. This is a rare example of surviving Soviet statuary in Budapest, though the bronze figures of Soviet soldiers that once stood at its base have been moved, like most other public monuments of that era, to the **Statue Park** (*see p86* **Socialist Budapest**).

The **National Gallery** – Magyar art from birth. *See p57.*

Don't miss Obscure Budapest

Agriculture Museum

Mezőgazdasági Múzeum
XIV. Vajdahunyad Castle in Városliget (363 5099). **Map** p247 F1.
Housed in a beautiful baroque wing of Vajdahunyad Castle, this museum dedicated to rural Hungary has stuffed animals and farm-related displays, including antique ploughs and an aerosol spray can labelled 'PIG SEX'.

Capital Sewerage Works Museum

Fővárosi Csatornázási Művek Múzeuma
II. Zsigmond tér 1-4 (335 4984).
Quite smelly building which is full of shiny black pumps.

Crime & Police History Museum

Bűnügyi és Rendőrség-történeti Múzeum
VIII. Mosonyi utca 7 (477 2183/ www.policehistorymus.com). **Map** p250 F4.
Various police uniforms and weapons from Habsburg times to today, with ghoulish re-creations of murder scenes featuring life-sized dummies 'bleeding' red paint and stuffed police dogs.

Ferenc Hopp Museum of Eastern Asiatic Arts

Kelet-Ázsia Művészeti Múzeuma
VI. Andrássy út 103 (322 8476/ www.museum.hu/budapest/hopp).
Map p247 E2.
In five trips around the world, Ferenc Hopp (1833-1919) amassed over 4,000 pieces of Asian art, including Lamaist scroll paintings and old Indian art influenced by ancient Greece.

Gizi Bajor Theatre Museum

Bajor Gizi Színészmúzeum
XII. Stromfeld Aurél út 16 (356 4294/ www.museum.hu/budapest/bajor).
This lovely, turn-of-the-century villa and former home of actress Gizi Bajor (1893-1951) houses an exhibition devoted to the history of early cinema and actors from the National Theatre.

György Ráth Museum

VI. Városligeti fasor 12 (342 3916).
Map p247 E2.
György Rath was an artist and Asian art historian who collected snuff bottles, scroll paintings, miniature shrines, Samurai armour

and a finely carved lobster on a lacquer comb from Japan. Detailed English texts, and a regular series of temporary exhibitions.

Hungarian Museum of Electrotechnics

Magyar Elektrotechnikai Múzeum
VII. Kazinczy utca 21 (322 0472).
Map p249 D4.
Inside a 1930s transformer station, men in white coats demonstrate things that crackle and spark, including the world's first electric motor, designed by a Hungarian Benedictine monk.

Museum of Commerce & Catering

Kereskedelmi és Vendéglátói Múzeum
I. Fortuna utca 4 (375 6249/www.mkvm.hu).
Map p245 A3.
Features adverts from the early 20th century, including Hungary's first electric billboard and a model dog atop an old phonograph that raps its paws against the glass case – as well as objects from old hotels and coffeehouses.

Museum of Firefighting

Tűzoltó Múzeum
X. Martinovics tér 12 (261 3586).
The first motorised water pump, brought to Hungary by Széchenyi's son Ödön in 1870, plus the original motorised dry extinguisher invented by Kornél Szilvay in 1928.

Telephone Museum

Telefónia Múzeum
I. Úri utca 49 (201 2243). **Map** p245 A3.
Old switchboards and telephones described in wonderfully useless Hunglish. Hungary's own Tivadar Puskás, a major influence on Thomas Edison, invented the telephone exchange.

Transport Museum

Közlekedési Múzeum
XIV. Városligeti körút 11 (273 3840).
Map p247 F2.
Antique cars, trams, a steam train, model boats and hands-on exhibits, plus a model train revved up every hour to whip through a realistic miniature Hungarian countryside.

Underground Railway Museum

Földalatti Múzeum
Deák tér metro station (461 6500).
Map p249 C4.
Original carriages from continental Europe's first underground, built in 1896.

Green Budapest

Sightseeing

Despite eating, drinking and smoking habits that border on suicidal, Hungarians extol the importance of fresh air. A day in the country is a weekend ritual for many Budapesters, but when they can't get that far, the city has plenty of green space that offers residents and visitors pleasant half-hour, or half-day, getaways.

Car-free Margaret Island (Margitsziget), set in the Danube between Buda and Pest, is the city's main pleasure garden. Literally a stone's throw from the heaving 4/6 tram carrying busy commuters overhead between the two halves of the metropolis, Margaret Island has been a place of refuge and relaxation since the Middle Ages. The ruins of a 13th-century Dominican church and convent – former home of Princess Margit, after whom the island is named – can still be seen, by a UNESCO-protected water tower and exhibition space. In the summer of 1989, hundreds of East German families camped out around the island before making their way to the open border with Austria.

Landscaped in the 19th century, the island was made accessible to the public with an extension of Margaret Bridge in 1901. A spa, hotel, rose garden and open-air café and restaurant provided entertainment under the shade of the 10,000 trees here; apart from an upgrade in facilities, little has changed since.

The spa hotels are now the attractively modern **Danubius Grand** and **Thermal Margitsziget** (*see p39* **Taking the waters**), swimming pools include the **Hajós Alfréd** and the **Palatinus** (*see p187*), and along with the rose garden, there's now a modest petting zoo, an open-air theatre and cinema, and tennis courts. Bikes and pedalos can be hired (bring a passport), and horse-drawn buggies carry you the three-kilometre stretch between Margaret Bridge and the northern tip at Árpád Bridge.

For more complete isolation, the Buda Hills are easily accessible by public transport. Catch the red No.21 bus from Déli station and ride the 20 minutes to the terminus at Normafa, where the forest begins. From there, you can wander the trails of Budakeszierdő Park, which pass by the Children's Railway and connect with other parks, or you can follow the signs for Budakeszi, which will lead you on an enjoyable, three-hour downhill hike through woods. You'll come out at Budakeszi, where you can catch a bus back to Moszkva tér.

Alternatively, take the red No.22 bus from Moszkva tér to the Budakeszi game reserve (Vadaspark), which stretches past the city limits into sprawling forest. Near the entrance is a small zoo. Beyond lie enough hiking hills and woods to keep you occupied all day. Take a good map and hiking boots, and watch out for rampaging wild boar.

There's also a strange network of eccentric forest transport. A cog-wheel railway runs from Szilágyi Erzsébet fasor, opposite the Budapest Hotel, up to the summit of Széchenyi Hill. There's a small park here, and you already feel as if you're out of the city. On the other side of the park is the narrow-gauge Children's

If you leave the Citadella by taking the path downhill in a southerly direction, heading towards the famous **Gellért Hotel** (*see p33*) at Gellért tér, you'll pass the **Cave Church**, an odd and somewhat spooky place of worship run by monks of the Hungarian Paulite order. Although the caves in this cliff were inhabited 4,000 years ago, the Cave Church was only dedicated in 1926 and expanded in 1931 by Count Gyula Zichy, archbishop of Kalocsa, who had helped re-establish the Hungarian Paulite order of monks. The monastery next door opened in 1934, and the monks resumed their work after an interval of 150 years. The Communist Party jailed the monks in the 1950s and the cave was boarded up for decades, reopening in August 1989.

At the Buda foot of Szabadság Bridge stands the four-star Gellért Hotel, an imposing art nouveau edifice with a complex of thermal baths and swimming pools behind. Even if you don't want to swim, soak or sleep here, it's worth poking your head round the entrance on Kelenhegyi út, just to observe the impressively ornate secessionist foyer. The café offers suitably elegant surroundings for breakfast, although one of Budapest's best bars can be found right round the corner on Budafoki út: the **Libella Café** (*see p112*).

Cave Church
Sziklatemplom
XI. Gellérthegy (385 1529). Tram 19, 47, 49/bus 7.
Open 9-10.30am, noon-4pm, 6.30-7.30pm daily.
Admission free. **Map** p249 C5.

Railway. This was once run by Pioneers, the Communist youth organisation whose membership supplied the conductors. Its charming trains, open to the breeze and still manned by children, snake hourly through wooded patches of the Buda Hills. The last station at Hűvösvölgy is near the end of the No.56 tram line and close to a modest amusement park in the Nagy-rét picnic area. The ever popular Náncsi Néni restaurant (II.Ördögárok út 80; 376 5809) is also nearby.

Alight earlier, or take a No.190 bus to its terminus, and you'll be on János-hegy, the city's highest hill, at 527 metres. Near the

bus stop is the station for the chairlift (*libegő*), which conveys you downhill into urban Buda, the city spread grandly before you as you ride. At the other end is the No.158 bus to Moszkva tér.

It's a short, steep hike to the top of János-hegy, where the view from the Erzsébet lookout tower puts the city in context: the rolling Buda Hills, the barely significant Castle Hill and, far across the Danube, the outskirts of Pest shade into a patchwork of fields that eventually disappear into a long, flat, dusty horizon – the beginning of the Great Hungarian Plain.

Citadella
XI. Gellérthegy. Bus 27. **Map** p248 B5.

Gellért Statue
XI. Gellérthegy. Tram 18, 19/bus 7. **Map** p248 B5.

Liberty Statue
Felszabadulási Emlékmű
XI. Gellérthegy. Bus 27. **Map** p249 C5.

Semmelweis Museum of Medical History
Semmelweis Orvostörténeti Múzeum
I. Apród utca 1-3 (375 3533/www.museum.hu/budapest/semmelweis). Tram 18. **Open** 10.30am-5.30pm Tue-Sun. **Admission** Ft250; Ft100 concessions; guided tour in English Ft500. EB Ft850-Ft1,000. **No credit cards.** **Map** p248 B4.

The Víziváros

From the north-east side of the Castle District, the ancient streets of the Víziváros ('Water Town') cascade down towards the Danube. This neighbourhood stretches along the river from Clark Ádám tér, by Chain Bridge, to the foot of Margaret Bridge. One of Budapest's oldest districts, Víziváros centres around Fő utca, which was built in Roman times.

This quiet neighbourhood is lined with medieval houses, baroque churches and narrow streets. George Maurois' **Institut Français**, built in 1992 at Fő utca 17, is one of the city's few decent postmodern buildings. It enjoys a prominent waterfront location, used for a flashy **Bastille Day** fireworks display every 14 July (*see p144*). The institute, home to a French library and myriad cultural events, is on a tiny square that connects Fő utca to Bem rakpart, a pleasant, tree-lined street.

North along the river is cool, shady Szilágy Dezső tér, site of a neo-Gothic Calvinist church. This is also the historical site of a massacre. In January 1945, after Nazi occupiers had already fled, members of the Hungarian Fascist Arrow Cross Party killed hundreds of Budapest's Jews and dumped their bodies into the river. A small plaque serves as a memorial to these victims (*see p76* **Jewish Budapest**).

Batthyány tér is the area's centrepiece, a pedestrianised square that is both a transport hub (it's the southern terminal of the HÉV line to Szentendre) and impromptu marketplace for second-hand goods. Fringed by 18th- and 19th-century architecture – including an otherwise disappointing indoor market – the square offers an excellent view of Parliament across the river. Perched on its southern side is the **Church of St Anne**, one of Hungary's finest baroque buildings. If you only visit one church in Budapest, this should be it. Construction began in 1740, to the plans of Jesuit Ignatius Pretelli. Máté Nepauer, one of the most prominent architects of Hungarian baroque, oversaw its completion in 1805. The façade is crowned by the eye-in-the-triangle symbol of the Trinity, while Faith, Hope and Charity loiter around the front door. The theatricality of the interior is typical of the style. Larger-than-life statues are frozen in performance on the High Altar, framed by black marble columns representing the Temple of Jerusalem. In the old presbytery next door is the atmospheric **Angelika Café** (*see p110*), its interior illuminated through the glow of stained-glass windows. There's a cool, shady terrace here in the warmer months.

Further along, Batthyány tér 4 was built in 1770 as the White Cross Inn, these days called Casanova House as he once stayed here. No.3 next door is a rare example of a late baroque style known as copfstil.

North along Fő utca, at Nos.70-72, is the Military Court of Justice, used as a prison and headquarters by both the Gestapo in the early 1940s and the secret police in the Stalinist 1950s. Here Imre Nagy and associates were tried in secret and condemned to death after the 1956 revolution. Just a block away is the **Király Baths** (*see p54* **Turkish Budapest** *and p148)*, another leftover from the Turkish days and, unlike the other Ottoman bathhouses, interesting to view from outside.

The street ends at Bem tér, where there's a statue of General Joseph Bem, a Polish general who led the Hungarian army in the War of Independence. His aide-de-camp was national poet Sándor Petőfi, whose verse is engraved on the pedestal. On 23 October 1956, this small square was the site of a huge demonstration against Soviet rule, held in sympathy of political changes in Poland at the time. It was the start of the revolution that ended with Nagy's trial in the Military Court, three blocks up the road. *See p18* **1956 and all that**.

Church of St Anne
Szent Anna templom
I. Batthyány tér 8 (318 5536). M2 Batthyány tér.
Open *Services* 6.45-9am, 4-7pm daily; 7am-1pm Sun and public hols. **Admission** free. **Map** p245 B3.

Moszkva tér & the Buda Hills

Ugly and dilapidated, Moszkva tér, a transport hub connecting the Buda Hills to the rest of town, bustles with a cross-section of Budapest. From 5am it's an unofficial labour market, where itinerant workers wait for someone to hire them. Hungarians from rural areas also cluster here, selling flowers, fruit and lace tablecloths.

The metro entrance and attached shops at Moszkva tér are done up in a tacky Socialist-era design, which is complemented by the tacky capitalist-era design displayed in the neighbouring **Mammut Center** mall (*see p129*) and the new events centre of **Millenáris Park**. Finished in 2001 on the site of the headquarters of the old Ganz works, a former foundry and electrical factory, some structures were renovated to make industrial-sized spaces for concerts and exhibitions.

The venue is also used for a children's playground (*see p150*), although the political motives behind its construction are more sinister: it was commissioned by the right-wing FIDESZ-MDF government to mark the millennium of the crowning of St Stephen. The park is shaped like a microcosm of Hungary, with a small pool intended to symbolise Lake Balaton, and a tiny cornfield and grape arbour symbolising the various agricultural regions (security guards prevent visitors from picking the grapes). Long-term exhibitions, like the one on great Hungarian innovators, are shamelessly pro-Magyar, but can be interesting nonetheless.

Amid the Magyar overkill and Mammut mall are still small hold-outs against postmodernity. In nearby Retek utca, the **Szent Jupát** restaurant (*see p93*) serves hearty platefuls deep into the night and **Auguszt Cukrászda** (*see p119* **Let them eat cake**) on Fény utca serves some of the city's finest cakes and pastries. Despite the bustle, Moszkva tér remains principally a tawdry transition zone.

Down near the Buda foot of Margaret Bridge, you can walk up the narrow, cobbled Mecset utca and come to the **Tomb of Gül Baba**

Musical miscellanea at the **Béla Bartók Memorial House**. *See p63.*

(*see p54* **Turkish Budapest**). Gül Baba was a Turkish Dervish and member of the Bektashi order. His name means 'father of roses' and, according to local folklore, he introduced the flower to Budapest, thus giving the name Rózsadomb (Rose Hill) to the area. Inside the mausoleum, recently renovated by the Turkish government, are verses inscribed by Turkish traveller Evliya Tselebi in 1663.

The tomb is at the foot of the Rózsadomb, for generations Budapest's ritziest residential area. It was said in Communist times that inhabitants of the airy Rózsadomb had the same life expectancy as in Austria, while the citizens of polluted Pest below had the life expectancy of Syria: two continents in one city. It isn't much less of a contrast today. Unless you're either staying here or visiting one of the area's garden restaurants, such as the **Vadrózsa** (*see p93*) or Remiz (II. Budakeszi út 5; 275 1396), there aren't many reasons to go to Rózsadomb.

The yurt houses designed by Imre Makovecz on Törökvész utca are one local architectural attraction. The Napraforgó utca housing estate, where each house is built in a different style, is another. Completed in 1931, the 22 houses here exemplify different styles of the modern movement, combining industrial production methods with traditional craftsmanship. Most of the estate, accessible by bus No.5 or tram No.56, is still intact.

Near the picturesquely decayed concrete bus terminal at Pasaréti tér stands the **Bartók Memorial House**, the composer's former residence and now a concert venue and museum (*see p167*). Artefacts from his travels around

Transylvania are the highlights here, along with a fob watch metronome. The composer himself, and his long-term colleague Zoltán Kodály, are buried in **Farkasréti Cemetery**, in the Buda Hills. Also here is Stalinist leader Mátyás Rákosi – he has a plaque near the main entrance – but the huge plot is best known for the mortuary chapel of Imre Makovecz, its wooden interior built in the form of a human ribcage. Look out for gravestone inscriptions in the runic Székely alphabet.

Further out, the Szemlő-hegyi (II. Pusztaszeri út 35; 315 8849) and Pálvölgyi (II. Szépvölgyi út 162; 388 9537) caves burrowed beneath the hills on the edge of this area offer a cheap, refreshing afternoon's entertainment.

Béla Bartók Memorial House

Bartók Béla Emlékház
II. Csalán utca 29 (394 2110). Bus 5. **Open** 10am-5pm Tue-Sun. **Admission** Ft400. **No credit cards**.

Farkasréti Cemetery

Farkasréti temető
XI. Németvölgyi 99 (319 3092). Tram 59 from M2 Moszkva tér/bus 8, 8A, 53. **Open** 7am-7pm Mon-Fri; 9am-5pm Sat, Sun. **Admission** free.

Millenáris Park

II. Fény utca 20-22 (438 5335/www.millenaris.hu). M2 Moszkva tér/tram 4, 6. **Open** 8am-8pm daily. **Admission** free. Check for ticket prices to concerts. **No credit cards**. **Map** p245 A2.

Tomb of Gül Baba

Gül Baba Türbéje
II. Mecset utca 14 (326 0062). Tram 4, 6. **Open** 10am-6pm daily. **Admission** Ft400; Ft200 concessions. **No credit cards**. **Map** p246 D1.

New Books Every Week!

Special Orders Taken

**French and English books
and magazines**

BESTSELLERS Bookstore
V. Október 6. utca 11
Tel. 312-1295
Open Mon-Fri 9:00-18:30,
Sat 10:00-18:00, Sun 10:00-16:00

Experience the Real Budapest

Absolute Walk
MORE THAN JUST CHURCHES & CASTLES!
DAILY @ 9:30 & 13:30
From June to Aug
DAILY @ 10:30
From Sept to May
No tours on Dec 25th & 26th
3500 HUF (Students)
4000 HUF (Others)

Hammer & Sickle Tour
THE WAY IT WAS, COMRADE!
**TOURS GO EVERY MON, WED,
FRI & SAT @ 10:30 AM**
From March to Dec, Jan & Feb Sat. Only
4500 HUF (students)
5000 HUF (Others)
Includes: A Visit in Our Own Block Flat & Guided Tour in the Statue Park

Absolute Pub Crawl
THE MAFIA & PORN INDUSTRY!
**TOURS GO EVERY MON, WED,
FRI & SAT @ 20:00 PM**
From March to Dec, Jan & Feb Sat. Only
4500 HUF (Students)
5000 HUF (Others)
Includes: Visit to pubs 3 Beers & 2 Shots

Info
Get 500 HUF off with this ad!
+36-(0)6-30-211-8861
IMAD@AXELERO.HU
ALL TOURS MEET AT THE CHURCH!
NO RESERVATIONS, JUST SHOW UP!
PRIVATE & GROUP TOURS AVAILABLE
MEET AT DEÁK SQ. ON STEPS
WWW.ABSOLUTETOURS.COM

YELLOW ZEBRA
FLYING BY THE SIGHTS
MEET NEW FRIENDS

THE TWO-WHEEL-TOUR!
AN ENTERTAINING RIDE AROUND BUDAPEST'S MAJOR SIGHTS!

NIGHT-RAMBLER-TOUR!
RIDE AMUCK AMONG THE MEDIEVAL LEGENDS AND SIGHTS!

TOURS MEET AT THE YELLOW CHURCH ON DEÁK SQ. (SEE MAP BELOW)

TOURS	TIMES	TOURS RUN	TOURS COST
DAY	11 AM	DAILY - MAY TO OCT.	4000 FT (STUDENTS)
NIGHT	8 PM	TUE, THUR + SUN - JUNE TO AUG.	4500 FT (OTHERS)

BIKE RENTALS BEACH CRUISERS+CITY BIKES!
1/2 Day 2000 Ft, Full Day 3000 Ft, 2 Days 5000 Ft, 3 Days 7500 Ft,
Note: A deposit of 20,000 Ft / 80 Euros is required to rent a bike

INTERNET POINT CHEAP INTERNET ACCESS!
Download your digi pics with our Smart / Flash Card Reader!
10 Ft / min. (600 Ft Hour) plus free coffee, tea or filtered water!

BIKE SHOP IN
COURTYARD
BEHIND THE
McDONALD'S +
TOUR OFFICE
AT SÜTÖ U. 2
+36-1-266-8777

Deák Sq. - In the center
On all 3 Metro Lines
Le Meridien Hotel — Deák
Deák Ferenc u. — Deák tér M M M
Store
Sütö u. 2
Yellow Church
Store Behind McD's
& Tour Info Office
Károly krt.

WWW.YELLOWZEBRABIKES.COM

Óbuda

This old Roman settlement is currently enjoying a retail revamp.

The oldest part of the city, Óbuda – Ancient Buda – was very much a separate entity until the unification of Budapest in 1873. Then a sleepy Danubian village of one-storey houses and cottages populated by Serb, German and Magyar fishermen and artisans, Óbuda still has the feel of a bygone era – and residents with strictly partisan sentiments.

Cheaper housing and new shopping centres have attracted the moneyed young to the area, generating a better class of bar and nightclub. They've even renovated the Roman museum.

The Romans established Aquincum, a town of some 4,000 people, in 35 BC, incorporating the surrounding region of Pannonia into the Empire in 14 BC. Little was known of their stay until archaeologists dug up its remains in the late 19th century. What can be seen today is mainly gathered at the **Aquincum Museum**. Its low walls composed of unearthed foundations, the venue is set in a large grassy area of scattered ruins, offset by a newly expanded museum. The highlight is a remarkable water-powered organ, the only one complete enough to be restored and played.

Further remains can be found nearby within the vast Flórián tér underpass, the so-called **Baths Museum**, unexciting ruins of Roman baths viewed from outside a glass enclosure. There's also a small amphitheatre by the HÉV station across the road, and parts of a military amphitheatre on the corner of III. Nagyszombat utca and Pacsirtamező utca.

Things are a little more lively down near Árpád Bridge. Around the focal cobblestoned square of Fő tér, old restored houses lend a certain grandeur to the village atmosphere. At No.4 is the **Zsigmond Kun Folk Art Collection**. Kun was an ethnographer whose 18th-century apartment now serves as a showcase for thousands of items of 19th- and early 20th-century Hungarian art he put together. Particularly notable are ceramics from his hometown Mezőtúr, in northern Hungary, and the replica of a peasant stucco oven.

Walking to the river from Fő tér, there is a small bridge leading to the southern tip of Óbuda Island – which at this end is known as Hajógyári Sziget ('Boat Factory Island'). The old factories and boatyards here are slowly being colonised by nightlife venues (such as the trendy **Dokk**, *see p178*) and movie studios

– there's even a golf driving range. One stop further up on the HÉV, at Filatorigát station, there's a footbridge leading to the northern end of Óbuda Island. For one week every August, the park is taken over by the massive **Sziget Music Festival** (*See p172* **Let's spend the week together**). For the rest of the year, most of the island is a spacious, empty park.

Equally secluded, away from the river up a quiet, wooded hill, is the **Kiscelli Museum**. This baroque Trinitarian monastery, built in 1745, now houses an important collection of Hungarian art from about 1880 to 1990. The works displayed upstairs include turn-of-the-century masters and paintings influenced by the impressionists, pre-Raphaelites, cubists and surrealists. Among them are Rippl-Rónai's *My Parents After 40 Years of Marriage*, János Kmetty's cubist *City Park*, and works by Alajos Stróbl, Károly Ferenczy, Margit Anna and many others. There are also engravings of 18th- to 19th-century Budapest – you'll recognise the vantage point from what is now Petőfi bridgehead in Pest in an 1866 engraving by Antal Ligeti, showing the newly built Chain Bridge, the church at Kálvin tér, Castle Hill, the Citadella and the twin domes of the new Dohány utca synagogue. The most atmospheric part of the complex is the ruined church, its bare brick walls left intact after World War II bombing and now transformed into a dim, ghostly gallery. These days it's often used to stage operas, fashion shows and other performances.

Aquincum Museum

Aquincumi Múzeum
III. Szentendrei út 139 (250 1650/www.aquincum.hu). HÉV to Aquincum. **Open** Oct-Apr ruins 9am-5pm, museum 10am-5pm Tue-Sun; May-Sept ruins 9am-6pm, museum 10am-6pm Tue-Sun. **Admission** Ft700; Ft300 concessions. Call to arrange guided tour in English, Ft3,000. EB Ft500. **No credit cards.**

Kiscelli Museum

III. Kiscelli utca 108 (430 1076/www.museum.hu/budapest/kiscelli). Tram 17 then bus 165. **Open** Nov-Mar 10am-4pm Tue-Sun; Apr-Oct 10am-6pm Tue-Sun. **Admission** Ft500; Ft250 concessions. EB Ft350-Ft3,920. **No credit cards.**

Zsigmond Kun Folk Art Collection

Kun Zsigmond Lakásmúzeum
III. Fő tér 4 (368 1138). HÉV to Árpád-híd. **Open** 10am-6pm Tue-Sun. **Admission** Ft200; Ft100 concessions. EB Ft300. **No credit cards.**

Pest

Dynamic engine of Hungary's capital.

Sightseeing

Little remains of medieval Pest, which hugged the river and spread inland as far as today's main drag, the Nagykörút. This five-kilometre stretch of tram track and tacky shopfront, built as one of three concentric ring roads in the great urban expansion of the late 1800s, brought together the previously disparate districts of downtown Pest. It also encircled a surprisingly compact area in which all of the city's daily business would be carried out: **Parliament**, the Stock Exchange, the **National Museum**, the **Opera House**, big international hotels, grand department stores and elegant coffeehouses.

It still holds true today. Pest is where people work, shop and bar-hop. Most of all, Pest is where people live. At the turn of the 19th century, its population was 30,000. By the dawn of the 20th, it was more than ten times that, as block upon block of Districts VI, VII, VIII, IX and X were thrown up to accommodate factory workers, civil servants, shopkeepers and their families. Only Chicago grew faster. Away from fussy, German-speaking Buda, here blossomed a Magyar culture: 21 newspapers a day, drama, poetry, novels, read and debated in any number of coffeehouses; huge houses of culture were constructed – an Opera House, a National Theatre and a **Music Academy**; then came the new arts of photography (*see p68* **Black-and-white Budapest**) and film (*see p156* **Moguls, ogres and misfits**). Pest was home to thriving Gypsy and Jewish cultures, both artistic and commercial (*see p85* **Roma Budapest** *and p76* **Jewish Budapest**). Truly, Pest was a very exciting place to be.

Hungary's demise was never better reflected than in the bullet-holed façades, scaffolding and sex bars seen around much of Pest today. It's not all grime and doom, however. City planning has seen fit to pave over parts of the inner city previously lost to choking traffic (*see p80* **Pedestrianised Budapest**). Significant islands of trendy nightlife thrive while once seedy Baross utca and Mikszáth Kálmán tér are being spruced up. The glitzy **Corinthia Grand Hotel Royal** (*see p36* **The empire strikes back**) and nearby **New York Café** (*see p111* **So good they built it twice**) will transform a grey section of the Nagykörút. Pre-EU property prices are spiralling for flats in Districts VI and VII, only a short journey to the centre.

The heart of Pest is District V, divided into the Belváros ('Inner City') in the south and Lipótváros to the north. Both lie inside the Kiskörút, the first of the concentric ring roads radiating from the centre.

The Belváros

The Belváros is bounded north-south between Chain Bridge and Szabadság Bridge, and east-west between the inner ring road of Károly körút and Múzeum körút, and the Danube.

At its centre is Vörösmarty tér, named after the poet of the same name, whose statue stands in the middle. The four sides of the square would be prime commercial space in any capital city; here, astoundingly, much is faceless office façade from the 1970s. The last of the old stores, **Luxus** (*see p129*), sits alone on one side. On another stands another famous institution, the **Gerbeaud** coffeehouse (*see p117*), a temple to gooey cakes. The outdoor restaurant offers dining options as well.

Neither is particularly cheap, but here you are deep in tourism central. Its apex, leading off Vörösmarty tér, is pedestrianised Váci utca, a stretch of cafés and shops catering almost solely to tourists: the only Hungarian voices you'll hear will be the ones serving. Most of the things on offer can be bought elsewhere for less.

The more recently pedestrianised southern stretch of Váci is more attractive. Dotted with strange collectors' shops – stamps, maps, small toys – this half of the street, decked out with café awnings in summer, is a fine place for a bar crawl. **Pauls Pub** (*see p121*) and nearby haunts along the tiny, narrow tributaries off Váci can provide entertainment until sun-up.

The mood of Váci changes when you go north of Kossuth Lajos utca at Ferenciek tere – named after the Franciscan church that stands near the University Library, but still known by its pre-1989 abbreviation of Felszab tér. This is Budapest's prestige shopping district, where high-priced boutiques and overpriced souvenir shops vie for the attention of the many hapless tourists strolling this pedestrian-only thoroughfare. The metro underpass, too, can be a hassle. Above ground, though, rises the beautifully elaborate edifice of Henrik Schmahl's Párizsi udvar, the 'Parisian Arcade' completed in 1913 and still functioning as a

Black-and-white Budapest

French lithographer Joseph Niépce invented modern photography in 1827. His partner, Louis Dauguerre, refined this process to plate photography, one of the great inventions of the 19th century. While the French were its masters, the camera played a subservient, documentary and pictorial role; painting and poetry held sway until the 1920s.

It would be a small band of Hungarians who, after fleeing the chaos of Budapest for Paris, would finally define photography as art. Among them were Andor – André – Kertész and Gyula Halász, known today as Brassai.

Kertész, born in Budapest in 1894, took up photography as a youthful hobby, recording Gypsies, peasants and Puszta landscapes, maturing when he took his Ica camera to the front while serving in World War I. His war photographs focused on the daily, banal lives of his fellow soldiers: 'We began to march at dawn. All of a sudden I saw a splendid image: a quartered battalion at daybreak, a foggy landscape with sleeping soldiers, dreaming civil dreams behind the heaps'. Composition meant ordering the forms and integrating atmosphere. Thanks to Kertész, combat photography became an art form, led by

Robert Capa, born André Friedmann in Budapest in 1913, the finest and most instinctive of his ilk to work in World War II.

Back in Budapest, Kertész contributed to the plethora of local press (*pictured*), taking cultural references from Lajos Kassák's influential magazine *Ma*. Already there is the sense of composition using light and diagonal that would set him as one of the great black-and-white visionaries, capturing the fragile and the lyrical out of everyday moments. He began to use audacious tilts and angles, and unusual framings – influenced by the work of *Ma* contributor László Moholy-Nagy.

One of the main proponents of photography as a legitimate expression of modern art, constructivist Moholy-Nagy fell in with the nascent Bauhaus movement. Inspired by the avant-garde futurists, Dada and his peer Surrealists, Moholy-Nagy worked in Paris and Berlin before founding the short-lived New Bauhaus – later the Chicago Institute of Design – in America.

Kertész moved to Paris in 1925, freelanced for the classic pictorial magazines of the day and hung out at the Café du Dôme with Henri Cartier-Bresson and emigrés Friedmann ('his

little child'), Moholy-Nagy – and Gyula Halász. Inspired by Kertész, the first to use of night-time photography, Halász developed the art of the photographer as late-night louche. Prowling the Paris underworld, he remade himself as Brassai (he was born in Brassó, now Brasov in Romania), the brash chronicler of whores, criminals and the demi-monde. He understood that the camera could profoundly distort society's vision of itself, and revelled in perceiving the beauty of the ugly.

Kertész moved to New York, where his stark and carefully composed work for *Vogue* and *Harper's Bazaar* became the standard on which American fine photography was built. He was also able to witness the birth and blossoming of their own artistic medium.

Friedmann reinvented himself as Capa, the dapper, gambling, womanizer of legend (Ingrid Bergman!!), who with his buddy Ernest Hemingway would capture the Spanish Civil War. Brave as a lion, Capa was the only photographer to wade through the sea of blood, bodies and bullets the morning of the D-Day landings, scuttling back from a foxhole on Omaha Beach to deliver *Life* magazine their seven-page exclusive.

Tired of exploitative magazine work, back in New York Capa formed an agency of top photographers: Magnum, after his favourite bottle. Cartier-Bresson was a key member. In 1954, Capa took one gamble too many in the first Vietnam conflict, a decade before the 'Nam of Tim Page and Don McCullin.

Why did Magyars come to dominate early art and feature photography? Perhaps the root lies in Hungarian itself. Emerging from a dynamic Pest of 21 daily newspapers and a virile avant-garde scene, these artists used an art form with no need for the unexportable Magyar tongue. They founded a universal language of writing with light, discovering a unity of aims in Paris, birthplace of the genre.

Hungarians describe things by active statements of opinion, a semantic world view perceived in black and white – hence the Magyar influence in maths, physics and visual art. This includes Gábor Dénes, inventor of holographs, and a slew of cinematographers, whose dominance in film history gave rise to the Hollywood adage: 'It's not enough to be Hungarian. You have to have talent, too'.

Classic Magyar photography can be seen at the **Mai Manó Fotógaléria** (*see p161*).

shopping arcade today. It began life as the Inner City Savings Bank, which is why bees, symbols of thrift, can be found throughout, an eclecticism continued with the detail of the interior and Miksa Róth's arched glass ceiling.

Another noteworthy building here, towards Elizabeth Bridge, is the **Inner City Parish Church**. Founded in 1046 as the burial site of the martyred St Gellért, this is Pest's oldest building, though little of its original structure remains. It's an extraordinary mixture of styles – Gothic, Islamic, baroque and neo-classical – testifying to the city's turbulent history. The beauty of its interior is in the light and shadow of the Gothic vaulting and most of the older detail is in the sanctuary, around the altar. Behind the high altar you'll find Gothic sedilias and a Turkish prayer alcove, surprisingly intact from when the church was used as a mosque. The remains of the Roman outpost Contra Aquincum lie to the north of the church.

The area south of here, on the other side of Kossuth Lajos utca, is one of Pest's most appealing quarters. The narrow, quiet streets around here feel like part of a waterfront district, even though the Danube is mostly invisible – except when streets running towards the river offer sudden, startling views of Gellért Hill.

Heading to the river, the main embankment, the **Korzó** is almost as busy as Váci utca. It begins at the convergence of Március 15 tér, with its stubby Roman ruins, and Petőfi tér, with its statue of the national poet. From here to Vigadó tér is the city's main gay cruise, though you wouldn't notice if you weren't looking for it. At Vigadó tér are zither-playing buskers, stalls selling folkloric souvenirs and the **Vigadó** concert hall itself (*see p168*). The Korzó follows up to Roosevelt tér, where statues of Deák and Széchenyi stand among the trees.

This walkway is lined with many of Budapest's most prestigious hotels, including the **Marriott** (*see p35*), many of them quite architecturally uninspiring. It is a far cry from a century ago, when the luxury hotels of the day – the Ritz, the Bristol and the Carlton, all of one height – fronted terrace cafés whose awnings would merge and form a colourful canopy under which *le tout Pest* would wander, to the sound of live Gypsy and jazz bands.

Today, the waterfront backdrop is barely used by bar owners. Apart from the Greek **Taverna Dionysos** restaurant (*see p101*), riverside entertainment is provided by the gay-and-mixed **Capella** dance club (*see p178*) and less well-known gay bars down the block.

A pity. This main stretch of riverbank is the track for the No.2 tram, a fabulous way to see

All is calm on pedestrianised **Hajós utca**. *See p80*.

Bold building – Lechner's extraordinary **Museum of Applied Arts**. *See p81.*

the city. When lit up and reflected in the river, the Chain Bridge and castle form one of the most magical urban landscapes in the world.

Inner City Parish Church

Belvárosi Plébiána templom
V. Március 15 tér (318 3108). M3 Ferenciek tere/bus 7. **Open** 9am-12.30pm, 6-7pm Mon-Sat; 6.30-7.30am, 6-7pm Sun. Latin Mass 10am Sun. **Map** p249 C4.

Párizsi udvar

V. Ferenciek tere 10-11/Petőfi Sándor utca 2-8. M3 Ferenciek tere/bus 7. **Map** p249 C4.

Lipótváros

Budapest gets down to business in Lipótváros, the northern part of District V: blocky, late 19th-century streets and austere neo-classical architecture provide a contrast to the smaller, twisty thoroughfares and baroque or secessionist whimsy that mark much of downtown Budapest. The neighbourhood maintains the grid pattern that was imposed on it by the Új Épület, the massive Habsburg barracks that once stood at what is now Szabadság tér. The barracks, where leaders of the nascent Hungarian nation were imprisoned and executed in 1849, were the base for Vienna's control over the city. Today, this is still the centre for business and bureaucracy.

The need to feed the business lunch crowd and downtown tourists has also made this a centre for a diverse array of restaurants,

offering choices like French at **Lou Lou** (*see p96*), sushi at **Tom George** (*see p102*), Asian dumplings at **Momotaro Ramen** (*see p101*), Asian noodles at the **Zebra One Noodle Bar** (*see p102*) and creative chatter with Hungarian-continental at **Café Kör** (*see p95*). It gets quieter in the evening, though there's a cluster of welcoming 24-hour bars and *presszók*, such as the classic **No. 1** (*see p121*) and the **Tulipán** (*see p178*), on Nádor utca round the corner from Parliament.

The **Basilica of St Stephen** points its façade down Zrínyi utca, towards the river. Budapest's largest church, it was designed in 1845 by József Hild, but only consecrated in 1905. Construction was so disrupted by wars and the deaths of its two major architects that one wonders if God actually wanted it built at all. The original dome collapsed in an 1868 storm. Miklós Ybl, the new architect, had the entire building demolished and rebuilt the original neo-classical edifice in the heavy neo-renaissance style favoured by the Viennese court. It was devastated by Allied bombing. Restoration began in 1980, the square facing the church converted from asphalt to cobblestone, with circular-patterned marble inlays.

The main attraction within is the mummified right hand of St Stephen, known as the 'Sacred Right', housed in its own side chapel. The gruesome relic is preserved in an ornate glass and lead trinket box that's shaped like

Art nouveau Budapest

Much of the cultural dynamism of turn-of-the-century, newly independent Budapest was born of a rejection of the staid Habsburg status quo and a search for Hungarian roots.

In music, this meant Béla Bartók delving around Transylvania for ancient folk harmonies that would be incorporated into a new musical form divorced from Germanic bombast.

In architecture it meant the secessionist movement, which would use bright motifs from mainly Transylvanian folk art to create coloured ceramics, folk motifs and sinuous curves. This became known as secessionism, although the style is recognisable as the art nouveau popular at the time.

Buildings had been created from pattern books of plain stucco until the secessionists came up with a new idiom. It was much less the product of outside influences than of the eccentric mind of Ödön Lechner (1845-1914). Neglected throughout the 20th century, he is now gaining recognition as a peculiar genius, comparable to Barcelona's Antonio Gaudí.

As a child, Lechner was taken to his family's brick factory, where his fascination for exposed brickwork began. His first project, the State Railway Pensioners Building (1881-

84, V. Andrássy út 25), deploys brickwork amid the graceful curves and decorative elements of a French renaissance structure. Although empty, this building is soon to be converted into a hotel. The smaller but more colourful Thonet House (1888-89, V. Váci utca 11A) is done in a Gothic style of abundant ornamentation. The blue ceramics are an early use of Zsolnay tiles, the first of Lechner's key ingredients. The second he found researching folk patterns and motifs.

His first major work in this new manner was the **Museum of Applied Arts** (1893-96, *pictured far left, see also p81*) prepared with Gyula Pártos. The sight of its shiny dome and roof as you drive in from the airport is the first indication that Budapest has buildings unlike any other city. Lechner deployed a wide array of Moorish and Indian designs – along with patterns taken from Hungarian folk culture.

From the explosion of colour at the tiled entranceway, Lechner designed every detail, in close collaboration with the Zsolnay ceramics factory in Pécs. Flowers also adorned the walls inside, until they were whitewashed in the 1970s. The floral motifs can still be seen in the archways and arcades.

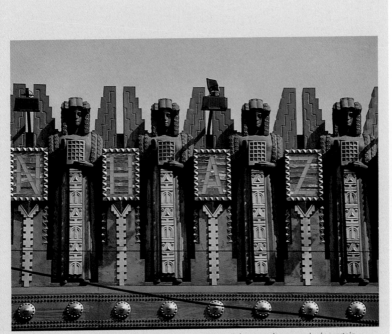

The abundant natural light owes its freedom to another daring architectural move, the decision to erect the building on a steel frame. At that time, no museum in Europe had been designed in anything other than a classicist style and the aged Emperor Franz Josef expressed as much unhappiness as he deemed polite when opening the building.

Lechner's crowning achievement is the **Former Royal Post Office Savings Bank** (1899-1901, *left*). You can visit this bank headquarters once a year (*see p75*). Outside, the orderly form is disguised by a brightly coloured façade of glazed brick and a freewheeling riot of line and pattern on the roof. The original function of the building is acknowledged by the beehives, symbols of thrift, at the corners, and the bees crawling towards them. Other decorative elements on the roof derive from Hungarian folklore and mythology. When it was put to Lechner that it was difficult to see these from the street, he answered: 'The birds will see them'.

Such exuberance was displeasing to the reactionary minister of culture, who immediately halted government funding for projects in this new style. Lechner would

never receive a major commission again. Lechner continued to work with his students and followers, unofficially, on smaller projects – most notably Armin Hegedűs's primary school (1906-06, VII. Dob utca 85).

Of all Lechner's students, Béla Lajta (1873-1920) did most to point Hungarian architecture towards its post-war future. Lajta also went on field trips to research folk motifs, then worked in his master's studio.

His most outstanding work is the **Új Színház** (1908-09, *above, see p191*) a building that still looks fresh almost a century later. It combines the playfulness of turn-of-the-century architecture, the lean aesthetic of modernism and elements typical of art deco, a style that did not catch on until the 1920s. It marks a watershed in Hungarian architecture.

Decoration faded from Lajta's work as he turned to more austere forms. Rószavölgyi House (1911-12, V. Szervita tér 5), with its stripped-down façade and horizontal accent, is now recognised as a landmark of European architecture, anticipating avant-garde style.

Lajta's achievements stand out as among the first manifestations of the dominant architectural style of the 20th century.

Sightseeing

Opulence abounds at Miklós Ybl's neo-renaissance **Opera House**. *See p81.*

Matthias Church. The hand lights up if you drop a coin into a slot next to the box. On 20 August, **St Stephen's Day**, the hand is marched around the square in a religious procession (*see p144*).

At the opposite end of Zrínyi utca, on Roosevelt tér, is the architecturally more appealing **Gresham Palace**, which offers an example of Hungarian-secessionist style on a grand scale. Built in 1906 by the Gresham Life Assurance Company of London, the building was designed by Zsigmond Quittner between 1904 and 1906. Renovation work has just been completed on the exterior, and the site is being converted into a luxury Four Seasons hotel by the end of 2003 (*see p26*). The original work involved some of the best-known artisans of the day: Miklós Ligeti did the statues symbolising the four seasons on the fourth floor. Visitors to the hotel should be able to go through the historic Peacock Gates for a peek at the beautiful glass cupola in the centre of the building.

Between the Gresham and the Basilica, on Nádor utca, is a complex of post-Communist institutions founded by Hungarian billionaire philanthropist George Soros. The complex includes the quirky **Centrális Galéria** (*see p159*), and Central European University, with the English-language bookstore **Bestsellers** (*see p126*).

North from here is Szabadság tér ('Liberty Square'), constructed during Hungary's brief flirtation with imperialism and conceived as the hub of the fin-de-siècle economy. It's still dominated by the Dual Monarchy's central bank (now the National Bank at No.9) and the Stock and Commodity Exchange (now the headquarters of Magyar Televízió at No.17). Completed in 1899, and meant to symbolise power and prosperity, the massive exchange building has a distorted perspective and exaggerated scale. In the 1920s Szabadság tér became the site of a Hungarian flag flown at half-mast over a mound of soil from territories lost at Trianon. After World War II, the Soviet army erected a large white obelisk commemorating its dead, right on top of the sacred mound. The obelisk still stands there, with a star on top and reliefs of Soviet soldiers besieging Budapest at its base. This is one of the few remaining Soviet-era monuments that hasn't been moved out to the **Statue Park** (*see p86* **Socialist Budapest**). A diagonal block away, down Aulich utca, on the corner of Báthory utca and Hold utca, the **Eternal Flame** commemorates Count Lajos Battyhány, the Prime Minister of the 1848 provisional government who was executed by firing squad here on 6 October 1849.

The **American Embassy** stands at No.12 and, nearby, a small statue of US General Harry Hill Bandholtz. An officer of the peacekeeping force in 1919, he saved the treasures of the National Museum from rampaging Romanian soldiers by 'sealing' the doors with the only official-looking seals he had to hand: censorship seals. The Romanians saw the American eagle and backed off down the steps.

The brightest spot in this sombre, officious quarter is Ödön Lechner's startlingly ornate and colourful **Former Royal Post Office Savings Bank**, now a bank headquarters (*see p72* **Art nouveau Budapest**). It's only open to the public once a year in September, but you can get a feel for Lechner's finest work by peeking into the lusciously designed lobby.

Between Szabadság tér and Kossuth Lajos tér, on Vértanúk tere, Tamás Varga's statue of Imre Nagy, tragic hero of the Uprising, stands at the crest of a small, symbolic bridge, looking towards Parliament and away from the Soviet obelisk (*see p18* **1956 and all that**).

Parliament defines Kossuth Lajos tér. Built, like the rest of Lipótváros, at a time when Hungary was getting a taste of empire, it was the largest parliament building in the world when it opened in 1902. Its 691 rooms have never been fully utilised, even in the 16 years before the Trianon treaty dismembered imperial pretensions. Governing Hungary today takes up only 12 per cent of the space.

Designed by Imre Steindl, the building was completed six years too late for the millennium celebrations it was intended to crown. It's beautifully sited: the prominence of its position on the curve of the Danube defines the city and exploits the elegance of the Danube sweep. The building itself, however, is an exercise in establishment kitsch. Guided tours (*see p48* **Tours**) pass the numbered cigar holders outside the Upper House, where members left their Havanas during debates. The Sacred Crown, a gift from the Pope to St Stephen in 1000 AD to mark Hungary's formation as a Christian state, was moved here from the National Museum by the patriotic FIDESZ-MDF government. The critical Socialists now in power have shown no sign of moving it back.

The **Museum of Ethnography**'s position opposite Parliament says much about how seriously Hungarians take their folk traditions.

Displays of Hungarian village and farm life, folk art and customs are accompanied by English texts. Originally constructed to serve as the Supreme Court, this monumental, gilt-columned edifice with ceiling frescoes by Károly Lotz is anything but folky.

Along Balassi Bálint utca to the north, the venerable **Szalai Cukrászda** (*see p119* **Let them eat cake**) serves coffees, pastries and snacks. Falk Miska utca, running parallel a block further away from the river, is a street of upmarket art galleries and antique shops such as the **Pintér Antik Diszkont** (*see p125*).

Basilica of St Stephen
Szent István Bazilika
V. Szent István tér 33 (317 2859). M3 Arany János utca. **Open** 9am-5pm Mon-Fri; 9am-1pm Sat; 1-5pm Sun. Treasury *1 Nov-31 Mar* 10am-4pm; *1 Apr-31 Oct* 9am-5pm. Tower *Apr-May* 10am-4.30pm, *June-Aug* 9.30am-6pm; *Sept-Oct* 10am-5.30pm. **Admission** *Treasury* Ft200; Ft150 concessions. *Tower* Ft500; Ft400 concessions. **Map** p246 C3.

Former Royal Post Office Savings Bank
Magyar Királyi Takarék Pénztár
V. Hold utca 4, entrance from Szabadság tér 8 (428 2600 ext 1532). M3 Arany János utca. **Open** Tours of building once a yr only; phone for details of open day in 3rd wk Sept. **Map** p246 C3.

Gresham Palace
V. Roosevelt tér 6 (266 8855/www.greshampalace.com). Tram 2. **Map** p246 C3.

Museum of Ethnography
Néprajzi Múzeum
V. Kossuth Lajos tér 12 (473 2400/www.neprajz.hu). M2 Kossuth tér/tram 2. **Open** 10am-6pm Tue-Sun. **Admission** Ft500; Ft250 concessions. Call to arrange guided tour in English, Ft6,000 for parties up to 25. EB Ft300-Ft2,800. **No credit cards**. **Map** p249 C4.

Parliament
Országház
V. Kossuth Lajos tér (441 4415). M2 Kossuth Lajos tér/tram 2. **Open** Tours in English 10am, noon, 2pm, 5pm daily. **Tickets** Ft2,000; Ft1,000 concessions from Door 11 to right of main entrance. EB Ft400. **No credit cards**. **Map** p245 B2.

Kiskörút

The southern half of Kiskörút, the inner ring road, follows the line of the old city walls – extant portions of which can be seen in Bástya utca behind Vámház körút and also a few yards down Ferenczy István utca off Múzeum körút.

It begins at Fővám tér. On the south side of the small square are the Budapest University of Economic Science and the **Great Market Hall** (Nagy Vásárcsarnok). The university was once the Main Customs Office, and an underground

Sightseeing

Jewish Budapest

On a Friday night, Hasidic men in black, wearing streiml hats with wide, fur-lined brims, can be seen strolling Klauzál tér, on their way from Sabbath services. On any weekday afternoon, old couples chatting in Yiddish can be encountered outside the kosher butcher at VII. Dob utca.

No, it's not like in 1900, when the 170,000 Jews living in Budapest made up a quarter of the city's population. But it's still evidence of a way of life that could not be wiped out by the Holocaust or made invisible by Communist-era policies encouraging assimilation.

Budapest's current Jewish population is estimated at just under 80,000, which makes it the largest Jewish community in Central Europe. The heart of this community remains in District VII, Erzsébetváros, bordered by the ring roads VI. Andrássy út and VII. Rákóczi út.

Budapest's Jewish quarter was established in Erzsébetváros in the 18th century, when Jews were still forbidden to live within the city walls. By the 1830s, a few Jewish families, notably Wodianer and Ullman, had begun to play an important role in the business world of Pest. They also played a political role, supporting the rebels in the 1848 Hungarian uprising against the Habsburgs. With the relative independence of 1867, the new leadership gave Jews civic and legal equality, a measure so unusual that Jews flooded in from Russia and southern Poland.

Jews soon became a vital part of the city's economy. Urbane and entrepreneurial, their commercial prowess saw Budapest become the largest financial centre east of Vienna before the end of the century. Along with the vast **Central Synagogue** (see p88), where Theodore Herzl founded modern Zionism, the city had Jewish clubs, Jewish restaurants, Jewish shops and Jewish workshops. A ghostly reminder of how things were then is afforded by the Gozsdu udvar – a linked series of courtyards running between VII. Dob utca 16 and VII. Király utca 15. Though today the passageway sits empty, awaiting development, you can look through the locked gates and imagine the scene in the early 1900s, when the courtyards bustled with Jewish-owned shops and businesses.

Between the wars, rising anti-Semitism, from Horthy's right-wing government and in general society, saw many prominent Jews flee to Paris and America.

Although the first years of the war saw little by way of the mass deportations suffered in Poland, by 1944 the Fascist Arrow Cross Party had begun to hound Jews into a walled-off area in the Jewish quarter, creating a Ghetto. Approximately 70,000 people, mostly women and children, were herded inside. Deportations of the menfolk were swift and aggressive. Some 700,000 Hungarian Jews were murdered in the Holocaust.

Jews fared better under Communism, though secularism and assimilation were strongly encouraged. Many Holocaust survivors found themselves under suspicion, the implication being that they avoided death by turning against their fellow Jews. District VII also became less and less Jewish. The many homes that had been emptied by the Holocaust were filled with non-Jewish workers, who were brought in from around the countryside to rebuild Budapest.

But the Jews did not disappear from Erzsébetváros, and today there is a 3,000-member Orthodox community, centred around the Orthodox Synagogue at VII. Kazincy utca 21 (pictured). Designed by Béla and Sándor Löffler in 1913, the building has a façade angled to fit the bends of this twisty street. The complex also has an entrance on VII. Dob utca. From here you can enter the courtyard to get to the Hanna kosher restaurant.

Outside, at VII. Dob utca 35, is the kosher butcher, who sells a goose kolbász sausage that's tasty enough to convert the most confirmed pork eater. Here also is the kosher Fröhlich Cukrászda, which sells the popular flódni, made of poppy seeds, ground walnuts and apple custard.

These businesses are remnants of a larger community, whose presence can be seen in memorials all around the neighbourhood. Adjacent to the Central Synagogue is the **Jewish Museum** (see p88). Behind it is the small Heroes' Temple. Built in 1931, based on a design by László Vágó and Ferenc Faragó, it was named after Jewish soldiers killed in World War I.

Connecting the Heroes' Temple and the Central Synagogue, a simple concrete arching colonnade encloses the Garden of Remembrance, now a mass grave for Jews massacred by fellow Hungarians in 1945. Imre Varga's moving weeping-willow memorial to those murdered in concentration camps is

visible from Wesselényi utca. The family names of the dead victims are delicately inscribed on every one of its leaves.

At VII. Dob utca 11, the statue of an angel swooping down the side of a building to help a fallen victim is to Swiss diplomat Carl Lutz, who gave passports to many Magyar Jews.

The synagogue at VII. Rumbach Sebestyén utca 11 was designed by Ottó Wagner and built in 1872, for Jews put off by the less traditional design of the Central Synagogue. Many synagogues and Jewish institutions in the neighbourhood are active, such as the Lubavits Hasidic synagogue, VI. Vasvári Pál utca 5. A number of organisations have their headquarters at VII. Síp utca 12, where the Goldmark Hall hosts Jewish theatre. Just past the Nagykörút is an active synagogue on VII. Bethlen Gábor tér, where the Oneg Sabbat Club was founded in the late 1980s. The organisation has played a significant role in a Jewish renaissance, which continues with the **Jewish Summer Festival** (*see p144*).

To learn more and see inaccessible sights, join an English-language walking tour:

Jewish Quarter Walking Tours

VII. Dohány utca 2 (317 2754/317 1377). M2 Astoria/tram 47, 49. **Tours** 10.30am, 1.30pm Mon-Thur; 10.30am Fri; 11.30am Sun. **Admission** Ft1,900-Ft4,900; *with kosher food* Ft5,600.

Mücsarnok – Budapest's palace of exhibitions. *See p84.*

canal used to run from the river, taking barges through the customs house and into the market. Opened in 1897, the three-storey hall was a spectacular shopping mall in its day, but fell apart under Communism. It was restored and reopened in 1994, with a new Zsolnay tile roof. In the basement the **Ázsia** store (*see p138*) provides exotic non-Hungarian foodstuffs.

Vámház körút leads up to Kálvin tér, named after the ugly Calvinist church on the square's south side. This was once the city's eastern gate and, with the pink, postmodern Hotel Mercure Korona (V. Kecskeméti utca 14; 317 4111) bridging Kecskeméti utca, still feels somewhat gate-like. Under the Korona, the large pedestrian underpass grants access across the square's busy intersection to the main roads of Baross utca and Üllői út, leading to Districts VIII and IX. Down here is the **ChaChaCha**

(*see p175*), a dance bar so packed after midnight that the crowd fills a section of the corridor in this labyrinthine underpass.

Above ground is bar-lined Ráday utca. The **Castro Bistro** (*see p116*), a few blocks away from the square at Ráday utca 35, is probably the best venue here, although the best bar hop is at the Kálvin tér end of the street.

Múzeum körút is named after the National Museum. Built to Mihály Pollack's neo-classical design between 1837-47, it was then so far out of town that cattle once wandered in. This was where poet Sándor Petőfi read his 'National Song' on 15 March 1848, the start of the revolt against Habsburg domination. The exhibitions cover Hungary from its foundation to the 20th century, the latter section including selections of contemporary propaganda, retro suites of furniture and shop window displays.

On the next corner is the century-old **Múzeum Kavéház** (see p92), where you can get fine examples of Magyar cuisine in elegant surroundings. Next door to the restaurant is the **Múzeum Cukrászda**, which serves cakes, coffees and harder stuff until the wee hours, and can fill up just before sunrise. Over the road is the **Központi Antikvárium** (see p126) and other second-hand booksellers.

Múzeum körút ends at **Astoria** (see p37), where the grand but faded 1912 hotel dominates the intersection to which it has lent its name. The **Astoria Café** (see p115) still has fine grandeur to burn and the **restaurant** (see p93) is an elegant spot for fine dining.

After Astoria, Károly körút continues on up to Deák tér, passing right by the vast **Central Synagogue** that guards the entrance to District VII (see p76 **Jewish Budapest**). Nearby Deák tér is where all three metro lines intersect, with the **Underground Railway Museum** (see p59 **Obscure Budapest**) by the ticket office.

Until a couple of years ago, the square above – Erzsébet tér, which merges into Deák tér – was mostly taken up by the parking lot for the central bus station. Plans to put the **National Theatre** here were scratched, and it was sited along the river instead (see p191). Now the area is home to a highly stylised small park. There's a glass-bottomed pool, with underground seating below it, so you can look up through the glass and the water in the pool to see oddly refracted sunlight. Below all this is the **Gödör Klub** (see p171), a nightspot that sometimes hosts decent music.

Great Market Hall

Nagy Vásárcsarnok
IX. Fővám tér (217 6067). Tram 2, 47, 49. **Open** 7am-6pm Mon-Fri; 7am-1pm Sat. **Map** p249 D5.

National Museum

Nemzeti Múzeum
VIII. Múzeum körút 14-16 (338 2122/www.hnm.hu). M3 Kálvin tér/tram 47, 49. **Open** winter 10am-5pm Tue-Sun; summer 10am-6pm. **Admission** Ft600; Ft300 concessions. Call to arrange guided tour in English, Ft500 per person. EB Ft2,500. **No credit cards. Map** p249 D4.

Nagykörút

At exactly 4,114 metres, the Nagykörút, or outer ring road, is the longest thoroughfare in the city, running from Petőfi Bridge in the south to Margaret Bridge in the north, and bisecting Districts IX, VIII, VII, VI and XIII en route. Trams 4 and 6 run its length, starting in Buda and ending up on the same side at Moszkva tér. A busy commercial boulevard built, like much

of 19th-century Pest, in eclectic style, it is here rather than on Váci utca that the everyday business of downtown Budapest takes place.

Most sections carry the name of a Habsburg. The first stretch, between Petőfi Bridge and Üllői út, is Ferenc körút. The ugly concrete building on the south-west corner of the Üllői út intersection is known as the Lottóház – its flats were given away as prizes in the 1950s.

The contrast with Ödön Lechner's extraordinary and colourful **Museum of Applied Arts**, just around the corner, couldn't be more complete (see p72 **Art nouveau Budapest**). This stunning building, decorated with ornate detail using Zsolnay tiles, opened for the 1896 Millennium. A statue of the architect sits outside this building, a masterful example of Lechner's efforts to create a Hungarian style. It was built to showcase Hungarian art objects and furnishings, which had already won international acclaim. Its permanent exhibition of furniture and objets d'art, 'Style Periods of the Applied Arts in Europe', is explained in English, with plenty of historical detail.

Just across this intersection is the site of the old Kilián barracks, and next to that, on the other side of Üllői út, is the old **Corvin theatre**, recently restored as a multi-screen cinema (see p158). During the 1956 revolution, the soldiers in the Kilián barracks were among the first to join the insurgents. Soldiers and rebels, some of whom were just children, took over the Corvin for tactical reasons: the theatre is in a half-enclosed area, just removed from the Nagykörút, so it offered a protected location from which to attack tanks advancing down the main street. A statue of a boy with a rifle outside the cinema commemorates the rebels who died here (see p18 **1956 and all that**).

Continuing north as József körút, the boulevard acquires a disreputable air as it passes through District VIII, being gradually being gentrified – note the twee new street lights along recently pedestrianised sections of Baross utca. Prostitutes are less visible after a 1999 law chased most of the business into mafia-controlled brothels. The most insalubrious patch used to be Rákóczi tér – a dusty square with a decorative old food market hall at the back – but the popular **Café Csiga** (see p115) has breathed new life into it.

Diagonally across the Nagykörút, down Krúdy Gyula utca, are a handful of other nightlife options, including the **Darshan Café** and the adjacent **Darshan udvar** (see p116).

At Blaha Lujza tér, Népszínház utca runs away south-east towards **Kerepesi Cemetery** (see p88). Rákóczi út cuts across the körút, heading south to Astoria and north to Keleti

Pedestrianised Budapest

While tourists and well-to-do residents in the Castle District have been enjoying car-free streets since the 1980s, most Pest citizens have been struggling with traffic fumes on their car-clogged pavements for a decade or more.

At the time, the only exception was Váci utca, Budapest's main tourist-friendly shopping street. When Gábor Demszky, a forward-looking former dissident spokesman for the post-Communist generation, became Budapest's mayor in the elections of 1990, his proposals for cleaning up the city began with cash payments to anyone trading in their Trabant.

Unable to part many Magyars from their Trabbie, Demszky then took the step of paving over the southern half of Váci in the mid-1990s, changing its feel from business-like to laid-back. At the same time, city planners turned to Liszt Ferenc tér (*pictured*), an otherwise underused passage between Andrássy út and Király utca. Bricks were laid down to close off the narrow lanes leading into the square, and its pedestrianisation saw a couple of cafés opened up, then a couple of others. A buzz was born.

Although only two blocks long, today on warm evenings there could well be close to 1,000 chairs crammed around the hundreds of café tables here, outside the **Buena Vista** (*see p115*), **Karma** (*see p118*) and the **Vian**

(*see p116*), among others. In turn, to compensate residents for the noise – although only currently the **Pesti Est** (*see p175*) opens until 2am – these ground-floor businesses were asked to pay for the renovation of the entire building. Car-free zones had the shiniest façades in Pest.

The same formula was employed on Ráday utca in 2000. Traffic was restricted, and the District IX council offered rent subsidies to new café owners. With the **Paris, Texas** (*see p121*) already established at one end, party wizard Hans van Vliet took over the **Castro Bistro** (*see p116*) at the other, packed the house, and soon a five-block stretch of brick-covered street had become the trendiest section in town. And it's not only bars – there are fine restaurants too, such as **Costes** (*see p95*) or the **Soul Café** (*see p123*). In summer, it could be somewhere on the Med.

Nearby in District VIII, Krúdy Gyula utca and Miksáth Kálman ter, and the stretch of Hájos utca behind the Opera House in District VI, anchored by **Picasso Point** (*see p121*) and the **Noiret** (*see p177*), are also enjoying pedestrianised rejuvenation.

Demszky, set to be in office until 2006, is now toying with the idea of banning cars from the Chain Bridge, an idea so radical it may turn the car-owning electorate against him. A panoramic bar stand, however, might just fit. Anyone for Daiquiris over the Danube?

station, its façade distinct from this vantage. This otherwise prosaic stretch of the ring road – note the ugly Centrum department store at the busy intersection – will get a shot in the arm once the historic **New York Café** is reopened by the end of 2003 (*see p111* **So good they built it twice**). Built in 1894 by Alajos Hauszmann, this handsome venue was a major meeting place for writers, artists, directors and Hollywood moguls. Its slow post-war demise will be reversed when it returns to its original splendour. Nearby, the reopened **Corinthia Grand Hotel Royal** (*see p36* **The empire strikes back**) has already added five-star glitz to once-prestigious Erzsébet körút.

Oktogon, where the Nagykörút crosses broad Andrássy út, is the grandest intersection and is, fittingly, octagonal. But the shape did not always dictate the name: in the Communist days this was 7 November Square; under Horthy it was named after Mussolini. The M1

metro stops here on its way underneath Andrássy út to **Heroes' Square** and the **Városliget** (City Park) beyond.

Teréz körút features the **Művész** (*see p156*), a good arthouse cinema, and the respectable **Radisson SAS Béke Hotel Budapest** (*see p32*). It finishes at the Nagykörút's most magnificent landmark: **Nyugati station**. Built by the Eiffel company of Paris in 1874-77, it's a pale blue palace of iron and glass. The panes in front allow you to see inside the station, making arriving and departing trains part of the city's streetlife. The introduction of a McDonald's in the iron-and-glass complex has since detracted from the steam-age romance. The mirror-glass frontage of the Skála opposite is oddly forbidding for a department store, despite attempts to enliven the square with concerts. The metro underpass has become a hangout for the seedy and the homeless – this is as heavy as street action gets downtown.

The centrepiece of this last stretch of körút is the stubbily baroque **Vígszínház** (Comedy Theatre, *see p191*). Built in 1896 and renovated in 1995, it staged performances by Budapest's top musical dramatists, such as Albert Szirmay, who worked with Gershwin in New York.

Szent István körút ends at Jászai Mari tér, terminus of the No.2 tram. Here traffic sweeps on to Margaret Bridge, which pedestrians can use to access the beautiful wooded park of Margaret Island (*see p60* **Green Budapest**).

Museum of Applied Arts

Iparművészeti Múzeum
IX. Üllői út 33-37 (456 5100/www.museum.hu/budapest/iparmuveszeti). M3 Ferenc körút/tram 4, 6. **Open** 10am-6pm Tue-Sun. **Admission** Ft500; Ft250 concessions. EB Ft750-Ft6,000. Tour in English Ft2,500 for parties up to 5. **No credit cards. Map** p249 D5.

Andrássy út & District VI

Andrássy út, a 2.5-kilometre boulevard built between 1872 and 1885, with the continent's first electric underground railway running underneath, is the spine of District VI. The development of the street, and many of the monuments along it, was part of the build-up for the country's 1896 millennium celebration. Intended as Budapest's answer to the Champs-Elysées, it even ends with its own version of the Arc de Triomphe: Heroes' Square monument in the City Park.

The first half of the boulevard, between Bajcsy-Zsilinszky and Oktogon, is narrower than the last half, and the trees lining the street here are taller, which makes this stretch pleasantly shady. This is the liveliest part of Andrássy and includes the venerable **Művész coffeehouse** (*see p121*), an elegant landmark, with shaded outdoor seating. The Goethe Institut, with its **Eckermann Café** (*see p117*), also provides a relaxing space. Restaurants like Belcanto (VI. Dalszínház utca 8; 269 2786) and the **Bombay Palace** (*see p97*) make this stretch a good place for lunch or a fancy dinner.

The most important building, though, is Miklós Ybl's neo-renaissance Opera House (*see p168*), built in 1884 to mark the Magyar Millennium. Its cultural importance has always been linked to Magyar national identity. Ybl supervised every detail, including the Masonic allusions of the smiling sphinxes. The interior features seven kilograms of gold and 260 bulbs in an enormous chandelier.

Opposite stands the former Dreschler Café and one-time State Ballet Institute, co-designed by Ödön Lechner (*see p72* **Art nouveau Budapest**) as an apartment block in 1883. Plans are afoot to restore it to its former glory as a hotel. Round the corner down Dalszínház utca is

There's more shopping to be had at the sprawling **Westend City Center** mall (*see p130*), the biggest in Central and Eastern Europe, located directly behind Nyugati and connected to the station via passageways lined with hawkers. The **multiplex** in this otherwise inconspicuous mall is often the most convenient place to find mainstream movies (*see p158*).

Views of Nyugati from the körút are spoilt by the unsightly road bridge carrying traffic over Nyugati tér towards the recently restored Lehel tér produce market. Szent István körút is the only section not named after a Habsburg, and the only one with much of interest at night. **Okay Italia**'s two restaurants are popular (*see p101*), while the **Trocadero** (*see p180*) is Budapest's only real Latin dance club. It divides Lipótváros from Újlipótváros, once a middle-class Jewish district, lively by day, with shops, a busy streetlife and peaceful Szent István Park pleasantly opening out on to the river.

one of the most striking examples of the work of one of Lechner's protégés, Béla Lajta. His extraordinary 1910 Parisiana nightclub, now the **Új Színház** (*see p191*), was restored to its art nouveau splendour in 1998. Its symmetrical geometric design features nine ceramic angels with gold inlaid wings, which carry turquoise mosaic plaques spelling out the letters of the word *Színház* ('Theatre'). The polished granite of its façade is punctuated by grey monkeys.

Nagymező utca, with the main MÁV railway office on the corner, is known as Budapest's Broadway (*see pp188-192*). Renovated theatre houses like the **Thália** and the **Operett** are complemented by nightspots such as the **Piaf** (*see p175*), an after-hours hangout for an older arty set. Nearby, at Liszt Ferenc tér, is the **Irók Boltja** ('Writers' Bookshop', *see p126*), an important centre for literary events. At the turn of the last century, this was the Café Japan, haunt of the leading artists of the day. Nearby, back on Nagymező is the **Mai Manó Fotógaléria** (*see p161 and p68* **Black-and-white Budapest**), the city's main photography gallery, once the studio of court photographer Manó Mai. Actors, artists and photographers would mingle around this elegant quarter in the early part of the 20th century, many later to flee to Berlin, Vienna, Paris and then New York or Hollywood as the political climate grew colder. Recent rumours of the Guggenheim Foundation looking at key buildings along this stretch have sparked talk of an artistic revival.

The area to the north and west of this section of Andrássy – a triangle also bounded by Teréz körút and Bajcsy-Zsilinszky út – is a dull commercial district by day, but by night offers a cluster of eccentric bars and restaurants. **Aloe Kávézó** (*see p115*), **Dzsungel Étterem** (*see p117*), **Marquis de Salade** (*see p99*), **Noiret** (*see p177*) and **Picasso Point** (*see p121*), among many others, are all around here.

More concentrated nightlife options can be found on bustling Liszt Ferenc tér, which leads from Andrássy up to the **Zeneakadémia** (*see p168*). Although only two blocks long – with a doleful statue of poet Endre Ady on one end and an effusive one of Franz Liszt on the other – the square buzzes with life on summer evenings as customers pack tables outside the more than half-dozen big bar-restaurants that fill the small space. (*see p80* **Pedestrianised Budapest**). Cafés include the **Buena Vista** (*see p115*) and the **Karma** (*see p118*). The **Pesti Est Café** (*see p175*) stays open latest.

Past Oktogon, the boulevard gets broader and noticeably brighter, as the tall shady trees are replaced by younger, smaller ones. From here you can make out the Archangel Gabriel atop his column at Heroes' Square.

Such a sight would have been a dreadful one to anyone being dragged up here by men in overcoats in the early 1950s, for here at No.60 were the headquarters of the ÁVO, the Secret Police. It was already a building with a dark past, for the right-wing Arrow Cross Party used it as a place to torture Jews and political opponents before and during the war. The ÁVO simply took over the premises. Shut down after the Changes, the once-unassuming façade is now easy to spot because of the huge stencil sticking out from its roof, with the slogan 'TERROR' in mirror-reverse: the new **House of Terror Museum**. The building's conversion in February 2002, just before national elections, caused a political storm. Questions have since arisen about whether the giant stencil violates the UNESCO landmark rules. The four-floor exhibition inside is intended to memorialise the cruelty of both these parties, but it has come under criticism for focusing too heavily on Communist oppressors while not giving enough attention to the Holocaust. The then right-wing FIDESZ-MDF Party in power used its opening for political gain against the Socialist Party, tarred with a Communist brush. Downstairs are cells, interrogation rooms and torture devices, many of which were used by both Fascists and Communists. There are video interviews with survivors from the Uprising, documentation, press clippings and samples of propaganda (*see p18* **1956 and all that**). The nearby **Lukács** café (*see p118*) at No.70, now a bright spot for coffee and cakes, was an old ÁVO haunt.

Around the corner on Vörösmarty utca is the **Franz Liszt Museum**, in the composer's former home. Over the road at No.69 is the neo-renaissance College of Fine Arts, once an exhibition hall and now housing the **Budapest Puppet Theatre** (*see p150*), designated by a big neon sign showing a crude outline of a doll.

Clustered around the corner of Rózsa utca is the **Kolibri**, a cellar bar that draws a student crowd and sometimes hosts English-language theatre (*see p189*), a couple of late bars, and the **Millennium Étterem** (*see p104*), which has a decor that faithfully recreates the metro stations of Andrássy's underground and serves good Hungarian and continental cuisine.

Kodály körönd is Andrássy's *rond point* and was clearly once very splendid. The palatial townhouses that enclose it are dilapidated but still fascinating. The composer Zoltán Kodály used to live in the turreted Nos.87-89, his old flat serving as the **Kodály Memorial Museum**.

The final stretch of Andrássy út feels wider than the rest of it, mostly occupied by villas set back from the road. This is Budapest's main

Into the dark ages at the **Terror Museum**.

diplomatic quarter and many embassies are here and in the surrounding streets. Benczúr utca is shady and quiet and full of art nouveau mansions, one of which houses the British Council, with its English-language library. The Yugoslav embassy where Imre Nagy holed up for a while in 1956 is the last building on the southern corner by Hősök tere.

There are two collections of Asian arts in the neighbourhood: the **Ferenc Hopp** on Andrássy út and the **György Ráth** on Városligeti fasor (*see p59* **Obscure Budapest**).

House of Terror Museum

Terror Háza Múzeum
*VI. Andrássy út 60 (374 2600/www2.terrorhaza.hu).
M1 Vörösmarty utca.* **Open** 10am-6pm Tue-Sun.
Admission *foreigners* Ft3,000; Ft1,500 concessions.
Hungarians Ft1,000; Ft500 concessions. **No credit cards.** Map p246 D2.

Franz Liszt Museum

Liszt Ferenc Múzeum
*VI. Vörösmarty utca 35 (322 9804 ext 16). M1
Vörösmarty utca.* **Open** 10am-6pm Mon-Fri; 9am-5pm Sat. **Admission** Ft360; Ft180 concessions.
No credit cards. Map p246 D2.

Kodály Memorial Museum & Archive

Kodály Emlékmúzeum és Archivum
*VI. Andrássy út 87-89 (352 7106). M1 Kodály
körönd.* **Open** 10am-4pm Wed; 10am-6pm Thur-Sat;
10am-2pm Sun. **Admission** Ft200. **No credit cards.** Map p247 E2.

Heroes' Square & City Park

A symbol of confident 19th-century nationalism, Heroes' Square (Hősök tere) is a monumental celebration of mythic Magyardom. Completed for the 1896 Magyar Millennium that celebrated the anniversary of Hungarian tribes arriving in the Carpathian Basin, it's flanked by the **Műcsarnok** and the **Museum of Fine Arts** and centred on the Archangel Gabriel, perched on top of a 36-metre column and staring boldly down Andrássy út. Perched in the pair of colonnades are statues of Hungarian kings and national heroes, from St Stephen to Lajos Kossuth. Now often crowded with teenage skateboarders, Heroes' Square has witnessed many key events in modern Hungarian history – most recently, the ceremony to mark the re-burial of Imre Nagy, leader of the 1956 revolution, the event that in June 1989 marked the rebirth of democracy in Hungary. Nagy's remains are at **Újköztemető Cemetery** (*see p88 and p18* **1956 and all that**).

While the National Gallery is Hungary's prime venue for Hungarian art, the country's major European display is here in the Museum of Fine Arts. The museum has a magnificent Spanish collection, the best outside Spain, featuring El Greco and his school, along with the Madrid and Andalusian schools. Other highlights are an excellent Venetian collection, a Dürer, several Breughels, a doubtful but beautiful Raphael and some Leonardos. The museum hosts important temporary exhibitions in the grand halls leading from the entrance.

Across Heroes' Square from the Museum of Fine Arts is the Műcsarnok (*see p161*), which hosts excellent rotating exhibitions and some good jazz concerts too.

Hősök tere is essentially the front gate to the City Park (Városliget) – Budapest's main area for rest and entertainment. Laid out by the French designer Nebbion, its amenities include a boating lake and **ice rink** (*see p186*), the **Széchenyi baths** (*see p148*), the **Zoo** (*see p151*), **Vidám** ('Amusement') **Park** (*see p152*), the **Transport Museum** (*see p59* **Obscure Budapest**) and **Petőfi Csarnok** concert hall (*see p171*), with its weekend flea market (*see p137* **A load of old junk**). Once the site of the 1896 Magyar Millennium exhibition, the place has a theme-park feel that survives in the Disneyfied **Vadjahunyad Castle**, a structure that incorporates replicas from pieces of various famous Hungarian castles throughout history. The castle's Transylvanian tower looms over the boating lake, and the baroque-style wing is home to the **Agriculture Museum** (*see p59* **Obscure Budapest**).

Vidám Park's beautiful Victorian merry-go-round is a protected landmark, but many of the other older rides in this amusement park have been replaced. Amid the dodgem cars and looping rollercoasters, there's one defiantly Hungarian ride: the János Vitéz Barlangvasút – a 'cave railway' featuring cutesy dioramas from Sándor Petőfi's children's poem *Kukorica Jancsi*, recited over speakers as you ride through. There's a toddlers' park next door.

Budapest's zoo, completed in 1911, was originally designed with buildings that placed every animal in an architectural surrounding supposedly characteristic of its place of origin. Noteworthy architecture includes Neuschloss-Knüsli's extraordinary Elephant House, the faux-Moorish Africa House complex and the Main Gate. The Palm House, built by the Eiffel company, is a beautiful indoor tropical garden, where exotic birds fly free around various large halls, each with creatures indigenous to jungle regions. Children can pet tame animals in the Állatsimogató ('stroking zoo'), open in summer.

Gundel (*see p103*), the most famous restaurant in town, is right next door to the zoo. Originally opened in 1894 as the Wampetics, it was taken over in 1910 by top chef Károly

Roma Budapest

Stereotypes of Hungary usually include the romantic Gypsy musician. The truth is that life is anything but romantic for Hungary's half a million Roma – the name they call themselves in their native Romanes, related to the northern Indian languages of Hindi and Punjabi.

The Roma are essentially a European nationality without a nation. The majority here are the 'Romungros', assimilated into the working and lower-middle class: they don't speak Romanes and by now have lost many of their ethnic and cultural characteristics. Ironically, these are the ones also referred to as 'Gypsy' musicians, after a long and renowned hereditary tradition of professional musicianship (see p173).

A smaller group, the Oláh or Vlach, speak several dialects of Romanes. Hungarian slang borrows their basic words for girl (csaj), guy (csávó), money (lóvé), food (kaja) and flat (kéró). They guard their traditions closely. Many came here after the abolition of slavery in Romania in 1855, and found menial work in Budapest. The Boyash are the third main group who live mostly in southern Hungary and speak an archaic form of Romanian.

Public opinion of all of them is low, and the local media's barely better. But with the accession of Hungary into the European Union in 2004, the situation of the Roma has been brought into focus.

There are several Roma organisations, political participation is slowly taking root and since 2001 Radio C, a Roma-only station, has been on the airwaves at 88.8 FM. Despite its popularity, stories of financial problems were all over the local press in March 2003.

The **Roma Parliament** (pictured, see p88) is an umbrella organisation and community centre with a broad cultural agenda. It houses a crowded, fascinating collection of paintings by Roma artists, and a gallery recently named after the late János Balázs, a Roma painter and poet of international renown.

A recent cultural revival in music has produced bands like Kalyi Jag, Ando Drom, Amaro Suno and the newly celebrated Parno Graszt playing traditional Roma music – vocals backed with guitars and milk-churn percussion. There's also the Roma rap of Fekete Vonat, named after the 'Black Train' that used to ferry Roma workers from the countryside to and from Budapest.

Socialist Budapest

Sightseeing

Scratch hard on the gleaming surface of today's Budapest and you'll find the hidden Socialist city underneath. Stray into the backstreets of Pest and the urban decor of the era is pretty much unchanged. Shopfronts are decorated in the faded greens and blues of low-tech design, dedicated to the sale of a single unlikely item – plastic buttons, safety visors, fizz machines – painstakingly displayed according to the archaic principles of Socialist window dressing.

To take the full plunge into 1958, ride the HÉV from Boráros tér to the industrial island of Csepel. Along with the metro, these suburban trains were all made in the Soviet Union, and the rattling journey is an opportunity to study the curious features of Socialist design: cramped seating, violent door-closing mechanism and discordant but reassuring chimes of the crackly intercom. The island has a proud history of heavy industry and proletarian activism, baptised 'Red Csepel' by the Communists. In addition to the huge factory complex, the suburb is full of housing blocks built for industrial workers. South from Csepel station, in a

Gundel, who transformed local cuisine by bringing in French influences. Nearby is the similarly fancy – and pricey – **Robinson** (*see p105*), perched on the edge of a duck pond. Gundel's cheaper branch, the **Bagolyvár** (*see p103*), serves fine food at more affordable prices. All three offer outdoor dining.

Museum of Fine Arts

Szépművészeti Múzeum
XIV. Hősök tere (363 2675). M1 Hősök tere. **Open** 10am-5.30pm Tue-Sun. **Admission** Ft800; Ft200 concessions. English tours (Ft4,000 for up to 20 people) can usually be arranged on the spot in summer; in winter call ahead. **No credit cards.** Map p247 E1.

Vidám Park

XIV. Állatkerti körút 14-16 (363 8310/ www.vidampark.hu). M1 Széchenyi fürdő. **Open** *winter* 9.45am-sunset daily; *summer* 9.45am-8pm daily. **Admission** Ft300; free for children under 120cm. **No credit cards.** Map p247 F1.

Zoo

Állatkert
XIV. Állatkerti út 6-12 (363 3710). M1 Széchenyi fürdő. **Open** *winter* 9am-4pm daily; *summer* 9am-6pm Mon-Fri, 9am-7pm Sat, Sun. **Admission** Ft1,000; Ft750 children. **No credit cards.** Map p247 E1.

Districts VII-X

Outside the Kiskörút, Districts VII, VIII, IX and X get on with their daily lives, as the emphasis of the neighbourhoods is less on monuments and more on residents. But the buildings can be as interesting as many of the sights in the centre of town.

District VII is Budapest's Jewish quarter, still referred to as 'the Ghetto', although it never was one until 1944-45, when Arrow Cross Fascists walled off this whole area and herded the Jewish community inside. The junction by the Central Synagogue was one of two entrances (*see p76* **Jewish Budapest**).

Dominating the estuary of Dohány utca into the Kiskörút, the Central Synagogue is grandiose and simply enormous – seating 3,000, it is too big to heat and it has never been used in winter. Designed by Lajos Förster and completed in 1859, this is the second-largest synagogue in the world, after New York's Temple Emmanuel. Newly cleaned brickwork glows in blue, yellow and red, the heraldic colours of Budapest. Interlaced eight-pointed stars in the brick detailing, continued in the stained glass and mosaic flooring inside, are a symbol of regeneration – appropriate once secluded corner of Béke tér, stands András Beck's impressive statue of a worker musing over a good book, his boot on a pile of bricks.

The statues that once loomed over downtown have now been removed and placed in Statue Park (*pictured*), out on Highway 70 in far District XXII, a discreet site where they can be tastefully stored and displayed. Highlights include Imre Varga's spectacular bronze, chrome, steel and copper monument to Béla Kun, showing the leader of the 1919 Hungarian Soviet surrounded by demonstrators. The gift shop sells Communist memorabilia, including CDs of the 'Red Csepel' anthem, and cans purporting to contain the 'Last Breath of Communism'.

Statue Park
Szobor Park
XXII. Balatoni út (227 7446). Bus 3 from tram 47, 49 Móricz Zsigmond körtér, then bus 50 to terminus. **Open** *Oct-Feb* 10am-dusk daily. *May-Sept* 8am-8pm daily. **Admission** Ft300. **No credit cards**.

again after a $10 million, ten-year facelift. The divisions of its central space are based on the cabalistic Tree of Life, giving it a similar floor plan to a Gothic cathedral. The ceiling entwines Stars of David outlined in gold leaf. A small **Jewish Museum** in one wing displays 18th- to 19th-century ritual objects from the region. The collection is arranged in three rooms according to function: Sabbath, holidays and life-cycle ceremonies. The fourth room covers the Hungarian Holocaust – one photo shows corpses piled up in front of this same building after a massacre by Hungarian Arrow Cross Fascists. Though founded in 1931, when Hungarian Jews were feeling fairly secure, many more objects were donated after their owners were murdered in the Holocaust. Exhibits are well documented in English.

Behind the Central Synagogue, the back streets of District VII are dark, narrow, tatty and full of odd detail. It's not as picturesque as Prague's Jewish quarter, but although 700,000 Hungarian Jews died in the Holocaust, enough survived to mean that District VII is still a living community. You can hear Yiddish on Kazinczy utca, or eat a kosher pastry at the Fröhlich Cukrászda on Dob utca (No.22; 321 6741). The Orthodox complex, including the

Carmel Pince restaurant (VII. Dob utca 31; 322 1834), is centred around the corner of Dob and Kazinczy – dominated by the 1910 synagogue whose façade gracefully negotiates the curve of the street. The Rumbach Sebestyén utca synagogue – a Moorish structure by Otto Wagner – can only be seen from the outside.

The community has survived both an exodus of younger, wealthier Jews into less noisy and congested districts, and post-war attempts by the Communist government to homogenise the area. If you'd survived the Holocaust, you got to keep your flat. Workers brought into Budapest to work on the reconstruction of the city were housed in the empty properties.

Many of these were Gypsies and District VII is now also a Gypsy quarter – although the heart of Gypsy territory is beyond the Nagykörút, an area of repair shops and dingy bars. Armin Hegedűs's 1906 primary school at Dob utca 85 is definitely worth a detour, though.

The heart of the Jewish quarter is Klauzál tér, with a park and playground in the middle, where old men play chess and cards in summer. Fresh food stalls spill out on to the square from the main covered market on Saturdays. Next to it, the cheap lunchtime **Kádár Étkezde** (*see p95*) serves great, home-style Magyar cuisine.

Király utca is a lively street worth delving into, 70 per cent Jewish in 1900. It's still full of character and commotion, with pristine Stalinist-style shop signs, curious courtyards and pavements dotted with unshaven hustlers peddling cheap watches and jewellery – although the recent introduction of Asian fusion restaurant **Ópium** (*see p101*) and IKEA-esque three-star **Hotel Fiesta** (*see p37*) have added somewhat to its street value.

This is a fine neighbourhood for drinking, from early afternoon until the wee hours. The unmarked **Wichmann** (*see p123*) on the corner of Király and Kazinczy, the **Szimpla** (*see p123*) on Kertész or the **Sark** (*see p122*) on Klauzál are all good places to start. The **Fészek** on the corner of Dob and Kertész, a classic old artists' club, offers peaceful summer dining (*see p95*) in a picturesquely tatty inner courtyard, or surreal after-hours drinking in the enticing nightclub downstairs (*see p177*). For outdoor drinking, there's the **Szimpla Kert** garden bar (*see p178* **Summer night city**) in the courtyard of an abandoned building on Kazinczy.

Beyond the Nagykörút, parts of District VII are more run-down, but there are also villas on Városligeti fasor, as it slowly merges into the diplomatic quarter towards City Park.

Busy Rákóczi út divides District VII from grimier District VIII. Although synonymous with crime, the area is a safe, if perhaps sad, place to walk around. And it's not all low-life.

Sightseeing

Bounded by Üllői út and Rákóczi, the urban pie-slice of Józsefváros, as District VIII is also known, has its point at the National Museum (*see p79*). In Pollack Mihály tér behind, former mansions rub shoulders with the Socialist-realist Magyar Rádió headquarters, scene of much bloodletting in the Uprising (*see p18* **1956 and all that**).

The section of the VIII District beyond the Nagykörút is vast and unpredictable. On and around Népszínház utca there are many fine buildings, such as Béla Lajta's 1912 Harsányi House at No.19 and the Trade School at Vas utca 11, designed by Lajos Kozma (*see p72* **Art nouveau Budapest**). Nearby Köztársaság tér boasts the **Erkel Színház** (*see p168*), the vast Socialist-style concert hall used for opera. Népszínház leads to **Kerepesi Cemetery**, where you'll find politicians, poets, novelists, singers and industrialists, a comprehensive overview of the Hungarian establishment of the last 100 years. Monumentally planned, it's a popular place for a stroll. Wide, leafy avenues direct you towards strategic mausoleums: novelist Mór Jókai and arch-compromiser Ferenc Deák, bourgeois revolutionary Lajos Kossuth and Count Lajos Batthyány. Nearby, music-hall chanteuse Lujza Blaha is tucked up in a four-poster bed, serenaded by adoring cherubs. Anarchist poet Attila József, thrown out of the 1930s Communist Party but rehabilitated during the 1950s, was buried here more than 20 years after his suicide.

Over Kerepesi's northern wall stands the city's main railway station, Keleti. Built as part of the great rail expansion of the 1800s, Keleti was the hub of an imperial network that kept its minorities dependent: all railway lines had to go through Pest. To this day there is no direct line from Zagreb to Vienna. Most traffic still comes through here, a grand old palace of a station, its departure boards beckoning with exotic and dangerous places, signposted in various alphabets on the sides of trains. Although renovated, and the money-changers who once haunted its corridors banished from the temple, Keleti can still be pretty seedy at night.

The heart of Józsefváros is the area south of Népszínház utca, centred on Mátyás tér. Eclectic façades are shabby, while overgrown inner courtyards buzz with a ragged, almost medieval life. The nearby **Roma Parliament** is headquarters for political activism on behalf of Roma and an arts centre, with plays in the Romany language and exhibitions by Roma artists (*see p85* **Roma Budapest**).

A little further out, down Kőbányai út, is the sprawling, seedy **Józsefvárosi piac** (*see p137* **A load of old junk**), an outdoor market. Many merchants are Chinese and, if the city ever

acquires a Chinatown, it will be in Józsefváros. Nearby is the home ground of 2003 Hungarian football champions **MTK** (*see p183*).

District IX, also known as **Ferencváros**, is a working-class neighbourhood, home to the football team of the same name (*see p182*), the great rivals of MTK a few tram stops away. Squeezed between Üllői út and the Danube, the district is similar in style to the neighbouring VIII, lined with grim grey housing blocks. Unlike the VIII, however, the IX can boast a major new arts centre: the **Trafó** (*see p189* **Sparking a cultural revolution**). Located in dowdy Liliom utca, this excellent multicultural venue, set in a former transformer building, offers performances in dance, theatre and music, with the occasional art exhibitions thrown in. Around it have sprung up a number of nightspots, including the **Jailhouse** (*see p179*), a fun dance club and favourite with the local African community.

Further down the Danube, the new **National Theatre** (*see p191*) offers superb riverside views from its gaudy interior. The surrounding new parkland is a pleasant place for a stroll, a rarity amid the grey and dusty tenements.

Just east of Ferencváros stretches the outer X District, most notable for **Újköztemető Cemetery**. People visit to see the final resting place of Imre Nagy, the Prime Minister who defied the Soviets in 1956 (*see p18* **1956 and all that**). You'll find him in Plot 301, along with 260 others executed for their parts in the revolution, in the farthest corner to the right of the entrance. Empty coach parks, a traffic barrier and a police guard let you know you've arrived. Transylvanian markers outline the mass grave behind a Székely gate proclaiming a 'National Pantheon'.

Central Synagogue/Jewish Museum

Nagy Zsinagóga és Zsidó Múzeum
VII. Dohány utca 2 (342 1335). M2 Astoria/tram 47, 49. **Open** *synagogue* 10am-3pm Mon-Fri, Sun; *museum* 10am-5pm Mon-Thur; 10am-2pm Fri, Sun. **Admission** *synagogue* by donation; *museum* Ft600; Ft200 concessions. Heroes' Temple prayer 6pm Fri, 9am Sat. **No credit cards**. **Map** p249 D4.

Kerepesi Cemetery

VIII. Fiumei út 14 (323 5100). M2 Keleti/tram 23, 24, 28. **Open** 7am-7pm daily. **Admission** free. **Map** p250 F4.

Roma Parliament

VIII. Tavaszmező 6 (210 4798). Tram 4, 6. **Open** varies. **Admission** varies. **Map** p250 E5.

Újköztemető Cemetery

X. Kozma utca 8-10 (433 7300). Tram 28, 37. **Open** dawn-dusk, hours vary depending on season; always open Aug-Apr 7.30am-5pm, May-July 7am-8pm daily. **Admission** free.

Eat, Drink, Shop

Restaurants

Quality improves, quantities decrease and prices stay low.

Eat, Drink, Shop

Eating well in Budapest is getting easier every year, thanks to outside influences lightening up traditionally heavy Hungarian cuisine and more new venues offering authentic foreign food.

These improvements in the local restaurant scene were direly needed, especially in a capital that relies so heavily on tourism. For decades, large portions were the yardstick of excellence, and low cost everything. And because Hungary maintained an isolated stance from trends in the rest of the world, the 1960s wave of lighter European cuisine never broke here.

Although Budapest's restaurant world at the turn of the century was famous, it was the preserve of the wealthy elite. For all its sins, Communist rule made eating out more accessible to the common person, but didn't, unfortunately, teach them what to look for. The situation was rough on visitors, but it didn't seem to bother the average Hungarian, who only ate out rarely, and considered doing so an occasional luxury.

Nowadays, the growth of disposable income and competition, plus greater openness to outside influences, means anyone can eat well in the city if they look for it. People seem to have learned that when it comes to serving non-Magyar cuisine, it's best to have an experienced chef using authentic ingredients. Miso soup prepared with paprika is, hopefully, a thing of the past. Meanwhile, more care is being put into preparation of local dishes.

Much of what is considered the best in Hungarian cuisine was developed in the early 1900s, when Joseph Maréchal, József Dobos, and János and Károly Gundel introduced a strong French influence into Budapest's kitchens. Since that time, not much has been done to expand or develop Hungarian food, but the new generation of independent, internationally aware chefs and restaurant owners may help to change that. Zoltán Kovács of the **Képíró** (see p95), for example, is one chef charting the future course of Magyar cookery. And places like **Café Kör** (see p95) have proved that it's possible to serve light, simple Hungarian food alongside international cuisine.

You can still find many places in Budapest where standards aren't very high and the service is decidedly poor, but with the help of this chapter you should also find a good number of memorable venues.

THE MAGYAR MENU

Innovation notwithstanding, the standard Hungarian fare that you will run into at the average street-corner restaurant will be predictable (see p103 **Top ten local dishes**). The colourful ethnic influences – Balkan, Jewish, Turkish, Central Asian and Central European – on local cuisine disappeared in the shortages, supply problems and general statis of state-run chain restaurants. As supplies improved, many chefs began aping, with less and less conviction and growing indifference, the pre-war Golden Age. The taste for fresh seasonal dishes got nudged aside amid the clamour for plenty – you will never leave a Hungarian table still hungry.

Paprika is ubiquitous, but that doesn't mean the food is especially spicy. In fact, Hungarian cuisine is rather bland by most standards. With exceptions, the paprika tends to be sweet and fragrant rather than hot, and in fried foods it is added more for decoration than flavour. It only comes into its own in dishes like *töltött káposzta* (stuffed cabbage) or *pörkölt* (what has come to be considered as Hungarian goulash), when meat and onions are stewed together in a fat flavoured with paprika. Like all cuisines with roots in peasant culture, Hungarian food tends to be very fatty – don't be surprised if you find a slab of lightly cooked pork fat on your plate next to the meat. Another source of fat is sour cream, which also provides the smooth piquancy in that other paprika-flavoured local classic, *paprikás* – a *pörkölt* thickened with a sour cream and flour mixture.

For Hungarians, goulash (*gulyás*) is a hearty beef soup named after the people who used to eat it (*gulyás* means 'herdsman'). Soup is an important component of the Magyar meal. Most tend to be a thin consommé with some form of dumpling or pasta to add ballast, but there are richer, heavier soups that are perhaps best kept for bleak winter evenings.

Many main courses on offer in a typical Hungarian restaurant are breaded and pan- or deep-fried. Restaurateurs like this style of cooking because it is quick and can employ that Hungarian favourite, pork. Deep-frying the meat means that it's easy to fry chips alongside it, and the two are often on offer together.

There's no point in thinking about seafood in a restaurant serving standard Hungarian fare.

Although more fresh ocean fish is making it to the tables of better restaurants in this land-locked country, simpler places won't serve seafood or will have it frozen. But fish lovers can enjoy *fogas*, the delicate pike-perch that is unique to Lake Balaton. Other popular fish include *harcsa* (catfish), often stewed *paprikás* style; *pisztráng* (trout), usually farmed but a revelation when fresh from a stream; and the fatty, bony *ponty* (carp), which is usually what the menu means when it just says 'fish'.

The situation in Budapest is improving for vegetarians (*see p107* **Vegging out**), but you won't notice this improvement on any bog-standard Hungarian menu. What locals call 'salad' is often a single vegetable in a light, oil-free dressing or something pickled: gherkins, peppers or cabbage. In many Hungarian places, vegetarians are forced to take refuge with starters like fried cheese or breaded mushrooms.

The portions are hefty, but, if you have room for dessert, traditional favourites are crêpes (*palacsinta*) and bready, dumpling-like creations with cream or jam. Chestnut purée, another local standard, is rich and filling.

PRACTICAL TIPS

Most restaurants serve guests in two sittings, a lunchtime and evening meal. Generally, it's not necessary to book a table, unless otherwise advised. You may have to share tables during the busy lunchtime period. Most menus have English and/or German translations – with the cheaper lunchtime special set menus at the top – and downtown restaurants will have at least one waiter able to communicate in either language.

The word for restaurant is *étterem*, although a *vendéglő* (and *kisvendéglő*) will do the same job. A *csárda* is a more traditional inn, its staff and decor done up with folk touches, with perhaps a band playing too. A *halászcsárda* is one that specialises in fish. The slowly disappearing *étkezde* is a cheap, family-run place generally catering to a lunchtime crowd.

Although some places now add a service charge to the bill – and also itemise it – in others it's customary to leave a tip of ten per cent or so. You do this by indicating how much you would like to be charged for when handing over the money, rounding up the total to the nearest applicable hundred. If the bill is, say, Ft3,600 (the price of an average two-course meal with drinks in a standard restaurant), then offering to pay Ft4,000 would be the norm.

You'll find that eating out in Budapest is far more affordable than in most European capitals. Our reviews attempt to give an idea of the costs of restaurants using the following comparative scale, based on the average cost of a starter and main course. Do be aware, though, that many places can charge a fortune for even an average wine ordered by the bottle:

€ – under Ft2,000;
€€ – Ft2,000-Ft4,000;
€€€ – Ft4,000-Ft6,000;
€€€€ – above Ft6,000.

Eat, Drink, Shop

California comes to Budapest at minimalist, fusionesque **Baraka**. *See p95.*

Fin-de-siècle styling at **Múzeum**.

Buda

Hungarian

Arcade Bistro

XII. Kiss János altábornagy utca 38 (225 1969/
www.travelport.hu/arkadbisztro). Tram 61.
Open 11am-midnight Mon-Sat. **Average** €€.
Credit MC, V.
This venue is the modern, upscale sibling of CaféKör
(*see p95*), catering to the same professional crowd.
It's also among the best restaurants in Buda, and
features great wines that are likely to show up in the
sauces. The offerings are freshly prepared international and Hungarian cuisine, with plenty of fish and
lighter-than-usual options on the menu. If your party
can't decide between Hungarian and something else,
this is a crowd pleaser. Reservations are a must for
dinner, especially at weekends. The decor is clean-
lined and unstuffy, with the odd abstract painting.
It's hard to spot, on the ground floor of a residential
building on a side street by the MOM Park complex.

Kacsa

I. Fő utca 75 (201 9992/www.kacsavendeglo.hu).
M2 Batthyány tér/bus 86. **Open** noon-3pm, 6pm-
midnight Mon-Fri; 6pm-midnight Sat, Sun. **Average**
€€€€. **Credit** AmEx, DC, MC, V. **Map** p245 B3.
Managed by an entrepreneurial young Leonardo
DiCaprio lookalike, this small, elegant establishment
specialises in duck (*kacsa*) dishes. The service is
almost ingratiating and the food and wine are rather
overpriced, but it can be pleasant for the pampered
atmosphere it evokes – all velvet, china and crystal.
Probably the best option here is the crispy half duck,
which takes a good approach to the fatty fowl. The
place could certainly use more innovation and more
vegetables – the food doesn't reach the level of the
restaurant's other trappings.

Múzeum

VIII. Múzeum körút 12 (267 0375). M3 Kálvin tér/
tram 47, 49/night bus 14É, 50É. **Open** 10.30-1.30am
Mon-Sat. **Average** €€. **Credit** AmEx. **Map** p293 D4.
High ceilings, tiled walls, tall windows providing
plenty of light and well-spaced tables embellish the
fin-de-siècle ambience at the ever-popular Múzeum,
next to the National Museum and founded in 1885.
The menu is impressive, with a large difference in
price from one dish to another – you can easily spend
a fortune in here or you can dine quite cheaply. The
Hungarian/international food is carefully prepared,
but presentation (artfully done to make vast portions
resemble nouvelle cuisine) just occasionally wins out
over culinary good taste. Smooth service and the
pleasant surroundings keep this old place buzzing.
Good spot for late dining.

Rivalda Café & Restaurant

I. Színház utca 5-9 (489 0236/www.rivalda.net).
Várbusz from M2 Moszkva tér/bus 16.
Open 11.30am-11.30pm daily. **Average** €€€.
Credit AmEx, MC, V. **Map** p248 B5.

Eat, Drink, Shop

A good place for light, modern Hungarian cuisine, Rivalda opened a few years ago atop Castle Hill, in a former monastery-cum-casino and theatre. In the spirit of its past incarnation, the rooms are done out with stage lights and curtains, and portraits of famous Hungarian performers decorate the walls. The Hungarian-American owner has managed to establish a place where Hungarian food has been updated and rendered in lighter form, but many of the lunchtime meals can be somewhat mediocre. There's also a large cobblestone courtyard outside and live music nightly.

Szent Jupát

II. Dékán utca 3 (212 2923). M2 Moszkva tér/tram 4, 6/night bus 6É, 49É. **Open** noon-6am daily. **Average** €. **No credit cards**. **Map** p245 A3.
They rarely change the grease in the frier, it seems and they serve more food than any normal person should sensibly eat, but if greasy and plentiful is what you're looking for at 4am, the bustling Szent Jupát can oblige. Share a booth with strangers in this small cellar space while you sober up with a rich bowl of smoky *Jókai bableves* (bean soup). Everything else is served on a mountain of fried potatoes. They also deliver.

Tabáni Kakas

I. Attila út 27 (375 7165). Tram 18/bus 5. **Open** noon-midnight daily. **Average** €€. **Credit** AmEx, DC, MC, V. **Map** p248 B4.
The menu proudly boasts that all dishes here are cooked with goose fat – and this ingredient really does make for decadently delicious meals. But it means that vegetarians are left out, and even most meat-eating regulars have to consider what eating here could do to their arteries. Still, it's a charming old one-room restaurant with a dimly lit interior of antiques and old pictures that look like they've been around for a while. Perennial standards on the menu include steak tartare, devillishly crunchy goose cracklings, classic fried goose leg with braised red cabbage and broken potatoes, and goose liver 'Hungarian style' with peppers, tomatoes, onions and paprika. Eschew the generally below-average wine list for draught beer instead. More often than not there's a singer/pianist providing appropriately old-fashioned music in the background.

Vadrózsa

II. Pentelei Molnár utca 15 (326 5817). Bus 11, 91. **Open** noon-3pm, 6pm-midnight daily. **Average** €€€€. **Credit** AmEx, DC, MC, V.
Occupying a sumptuous villa and garden on Rózsadomb, Budapest's ritziest peak, this place has prices to match its posh surroundings. Guests are proffered a tray of raw fish, viands and delicacies, and these are whipped up at their pleasure (with suggestions, of course) if they don't see what they want on the menu. The kitchen is particularly known for its fine preparations of steak, pheasant and venison. If you're willing to shell out, you'll eat well here, but you can find better value around town.

International

Arany Kaviar

I. Ostrom utca 19 (201 6737/225 7370/06 30 954 2600/www.aranykaviar.hu). M2 Moszkva tér/tram 4, 6. **Open** noon-midnight daily. **Average** €€€. **Credit** AmEx, DC, MC, V. **Map** p245 A2.
Excellent Russian food, prepared by a Hungarian-Russian chef trained at top hotels in the Motherland. It offers Beluga or Sevruga caviar at some of the cheapest prices around, and fantastic sturgeon, though that's supposed to be an endangered species. Anyway, unless you're with at least two others, you won't be able to finish both the well-laden caviar 'boat', with fixings, and a main course: fantastic home-smoked Kamchatka salmon, delicious beef tenderloin or goose liver-stuffed *pirogi*, wrapped in tender pastry with a slathering of fresh minced herbs bathing the meat beneath. The portions are generous, vodka aficionados won't be disappointed, and the wine list is from the Budapest Wine Society around the corner. Highly recommended.

Downtown Pest

Hungarian

Alföldi Vendéglő

V. Kecskeméti utca 4 (267 0224). M3 Kálvin tér/ tram 47, 49. **Open** noon-midnight daily. **Average** €. **No credit cards**. **Map** p249 D5.
Inexpensive place brings rural atmosphere to the centre of town with slow service, low-frills decor and 'country-style' cuisine – a satisfying example of hearty high-cholesterol Hungarian, with the accent on meat. Its Hortobágyi *palacsinta*, a meat-stuffed pancake with creamy paprika sauce, is as good as anyone's. Tasty soups are served in generous, bat-tered aluminium tureens. The excellent *Kolozsvári töltött káposzta* consists of stuffed cabbage rolls with sausage, bacon and a pork chop served alongside. Wash it all down with sweetish brown beer.

Astoria Empire

V. Kossuth Lajos utca 19-21 (484 3222). M2 Astoria/tram 47, 49/bus 7. **Open** noon-3pm, 6.30-11pm daily. **Average** €€€. **Credit** AmEx, DC, MC, V. **Map** p249 D4.
Often overlooked fine dining in the restaurant of the Hotel Astoria (*see p37*). Like the hotel, this elegant establishment is reminiscent of the age of the Orient Express, and offers far more elaborate preparations than the average Hungarian venue. The menu includes lots of game and goose liver, and quite sumptuous set Hungarian menus, all elegantly presented. Check the specials card for seasonal items like asparagus. For some reason the interior isn't as gorgeous as the adjoining café (*see p115*), which gleams with wood and brass. Ironically, the place doesn't seem to be overrun by tourists, who flock to far more expensive restaurants with far worse food instead. Live music in the evenings.

Eat, Drink, Shop

A venue with spirit...

KÁRPÁTIA
RESTAURANT & BRASSERIE

Original turn-of-the-century dining experience in a
magnificent environment
Classic and contemporary Hungarian food and wine
Hungarian gypsy music every evening
Terrace in the courtyard of the Franciscan monastery
Open daily 11 am to 11 pm

Ferenciek tere 7-8., 1053 Budapest
Telephone: 317-3596, Fax: 318-0591
E-mail: restaurant@karpatia.hu. Website: www.karpatia.hu

PREMIER
RESTAURANT
&TERRACE

A venue with style...

- The premier art nouveau restaurant of Budapest
- Contemporary Hungarian and International food
- Relaxed outdoor dining experience
  on the corner of Andrássy út and Bajza utca
- Open daily 10 am to 11 pm

- Andrássy út 101., 1062 Budapest
- Tel.: 342-1768
- premier-restaurant@axelero.hu
- www.premier-restaurant.hu
- Operated by the Kárpátia Restaurant

Rivalda Café & Restaurant

Best OF BUDAPEST 2000
Best OF BUDAPEST 2001
Best OF BUDAPEST 2002

Experience classic Castle Hill dining...

◆

*Creative, contemporary cuisine
in the casual-chic restaurant
or the charming centuries old
cobblestone courtyard.*

1014 Budapest, Színház u. 5–9. (Next to the National Dance Theatre)
Open daily: 11:30-23:30 • Reservations: 489-0236 • www.rivalda.net • rivalda@nextra.hu

Baraka

*V. Magyar utca 12-14 (483 1355). M2 Astoria/tram
47, 49/bus 7.* **Open** 6-11pm Mon-Sat. **Average** €€.
Credit AmEx, DC, MC, V. **Map** p249 D4.
Slip down a sidestreet near the Astoria intersection
and suddenly you're in a culinary outpost of
California. Owners Leora and David tend to you in
this outstanding restaurant invariably filled with
repeat customers. Refreshingly lighter than typical
Hungarian fare, the food here is mostly fusionesque,
richly embellished with Asian seasonings and
piquant spices. Fish and seafood sit centre stage, but
there are creative specials like pan-fried goose liver
slices layered between crispy wonton skins in a pool
of ginger-infused sauce. The mostly Hungarian wine
selection is top notch. David worked at the City
Bakery in New York, and his delicious breads and
desserts are not to be missed. The sleek, minimalist
interior is surprisingly intimate.

Café Kör

V. Sas utca 17 (311 0053). M3 Arany János utca.
Open 10am-11pm Mon-Sat. **Average** €€.
No credit cards. Map p246 C3.
The ever-popular Café Kör offers a comfortable,
bistro-like atmosphere more reminiscent of Vienna
or Berlin than Budapest. There's a great bar, with a
fine selection of local wines, and some small café
tables as well as a more formal dining space.
Furnishings have been chosen with care and a
refreshingly simple Hungarian international menu
is complemented by daily specials. Service can be
slow but is generally friendly and knowledgeable.
One of the few places in Hungary to offer a truly first-
class steak. Excellent grilled goat's cheese is one of
the few vegetarian options. Good spot for breakfast,
served until 11.30am. Book ahead for dinner.

Costes

*IX. Ráday utca 4 (219 0696). M3 Kálvin tér/tram
47, 49.* **Open** 11am-midnight daily. **Average** €€€.
Credit MC, V. **Map** p249 D5.
The best and priciest restaurant on bar-starred
Ráday utca serves mainly continental cuisine that
transcends Hungarian offerings, as well as some local
dishes. The menu is extensive and covers everything
from pheasant to prawns, the preparation pleasingly
elaborate and fresh. Fabulous filet mignon is served
with morel sauce set atop a cushion of couscous-
stuffed Savoy cabbage. Offers proper salads, hard to
find anywhere in Budapest. There are great desserts,
such as *arany galuska*, a recommended frequent special: lumps of rich yeast dough are dipped in butter
and ground walnuts, wedged into a pan and baked,
then served warm with crème anglaise. You might
have to wait a while for your meal during peak hours.

Fészek

*VII. Kertész utca 36 (322 6043). Tram 4, 6/night bus
6É.* **Open** noon-2am daily. **Average** €. **Credit** AmEx,
MC, V. **Map** 246 D3.
Recently changed to be open late, this place has been
an artists' club since the turn of the century but in

practice is open to anyone (with a Ft200 entrance fee
in the evening). 'The Nest' offers stylish dining at
bargain prices. The ornate high-ceilinged main room
is attractive enough, but the real bonus is outside,
an appealingly dilapidated Venetian-style courtyard, formerly a monks' cloister and one of the most
beautiful places in central Pest to while away a long
summer lunchtime. Service can be rather slow and
inaccurate and the menu is simply too extensive to
excel at anything, but the price is right and the
atmosphere is relaxing and unique. Downstairs is a
semi-exclusive club – they'll admit you after you
plead a little – and late-night haunt (*see p177*).

Kádár Étkezde

VII. Klauzál tér 10 (321 3622). Tram 4, 6. **Open**
11.30am-3.30pm Tue-Fri. **Average** €. **No credit
cards. Map** p246 D3.
Zero frills and delicious Hungarian home cooking
fuse in this institution in the heart of the old Jewish
quarter. Autographed photos of Hungarian showbiz
stars adorn the walls and each table has its own
(dangerously high-powered) soda siphon. Share a
table with a stranger and keep an eye out for daily
specials, like goose leg (*libacomb*), served with red
cabbage and mashed potatos, or the fabulous Jewish
dish *sólet*, made of smoked goose breast and baked
beans. A fine place to find *főzelék*, a puréed vegetable
stew served with a fried egg on top. Pay for your
meal at the door on your way out.

Károlyi Étterem Kávéház

*V. Károlyi Mihályi utca 16 (328 0240). M3 Ferenciek
tere/bus 7.* **Open** 10am-11pm daily. **Average** €€.
Credit AmEx, DC, MC, V. **Map** p249 C4.
Café/restaurant recommended for its traditional
Hungarian menu at fair prices, in the courtyard of
the beautifully restored Károly Mansion, providing
outdoor seating in a peaceful garden just off bustling
Váci utca. Catfish (*harcsa*) *paprikás* with cottage
cheese noodles is a hearty change from the chicken
version. Similarly, the *Kalotaszegi húsos palacsinta*,
a meat-stuffed pancake flavoured with dill, is a twist
on the standard *Hortobágyi palacsinta*. A veggie
main course for two is always on the menu. Some
elegant, upscale dishes dot the selection, and the
wine list is excellent.

Képíró

*V. Képíró utca 3 (266 0430/www.kepiro
restaurant.hu). M3 Kálvin tér/tram 47, 49.* **Open**
noon-3pm, 6pm-midnight Mon-Fri; 6pm-midnight
Sat. **Average** €€€€. **Credit** MC, V. **Map** p249 D5.
A peek into the future of Hungarian cuisine, Képíró's
mandate is also to resurrect the great Hungarian
dishes elaborated by Escoffier and other great chefs.
The constantly morphing menu is sophisticated and
makes use of top-quality Hungarian ingredients
such as mushrooms, truffles, organic steaks from
heritage Hungarian grey cattle and the like created
by Képíró's indefatigable young chef, Zoltán
Kovács. Teeny portions at high prices might be a
drawback, but there are several set menus.

Oenophiles should look into the wine tasting menus, consisting of many fine successive small courses or cheeses, with an appropriate wine to match each one. A serious venue for gastronomes, in which you'll be well looked after by the management.

Lou Lou

V. Vigyázó Ferenc utca 4 (312 4505). M1, M2, M3 Deák tér/tram 47, 49. **Open** noon-3pm, 7-11pm Mon-Fri; 7-11pm Sat. **Average** €€€€. **Credit** AmEx, MC, V. **Map** p249 C4.

Prices have risen since its inception, but this is still one of the cleverest choices for dinner in Budapest. Cherub-faced owner Károly Rudits stays on top of what's hot internationally. Expertly prepared, mainly continental cuisine, heavily inspired by French and Italian, with modern interpretations of Hungarian fare. Originally more of a bistro-style place, the menu has become more sophisticated, and includes items like Irish smoked salmon, scallops in rosé sauce, sweet and savoury pairings of game steaks with forest fruits or goose liver with honey. Good selection of the better Hungarian wines, some of which can be pricey. Agreeable service and quaint interior with just seven tables. Booking essential.

Oroszlános Kút

V. Vörösmarty tér 7 (429 9023). M1 Vörösmarty tér/tram 2. **Open** *Oct-May* 11am-3pm, 6-11pm Mon-Sat. *June-Sept* 11am-11pm daily. **Average** €€€. **Credit** AmEx, DC, MC, V. **Map** p249 C4.

The famous Gerbeaud, a venerable institution for coffee and cakes (*see p117*), was serious when it decided to add on a fine-dining arm. It obtained an

What's on the menu?

Eat, Drink, Shop

Useful phrases

Are these seats taken? *Ezek a helyek foglaltak?*
Bon appétit! *Jó étvágyat!*
Do you have...? *Van...?*
I'm a vegetarian. *Vegetáriánus vagyok.*
I'm diabetic. *Diabetikus vagyok.*
I'd like a table for two. *Két fő részére kérek egy asztalt.*
I'd like the menu, please. *Kérem az étlapot.*
I didn't order this. *Nem ezt rendeltem.*
Thank you. *Köszönöm.*
The bill, please. *Számlát kérek!*

Basics (Alapok)

Ashtray *Hamutartó*
Bill *Számla*
Bread *Kenyér*
Cup *Csésze*
Fork *Villa*
Glass *Pohár*
Knife *Kés*
Milk *Tej*
Napkin *Szalvéta*
Oil *Olaj*
Pepper *Bors*
Plate *Tanyér*
Salt *Só*
Spoon *Kanál*
Sugar *Cukor*
Teaspoon *Kiskanál*
Vinegar *Ecet*
Water *Víz*

Meats (Húsok)

Bárány Lamb
Bográcsgulyás Thick goulash soup

Borjú Veal
Comb Leg
Jókai bableves Bean soup with pork knuckle
Kacsa Duck
Kijevi pulykamell Butter or cheese-filled turkey in breadcrumbs
Liba Goose
Máj Liver
Marha Beef
Mell Breast
Nyúl Rabbit
Pulyka Turkey
Sonka Ham
Szarvas Venison

Fish/Seafood (Hal/Tengeri gyülmölcs)

Fekete kagyló Mussels
Halfilé roston Grilled fillet of fish
Harcsa Catfish
Homár Lobster
Kagyló Shellfish, mussels
Lazac Salmon
Pisztráng Trout
Ponty Carp
Rák Crab, prawn
Tonhal Tuna

Salads (Savanyúság)

Cékla Beetroot
Fejes saláta Lettuce salad
Paradicsom Tomato
Uborka Cucumber
Vitamin saláta Mixed salad with mayonnaise

Vegetables (Zöldség)

Gomba Mushrooms
Karfiol Cauliflower

excellent chef who oversees the highly recommended Hungarian cuisine, with the occasional twist, as well as upscale international dishes. The marble-clad interior and nice outdoor seating are impressive, even in this glitzy part of town. The tendency here to treat everyone as a moneyed tourist can be quite off-putting, especially the elaborate and expensive recommendations from the staff.

Pilvax

V. Pilvax köz 1-3 (266 7660/www.taverna.hu). M3 Ferenciek tere/bus 7. **Open** 11am-11pm daily. **Average** €€€. **Credit** AmEx, DC, MC, V. **Map** p249 C4.

This is where the revolutionaries of 1848 gathered to demand independence from the Habsburgs, but this newly established hotel/restaurant (*see p35*)

Kukorica Sweetcorn
Lencse Lentils
Paprika Pepper
Sárgarépa Carrot
Spárga Asparagus (white/*fehér*, green/*zöld*)
Spenót Spinach
Zöldbab Green beans
Zöldborsó Green peas

Fruits, Nuts (Gyümölcs, Dió)

Alma Apple
Cseresznye Cherry
Dió Nut, walnut
Dinnye Melon
Eper Strawberry
Gesztenye Chestnut
Mák Poppyseed
Málna Raspberry
Mandula Almond
Meggy Sour cherry
Narancs Orange
Őszibarack Peach
Sárgabarack Apricot
Szeder Blackberry
Szilva Plum

Drinks (Italok)

Ásványvíz Mineral water
Bor Wine
Édes bor Sweet wine
Fehér bor White wine
Kávé Coffee
Narancslé Orange juice
Pálinka Fruit brandy
Pezsgő Sparkling wine
Sör Beer
Száraz bor Dry wine
Vörös bor Red wine

---

is a little different to the café of 150 years ago. Nevertheless, patriotic souls still flock here as part of Independence Day celebrations every 15 March. Aware of its importance to tourists, the place offers an elegant interior and well executed classic Hungarian cuisine with a historic bent. There are also various interesting continental offerings. A pleasant terrace makes this a fine choice for outdoor dining near tourist-heavy Váci utca.

International

Al-Amir

VII. Király utca 17 (352 1422). M1 Opera. **Open** noon-11pm Mon-Sat; 1-11pm Sun. **Average** €. **No credit cards**. **Map** p249 C4.

This sound Syrian restaurant with friendly service is a favourite among vegetarians seeking to escape the meat-heavy menus found around town. Also a fine place for the teetotal, as it serves good teas – and no alcohol. You can make a decent meal out of an assortment of the many tasty appetisers, which include houmous and aubergine cream. It also does good lamb dishes and kebabs, and the baklava is exquisite. The television tuned to Middle Eastern cable channels constantly shows melodramatic Arabic music videos. The window in the front sells falafel and kebabs to street eaters.

Arigato

VI. Ó utca 3 (353 3549). M3 Arany János utca. **Open** noon-3pm, 5-11pm Mon-Sat. **Average** €€. **Credit** AmEx, DC, MC, V.

This family-owned Japanese restaurant and bar, carefully watched over by chef Kaoru Uehara and his wife Tomoko, offers the biggest selection and the best prices for sushi and Japanese food in Budapest. *Tonkatsu-don* (rice topped with fried pork, egg and caramelised onions) is highly recommended. Specials, like curried rice or noodles available on Fridays, make for happy surprises. The daily lunch specials are economical but the portions are small – especially by local standards – and you may want to add a side dish. Renovation of parts of the vast cellar space, formerly a bar, is ongoing, hence the anachronistic nautical hardware in the restroom area. Construction of a tatami room is planned.

Bombay Palace

VI. Andrássy út 44 (332 8363/331 3787). M1 Oktogon/tram 4, 6. **Open** noon-2.45pm, 6-11.30pm daily. **Average** €€€. **Credit** MC, V. **Map** p246 D3.

Hungary's best Indian, but also its most formal and expensive. This branch of an international chain is set in suitably palatial premises, with marble floors, chandeliers and almost too many service staff. The fare is usually good, displaying no particular regional bias. There's a fair tandoori selection but vegetarian options are the wiser choice for both quality and price. Also provides a fine basket of assorted naan breads to complement the dependably good classic main dishes.

Eat, Drink, Shop

Unknown pleasures

Right now Hungary is producing world-class wines in all categories, but because it's shamelessly negligent in promoting them abroad, a visit here remains the best opportunity to enjoy them. *See also p207* **Touring the vineyards**.

Top-quality Hungarian white wines are a revelation, bringing forth varietal clarity within a mantle of clean, refreshing acidity – even more so when they're native varieties, such as the fruity, blossomy Cserszegi Fűszeres. The Hilltop Neszmély winery has made 'Woodcutter's White' popular in the UK using this grape, also marketed under the Unpronounceable Grape label. Irsai Olivér is a similar variety, but it's still fairly rare to come across these two.

The region around Lake Balaton is almost exclusively white wine territory, with Olasz Rizling (in actual fact not a true Riesling) dominating production. Most of it is horrible, reeking of mothballs. It's best to gravitate toward winemakers Ottó Légli, Mihály Figula, Huba Szeremley/Szent Orbán and Öregbaglas from that region. But on the up and up is the Etyek region near Budapest, historically a Chardonnay producer for sparkling wines. Etyeki Kúria is fast becoming a major proponent of that grape. Other popular whites include Szürkebarát (Pinot Gris), creamy Királyleányka from Eger, and Sauvignon Blanc.

Tokaj is best known for its sweet Tokaji Aszú, but dry versions of the varieties used to make it – Furmint, Hárslevelű and Muscat Lunel – are also made by most of the big new wineries there (Oremus, Disznókő, Hétszőlő,

Királyudvar, Degenfeld). As for Tokaj Aszú, you can't go wrong with the above-mentioned either. Just remember that the higher the *puttony* number (usually from 4 to 6), the sweeter the wine.

Hungary's most widely grown red grape is Kékfrankos (Blaufränkisch), a feisty, hard red that's often sour. Austrian Franz Weninger's Kékfrankos from the Sopron region is a supreme expression of the potential of this grape, and it's available in barrique versions.

The Villány region sits securely at the top of the red wine-growing heap, but it's a position that's increasingly relying on reputation as other regions gain prominence. Wonderful red cuvées (blends, usually containing Cabernet Sauvignon and the region's flagship grape, the round and lush, easy-drinking Kékoportó, among others) are to be had from Attila Gere/Gere & Weninger, Vylyan, Malatinszky Kúria, Tiffán and József Bock. Attila Gere's Kopár is arguably the best red in Hungary.

Eger winemakers are proficient at crafting both whites and reds. The cream of the crop include Tibor Gál, Tamás Pók and Vilmos Thummerer. The famous 'Bull's Blood' (Bikavér) blend hails from here, as does the Szekszárd, whose better wineries include Heimann, Vesztergombi, Baron von Twickel/Chateau Kajmád/Liszt/Gróf Zichy, Péter Vida and Tamás Dúzsi.

One final point: run screaming from red wine labelled *félszáraz* or *édes*. Many Hungarians prefer sweet wines – including reds. But the better wineries don't dabble in such sacrilege, and you needn't worry about accidentally buying any in a reputable shop.

Eat, Drink, Shop

Mokka – North African/modern French cuisine.

Le Bourbon

Hotel Le Meridien, V. Deák Ferenc utca 16-18 (429 5500). M1, M2, M3 Deák tér/tram 47, 49. **Open** 6.30am-11pm daily. **Average** €€€. **Credit** AmEx, DC, MC, V. **Map** p249 C4.

The excellent restaurant of the Hotel Le Meridien (*see p30*), with French food both classic and new. Young chef Laurent Vandenmeele is in charge of a seasonally changing menu of high French cuisine, with pastry chef Alain Lagrange creating breathtaking desserts. The menu usually includes fresh or hot oysters, duck confit and exquisite fish dishes. The hushed, elegant wood-panelled interior features the odd antique and a gorgeous behemoth of a flower arrangement. Vast Sunday brunch spread, promotional specials on Fridays, fresh assorted seafood on Saturdays and 'Chocaholic Night' Thursdays.

Fausto's

VII. Dohány utca 5 (269 6806). M2 Astoria/tram 47, 49. **Open** noon-3pm, 7-11pm Mon-Sat. **Average** €€€€. **Credit** AmEx, DC, MC, V. **Map** p249 D4.

Undoubtedly one of the best restaurants in Budapest. Fausto's is small, slick, elegant and offers inventive Italian dishes that make good use of local ingredients. Friulian chef Fausto DiVora is a fine host and brilliant cook, creating excellent, unusual pastas, delicate seafood, succulent viands and wild desserts. Excellent wine list has Hungarian and Italian vintages. The waiters are well trained, and portions justify the prices, but be prepared to sell an organ to finance your meal – or enjoy one of the less expensive lunch specials. Booking is essential.

Kempi Brauhaus

Kempinski Hotel Corvinus Budapest, V. Erzsébet tér 7-8 (429 3777/www.kempinski.hu). M1, M2, M3 Deák tér/tram 47, 49. **Open** noon-3pm, 7-11pm Mon-Fri; 7-11pm Sat. **Average** €€. **Credit** AmEx, MC, V. **Map** p249 C4.

The talented chef at the Kempinski Hotel (*see p32*) is Alf Wagenzink, a Bavarian who has created this interesting and inexpensive pub restaurant inside the luxury hotel. You can choose from main-course salads, beer savouries, vegetarian dishes and, of course, traditional Bavarian food of beer and homemade sausages. Seasonal treats might provide the odd surprises like Christmas goose, filled pancakes towards Lent and fish on Fridays. The inexpensive daily changing lunch menu for Ft1,750 includes two courses and a drink. A laid-back atmosphere can hardly be generated by the daft wench-and-publican costumes of the staff, but there's at least a big screen for televised sports, an all too rare find downtown. Broadband laptop connection at every table.

Marquis de Salade

VI. Hájos utca 43 (302 4086). M3 Arany János utca. **Open** 11am-midnight daily. **Average** €€. **No credit cards. Map** p246 C3.

Owned by Sevà, a gracious Azeri woman, this venue offers a selection of salads, augmented by assorted dishes from Italy, China, North Africa, Bangladesh and the former Soviet Union. This is where the Marquis excels, the Azeri and Georgian lamb soups and stews the best items on the menu. There's an excellent vegetarian selection – this was one of the first restaurants in Budapest to set up a salad bar – but Sevà has plenty to please carnivores. Such is the popularity of the Marquis that it soon expanded into the adjacent spaces and eventually the vaulted brick cellar. One of the cosiest nooks here is the oriental carpet-lined room in the cellar, which seats up to a dozen diners. Book it in advance.

Mokka

V. Sas utca 4 (328 0081). M1, M2, M3 Deák tér/tram 47, 49. **Open** 11am-midnight Sun-Fri; 6pm-1am Sat. **Average** €€€. **Credit** AmEx, DC, MC, V. **Map** p246 C3.

Authentic Hungarian

restaurants

These restaurants guarantee the high quality of their service and the fair prices.

in Budapest

- Make unique gastronomic experience in Budapest's downtown
- Choose from the delicious traditional Hungarian cuisine
- Taste the historical wines
- Listen to the Hungarian melodic music
- Enjoy the famous Hungarian hospitality

Mátyás Pince Restaurant
V. Budapest, Március 15. tér 7.
Open: 11.00 am 01.00 am

Pilvax Restaurant
V. Budapest, Pilvax köz 1-3.
Open: midday to midnight

Százéves Restaurant
V. Budapest, Pesti Barnabás u
Open: midday to midnight

More information: www.taverna.hu

Modern French cuisine with North African accents is the draw at this stylishly designed resto and bar. Co-owner Fred Rol is a Moroccan-born Belgian whose senses are finely tuned to his customers' tastes, and he has no qualms about changing the interior or the menu to reflect them. There's a wide range of business lunch options – choose two or three courses for a set price. Seven-hour leg of lamb in peach broth pleases the palate and satisfies the tummy. North African specialities are supplemented by a few Hungarian dishes to keep mixed parties happy. Brunch on Sundays.

Momotaro Ramen

V. Széchenyi utca 16 (269 2037). M2 Kossuth tér/ tram 2. **Open** noon-11pm daily. **Average** €. **No credit cards. Map** p246 C3.

Notable for its noodle soups from fresh ramen made on the premises, dim sum and great dumplings, which are hard to find in Budapest. This twee, one-room no-nonsense pitstop has clunky furniture, quite awesome sesame chicken toasts and Chinese desserts like sweet, sticky 'Eight Treasure' rice and glutinous rice balls. If you're vegetarian, emphasise that you would like your vegetable ramen made without meat or chicken broth. You'll probably have to share a table during the lunchtime rush, and don't be bashful about staring at your neighbour's food – the clientele is generally made up of cosmopolitan regulars who know the menu, so if you see something tasty, ask what it is.

Okay Italia

XIII. Szent István körút 20 (349 2291/ www.okayitalia.hu). **Open** 11am-11.30pm Mon-Fri; noon-11.45pm Sat, Sun. **Average** €. **Credit** AmEx, DC, MC, V. **Map** p246 C2.

The workhorse of the crowd that dines out on most days of the week, Okay Italia offers inexpensive and satisfying Italian food served by waitresses in tiny skirts. The two sister locations are only about a block apart and have slightly different menus, with more northern food (including an excellent Cordon Bleu) at this branch, and the one by Nyugati train station serving up more southerly fare. Silly cheesy frescoes of Italian landscapes are common to both restaurants. The pizzas, though, are trustworthy, and there is ample roughage – in the form of a simple bowl of rucola and shaved grana, for example – and many meatless pastas. No reservations, very few disappointments, and a real lifesaver. **Branch**: XIII. Nyugati tér 6 (332 6960).

Ópium

VI. Király utca 34 (413 2949). M1, M2, M3 Deák tér/tram 47, 49. **Open** noon-midnight daily. **Average** €€. **Credit** AmEx, DC, MC, V. **Map** p246 D3.

Asian fusion cuisine served in an opulent downtown space with dramatic Chinese-style decor using a lot of blacks. The Western ownership is evident in the attention paid to service and presentation. Imaginative dishes are loosely inspired by various

Asian ingredients and cuisines, such as *char siu* duck ravioli and Cajun seared tuna. The mixed dumpling appetiser is tasty. But the more unusual creations can sometimes be bland, and the spices all seem to be toned down. The wasabi sauce is weak and the sesame should be more overpowering. Chic bar area, with exotic cocktails – and probably the fanciest toilets in town.

Papageno

V. Semmelweis utca 19 (485 0161). M2 Astoria/ bus 7. **Open** 11.30am-midnight Mon-Fri; 6.30pm-midnight Sat. **Average** €€. **Credit** AmEx, MC, V. **Map** p249 D4.

An under-appreciated, intimate but cheery place on a quiet side street near Astoria is a useful venue for escaping tourist traps in the area. Although pastas are a mainstay, the fresh, light, cooked-to-order food tends to be more French than Italian. The excellent salads are embellished with beef carpaccio, steak bits or forest mushrooms. Dishes prepared with *fogas*, Hungarian pike-perch, are pretty trustworthy choices. A classic range of French desserts include crème catalane, tarts, and every so often pineapple with sabayon. The good-value lunch specials include a veggie option. Sturdy wine list.

Sala Thai Rim Naam

V. Apáczai Csere János utca 4 (266 4363/267 4168). M1 Vörösmarty tér/tram 2. **Open** noon-11pm daily. **Average** €€€. **Credit** AmEx, DC, MC, V. **Map** p249 C4.

Perhaps the most gracious service in town is to be found in this modest Thai restaurant, where Fone the waitress remembers your last visit and favourite dishes, and the pleasant owner, Mr Yamnarm, fixes Thai coffee and tea behind the bar. The crispy fish in tamarind sauce is excellent, and mussel fans will be delighted with the huge, plump specimens cooked with Thai aromatics as an appetiser. It can get pricey to call up several individual dishes, but an order of Pad Thai and a Thai iced tea will successfully fill you up. The dark glass front is easy to pass by, as it doesn't look much like a restaurant from the outside. Memorable view of the Danube and Castle Hill from the tables inside.

Taverna Dionysos

V. Belgrád rakpart 6 (318 1222). Tram 2. **Open** noon-midnight daily. **Average** €€. **Credit** AmEx, MC, V. **Map** p249 C4.

Over-the-top whitewash-and-blue decor informs you that your dining experience will be Greek, and a bustling place it is too, offering acceptable versions of Aegean standards. The waiters seem harried at times, as they try to serve the many tables in this large, airy two-floor restaurant with a busy terrace. The huge mixed fish and seafood platters will feed a hungry couple well, as will the barbecued meat platters. Vegetarians are well cared for, and they can make a meal out of the many starters on offer. Book ahead on warm evenings for scenic dining overlooking the Danube and Castle Hill.

Eat, Drink, Shop

Shalimar

VII. Dob utca 50 (352 0305). Tram 4, 6.
Open noon-4pm, 6-11pm daily. **Average** €€.
Credit MC, V. **Map** p246 D3.

A humble, cellar-level warren situated in the Jewish quarter near Klauzál tér, decorated with a number of Indian statues and trinkets. The cooks are Indian and the waiting staff Hungarian – meaning that the service tends to be next-to-useless and the food excellent, including an excellent selection of tandoori dishes, eight types of bread and many vegetarian options. Butter chicken and *palak paneer* are the real highlights at the Shalimar. Spice levels are usually set at low-to-medium, to suit the uninitiated, so you need to speak up if you want your food to bite back – and on busy nights, be prepared to wait up to an hour for it to arrive.

Taverna Pireus Rembetiko

V. Fővám tér 2-3 (266 0292). Tram 2, 47, 49.
Open noon-midnight daily. **Average** €€. **Credit** AmEx, DC, MC, V. **Map** p249 C5.

This Greek taverna is named after the port of Athens where the gritty, tortured music of its title was born. It's often played live here on Friday and Saturday evenings. This small place across the square from the main market hall sports the seemingly requisite royal blue paint trim and the half-heartedly executed trappings of the Greek restaurant interior. Expect reasonable batter-dipped calamari and mixed grills here, although the menu is somewhat brief. You can order retsina from the barrel or a whole slew of imported Greek wines. Probably catches a lot of overflow from the nearby Taverna Dionysos (*see above*) and the food is somewhere on a par with it.

Tom-George Restaurant & Café

V. Október 6 utca 8 (266 3525). M1, M2, M3 Deák tér/tram 47, 49. **Open** noon-midnight daily. **Average** €€€. **Credit** AmEx, DC, MC, V. **Map** p246 C3.

The somewhat strained attempt at trendy decor here is painfully obvious, especially in dusty old downtown Budapest, and some of the fusion dishes also seem to have too much thought put into them. The menu covers a lot of culinary and economic ground, with inexpensive lunch specials and gourmet sandwiches for the office crowd. The bulk of the food is Asian, mostly Thai and Indonesian, some of it served in dramatically overlarge bowls, with the odd Hungarian/international fusion and Aussie steak thrown in. Chef Hokama Yusei mans the sushi bar. A smoking area is located to the left of the entrance, and there's outdoor seating available. The service can be rather indifferent.

Zebra One Noodle Bar

V. Október 6 utca 19 (373 0092/www.zebraone.hu). M1, M2, M3 Deák tér/tram 47, 49. **Open** 11.30am-midnight Mon-Sat. **Average** €€. **No credit cards**. **Map** p246 C3.

This has got a snazzy, minimalist interior, a classy café/bar smoking area and what the management thinks is a snazzy English name. But, with the honourable exception of spring rolls, dumplings and other such titbits, the food is generally no great shakes. On the plus side, it's centrally located and has many vegetarian options. The menu favours starchy staples of many Asian nations – rice and noodle dishes from Thailand, China, Indonesia and Japan. The French desserts seem incongruous, but they may be a Vietnamese colonial holdover.

Ópium – great décor, shame about the wasabi sauce. *See p101.*

Nagykörút & Outer Pest

Hungarian

1894 Food & Wine Cellar
XIV. Állatkerti út 2 (468 4044/www.gundel.hu/ 1894_borvendeglo). M1 Hősök tere. **Open** 6-11pm Tue-Sat. **Average** €€. **Credit** AmEx, DC, MC, V. **Map** p247 E1

The newest, vinous arm of Gundel (*see below*), is a casual, brick-lined wine cellar where you can choose from more than 100 Hungarian wines by the glass or bottle. A sommelier is on hand to guide you through the country's wine regions. Food is perhaps secondary here, but this being Gundel's, it is still excellent. Traditional Hungarian snacks such as goose cracklings, fillet of smoked trout or *lángos* – fast dough which is usually deep-fried, but here is baked, the old-fashioned way, and topped with bits of bacon and Hungarian smoked sausage. Good main courses include 'Tycoon's goulash', a good beef stew, and duck with sour cherry sauce. There are also special wine tasting menus.

Bagolyvár
XIV. Állatkerti út 2 (468 3110/www.bagolyvar.com). M1 Hősök tere. **Open** noon-11pm daily. **Average** €€. **Credit** AmEx, DC, MC, V. **Map** p247 E1.

Gundel's attention to quality is applied to rather less expensive, homier meals in a mock Transylvanian castle attached to the main restaurant and owned by the same people. All the staff are women, because owner George Lang reckons that they're the best home cooks. The menu varies daily and features some very good soups and other basic offerings, such as the roulade of fresh breads, served with various spreads, that is part of the starter. There's also a secluded terrace, shaded in summer.

Gundel
XIV. Állatkerti út 2 (468 4040/www.gundel.hu). M1 Hősök tere. **Open** 6.30pm-midnight Mon-Sat; brunch only (11am-2pm) Sun. **Average** €€€€. **Credit** AmEx, DC, MC, V. **Map** p247 E1.

Still the city's most famous and elegant restaurant. Originally opened in 1894 as the Wampetics, it was taken over in 1910 by top chef Károly Gundel. He proceeded to Frenchify Hungarian cuisine, by

Top ten Local dishes

Bécsi szelet
Wiener schnitzel, except here it's usually made with pork instead of veal (for the latter, ask for *borjú bécsi*). Hammered flat until it's the size of a plate, it can stay with you for days.

Csirke paprikás
Probably the second most popular dish outside of Hungary's borders, it's hard to find a bad rendition of 'Chicken Paprika', a chicken drumstick and thigh in thickened paprika sauce with *galuska* (little dumplings) and sour cream.

Gulyás
The best-known Hungarian export after the Gábor sisters, goulash is a semi-spicy soup of diced beef, onions, garlic and paprika. Can be made thicker and spicier in a cauldron – *bográcsgulyás*. Do not confuse with *pörkölt*, a meat stew.

Halászlé
'Fisherman's soup' stars that bony pig of the water, the carp, which is mercifully drowned in paprika.

Hortobágyi palacsinta
A crepe stuffed with minced pork paprika stew, the sauce of which is mixed with sour cream. A superb appetiser.

Jókai bableves
A lusty, rich bean soup with chunks of smoked ham hock, sliced sausages and vegetables. Usually flavoured with a substantial dollop of sour cream.

Lángos
Hungary's own fast food, sold in market halls, train stations and lidos. The term 'fried dough' barely does justice to this piping hot delicacy, a puffy, chewy disc brushed with garlic (*fokhagymás*) or other toppings. Will keep you full for hours at a rock-bottom price.

Libamáj
Goose liver, served cold as an appetiser with its own fat (*hideg libamáj*), or 'Hungarian style' with peppers, tomatoes and onions stewed in paprika sauce. Cholesterol-laden ambrosia.

Somlói galuska
Rum-soaked sponge bathed in chocolate sauce, walnuts, raisins and crème anglaise, hidden under a glacier of whipped cream. Dissolves deliciously in the mouth.

Sült libacomb (or libasült)
Fried goose leg with braised sweet red cabbage and oniony broken potatoes. Hard to resist the crispy skin once bitten.

Eat, Drink, Shop

... for meeting the locals

Share your table with strangers for a simple, home-cooked lunch at **Kádár Étkezde** *(see p95)* or a carbohydrate binge at **Szent Jupát** *(see p93)*.

... for personal service

Even if you forget, the waitress at **Sala Thai Rim Naam** *(see p101)* will remember what you ordered last time.

... for eye-opening innards

Spicy tripe and duck heart at **China Lanzhou Restaurant** *(see p106)* will turn you into a variety meat acolyte.

... for splashing out

Spoil yourself at **Fausto's** *(see p99)*, where you'll get what you pay for and you may not even be able to finish it all.

... for cheesy music

Old standards played with misremembered lyrics and cocktail-lounge melodrama by the keyboardist at **Tabáni Kakas** *(see p93)*.

... for outdoor dining

Károlyi Étterem Kávéház *(see p95)* and **Fészek** *(see p95)* both have pleasant,

secluded gardens in the middle of town. The terrace of the **Taverna Dionysos** *(see p101)* overlooks the Danube with Gellért Hill as the backdrop.

... for a taste of the future

The creative cuisine at **Képíró** *(see p95)* may be setting the course for Magyar cuisine in the new millennium.

... for getting drunk

The competition is pretty stiff in this category, but the nod may go to **A Kis Sün** *(see p105)* where the vodka-soaked revellers can turn the aisle into a dancefloor.

... for an excuse to dress up

Jacket and tie are definitely required for **Gundel** *(see p103)*, Budapest's most prestigious restaurant.

... for restrooms

The toilets at the **Ópium** *(see p101)* simply ooze opulence.

...for affordable Magyar cuisine

Every street corner has a place serving domestic cuisine, but the **Millennium** *(see p104)* on leafy Andrássy does it with aplomb and little grease.

inventing many now standard dishes, such as the ubiquitous Gundel pancakes. A tourist trap under Communism, in 1991 it was acquired by restaurant impresario George Lang (of the Café des Artistes in New York) and Ronald Lauder (son of Estée), and given an expensive makeover with the aim of recreating the glory days. It's a huge place, set in an art nouveau mansion by the zoo, with a ballroom, garden and terrace, and several private dining rooms, as well as the large main room hung with paintings by Hungarian masters. Tables are laid with Zsolnay porcelain and sterling silver. The Gypsy band is slick. The menu is, not surprisingly, a little old-fashioned, and starters and desserts almost outshine the main courses. These feature fine versions of Hungarian standards, as well as Magyar versions of international dishes, such as the Tournedos Franz Liszt, made with local goose liver. Chef Kálmán Kalla renders lighter versions of Hungarian favourites, like chicken *paprikás*, to please modern palates. Sunday brunch deals are more affordable. A long and authoritative list of Hungarian wines is rounded off with excellent sweet Tokaj from the restaurant's own vineyard. Service is smooth and formal, and men must wear a jacket and tie. Dress up for it, as it's not every day that you eat at Gundel.

Millennium

VI. Andrássy út 76 (354 0575). M1 Vörösmarty utca. **Open** 11pm-1am daily. **Average** €. **Credit** MC, DC, V. **Map** p246 D2.
A decade ago, when you wanted to eat Magyar, you had two choices: the greasy corner diner served cheap, hearty (read: lardy) meals on a stained checked tablecloth, and the top-end restaurant put on airs (mostly stale) and served pretty much the same food on a white tablecloth that may or may not have been clean. A decade later, the Millennium straddles the two. It's a good, affordable, mostly Hungarian restaurant. The premises are clean (including the tablecloths) and modestly decorated, the interior copying the cutely tiled stations of the renovated Millennium metro that runs nearby. A friendly service adds to the pleasure of eating well-prepared dishes: the peasant potato soup is a cut above the average version and stained red with paprika, full of authentic Hungarian sausage and vegetables. Standards like chicken *paprikás* and batter-fried veal are handled with care. Fish dishes, such as salmon steak or smoked trout, are consistently pleasing, as a starter or a main. There's also several vegetarian options. Decent wine selection to boot, and Staropramen on tap.

If you can't decide what to have at **Chez Daniel**, just ask the chef. *See p106.*

Premier

VI. Andrássy út 101 (342 1768/www.premier-restaurant.hu). M1 Bajza utca. **Open** *Oct-Apr* 10am-11pm Mon-Sat. *May-Sept* 10am-11pm daily. **Average** €€. **Credit** AmEx, DC, MC, V. **Map** p247 E2.

The pleasant terrace along tree-lined Andrássy út is the big draw here, but there are also nice surprises on the menu, with Hungarian dishes augmented by enough international ones to please most palates and even vegetarians. The mozzarella in the caprese salad is sumptuously smoked, the 'sportsman's salad' is quite substantial, and there are other fine meatless offerings. Carnivores can enjoy smoked clam and prawn tails marinated in olive oil with aubergine cream, oxtail essence with sherry and vegetable-semolina gnocchi or even Balaton catfish with mushroom-paprika sauce.

Restaurant Robinson

XIV. Városligeti tó 5 (422 0222/422 0224). M1 Széchenyi fürdő. **Average** €€€. **Open** noon-4pm, 6pm-midnight daily. **Credit** AmEx, DC, MC, V. **Map** p247 E1.

A light-filled venue that gets its name from being situated on an 'island' (only about a yard from the shore) in the City Park duckpond, Restaurant Robinson is a living reproach to the 'location, location, location' theory of restaurant management. In spite of its wonderful terrace and winter garden, and occasionally inspired kitchen, this restaurant has lost the reputation it once had of being one of the city's best. The service is bumbling, the wines are expensive, as reflected in the bill. The food is still very good, with a menu that is catch-all

Mediterranean/international, dotted with Hungarian, which roughly translates as pastas, grilled fish, and duck and goose liver dishes.

International

A Kis Sün

VI. Podmaniczky utca 29 (269 4072). M3 Nyugati pu./tram 4, 6. **Open** 11am-11pm daily. **Average** €. **No credit cards**. **Map** p246 D2.

The unobtrusive 'Little Hedgehog' resembles the scores of other Hungarian pub-style eateries, but is actually a gem of home-style Russian cooking. Skip past the Hungarian standards in the immense menu and spoil yourself with caviar, herring salad, grilled sturgeon, various Russian dumplings, classic Russian soups, blinis and plenty of stick-to-your-ribs vegetarian food. Made-to-order dishes can take a while but are worth the wait. For the full experience, forget the wine and get an iced bottle of Stolichnaya. The customers are mostly Russian, and they think dancing in a restaurant normal, although the rather cheesy standards played by the DJ may grate.

Brasserie Royal

Corinthia Grand Hotel Royal, VII. Erzsébet körút 43-49 (479 4850). Tram 4, 6. **Open** 7am-11pm daily. **Credit** DC, MC, V. **Average** €€€. **Map** p246 D3.

This lavish, cavernous but comfortable and bright space is the flagship French restaurant in the new Corinthia Grand Hotel Royal (*see p36* **The empire strikes back**). It has recently opened, and the menu is still being tweaked, but current offerings include lobster and artichoke salad with truffle vinaigrette,

Eat, Drink, Shop

Go Goan at **Taj Mahal**.

Provençal yellow and blue is lovely. Service is knowledgeable but shambolic. Table reservations are recommended in the evenings.

China Lanzhou Restaurant

VIII. Luther utca 1B (314 1080). M2 Blaha Lujza tér/tram 4, 6/bus 7. **Open** noon-11pm daily. **Average** €. **No credit cards. Map** p250 E4.
Never mind that it's hard to find on a long street beside a shabby neighbourhood and is decorated cheaply with mirrors and paper cutouts, this venue probably has the best Chinese food in town – and definitely the best in this price range. The menu has surprisingly delicious offbeat meat dishes like spicy tripe, duck heart and tongue 'salad'. But there's lots for vegetarians too, including the potato salad of quick-blanched potato shreds simply seasoned with a few drops of sesame oil. The sinfully tasty sweet-and-sour aubergines stuffed with Chinese mince are also excellent. The chef even turns the dreaded carp into a fine dish, steaming it whole with chilli sauce.

Taj Mahal

VI. Szondi utca 40 (301 0447/www.tajmahal.hu). M3 Nyugati pu./tram 4, 6. **Open** noon-11pm Tue-Sun. **Average** €. **No credit cards. Map** p246 D2.
Tucked away on a side street near Nyugati station is the only Indian restaurant in Budapest to offer south Indian breads and fermented rice batter pancakes, including enormous uttappams wrapped around a vegetarian filling and served with sambar vegetable sauce. The menu spans all the Indian regions and cooking styles, and the range of spicy Goan dishes is another advantage over other Indian restaurants. Delicious desserts include cardamom-flavoured Indian 'ice cream' and *burfi* ('milk fudge'). The interior is airy and comfortable and they deliver, unusual for good restaurants in Budapest.

Óbuda

Hungarian

Kisbuda Gyöngye

III. Kenyeres utca 34 (368 6402). Tram 17. **Open** noon-midnight Mon-Sat. **Average** €€€. **Credit** AmEx, DC, MC, V.
Moved from its original location further north into Óbuda about ten years ago, the 'Pearl of Kisbuda' is part of the standard restaurant circuit for visitors to town. Walls are panelled with parts of old wardrobes and the seating is an assortment of old and not always terribly comfortable kitchen chairs. A run-of-the-mill Hungarian menu features interesting daily specials. The venison fillet comes with wild mushrooms and brandy sauce, and demonstrates the best of the perhaps overrated kitchen. The waiters, though, are wonderful.

Kéhli Vendéglő

III. Mókus utca 22 (250 4241/www.regisipos.hu). Bus 86/HÉV to Timár utca. **Open** noon-midnight daily. **Average** €€. **Credit** AmEx, DC, MC, V.

lobster bisque flavoured with cognac, and cheesecake with fudge sauce for dessert. Chef Philippe Derien has a passion for fish dishes, and his nimble fingers also prepare popular Hungarian standards to please parties divided over which national dish to consume. The kitchen is discreetly open plan and there is seating in the impressive atrium adjacent. The Sunday brunch, accompanied by live jazz, is outstanding, especially the cold catering area with fish preparations and terrines.

Chez Daniel

VI. Szív utca 32 (302 4039). M1 Kodály körönd. **Open** noon-3pm, 7-11pm daily. **Average** €€€. **Credit** AmEx, DC, MC, V. **Map** p246 D2.
Careful and curmudgeonly chef Daniel Labrosse presides over this popular French restaurant, with cooked-to-order Gallic dishes by the dozen, enhanced and embellished by the luxurious foodstuffs Daniel himself scouts out from the markets. He's got his own truffle supplier and makes the best goose liver terrine in town. Don't bother with the menu; it's the illegible specials board you're after – or even better, ask Daniel. Many change seasonally, but the duck parmentier – buttery, silky-smooth mashed potatoes studded with duck confit – is a perennial pleaser, as is the veal chop in mustard sauce and monkfish with butter and capers. The little courtyard terrace in

The best Vegging out

In Hungary, pork rules. The following places can provide excellent, meat-free fare:

Al-Amir
Syrian restaurant carries all Middle Eastern classic dips and salads, with great cheese and spinach-stuffed flatbreads (*see p97*).

Bombay Palace
Best Indian in town (*see p97*) offers a great selection of assorted naan breads to go with your veg options. If that's too expensive, the **Shalimar** (*see p102*) has extensive vegetarian options – if you're prepared to wait for them to arrive from the kitchen.

Fausto's
Of the higher-end international restaurants, Fausto's (*see p99*) is the best, with imaginative Italian options. **Mokka** (*see p99*) combines French with North African specialities.

Marquis de Salade
The first salad bar takes a culinary trip to Central Asia to bring back a massive menu of vegetarian options (*see p99*).

Momotaro Ramen
Vegetable ramen noodle soup (make sure to ask about the broth) and vegetable dumplings are among the meatless offerings (*see p101*).

Okay Italia
Salads, pastas and pizzas from a chef who knows that simple really can be beautiful (*see p101*).

Taverna Dionysos
Dine veggie here (*see p101*) with a view of the Danube – a selection of starters should satisfy the hungriest vegetarian. If full, try the Taverna Pireus Rembetiko (*see p102*) round the corner for more aubergine dips and cooked vegetables.

Every Budapester knows about the legendary Kéhli, and many claim that it to be the best Hungarian restaurant of all. The century-old walls are dripping with nostalgia: this was the favoured feeding place of fin-de-siècle novelist and gastronome Gyula Krúdy, his table commemorated with a plaque, although today the restaurant is set in grey Socialist-realist surroundings. The main area with its Gypsy band is difficult to get into without booking, but there are several other rooms in which to perch – although avoid the awful cellar with its hideous red plastic candles and armchair-style seating. One of the specialities is a rich bone marrow soup: first drink the soup, then scrape out the marrow and spread it on toast with garlic. The portions are absolutely mountainous. Excellent value too.

Régi Sipos Halászkert
III. Lajos utca 46 (250 8082). Tram 17/bus 86/HÉV to Szépvölgyi út. **Open** noon-midnight daily. **Average** €€. **Credit** AmEx, DC, MC, V.
Considered by many to be the best of the Hungarian fish restaurants, it was forced to move here from its original location nearby. Since then regulars have predictably whinged that it's not as good as the old one. But it still makes the best *halászlé* (fisherman's soup), which contains boned fillets – as well as the roe and offal, the real benchmarks of a quality preparation. There's more to the menu than fish, however. It's worth sampling one of the many kinds of Hungarian stews, noodle dishes and desserts on offer, especially the *túró gombóc* (warm curd cheese dumplings with sour cream). Garden seating also available.

International

Mennyei Ízek
III. Pacsirtamező utca 13 (388 6430/06 30 992 1945). Bus 86. **Open** noon-9pm daily. **Average** €. **No credit cards.**
This simple, family-run place is the best Korean restaurant in Budapest, with a complete Chinese menu as well. Meats grilled at your table, including the delicious *bulgogi*. This beef fillet is ingeniously marinated with mashed kiwi fruit, which tenderises the meat and causes it to caramelise as it is grilled in front of you. Fantastic Korean broiled fish and a full complement of homestyle *kimchi* – the spicy, garlicky fermented cabbage pickle that is Korea's national dish. There is also a range of *kimchi*-style dishes made from fresh vegetables. And everything is reasonably priced. Delivery also available.

Okuyama Sushi
III. Kolosy tér 5-6 (250 8256). Bus 86. **Open** 1-10pm daily. **Average** €€. **No credit cards.**
Chef Okuyama is a real professional, and his Japanese regulars know it. They're not there for the sparse decor, but rather for the Osaka-style sushi – like the orange-mottled shrimp, glazed with a greenish translucent fish aspic pressed into a rectangular form and cut into squares. Sushi and sashimi are also available, and there are good, inexpensive cooked mackerel and herring dishes. Located in the cellar of a shopping complex, it's hard to find, as there's only a sign in Japanese above the building entrance. Go straight to the back and down the stairs to the left.

Eat, Drink, Shop

Cafés & Bars

Dingy, designer or elegant, Budapest has a drinking hole to meet every need.

Set between the beery expanses of Germanic
Europe and the spirit-swilling realm of the
Slavs, with a coffeehouse culture instigated
a century before Vienna's, wine-guzzling
Hungary has much to offer the visiting bar-
goer. Indeed, Budapest can boast a watering
hole of some kind on nearly every street corner.

Downtown this is a blessing, especially now
that modern design has come to many Budapest
bars, and owners are far more choosy about the
kind of music that gets played in them. Enjoy a
summer evening amid the terrace café-bars of
trendy Liszt Ferenc tér or Ráday utca (*see p80*
Pedestrianised Budapest) and you could
be in any cosmopolitan hub of Central or
Mediterranean Europe. The range and quality
of food and drink on offer these days would
not be put to shame by similar spots in, say,
Munich or Marseilles.

Andrássy út and Districts VI and VII also
boast fine establishments of either grand
tradition or trendy taste. Sadly, the stretches
that would benefit most from being given over
to the rapid gentrification of bar culture – the
Danube embankment in Pest and Nagykörút –
are criminally underused. Gone are the days
when the Duna Korzó shone with the bright
awnings of elegant riverside cafés; the shop-
lined main ring road will at least welcome the
reopening of the prestigious New York Café by
2004 (*see p111* **So good they built it twice**).

Elsewhere in town, drinking is plentiful if
hardly discerning. The average corner bar will
have little else to recommend it other than its
convenience; it will be open either before dawn
or past midnight, will be generally welcoming
to foreigners – and be dangerously cheap. You
can still get flat-face drunk for a fiver.

Café society returns
to Liszt Ferenc tér.

Eat, Drink, Shop

WHERE TO DRINK

Venues break down into five main categories:
the classic Viennese-style café; the corner
borozó and *söröző*; the dowdy *presszó*; and the
continental-style café-bar with summer terrace.
The rapid influx of the latter has spelled the
death of many a standard *borozó*, a bar selling
bor, or wine, and *söröző*, a bar selling mainly
sör (prounounced *'shur'*), or beer.

The slower pace of life in Budapest lends
itself perfectly to the *kávézó*, or coffeehouse.
Coffee arrived in Hungary with the Ottomans,
and coffeehouses were a feature in Budapest
long before they appeared in Paris or Vienna.
Budapest coffeehouses soon developed along
Viennese lines, reaching their heyday with the
Dual Monarchy. In 1900 the city numbered 600
of them. They both embodied a Habsburg ideal
– that people of all classes, races and nations
could mingle under one roof – and were a
breeding ground for burgeoning Magyar
culture. A list of regulars at the Café Japan,
now the Írok Boltja bookstore (*see p126*), reads
like a who's who of Hungarian painting. Local
writers and filmmakers mingled with
Hollywood moguls at the New York Café. Even
the 1848 revolution against Habsburg rule

started in a coffeehouse, the **Pilvax**, now a
hotel (*see p35*) and restaurant *(see p97)*.

Combining the neighbourliness of a local
pub, the facilities of a gentleman's club and
the intellectual activity of a free university,
coffeehouses were places to feel at ease.
Fascism, war and Communism destroyed not
just the actual coffeehouses, but also the social
classes and independent artistic scene that had
brought them to life. Their postmodern
reinvention, the designer café found in up-and-
coming areas of town, offers decent service,
good light meals and an imaginative selection
of drinks. Their regulars tend to be either
foreigners or moneyed young Budapesters.

Straddling the blurred line between café and
bar is the *presszó*, a paean to 1960s tackiness
serving coffee and daytime meals, although
their era, like the waitresses once employed to
put customers' money in the jukebox, has gone.

WHAT TO DRINK

Wine is the opium of the masses (*see p98*
Unknown pleasures). The stuff ladled out of
tureens in a dark wine cellar, or *borozó*, will
certainly be Magyar but may not be wine alone
– although it should cost you less than a daily

newspaper in the West. If not for the quality of wine, the *borozó* is ideal for a pre-dawn anthropological experience. Its doors open at birdsong to accommodate a steady stream of shift workers and professional drinkers. Given the early opening, most will be shut (and the clientele slaughtered) by 8pm, but it will allow you to observe the strange combinations in which wine is served here. A *házmester*, *hosszú lépes* and *nagy lépes*, the housemaster, long step and big step, are glasses of differing amounts of wine and soda. The occasional female customer may order a VBK, or *vörös boros kóla*, red wine and coke. A normal spritzer is a *fröccs*. A small selection of spirits will include Unicum (*see p113* **Kill or cure**) and fruit brandy, *pálinka*. The plum (*szilvapálinka*) and pear (*körtepálinka*) varieties are the most common. Go easy if you wish to do anything the next day, and if someone fishes the *házi* (home-made *pálinka*) from under the bar all bets are off.

Bar snacks amount to little more than a *pogácsa* (a cheesy/salty scone) or *zsíroskenyér* (goose fat on bread topped with red onions and a sprinkle of paprika). There may even be a *meleg szendvics* – the Hungarian toastie.

The *söröző* offers much the same, plus at least one domestic brew on tap (usually Dreher or the superior Borsodi) and one from Germany, Austria or former Czechoslovakia. Although inferior to their beer halls – entire generations of Magyars before this one were raised on wine – Hungarian venues now at least boast a little variety. There is even the odd Belgian bar. Beer is sold by the half-litre, *korsó*, or smaller glass, *pohár*. An average bar will charge about Ft350-Ft500 for the former. Ask for a coffee, *kávé*, and you'll get a small glass of strong black liquid, without milk. Bars attracting expatriates, either overpriced pretend pubs or bohemian hives, tend to be dearer. *Egészsegedre!* Cheers!

For cafés and bars that come to life after midnight, *see pp175-181*.

Buda

Angelika
I. Batthyány tér 7 (212 3784). M2 Batthyány tér. **Open** 10am-midnight daily. **No credit cards.** **Map** p245 B3.
Located in the former crypt of St Anne's Church on the south side of Batthyány tér, this refined café attracts Buda ladies who gossip. Of a late September afternoon, when the sun's streaming through the stained-glass windows, it's an atmospheric spot for coffee and cakes. The terrace affords a fine view of Parliament across the river.

Avar Presszó & Sörkert
XII. Avar utca 31 (209 1758). Bus 112. **Open** 2pm-midnight daily. **No credit cards.**

Time stands still at the **Bambi Presszó**. *See p111.*

So good they built it twice

The complete renovation of Budapest's most famous café, the New York, will bring history full circle more than a century after this historic venue first opened.

The stylish, contemporary look planned by renowned international interior designer Adam Tihany will be blended with its historic, original features, producing a creation relevant to both 1894 when it opened and 2004 when it reopens. Coupled with the **Corinthia Grand Hotel Royal** (*see p36* **The empire strikes back**), the New York will provide prestige to this otherwise prosaic stretch of the city's main ring road.

For the first half of the last century, this was *the* place to be. The same architect responsible for the reconstruction of the Royal Palace, Alajos Hauszmann, also created the fabulous bronze-and-marble interior of the New York. Decorated with frescoes by the leading painters of the day, the New York was the epitome of coffeehouse culture, where leading literary figures of the day would mix and share their ideas. Between the wars, visiting Hollywood moguls were as vital to the atmosphere as the literary set, mingling with the stars of stage and silent film to offer lucrative contracts in America (*see p156* **Moguls, ogres and misfits**).

The post-war demise of the coffeehouse was never better illustrated than here. As if to add injury to insult, the building was rammed by a Soviet tank during the 1956 Uprising. Until recently, the shaken façade was propped up by heavy wooden scaffolding, and the café below – having also served time as a sports shop – became a shoddy tourist trap.

Its renovation is in the trusty hands of a Hungarian. Tihany, born in Transylvania of Magyar descent, has run his own design company since 1978. As past triumphs feature New York's Le Cirque restaurant and the Mandarin Oriental bar in Knightsbridge, it seems safe to assume that the new interior planned by Tihany for the New York wouldn't look out of place in either city.

And Tihany's blueprint is most certainly ambitious: an 80-seat bar will be shadowed by a lighting sculpture entirely manufactured from Martini glasses; the cocktail tables in a raised area above will glow in the dark, and the surrounding fabric curtains will be dramatically up-lit.

As for the fixtures and fittings, Tihany aims to provide bold juxtapositions between the original neo-baroque interior of tall arches and grand staircases and the modern, custom-designed furniture and lighting. 'The interior and the frescoes will be restored to their original glory,' said Tihany. 'The old New York will be instantly recognisable. It will be a complete restoration with contemporary furniture.'

Further restoration work is also being carried out on the New York Palota, the building surrounding the coffeehouse. These old insurance offices are set to be converted into a 235-room five-star hotel by the Italian Boscolo group.

Dingy though friendly little bar out in the XII, the inside of the Avar is standard issue *presszó* – three formica booths, an old telly, two fruit machines and a toilet that takes a fair degree of bravery. What does give the Avar ('carpet of leaves') a nice edge is its summer beer garden nestling under four ancient chestnut trees – and a Ft280 pint of cold Dreher. Once a popular haunt of boho Buda, the Avar has clearly suffered over the years and when the garden furniture was last replaced is anyone's guess. Furthermore, given its position on the corner of the now racetrack-like Hegyalja út, the main route out of town towards the Balaton and Vienna, the once-peaceful garden now feels like the grandstand at the Hungaroring. A sign over the door proclaims 'until we meet again', once a Hungarian hostelry staple but unfortunately now seldom seen and indicative of the way that modern Budapest has passed the place by.

Bambi Presszó

II. Frankel Leó út 2-4 (212 3171). Tram 4, 6/ bus 60, 86. **Open** 8am-9pm Mon-Fri; 9am-8pm Sat, Sun. **No credit cards. Map** p245 B2.

Something of a Budapest tradition, the Bambi is the perfect example of the Communist-era *presszó*, and a place where time has stood still. Ancient plastic plants and the background noise of dominoes being slapped on to mosaic-topped tables by unsmiling locals complement designer touches from 1965. The service can be hit and miss, more often miss, but the beer's cold and the *meleg szendvics* and omelettes rock. There's even a view of the Danube (just) from the summer terrace – and the prices are in a similar time warp to the decor and clientele.

Belgian Brasserie

I. Bem rakpart 12 (201 5082). M2 Batthyány tér/ tram 19/bus 86. **Open** noon-midnight daily. **Credit** MC, V. **Map** p245 B3.

Eat, Drink, Shop

Although a reasonable restaurant in its own right, the *raison d'être* for this fine if pricey establishment is its extensive beer menu. The best Belgium has to offer – Kriek, Chimay, Hoegaarden – can be enjoyed on the riverside terrace, a sad rarity in Buda. The two-room interior, too, is done out in reasonable taste, old publicity posters from way back when.

Café Gusto

II. Frankel Leó utca 12 (316 3970). Tram 4, 6. **Open** 10am-10pm Mon-Sat. **No credit cards. Map** p245 B2.
Classy joint a short walk from Margaret Bridge, with a terrace overlooking a quiet, tree-lined side street. Inside, it's the kind of place you wouldn't feel too embarrassed to take an Italian friend to, with coffee to match. Excellent selection on the menu, including fish and other seafood, fresh orange juice, decent salads and a good wine list.

Café Miró

I. Úri utca 30 (201 5573). Várbusz from M2 Moszkva tér/bus 16. **Open** 9am-midnight daily. **No credit cards. Map** p245 A3.
Although, like everywhere in the Castle District, mostly frequented by tourists, the Miró has resisted the temptation towards the phonily historical. Decor and furniture have been designed in the shapes and colours of the artist himself. The green metal chairs look crazy but are surprisingly comfortable; extra-ordinary sofas and hat stands impel you to pause and admire. Service ranges from cute to competent, but there's a fine selection of cakes and snacks, plus a small summer terrace.

Café Ponyvaregény

XI. Bercsényi utca 5 (209 5255). Tram 18, 19, 47, 49/night bus 3É. **Open** 10am-2am Mon-Sat. **No credit cards.**
As its name ('Pulp Fiction') suggests, this cellar café has a theme, although from the outside, with its tiny frosted window panes, it resembles more the Old Curiosity Shop than Tarantino's diner. It's popular with the nearby technical college students, who sit among the stuccoed, book-lined walls and flip through the daily papers or indulge in a quiet game of chess. Live music on Wednesdays.

Café Zacc

XI. Bocskai utca 12 (209 1593). Tram 18, 47/bus 7/night bus 3É. **Open** noon-2am daily. **No credit cards. Map** p248 B6.
Modest but fun-loving bar a short hop from Móricz Zsigmond körtér. The decor wavers between Pop Art and a local youth club, with customers to match. Decent sounds, much football talk and a grimly imaginative range of cheap and lethal cocktails served in heavy, school-canteen glasses. Can get pretty smoky, but there's tables outside in summer.

Calgary

II. Frankel Leó utca 24 (316 9087). Tram 4, 6, 17/night bus 6É. **Open** noon-4am daily. **No credit cards. Map** p245 B2.

Beguiling little bar on the Buda side of Margaret Bridge, the Calgary is halfway between a pub and an antiques shop. Landlady Vicki is an eccentric old bat and her mood varies from accommodating to rude. A former concert pianist bangs out 1940s melodies on a criminally out-of-tune piano, suffered by a mix of artists and fruitcakes. Draught Radeberger and a good array of spirits complement the antique dolls and bric-a-brac.

Erzsébet híd Eszpresszó

I. Döbrentei tér 2 (212 2127). Bus 5, 7/tram 18. **Open** 9am-11pm daily. **No credit cards. Map** p248 B4.
Refurbished but still cramped inside, the attraction here is the terrace by the tramlines, looking out over the Danube and the busy flyover above. The usual clientele is mixed, the decor in the narrow bar area kitsch, the cake selection minimal and the service sluggish, but the Buda bank of the river is so underused as a drinking venue that even the most modest *presszó* will do on a baking hot afternoon.

Kőbüfé Söröző

XII. Rege utca 21 (275 5195). Cog-wheel railway terminus. **Open** 7am-10pm daily. **No credit cards.**
When downtown gets too much, take the cog-wheel railway to its terminus at Széchenyi-hegy, walk 100 metres up to the hill's summit and discover the delights of the Kőbüfé ('Stone buffet'). Little has changed here since the 1950s, which goes for the staff, furniture, prices, and surrounding forest and fresh air. Healthy-minded families are joined by mountain bikers in full Day-Glo kit by day, and hill-dwelling drinkers by night. Worth the hike for a drought-breaking beer in summer, or a warming mulled wine (*forralt bor*) in winter.

Libella

XI. Budafoki út 7 (209 4761). Tram 18, 47, 49/night bus 6É. **Open** 8am-2am daily. **No credit cards. Map** p249 C6.
Friendly and unpretentious café-bar just around the corner from Gellért tér. Perfect for a quiet afternoon beer, a newspaper and arguably the best *meleg szendvics* toastie in town, the Libella gets rowdier as the night progresses with a strange mix of check-shirted engineering students from the nearby college lashing back the red wine and colas and a table of old denizens playing a card game that appears to have been going on for at least ten years. A TV goes up for any football worth watching on the terrestrial channels, there's good, cold HB and Dreher Bock (Hungary's answer to Boddington's Mild) on tap, occasionally deadly *házi pálinka* and the pièce de résistance, fantastic pickled eggs.

Móri Borozó

I. Hattyú utca 16 (214 9216). M2 Moszkva tér. **Open** 2-11pm Mon-Fri; 2-9pm Sat, Sun. **No credit cards. Map** p245 A2.
Comfortable wine bar singled out by its younger clientele. In the 1970s Moszkva tér was a meeting place for young rockers with nowhere else to go. The

Kill or cure

It takes something singular to earn the title of National Drink in a nation of drinkers like Hungary. And, most certainly, Unicum is as singular as it gets.

Unicum baffles the first-time imbiber. In a bottle shaped like an anarchist's bomb, this dark brown herb liqueur smells like a hospital corridor and packs a punch like László Papp. Its foul aftertaste is coupled with the feeling that it must be good for you; cough medicine that tasted like this went out with the bubble car.

The rule of thumb is not to drink more than three in an evening – but, of course, everyone does and the hangovers can be spectacular. No problem, as Hungarians consider Unicum to be the premier hangover cure.

Its name comes from Habsburg King Josef II's reaction to tasting it for the first time in 1790. 'Das ist ein Unikum,' he was heard to say, referring to the royal physician's concoction as a 'curiosity'. The chap was a certain Dr Zwack, and the recipe stayed in the family until a young József Zwack opened a liqueur factory in Budapest in 1840.

Zwack himself was a Moravian, who firmly believed in producing spirits using organic raw materials and not synthetic substitutes. He set up a distillery in 1854 and by the late 19th century Unicum had become a household name across Central Europe. By then it was being sold in its characteristic bottles. In 1915 Sándor Bortnyk, one of the leading figures in the avant-garde art movement, designed the famous advert that can still be seen in bars today, of the drowning man saved by a bottle of Unicum bobbing around him in the sea.

With their factory bombed by the war, and unwilling to have their company nationalised, the Zwacks had to leave Hungary after 1947, smuggling out their secret recipe with them. Having set an international precedent with his lawsuit against the Hungarian state for using the Zwack trademark, Péter Zwack then started producing the original drink again in Italy in 1969. Twenty years later, a joint venture with Germany company Underberg allowed Zwack to buy back their original factory in Budapest.

Today, four million litres are drunk every year, and not just in Hungary. It is considered an exotic delicacy in Italy, a cure-all to homesick Hungarians in obscure bars across

America and a cause of much curiosity to Japanese businessmen presented with it in corporate gift boxes. A clever publicity campaign, not unlike that of Guinness in the West, plays up the drink's long tradition, using classic images from the golden age of Bortnyk and the avant-gardists. You can even buy (www.zwackunicum.hu) Unicum hats, Unicum T-shirts and Unicum umbrellas. What they can't do is give you the taste for it.

Buena Vista – decent cocktails and perfect posing territory. *See p115.*

Eat, Drink, Shop

Móri still attracts the leather waistcoat brigade, one generation down from the messy mac merchants who usually frequent these joints. Friendly but smoky atmosphere, Innstadt beer on draught, cheap wine and a Budapest rarity – a pinball machine.

Mosselen Belgian Beer Café

XIII. Pannónia utca 14 (452 0535). Tram 4, 6. **Open** noon-midnight daily. **Credit** AmEx, MC, V. **Map** p246 C2.

Nestled in the heart of the architecturally rich District XIII, the Mosselen (Flemish for 'mussel') is a celebration of all good things Belgian: Chimay, Hoegaarden, Duvel, Kriek, steak with béarnaise, crispy fries and mussels. The classy decor features a beautiful, long mirror-backed bar, heavy wood furniture and some retro Belgian brewery ads. Attentive and swift staff complement the 25-plus bottled Belgian beers and an extensive menu littered with odd names for standard dishes – 'Beside the Fireplace' is, of course, steak and green pepper sauce. The highlight is the excellent mussels; served with big, fat steak chips and washed down with a pint or two of draught Leffe.

Oscar Café

II. Ostrom utca 14 (212 8017). M2 Moszkva tér/tram 4, 6/night bus 6É. **Open** 5pm-2am Mon-Thur, Sun; 3pm-4am Fri, Sat. **No credit cards. Map** p245 A3.

Dark, cinematically themed pub a short hop from Moszkva tér, whose main feature is its irresistibly long bar counter. Silly 'Nam corner is decked out in camouflage nets, but otherwise classic shots, stills and stars from the world of Hollywood and Magyar movies make for a pleasant backdrop. Mixed, well-heeled young crowd and a fairly decent selection of cocktails.

Ruszwurm Cukrászda

I. Szentháromság utca 7 (375 5284). Várbusz from M2 Moszkva tér/bus 16. **Open** 10am-7pm daily. **No credit cards. Map** p245 A3.

Founded in 1827, Hungary's oldest *cukrászda* (café-cum-pastry shop, *see p119* **Let them eat cake**) has a warm interior that retains some of the 1840s Empire-style cherrywood fittings. Its history and Castle District location guarantee its popularity with tourists, and the handful of tables, inside and along the pavement, are often full. The kitchen produces masterful pastries, freshly made ice-cream and quite delicious *pogácsa* scones. Good espresso too.

Soho Café

I. Fő utca 25 (201 3807). M2 Batthyány tér, then tram 19/bus 186. **Open** 7.30am-9pm Mon-Fri; 10am-9pm Sat, Sun. **No credit cards. Map** p245 B2.

English-owned orange coffee shop on busy Fő utca, and a fine place to take a *macchiato*, kick back on a sofa and browse a newspaper or delve into one of the English-language novels from the bookshelves. Friendly staff, one computer with internet access and a good line in coffee and tea specialities and light sandwiches. In short, ideal for breakfast. Owner plays a cool jazz selection later on.

Pest

Akali Borozó

XIII. Szent István körút 2 (340 4354). Tram 2, 4, 6.
Open 5.30am-11.30pm Mon-Fri; 8am-10.30pm Sat;
7am-9.30pm Sun. **No credit cards. Map** p246 C2.
Friendly *borozó* on the Pest side of Margaret Bridge.
Wine tureens, bread and dripping are devoured by
a morning clientele with faces like let-down balloons.
The Akali's attractive late-opening hours (for a
borozó) draw a more refined crowd later in the day.
Good views of the busy körút action outside.

Aloe Kávézó

*VI. Zichy Jenő utca 37 (269 4536). M1 Opera/M3
Arany János utca/night bus 14É, 50É.* **Open** 4pm-
2am daily. **No credit cards. Map** p246 C3.
Comfortable warren-like cellar bar with sofas and
armchairs for a young, vaguely literary and rowdy
student crowd. Old radios, period posters and tatty
rugs make up the decor. Toasted sandwiches and
instant soups complement a drinks menu with lethal
cheap cocktails. Friendly place.

Astoria Café

*V. Kossuth Lajos utca 19-21 (484 3222). M2
Astoria/tram 47, 49/bus 7.* **Open** 7am-11pm daily.
Credit AmEx, DC, MC, V. **Map** p249 D4.
Elegant but not overbearing, the high-ceilinged café
of the Astoria Hotel (*see p37*) has picture windows,
comfortable chairs and offers basic coffee, cakes and
snacks. The haunt of Nazi and Soviet officialdom,
although a state chain hotel for decades, the Astoria
has managed to retain its turn-of-the-century feel.

Bar Martinez

*VII. Dohány utca 1 (266 7226). M2 Astoria/night
bus 14É, 50É.* **Open** 11am-2am Mon-Fri; 6pm-2am
Sat. **No credit cards. Map** p249 D4.
This bar specialises in cocktails, in a town where
that's still unusual. The frozen Daiquiris, Margaritas
and fruit Coladas are quite inspired, the waitresses
are unusually friendly for such a hectic downtown
venue, and service of strong Italian coffee on the
shaded pavement terrace is swift and efficient. On
the edge of District VII's burgeoning drinking zone,
so a handy jumping-off point for a bar crawl.

Beckett's

*V. Bajcsy-Zsilinszky út 72 (269 3137). M3 Nyugati
pu./tram 4, 6/night bus 6É, 14É, 50É.* **Open** noon-
1am Mon-Thur; noon-2am Fri-Sun. **Credit** AmEx,
DC, MC, V. **Map** p246 C2.
This huge place was Budapest's first large-scale
expat hangout. Serves decent, if pricey, pub food and
a passable Irish breakfast, but it's the well-kept
Guinness and Sky Sports that draw in the punters.
Somehow continues to get away with extortionate
prices for local staples such as Zlaty Bazant lager.
Older crowd is comprised of overseas consultants
and chancers, plus the odd affluent Hungarian. At
weekends, each genre dances like dads at a wedding
to an atrocious Beatles cover band.

Box Utca

*VI. Bajcsy-Zsilinszky út 21 (354 1444). M3 Arany
János utca.* **Open** 8am-midnight Mon-Fri; 10am-
midnight Sat. **Credit** MC, V. **Map** p246 C2.
Former world featherweight champ István 'Ko-Ko'
Kovacs, a huge local celebrity, is a frequent visitor
to the new bar-restaurant he owns, a posh-looking
place with not-so-posh prices. A variety of sports
show all day on 16 televisions around the spacious,
sumptuously decorated bar, dining room and 'club
room'. No UK cable, though, so Beckett's (*see above*)
remains the only option for live Premiership action.
The food is Hungarian/continental nouvelle.

Buena Vista

*VI. Liszt Ferenc tér 4-5 (344 6303). M1 Oktogon/
tram 4, 6.* **Open** *restaurant* noon-midnight daily;
café 11am-1am daily. **Credit** MC, V. **Map** p246 D3.
The latest in the clutch of flashy cafés on Liszt
Ferenc tér, the Buena Vista is classy indeed. Nordic
woods and carved stone comprise a stylish interior
that pays homage to 1970s concepts in organic
design. The light, continental food (Mediterranean
grilled meats, inventive pasta, Caesar salads and the
like) is well done if a touch pricey. The cocktail mixer
actually knows what he's doing and on summer
nights the terrace is packed with the well-heeled
posers of Budapest sipping his creations.

Café Csiga

*VIII. Vásár utca 2 (210 0885). Tram 4, 6/night bus
6É.* **Open** 11am-1am Mon-Sat. **No credit cards.**
Map p250 E4.
With picture windows overlooking the former red-
light district of Rákóczi tér – now peopled by jobless
pimps playing cards and pensioners walking assault
dogs – the Csiga (pronounced 'Chigah', meaning
snail) is the latest venture from the people who
brought you the original Sixtus (*see p122*). In other
words, it's another island of misfit expats, but the
spacious main dining area bathed in natural light
also attracts many a Magyar. Its high ceilings are
decorated in bold colours; bric-a-brac furniture and
huge crepe paper lampshades with the cheesy smile
of Silvio Berlusconi moulded on to a TV set provide
a boho backdrop. The smaller, intimate bar area –
those who frequented the old Sixtus will spot the
ranting Shane MacGowan photo – successfully
recreates its friendly conspiracy. The market next
door informs the excellent menu (tasty home-made
seasonal soups, quiches and a good BLT), there's
Staropramen on tap and the crowd is a tipsy mix of
students, traders and layabouts. Occasional live
music, DJs and exhibitions.

Café Eklektika

*V. Semmelweiss út 21 (266 3054). M2 Astoria/
tram 47, 49.* **Open** noon-midnight Mon-Fri; 5pm-
midnight Sat, Sun. **No credit cards. Map** p249 D4.
Announced by a chair stuck precariously on to the
front of the building, Eklektika sits on one of the
quietest tree-lined streets in the busy belváros. With
high vaulted ceilings, soft orange decor, 1960s-70s

Eat, Drink, Shop

furniture and beautiful floor-to-ceiling windows, the Eklektika has carved out a reputation as a lesbian bar, and indeed does host a monthly lesbian party, (see p165), but by and large the clientele is a pretty straight, glamorous mix of arty students and actors. Light lunch and slightly skimpy evening meals are complemented by draught Tuborg and cocktails, along with well-chosen background music. Between the CDs you'll catch snippets of classical musicians limbering up in the nearby Music Academy.

Café Vian

VI. Liszt Ferenc tér 9 (268 1154). M1 Oktogon/tram 4, 6. **Open** *9am-midnight daily.* **No credit cards.** **Map** *p246 D3.*

A pink revamp of the old coffeehouse, catering to a classy crowd on heaving Liszt tér. The decor's a bit over the top and it's hardly the cheapest place in town, but it does offer an imaginative selection of salads and sandwiches, plus milkshakes, fresh juices and a cocktail menu, in an ambience suitable for relaxed supping, chatting and gawping.

Café Zaccos

V. Arany János utca 27 (no phone). M3 Arany János utca. **Open** *10am-11pm Mon-Sat.* **No credit cards.** **Map** *p246 C3.*

With lovely big windows that deserve more than the view of a monolithic bank centre, this cosy split-level café-bar is run by an ex-female bodybuilder – so be advised to tow the line. Cheap lunches of standard Hungarian fare on offer, along with a few unusual spicy meat dishes from Indonesia and Crete, plus Guinness, Tuborg and Leffe on tap. The place looks like somebody emptied their attic and nailed it to the wall, but space is allowed for maxiscreen football. The handy music timetable scored on an antique mirror means you can't say you weren't warned if you turn up halfway through Cher hour (5-6pm).

Castro

IX. Ráday utca 35 (215 0184). M3 Ferenc körút/ tram 4, 6. **Open** *10am-midnight Mon-Thur; 10am-1am Fri; 2pm-midnight Sat, Sun.* **No credit cards.** **Map** *p249 D5.*

Arguably the starting point of the Ráday utca renaissance, in 1999 the Castro was a dodgy Cuban theme bar aimed at the dreaded Magyar yuppie. Thankfully, after a lean few months, the owners saw sense; out went the £15 cigars and po-faced service, and in came Hans, the Dutch ex-manager of the Sixtus (see p122), with his Chet Baker picture under his arm, West Coast jazz for the stereo and a sense of fun hitherto sadly lacking. Now cool and calm in the daytime, popular with students for its cheap ham and eggs and internet access, the Castro undergoes a transformation every evening when the lovely long bar heaves with a youngish international crowd eating, drinking and making merry. Add in a little summer terrace, authentic Serb meat dishes from a chef who fits the part, and well-kept draught beer (Dreher and Pilsner Urquell), and the Castro is truly a bar for all seasons.

Centrál Kávéház

V. Károly Mihály utca 9 (266 4572). M3 Ferenciek tere/bus 7. **Open** *7am-1am daily.* **Credit** *AmEx, DC, MC, V.* **Map** *p249 C4.*

The recently reopened Centrál Kávéház, once a gathering place for intellectuals at the turn of the century, is poised to take its place back alongside the finest old-style coffeehouses of Budapest. Its open space right downtown, offset with carefully recreated 19th-century decor, encourages intimate discussions on lofty topics. Delicious cakes, well-priced coffees and stronger drinks, plus warming coffee cocktails, help fuel conversation. Full meals of Hungarian provenance also available, and, as if replacing the free sheets of writing paper commonplace to coffeehouses 100 years ago, there's an internet facility downstairs.

Champs Sports Pub

VII. Dohány utca 20 (413 1655). M2 Astoria/tram 47, 49/bus 7/night bus 14É, 78É. **Open** *noon-midnight Mon, Sun; noon-2am Tue-Sat.* **Credit** *DC, MC, V.* **Map** *p246 D4.*

Owned by a consortium of five Hungarian Olympic champions, this labyrinthine brick-lined cellar – complete with 35 televisions and two giant screens – is, as the name would suggest, dedicated to sport of the televised nature. Mid-priced Tex-Mex bar food, draught Guinness, Dreher, Pilsner Urquell and Kilkenny are served by scantily clad waitresses who seem more interested in their nails and hairdos. The decor is standard sports toot, along with a pommel horse, in case you're feeling game.

Cream Café

VII. Dohány utca 28 (413 6997). M2 Astoria/tram 47, 49/bus 7/night bus 14É, 50É, 78É. **Open** *noon-midnight Mon-Thur, Sun; noon-4am Fri, Sat.* **Credit** *AmEx, MC, V.* **Map** *p246 D4.*

Huge new cellar café-bar apparently run by, and for the pleasure of, local gold chain-wearing fatnecks, but when it's packed you can almost ignore them. Mediterranean cuisine, a good array of draught and bottled beers and, oddly enough, not a bad choice of single malt whiskies. The big brick cellar pumps with Ibiza-inspired Euro-house as the boys and their bimbos strut their not-too-funky stuff.

Darshan Café

VIII. Krúdy Gyula utca 8 (266 7797). M3 Kálvin tér/tram 47, 49. **Open** *8am-midnight Mon-Fri; noon-midnight Sat; 4pm-midnight Sun.* **No credit cards.** **Map** *p249 D5.*

Imaginatively designed, laid-back and with half-decent ambient and acid jazz, the Darshan could do with a better drinks selection – only one beer and a few desultory spirits. The Gaudi-ish mosaic entrance and gallery space are cool, though, and it's a better daytime option than Darshan Udvar opposite (see below). Slow counter service only.

Darshan Udvar

VIII. Krúdy Gyula utca 7 (266 5541). M3 Kálvin tér/tram 47, 49/night bus 6É, 14É, 50É. **Open**

Eat, Drink, Shop

10.30am-1am Mon-Wed; 10.30am-2am Thur, Fri;
6pm-2am Sat; 6pm-midnight Sun. **No credit cards**.
Map p249 D5.
The beating heart of up-and-coming Krúdy Gyula
utca, this huge, popular studenty pub occupies the
centrepiece for the mock Mongolian courtyard of the
same name. Along with two other bars, you'll also
find a Buddhist bookshop and Indigo music. Menu
of daily specials, plus soundtrack of world music,
reggae, jazz, dub, ambient and 'alternative'.

Dzsungel Étterem

*VI. Jókai utca 30 (302 4003). M3 Nyugati pu./tram
4, 6.* **Open** 10am-1am daily. **No credit cards**.
Map p246 C2.
The name and long row of beer signs outside refer
to the ridiculous choice of drinks: up to 18 types of
draught beer, nearly 100 bottled beers and some
50 cocktails. Housed in a long cellar, the place is
divided into two restaurant areas serving pizzas and
Hungarian standards, two bars, an area for live
music and karaoke, and an improbably bad jungle
theme room – the purpose of which escapes us.

Eckermann

VI. Andrássy út 24 (374 4076). M1 Opera. **Open**
8am-10pm Mon-Fri; 9am-10pm Sat. **No credit
cards**. **Map** p246 D3.
The Goethe Institut café seems to have attracted the
literary locals, who used to occupy the now tourist-
dominated Művész opposite *(see p118)*. Excellent
coffee (including gigantic bowls of *Milchkaffee*),
Hungarian and German newspapers, light snacks of
pastries and sandwiches, and in the far corner, three
busy computers for surfing.

Előre 57

*VII. Akácfa utca 57 (341 0608). Tram 4, 6/night
bus 6É.* **Open** 10am-2am daily. **No credit cards**.
Map p246 D3.
New bar from the owners of ChaChaCha *(see p175)*,
the 57 has cracked the seemingly impossible and
successfully fused a neighbourhood *borozó* with a
young, trendy dance bar. Downstairs the *borozó* of
old has been left pretty much as it was, although the
staff are friendlier, the toilets usable and the wine
drinkable. A nice touch has been to keep the tureens
for the wine and, as yet, there appears to be no active
policy of driving away the old soaks. Walk up the
metal stairs past a disarming mannequin and an
antique bike, and the gallery opens into two largish
rooms with 1960s Pop Art furniture and interesting
photo-montages of old Budapest on the wall. With
cheap booze and weekend DJs, the 57 could soon
become as much of an icon as ChaChaCha.

Gerbeaud

*V. Vörösmarty tér 7 (429 9000). M1 Vörösmarty
tér/tram 2.* **Open** 9am-9pm daily. **Credit** AmEx, DC,
MC, V. **Map** p249 C4.
On this imposing site since 1870, and with handsome
turn-of-the-century fittings, these days Gerbeaud's
elegance is mostly reserved for tourists, who stop
off for refreshment after a shopping trip down Váci.

Castro – no more Cuban cigars, but well-kept beer and a cute summer terrace. *See p116.*

It was here that Émil Gerbeaud invented the cognac cherry and there's still a great choice of pâtisserie items, both Hungarian and Viennese (*see p119 Let them eat cake*). Service runs from rude to efficient in dealing with the scores of outdoor tables, which are set against the slipstream of Budapest's busiest downtown square.

Grinzingi

V. Veres Pálné utca 10 (317 4624). M3 Ferenciek tere/bus 7/night bus 14É, 50É, 78É. **Open** *borozó* 9am-1am Mon-Sat; 3-11pm Sun; *cellar* 1pm-1am Mon-Fri; 6pm-1am Sat. **No credit cards. Map** p249 C4.

Large, busy establishment on the corner of Irány utca and Veres Pálné, the Grinzingi is probably the best *borozó* in Budapest. Upstairs, big street-level windows and marble-topped tables screwed to the floor form a horseshoe around the large bar, where passers-by, dedicated locals and the odd tourist neck *fröccs* and bottled lager. Downstairs is cramped, smoky and rammed with students counting out their last forints for a glass of wine. Cheap though it is, the wine has at least seen grapes and won't give you the twisted-balloon intestine that accompanies many *borozó* outings. Moreover this great bar does the best fried egg sandwich in town. Recommended.

Hat-három (6:3) Borozó

IX. Lónyay utca 62 (217 0748). Tram 2, 4, 6. **Open** 7am-10pm Mon-Sat; 7am-8pm Sun. **No credit cards. Map** p249 D6.

This intimate wooden sit-down wine bar is a temple to the greatest victory in the history of Hungarian football, the 6-3 (*Hat-három*) trouncing of former masters England at their own temple of Wembley stadium in 1953. In its 50th anniversary year, the legendary match is occupying page after page of the local football press, happy to seize any chance to evoke its memory. Three framed sepia photographs decorate the walls of this old *borozó*, the best being the one of a gaggle of celebrating Magyar players running away laughing from a recently filled English net. The one English defender to be picked out from the November fog, looking in desperation at another score increase, is Alf Ramsey, who would gain revenge of a sort by managing a dull English team to World Cup victory 13 years later. Here fans can order the usual array of wines, sodas and hard spirits to celebrate either football victory.

Ibolya

V. Ferenciek tere 5 (267 0239). M3 Ferenciek tere/bus 7. **Open** *Winter* 7am-10pm Mon-Sat; noon-8pm Sun.*Summer* 8am-11pm Mon-Sat; noon-10pm Sun. **No credit cards. Map** p249 C4.

Opposite the ELTE University Library, the Ibolya ('Violet') is among the best and most central of the surviving Communist-era *presszók*. The staff are slow, but wait a while and you can be served fine salads and sandwiches from the glass display by the cash registers. Avoid the microwaved meat. Cheap drinks, too. In summer, take a seat on the terrace if you prefer traffic fumes to cigarette smoke.

Iszaki Borozó

V. Belgrád rakpart 18 (318 1970). Tram 2. **Open** 7am-10pm Mon-Sat; 8am-10pm Sun. **No credit cards. Map** p249 C5.

No doubt about it, this place is a first-class dive but it's worth a visit for both the wonderful view of the river and Gellért Hill, and its weird mix of clientele. Downstairs, toothless pros stand silently with their *fröccs* and gawp at the TV, while their shackled mutts howl incessantly outside. Walk upstairs and you'll find rumours of the death of punk greatly exaggerated, in District V at any rate. Under-aged, safety-pinned spiky tops chain-smoke, wolf cheap wine and nod to the punk/metal-themed jukebox.

Karma Café

VI. Liszt Ferenc tér 11 (413 6764). M1 Oktogon/ tram 4, 6/night bus 6É. **Open** 9am-1.30am daily. **No credit cards. Map** p246 D3.

Another latest newcomer to Liszt tér, the Karma appears to have something of an image problem. The patio-doored front area feels like a tapas bar, despite the best efforts of the assorted Buddhist paraphernalia, the cosy back room complete with floor cushions and chaises longues looks Moorish, and the gallery restaurant, with its huge cast-iron chandelier, looks like a set from *The Three Musketeers*. Design schizophrenia aside, the Karma does mid-priced café-bar standards (grilled lemon chicken, creamy salmon pasta, salads), a good range of well-mixed cocktails and draught Guinness. The staff are courteous and efficient, and flit around the terrace, which blends into other ones on the square.

Lukács

VI. Andrássy út 70 (302 8747). M1 Vörösmarty utca. **Open** 9am-8pm Mon-Fri; 10am-8pm Sat, Sun. **Credit** MC, V. **Map** p246 D2.

This historically infamous *kávéház* is now part of the main office for CIB Bank – but for a dark decade it was a meeting place for Rákosi's secret police, the dreaded ÁVO whose headquarters were nearby at No. 60 (*see pp18-19* **1956 and all that**), today the themed Terror Museum. Lukács' present-day stab at elegance is spoiled by the correct impression that you're walking into a bank. Not even the gooey cake display by the main entrance, the tea-time piano player and friendly waitresses in frilly uniforms can persuade you otherwise.

Manchester Darts Pub

VI. Izabella utca 36 (342 5530). M1 Vörösmarty utca/night bus 6É. **Open** 4pm-2am daily. **No credit cards. Map** p246 D2.

Don't expect Lowry prints, a scale model of Maine Road in toothpicks or a signed Happy Mondays tour poster, but be prepared for a spit and sawdust-style bar with wooden booths, decent Hungarian grub and beer, a Radio 2 drivetime jukebox and five Harrow championship bristle dartboards. In fact, if you can find anything that relates to Manchester in the whole place, please let us know. That aside, the Manchester is a friendly darts-oriented cellar bar,

Let them eat cake

Along with coffee, baths and paprika, the Turks were responsible for bringing Hungary one of its greatest treasures: sweet cakes.

In the 1600s sorbets and honey cakes were all the rage in Buda, before the arrival of French and Swiss confectioners to add a little Gallic style to cake-making. Once gooey cakes became fashionable in Vienna, confectioners in Budapest took to giving a Germanic touch to their creations, adding more cream and replacing the French-sounding names for them.

Recipes for classic cakes were passed down from generation to generation. Hungarian cake (*torta*) creators included József Dobos, responsible for the creamy-layered, caramel-topped *dobos torta*, and restaurateur Károly Gundel, who came up with various sticky takes on the pancake, or *palacsinta*. Renowned Swiss confectioner Emil **Gerbeaud** invented a walnut, apple, apricot and chocolate fantasy known as the *zserbószelet*: the Gerbeaud slice. The windows of his elegant café are still filled with his creations (*see p117*).

Cake shops, *cukrászdák*, are small, beautiful, idiosyncratic, family-run establishments, tucked away in the side streets. Sadly fewer and farther between than they once were, one can still be found in most neighbourhoods. Plates and forks are provided for you to eat on the premises, occasionally standing up. If you take away, the wrapping is as delicate as the delicacy itself. Coffee will also be served, and some *cukrászda* also function as cafés in their own right – the **Ruszwurm** (*see p114*) being the classic example.

Hungary's classic cakes and pastries use traditional ingredients, especially lard. Strict vegetarians should be aware that the god-like pig provides the fat for rich flaky pastry, often stuffed with soft peppered cabbage seeded with caraway and a morsel of sausage (*káposztás roló*). It's also indispensable for the small savoury scones (*pogácsa*) baked with cheese, potato or pork crackling. Cottage cheese (*túró*) is used everywhere, finding its way into the warm pockets of sweet pastry (*túrós táska*) or moistening layers of sponge in cakes dotted with raisins; it turns up in ice-cream, in little fingers covered in chocolate (*túrórudi*) and even in savoury pastries.

Poppyseed (*mák*), with its strong earthy taste much loved across Central Europe, is often used with sour cherry to stuff pies served from vast black baking trays or to fill skilfully fashioned crescents of shortcrust pastry (*mákos kifli*). Chestnut purée (*gesztenye*) is eaten in vermicelli with whipped cream or strewn on cakes. Hungary's summers are bounteous; apples, peaches, apricots, plums, raspberries and strawberries all find their way to the *cukrászda*, fresh, in ice-cream, or in jam for biscuits and sweet glazes.Other classic desserts on offer include the *francia kremes*, a square of cream and coffee, the spongy *somlói galuska* and the *rétes*, closely related to the Viennese strudel. To enjoy them, the following are classic *cukrászdák*:

Auguszt Cukrászda

V. Kossuth Lajos utca 14-16 (337 6379). M3 Ferenciek tere/bus 7. **Open** 10am-6pm Mon-Fri. **No credit cards. Map** p249 C4.
Run by the Auguszt family since 1870, their cakes are coveted for special occasions. **Branch**: II. Fény utca 8 (316 3817).

Kovács Cukrászda

VIII. Brody Sándor utca 23 (no phone). M2 Blaha Lujza tér/tram 4, 6. **Open** 10am-6pm Tue-Fri; 10am-2pm Sat. **No credit cards. Map** p249 D4.
Well executed pastries make it worth taking one of the three tables in this tiny spot.

Nádori

IX. Ráday utca 53 (215 8776). M3 Ferenc körút/tram 4, 6. **Open** 8am-7pm Mon-Sat. **No credit cards. Map** p249 D5.
A speciality here is the *medvetalp*, a 'bear paw' of orange-and-walnut sticky cookie.

Pálmai

VII. Garay tér 8 (322 8915) M2 Keleti pu./ bus 7. **Open** 9am-4pm Mon-Fri; 8am-1pm Sat. **No credit cards. Map** p247 F3.
Pálmai offers delicious reasons to visit this quiet market square.

Szalai

V. Balassi Bálint utca 7 (269 3210). M2 Kossuth tér/tram 2. **Open** 9am-7pm Mon, Wed-Sun. **No credit cards. Map** p246 C2.
Family-run for generations, the excellent Szalai deserves its superb reputation for fine sweets and friendly service.

Eat, Drink, Shop

Sark – from the people behind Tilos Rádió. *See p122.*

busy in the evenings with the vagaries of the local arrows league, but a welcoming place to take the oche of an afternoon at a mere Ft300 per hour.

Művész

VI. Andrássy út 29 (352 1337). M1 Opera. **Open** 9am-midnight daily. **No credit cards.** **Map** p246 D3.

Although its unpretentious period decor still has a turn-of-the-century feel, new management at the Művész has cashed in on its reputation, upping prices and replacing friendly staff with sullen ones, forcing out regulars to the nearby Eckermann and beyond. Limited selection of cakes, savouries and ice-creams. The summer terrace is still a grand spot.

Natasha B

VI. Paulay Ede utca 5 (06 30 655 3848). M1, M2, M3 Deák tér/tram 47, 49/night bus 14É, 50É. **Open** 11am-2am Mon-Fri; 6pm-2am Sat, Sun. **No credit cards.** **Map** p246 D3.

Smallish Mediterranean-style café-bar on two levels – upstairs is a light, airy tiled bar area and a chillout room with sofas and books, downstairs an oxygen-free cellar with a bar and DJs playing reggae and funk. Intimate, friendly and cheap. Pilsner Urquell on tap, good sandwiches, a fun young crowd and, given its popularity among the party folk of Budapest, a fine place to find party flyers.

No. 1 Presszó

V. Sas utca 9 (267 0235). M3 Arany János utca. **Open** 9am-midnight Mon-Fri; 6pm-midnight Sat. **No credit cards. Map** p246 C3.

Fine *presszó* slap-bang in the middle of Budapest's business quarter. The prominent bar counter is off-set by a spacious room of brown furniture, set against incongruous paintings and signed photos of theatre stars. Zipfer and cocktails of questionable parentage share the menu with toasted sandwiches and cappuccinos. As far from the city beat as it's possible to get in the same postal district.

Operett Söröző-Kávéház

VI. Nagymező utca 19 (269 5001). M1 Opera. **Open** 8am-1am Mon-Sat; 9am-midnight Sun. **Credit** AmEx, MC, V. **Map** p246 D3.

Pleasant and leafy annexe to the Operett Theatre on Budapest's quickly reviving Broadway, with a tree-lined terrace and wooden interior. Great spot for breakfast, served until noon, lunches and main meals thereafter. Mainly used as a meeting place for actors making drinks stretch between jobs.

Paris, Texas

IX. Ráday utca 22 (218 9323). M3 Kálvin tér/tram 47, 49/night bus 14É, 50É. **Open** 10am-3am Mon-Fri; 4pm-3am Sat, Sun. **No credit cards. Map** p249 D5.

Decent venue on lively Ráday, Paris, Texas is dolled up with period portrait photos, not unlike an Amsterdam café. Upstairs is a relaxed bar area, downstairs pool and occasional live music. Tables outside in summer. Pizza and pasta can be ordered from the partner restaurant next door.

Pauls Pub

V. Nyári Pál utca 5 (266 8724). M3 Ferenciek tere/bus 7. **Open** 7am-midnight daily. **No credit cards.** **Map** p249 C5.

The last remaining old-style boozer in the touristy, pedestrianised area of south Váci, Pauls is a smoky one-room pub with a no-frills wooden bar, a pair of bleeping poker machines and a mix of friendly locals and antique dealers from the street's many curio shops. *Pogácsa* and *zsíroskenyér* accompany the cheapest beer on the street, and a terrace in summer.

Picasso Point

VI. Hajós utca 31 (312 1727). M3 Arany János utca/night bus 14É, 50É. **Open** noon-2am Mon-Wed; noon-2am Thur; noon-4am Fri; 4pm-4am Sat. **No credit cards. Map** p246 C3.

The pedestrianisation of Hajós utca has helped usher in the latest incarnation of this decade-old bar that manages to draw a new crowd every few years without changing ownership – or much else. A lot of comfy chairs and tables upstairs encourage gabbing with friends and some mingling, though many of the patrons seem too young and polite to chat up strangers. Folks loosen up at weekends, when the downstairs games room of darts and table football becomes a dancefloor, house DJs spinning trip hop, disco classics and pot luck. Decent, affordable fare includes Hungarian-style standards.

Potkulcs

VI. Csengery út 65B (269 1050). M3 Nyugati pu./tram 4, 6/night bus 6É, 14É, 50É. **Open** 5pm-2.30am Thur-Sat; 5pm-1.30am Sun-Wed. **No credit cards. Map** p246 D2.

The Potkulcs ('Spare Key') inhabits a former light engineering workshop, hidden behind a wall in the middle of a residential district near Nyugati station. Walk through the metal door and you'll find yourself in a pleasant beer garden, with a cellar-style area to the left with sofas and *csocsó* (table football). Straight ahead is a large one-room bar area spartanly decorated to evoke its past as a workshop – industrial lighting, functional brick bar, wire meshed skylights, etc. Popular with students, backpackers and younger expats, the Potkulcs has acceptable pub food, occasional DJs, recitals and plays and cheapish booze. Worth finding.

Portside

VII. Dohány utca 7 (351 8405). M2 Astoria/bus 7/tram 47, 49/night bus 14É, 50É. **Open** 11am-2am Mon-Sat; 4pm-2am Sun. **Credit** AmEx, V. **Map** p249 D4.

Huge British-run cellar pub with a vaguely nautical theme. Early evenings it's patronised by a smart, youngish anglophone crowd from financial services – guys in suits and ties, and women who like guys in suits and ties. At some point later on the brokers undo their Windsor knots, slip off their braces and let their thinning hair down as the place descends into a hellish pastiche of a City meat market. Efficient staff preside over an extensive menu with decent pub

Eat, Drink, Shop

Eat, Drink, Shop

For al fresco drinking

Enjoy a drink in the chestnut-tree shade of the **Avar** beer garden (see p110) or sip a quiet *fröccs* surrounded by forest and fresh air at the **Kobüfé Söröző** (see p112).

For death-wish drinking

Getting zonked at the **Zacc** (see p112) or plastered at the **No.1 Presszó** (see p121) involve the kind of lethal cocktails perhaps considered by Gottlieb Daimler for early automotive transport.

For the best gooey cakes

The **Ruszwurm Cukrászda** (see p114) is Hungary's oldest, but the **Auguszt** (see p119) offers the most coveted cakes – and the **Szalai** (see p119) has the best sweets.

For the worst jukebox on Earth

The one in the **Víg Söröző** (see p123) has to be heard to be believed. Do these people have no shame?

For bar games

Picasso Point (see p121) boasts darts and table football, while the **Paris, Texas** (see p121) has a pool table; the table football gets wicked at the **Potkulcs** (see p121) and the **Sark** (see below), while the **Móri Borozó** (see p112) has that rarity, a pinball machine. The **Manchester Darts Pub** (see p118) tops the lot with five classic Harrow-championship bristle boards for hourly hire.

For zaniest furniture

The **Café Miró**'s chairs (see p112) are as if constructed by the artist himself; no two chairs are alike at the eclectic **Café Eklektika** (see p115), while the **Szimpla/Dupla** (see p123), the **Calgary** (see p112) and the **Café Zaccos** (see p116) are all fierce followers of flea-market chic.

For not knocking over the landlord's pint

Box Utca (see p115) is owned by boxer Kókó Kovács, the **Café Zaccos** (see p116) is run by an ex-bodybuilder, while ex-champion canoeist Tamás **Wichmann** has his eponymous bar (see p123) guarded by fearsome Alsatians.

For grim ex-regulars

The **Astoria Café** (see p115) was frequented by Nazi officials and Soviet apparatchiks, while the **Lukács** (see p118) was the haunt of the Hungarian secret police in the 1950s.

For laddish bar snacks

The **Libella** (see p112) serves fine toasted sandwiches and pickled eggs, the **Bambi Presszó** (see p111) does a mean omelette, while the **Grinzingi** (see p118) can rustle up a demon fried egg sandwich.

For range of beers

The **Belgian Brasserie** (see p112) may boast Kriek and more, but the **Dzsungel** (see p117) has 18 on draught and 100 bottled types.

---

food, pool tables and dull disco standards cranked up a notch over bearable. Packed at weekends and living proof that money is the root of all eejits.

Sark

VII. Klauzál tér 14 (328 0753). Tram 4, 6/night bus 6É. **Open** 10am-2am Mon-Thur, Sun; 10am-3am Fri, Sat. **No credit cards. Map** p246 D3.
New venture from the people behind Tilos Rádió, the Sark is a welcome addition to this increasingly pub-crawl-friendly district. Sited in an old *borozó* on a corner of Klauzál tér, where the Arrow Cross Fascists stacked the bodies of the district's dead in the winter of 1944, the Sark is an atmospheric café-club on two levels. Upstairs is an airy bar area with large windows, a ceiling-to-floor multiple Warholian portrait mural and a gallery replete with cushions for those who've had a tad too much; below is a big, smoky cellar with table football and DJs from Tilos. Uncomfortably busy at the weekends with a cool twentysomething crowd, it's also a pleasant daytime coffee bar near a busy fruit and vegetable market.

6tus (Sixtus)

VII. Nagy Diófa utca 26-28 (413 6722). M2 Blaha Lujza tér/tram 4, 6/bus 7/night bus 6É, 78É. **Open** 5.30pm-1am Mon-Sat. **No credit cards. Map** p249 D4.
A subtle semantic change to the sign, a new smiling face behind the bar and the addition of a perspective-deficient Ikarus mural (quite why he has bananas stuck to his arms is beyond us) aside, everything remains pretty much the same at the old Sistine Chapel – it's a small, poky, smoky, dangerously fun bar in the depths of District VII. Well-chosen music, anywhere from Curtis Mayfield to Iggy and the Stooges, popular with an oddball arty/clubby crowd and local lags, the 6tus has been a mainstay of the alternative scene since the mid-1990s. No food, but staff will order you anything you want from an array of takeaway menus, Dreher on tap, bottled Pilsner Urquell, good wine and a killer Cocaine cocktail. And yes, don't worry, staff and regulars still dance on the bar counter when the mood takes.

Soul Café

IX. Ráday utca 11-13 (217 6986). M3 Kálvin tér/tram 47, 49. **Open** noon-1am daily. **Credit** AmEx, MC, V. **Map** p249 D5.

Situated in the old El Greco café at the top end of Ráday utca, the Soul is a refined café-bar serving Med cuisine, ideal for a summer salad and a glass of wine from the well-chosen list. Tables outside for al fresco dining, inside a lovely high, vaulted room done out in cool shades of orange, with Charles Rennie Mackintosh-style fittings and features. Home-made soups make it attractive in winter too. Fast and friendly English-speaking staff.

Szilvakék Paradicsom Café Bar

XIII. Pannónia utca 5-7 (339 8099). Tram 2, 4, 6. **Open** noon-midnight daily. **Credit** MC, V. **Map** p246 C2.

Large American-style restaurant-bar opposite the Mosselen (*see p114*), the venue's attractions are its cheap and hearty Hungarian/Tex-Mex food, a wide range of draught beers (Bak, Lauterbacher, Pilsner Urquell, Guinness) and a fun, unpretentious crowd enjoying themselves. Occasional live music, a jukebox plus a large terrace area. Decor is standard issue 1930s/1940s Americana nailed to the wall. Cheap all-you-can-eat Sunday buffet brunch.

Szimpla/Dupla

VII. Kertész utca 48 (342 8991). Tram 4, 6/night bus 6É. **Open** noon-2am daily. **No credit cards**. **Map** p246 D3.

A café-bar, Szimpla ('single'), and a cheap eaterie, Dupla ('double'), with a large, smoky cellar bar that connects the two. Part of a growing District VII empire that also includes the **Szimpla Kert** (*see p179*), these two places conform to a pretty simple formula: fire-sale furniture, squeaky floorboards, cheap fare and decent music. The place is rammed on a Friday with a mix of students, backpackers and musicians, here for the live music. Bar service only.

Time Café & Lounge

IX. Ráday utca 23 (476 0433). M3 Kálvin tér/tram 47, 49/night bus 6É, 14É, 50É. **Open** 11am-1am Mon-Wed; 11am-2am Thur, Fri; 1pm-2am Sat; 1pm-1am Sun. **No credit cards**. **Map** p249 D5.

One of the oldest of Ráday's chic bars, the Time is split into a downstairs of comfy leather and dark wood booths, tables and an oval bar, and an upstairs of leather upholstered sofas – a bid to recreate a lounge club feel. DJs and live acts play a West Coast jazz-based selection at a volume to help the atmosphere along rather than kill it, along with well-made cocktails. The name springs from the glass-covered clock set into the floor. Outdoor tables in summer.

Toldi Mozi Kávézó

V. Bajcsy Zsilinszky út 36-38 (472 0397). M3 Arany János utca/night bus 14É, 50É. **Open** 11am-2am daily. **No credit cards**. **Map** p246 C3.

The Toldi (*see p157*) is an arthouse cinema right next to Arany János utca metro, also boasting a book and CD shop. The lively café serves cheap booze,

Simple fare, cheap prices at **Szimpla/Dupla**.

healthfood nibbles and cakes. Runs a no-smoking policy, but there are seats outside for those who need them. The clientele is a young, film buff/alternative crowd. Hosts great one-off parties in the foyer.

Víg Söröző

XIII. Ditrói Mór utca 1 (no phone). Tram 4, 6/night bus 6É. **Open** 24 hrs daily. **No credit cards**. **Map** p246 C2.

The Víg leads a double life. In winter it's a small, smoky *söröző*, patronised by the bouncers and staff of the strip joint across the street filling up on Red Bull and listening to possibly the worst jukebox on the planet. In summer, however, it's a pleasant and cheap terrace to enjoy an aperitif before a show at the Vígszinház (*see p191*) next door. As it's open all night, it's also a fine place for a post-mortem on your night while waiting for trams to start running again.

Wichmann

VII. Kazinczy utca 55 (342 6074). M1, M2, M3 Deák tér/tram 47, 49/night bus 14É, 50É. **Open** 6pm-2am daily. **No credit cards**. **Map** p249 D4.

Owned by former world champion canoeist Tamás Wichmann, this rough and smoky bar with no sign outside (it's 50m from the corner with Király utca) seems largely untouched by recent history. Wine is appallingly cheap, young customers cluster round big and sociable wooden tables and the staff are friendly, if a bit mental. Perhaps it's Wichmann's nosy Alsatians. Nonetheless, a fine establishment.

Eat, Drink, Shop

Shops & Services

Local mavericks survive amid the malls and megastores.

Eat, Drink, Shop

Somewhere between the tacky folklore and the omnipresent Western brands, tradition has survived and defied the market forces that have shut down much of the old service industry. Budapest's mall mania – which has dotted the city with grey-and-glass shopping centres, all in the guise of 'neighbourhood regeneration' – has siphoned stores away from the traditional style mile, the Váci utca area, where only a few mass-market brands remain among the empty shop windows and 'to lease' signs.

Western brand stores feature a fragment of their collections and with a longer shelf life, because the local clientele can't afford to keep up with the change of seasons at Zara speed. Even at the luxury end of the scene, tag-land will more likely have bits and bobs than a full collection of sizes, models and colours. It leaves the shopping traveller in a local time warp. Budapest's treasure hunts will generally fill your shopping cart with adorable antiques, precious porcelain, fabulous fashion and smart arts and crafts, all testimony to a long-standing tradition – and somewhat stuck there too. There's hope for that tradition to surface in the avant-garde work of a new generation of artists, but their output largely depends on individual commissions, and their exposure is limited to the wrought-iron powerhouse of **Hephaistos** and the Hungarian showcase of **Magma** (see *p129* **Smart art**), the stores most successful in aligning local talent with commercial demand. Most here is handmade and original, and a lack of access to mass production keeps things specially and personally Hungarian.

Váci utca and its pedestrianised sidestreets host most of the treasure. It's here that the old store fronts and their owners' trades still survive – although sadly most of it is pre-extinction, be it handmade gloves, hats, decorative objets, made-to-measure shoes or clothes. The tiny spaces are swamped by a tide of uniform folk stores, all flogging faux folksy memorabilia: shirts, umbrellas, keychains, jugs, whips. Although there are antique stores in this most central area, the real trade transpires on Falk Miksa utca and the markets on the outskirts, with **Ecseri** (*see p137* **A load of old junk**) setting the local standard in absolute antique as well as genuine junk.

Prices vary: taxis are still cheap, but dry-cleaning could set you back a fortune. A private

beauty treatment or massage will cost next to nothing, while the price of local wine compares to expensive imports. In general, services mainly catering to foreigners will charge Western prices, while what locals can afford should be cheap for the visitor.

More and more assistants speak English; a fledgling service mentality has surfaced from the knee-jerk urge to earn a tip. Still, there may be attempts to cheat and Lake Balaton is notorious for overcharging foreigners.

OPENING HOURS
Standard opening hours are 10am-5pm or 6pm on weekdays and 10am-1pm on Saturdays. In touristy areas, stores stay open later as well as on Sundays. Malls also have extended hours and are open seven days a week. For basic necessities at all hours, there's a non-stop in every neighbourhood. Most places are closed around major holidays, including 15 March, Easter Monday, Pentecost, 20 August, 23 October, Christmas and New Year's Day.

VAT
On 1 May 2004, Hungary will join the European Union, which practically ends VAT refunds for EU citizens. Non-EU citizens will still be able to reclaim the VAT on purchases over Ft50,000 that don't qualify as a commercial quantity. Whether or not shops and stores choose to join the refund scheme at all is entirely up to them. Furthermore, they're not required to return the full 12 or 25 per cent VAT either – the amount you can reclaim will vary from store to store.

Stores participating in the refund scheme will fill in a form for you, which you need to have stamped at your point of departure. Some will deduct the amount from the total in the shop, in which case you'll have to send the stamped refund form back to the store. Otherwise, they'll furnish you with a pre-addressed envelope, and you'll receive the VAT amount via bank transfer. For more information, contact the Hungarian Customs Office (XIV. Hungária körút 112-114 (470 4118, vam.info@vpop.hu).

DIRECTORY SERVICES
For English-language lists, www.superpages.hu has an English option. In Hungarian, www.mtt.hu, www.telefonkonyv.hu and www.aranyoldalak.hu have search tools.

CONSUMER PROTECTION
Complaints can be lodged at the Consumer Protection Authority, VIII. József körút 6 (459 4800/4999).

Antiques

Antik Bazár
VII. Klauzál utca 1 (322 8848/06 30 944 2929). M2 Blaha Lujza tér. **Open** 10am-6pm Mon-Fri; 10am-2pm Sat. **No credit cards. Map** p249 D4.
Also known as Nosztalgia, this store is a little shop of horrors from eras long gone – an indoor flea market from dubious chapters in the history of taste.

Antik Emma
XIII. Pozsonyi út 59 (06 30 970 7455). Bus 15. **Open** by appointment. **No credit cards. Map** p246 C1.
Full of antique fabrics and complete with design services, Antik Emma also features Ildikó Fáczány's clothes, inspired by old lace and silk. Bedding too.

BÁV
V. Bécsi utca 1-3 (317 2548). M3 Ferenciek tere/tram 2/bus 7. **Open** 10am-6pm Mon-Fri; 9am-1pm Sat. **Credit** AmEx, DC, MC, V. **Map** p249 C4.
BÁV stores are state-run pawn shops. Outlets all over the city buy and sell everything from high-quality antiques to used refrigerators and can be recognised by a maroon-and-white Venus de Milo sign. This central location flogs a wide range of random treasures, from paintings to jewellery, while an adjacent sister store at V. Bécsi utca 3 (318 4403) specialises in contemporary Hungarian art . For auction schedules, call the central office at IX. Lónyay utca 30-32 (455 7700/455 7439) or pick up times at the major branches.
Branch: V. Szent István körút 3 (473 0666).

Detre & Ferenczy Antikvitás
V. Váci utca 51 (317 7743/235 0217). M3 Ferenciek tere/bus 7. **Open** 10am-6pm Mon-Fri; 10am-1pm Sat. **Credit** MC, V. **Map** p249 C5.
The strength of the selection lies in silver and bronze antiques, old Zsolnay and Herend porcelain, as well as glass. Two auctions held every year. Payment in cash preferred, especially if you intend to haggle.

Ecclesia
V. Ferenciek tere 7-8 (317 3754). M3 Ferenciek tere/bus 7. **Open** 9.30am-5.30pm Mon-Fri; 9.30am-1pm Sat. **No credit cards. Map** p249 C4.
Christian artefacts and divine memorabilia tend to dominate this spacious downtown store, which offers old devotional art and icons too. It's also the ideal place for inexpensive oversized candles.

Judaica Gallery
VII. Wesselényi utca 13 (267 8502). M2 Astoria/tram 47, 49/bus 7. **Open** 10am-6pm Mon-Thur; 10am-1.30pm Fri. Closed on Jewish holidays. **Credit** AmEx, MC, V. **Map** p249 D4.
Articles related to Hungarian Jewish culture: old prayer books, illustrative work by local Jewish

artists and village pottery with Hebrew sayings and Haggadahs. Also stocks a good selection of books in English on Jewish themes.

Mő-Terem Gallery
V. Falk Miksa utca 30 (312 2071). Tram 2, 4, 6. **Open** 10am-6pm Mon-Fri; 10am-1pm Sat. **Credit** MC, V. **Map** p246 C2.
An array of 19th- and 20th-century paintings and their exhibitions make up the best of this often-changing stock, with a strong collection of antique art deco Zsolnay porcelain.

Pintér Antik Diszkont
V. Falk Miksa utca 10 (311 3030). Tram 2, 4, 6. **Open** 10am-6pm Mon-Fri; 10am-2pm Sat. **Credit** MC, V. **Map** p246 C2.
In a former World War II bomb shelter, 1,800sq m of recently expanded floor space boasts antique furniture and new crystal chandeliers by Bohemia Salon. The Pintér Szonja Gallery specialises in contemporary Hungarian painting and sculpture, and there's also a coffee shop – a welcome relief after winding through the maze of rooms.

Relikvia
I. Fortuna utca 21 (356 9973). Várbusz from M2 Moszkva tér/bus 16. **Open** 10am-noon, 1-6pm daily. **Credit** AmEx, DC, MC, V. **Map** p245 A3.
Specialises in fine furniture, paintings and porcelain. The smaller branch in the Hilton sells new Ajka crystal and Hungarian porcelain. Don't expect many bargains, but this is certainly the best antique shop you'll find in the Castle District.
Branch: Hilton Hotel, I. Hess András tér 1-3 (488 6886).

Art supplies & stationery

Ápisz
V. Kossuth Lajos utca 2 (266 1957). M3 Ferenciek tere/bus 7. **Open** 9am-6pm Mon-Fri; 9am-1pm Sat. **Credit** MC, V. **Map** p249 C4.
Ápisz, with its cutesy lilac logo, is the local paper expert – stocking anything from toilet paper to calendars, wrapping paper to decorations. Non-paper items include pens, office supplies, baking tins, small toys, diskettes, string, elastic bands and plastic cups; all Hungarian-made, all cheap. The branches listed below specialise in art supplies.
Branches: V. Szent István körút 21 (312 0425); VIII. József körút 11 (338 4381); V. Bajcsy-Zsilinszky út 60 (311 0678).

Intérieur Studio
V. Vitkovics Mihály utca 6. M2 Astoria/tram 47, 49. **Open** 10am-6pm Mon-Fri; 10am-1pm Sat. **No credit cards. Map** p249 C4.
Handmade paper goods, fancy gift trimmings, dried flowers and local handicrafts compose the attractive stock of this tiny shop. Bath oils, delicate hand-dipped candles, paper boxes and pretty baskets fill the rest of the space.
Branch: Pólus Center, XV. Szentmihályi út (419 4166).

Eat, Drink, Shop

Művészellátó Szaküzlet

VI. Nagymező utca 45-47 (332 6163/311 7040). M3 Arany János utca. **Open** 9am-6pm Mon-Fri; 10am-1pm Sat. **Credit** AmEx, DC, MC, V. **Map** p246 C3.
The best stock of art supplies in town. Branches specialise in equipment for children and hobbyists. **Branches:** II. Margit körút 3 (212 2807); VIII. Üllői út 36 (266 1938).

Auctions

Kieselbach Galéria

V. Szent István körút 5 (269 3148/269 3149). Tram 2, 4, 6. **Open** 10am-6pm Mon-Fri; 10am-1pm Sat. **Credit** AmEx, DC, MC, V. **Map** p246 C2.
The city's most successful auction house, Kieselbach holds three auctions yearly of about 200 select works, mostly Hungarian of the 1850-1950 period.

Nagyházi Galéria

V. Balaton utca 8 (475 6000). Tram 2, 4, 6. **Open** 10am-6pm Mon-Fri; 10am-2pm Sat. Exhibitions can affect opening hours. **Credit** AmEx, DC, MC, V. **Map** p246 C2.
One of the city's biggest auction houses holds four auctions in spring and autumn, plus a collection of antique furniture, paintings and old masters. **Branch:** V. Kálmán Imre utca 15 (312 1277).

Books, maps & newsagents

A Világsajtó Háza

V. Városház utca 3-5 (317 1311). M3 Ferenciek tere/bus 7. **Open** 7am-7pm Mon-Fri; 7am-4pm Sat; 8am-2pm Sun. **No credit cards. Map** p249 C4.
Part of the Sajtó Pont network, these branches carry no fewer than 2,000 international titles. **Branch:** V. Kálvin tér 3 (266 9730).

Bestsellers

V. Október 6 utca 11 (312 1295). M3 Arany János utca. **Open** 9am-6.30pm Mon-Fri; 10am-5pm Sat; 10am-4pm Sun. **Credit** AmEx, DC, MC, V. **Map** p246 C3.
Budapest expats' favourite bookstore offers the widest selection of foreign literature. Popular foreign newspapers and magazines are also available.

CEU Academic Bookshop

V. Nádor utca 9 (327 3096). M3 Arany János utca. **Open** 9am-6pm Mon-Fri; 9am-6.30pm Wed; 10am-4pm Sat. **Credit** AmEx, DC, MC, V. **Map** p246 C3.
The academic branch of Bestsellers (see above), in the Central European University, stocks works on Central and Eastern Europe and the former Soviet Union. Ten per cent discount on cash purchases during 'happy hour' every Wednesday 4.30-6.30pm.

Írók Boltja

VI. Andrássy út 45 (322 1645). M1 Oktogon/tram 4, 6. **Open** 10am-6pm Mon-Fri; 10am-1pm Sat (Sept-June). **Credit** AmEx, MC, V. **Map** p246 D3.
All Hungarians in English translation are available here, and the albums selection is extraordinary.

Although the 'Writers' Bookshop' offers only the basics in foreign languages, it remains the most intellectual of all local bookstores, complete with matching atmosphere and modest coffee corner.

Antiquarian bookshops

Bibliotéka Antikvárium

VI. Andrássy út 2 (475 0240). M1 Bajcsy-Zsilinszky út. **Open** 10am-6pm Mon-Fri; 9am-1pm Sat. **Credit** AmEx, DC, MC, V. **Map** p246 C3.
Large stock of over 25,000 books. Rare editions upstairs and knowledgeable staff. Good selection of engravings, maps and postcards.

Forgács

V. Erzsébet tér 7-8 (429 3379). M1, M2, M3 Deák tér/tram 47, 49. **Open** by appointment. **No credit cards. Map** p249 C4.
This tiny store in the Kempinsky's shopping arcade offers rare books and prints, and some antiques for the cerebrally inclined.

Központi Antikvárium

V. Múzeum körút 13-15 (317 3514). M2 Astoria/tram 47, 49. **Open** 10am-6.30pm Mon-Fri; 10am-2pm Sat. **Credit** AmEx, MC, V. **Map** p249 D4.
Spacious collectors' shop, especially good for old books, maps and engravings. Also includes a strange selection of second-hand books in various obscure foreign languages.

Carpets

Aga's Oriental Carpet Shop

VI. Hajós utca 1 (341 3229). M1 Opera. **Open** 10am-6pm Mon-Fri; 10am-2pm Sat, Sun. **Credit** AmEx, DC, MC, V. **Map** p246 C3.
The range of creativity is breathtaking in this showcase of mostly Afghan, Iranian and Turkish rugs and handicrafts. Tribal rugs and kilims are also available.

Heriz Galéria

V. Március 15 tér 8 (266 7893). Tram 2. **Open** 10am-6pm Mon-Fri; 10am-1pm Sat. **Credit** MC, V. **Map** p249 C4.
In an exquisite location just off the Danube, this atmospheric family-run store with generations of experience in Germany stocks colourful oriental rugs from the Caucusus and Tabriz.

Children

Clothes

Benetton Zerododici

V. Váci utca 6 (266 2393). M1, M2, M3 Deák tér/tram 47, 49. **Open** 10am-9pm Mon-Sat; 10am-6pm Sun. **Credit** AmEx, DC, MC, V. **Map** p249 C4.
True to form, the Italian wizard of the uniformed multi-culti brings a no-nonsense collection of infant gear to Benetton's Central European megastore.

Eat, Drink, Shop

Írók Boltja: 'Writers' Bookshop'. *See p126.*

Mall therapy at **MOM Park**. *See p129.*

Götz Bababolt

V. Váci utca 11A (318 3115). M1, M2, M3 Deák tér/tram 47, 49. **Open** 10am-6pm Mon-Fri; 10am-4pm Sat. **Credit** AmEx, DC, MC, V. **Map** p249 C4.
Central location for all baby and toddler supplies.

Sonia & Oliver

V. Régiposta utca 11 (318 2515). M1, M2, M3 Deák tér/tram 47, 49. **Open** 10am-7pm Mon-Fri; 10am-3pm Sat. **Credit** MC, V. **Map** p249 C4.
Haute outfitting for chic children in a microcosm of Baby Dior, Moschino Junior and the like.

Toys

Burattino

IX. Ráday utca 47 (215 5621). M3 Kálvin tér/tram 47, 49. **Open** 10am-6pm Mon-Fri; 10am-1pm Sat. **No credit cards. Map** p249 D5.
Great selection of wooden blocks, trains and puzzles.

Fakopáncs Fajátékbolt

VIII. Baross utca 46 (337 0992). Tram 4, 6. **Open** 10am-6pm Mon-Fri; 9am-1pm Sat. **No credit cards. Map** p250 E5.
Great wooden trains, garden tools and looms.

Gondolkodó Logikai Játékok Boltja

II. Fény utca 10 (316 4082). M2 Moszkva tér. **Open** 10am-1pm, 1.30-6pm Mon-Fri; 9am-1pm Sat. **No credit cards. Map** p245 A2.
This store concentrates on an excellent collection of games to facilitate motor skills and learning.

Gondolkodó Toy Store

VI. Király utca 25 (322 8884). M1 Opera. **Open** 10am-6pm Mon-Fri; 9am-1pm Sat. **No credit cards. Map** p246 D3.
Games from chess software to beautiful wooden puzzles and local hero Rubik's latest inventions.

Puppet Show

V. Párizsi utca 3 (318 8453). M3 Ferenciek tere/bus 7. **Open** 10am-6pm Mon-Fri; 10am-1.30pm Sat. **No credit cards. Map** p249 C4.
A little shop with lots of cute animal puppets. Friendly staff demonstrate how to make them move.

Totyi & Tini

V. Bárczy István utca 1-3 (317 9429). M1, M2, M3 Deák tér/tram 47, 49. **Open** 10am-6pm Mon-Fri; 10am-1pm Sat. **Credit** AmEx, DC, MC, V. **Map** p249 C4.
Hungarian-designed dress-up and play clothes.

Amsterdam Andalucia Bangkok Barcelona Berlin Boston

Brussels Budapest Buenos Aires Chicago Copenhagen Dublin

Edinburgh Florence Havana Hong Kong Istanbul Las Vegas

Lisbon London Los Angeles Madrid Marrakech Miami

Milan Naples New Orleans New York Paris Patagonia

Prague Rome San Francisco South of France South West England Stockholm

Sydney Tokyo Toronto Venice Vienna Washington, DC

Time Out City Guides

Available from all good bookshops and at www.timeout.com/shop

www.penguin.com

Time Out City Guides

www.timeout.com

Department stores & malls

Budagyöngye

*II. Szilágyi Erzsébet fasor 121 (275 0839). M2
Moszkva tér, then bus 56.* **Open** *Shops* 9am-7pm
Mon-Fri; 9.30am-2pm Sat; 10am-1.30pm Sun.
Buda's most functional mall deters with a chaos of
smaller stores, but attracts with its comprehensive
services catering to its better-heeled customers.
Good for fresh fish and decent selection of imported
cheese and vegetables.

Luxus Áruház

V. Vörösmarty tér 3 (318 2277). M1 Vörösmarty tér.
Open 10am-7pm Mon-Fri; 10am-5pm Sat. **Credit**
MC, V. **Map** p249 C4.
One of the last old stores standing, Luxus occupies
a landmark building on prime retail space –
Vörösmarty tér – and offers an excellent selection of
toiletries on the ground floor, with men's and
women's apparel on the first. The wonderfully
old-fashioned staff are fully conversant with the
stock and the customers.

Mammut

*II. Lövőház utca 2-6 (345 8020). M2 Moszkva tér/
tram 4, 6.* **Open** 10am-9pm Mon-Sat; 10am-6pm Sun.
Map p245 A2.
Two massive wings make up the Mammut mall, the
newer one boasting more megastores like Benetton
and Mango, compared to the older wing's myriad
smaller shops. There's a huge food store, Smatch, in
the basement. Adjacent is the Fény utca market for
fresh produce. If it gets too much, there's a fine view
of the Moszkva tér rooftops from the food court.

MOM Park

XII. Alkotás út 53 (487 5500). Tram 61. **Open**
10am-7pm Mon-Sat; 10am-4pm Sun.
This most recent of malls has Goa in interior design
and a branch of the Vista travel agency (*see p140*)
which is less crowded than the one downtown.

Rózsakert

*II. Gábor Áron út 74-78 (391 5998). M2 Moszkva
tér, then bus 49.* **Open** 10am-8pm Mon-Fri; 10am-
7pm Sat; 10am-4pm Sun. **Map** p245 A2.

Smart art

Boldly defying the sign of the times when
markets are mass, and uniform ubiquitous,
Magma (*see p130*) exclusively nourishes the
original talent of Hungarian artisans. Opened
with the enthusiasm of the millennial élan in
2000, this spacious store showcases
decorative items for the home as well as
the self, all inimitable in their creators'
commitment to uniqueness.

The selection ranges from furniture to
jewellery, and all the items are individual.
Tünde Valkovics's ceramics feature sets in
the abstracted shape of a cat and sensual

vases. Judit Karsay takes inspiration from
birds, and Zsófia Karsai blends ceramic art
with cerebral games.

Glass is used for wall decoration in Márta
Edőcs's collection, while Péter Borkovics
pours art into his schnapps glasses. Anna
Regős designs tablecloths out of her own
textiles, and a novel individuality dominates
the fashions of Mónika Varga and Szilvia
Vereczkey. For a different take on pendants,
chains and rings, István Holló, Fanni Király,
Krisztina Stomfai, Klára Abaffy and József
Bozsits present their silver jewellery.

Eat, Drink, Shop

Ékes Kesztű. *See p131.*

Rózsadomb's pet mall features all the neighbourhood haute bourgeoisie requirements, with beauty and fitness services, even a medical centre.

Westend City Center

VI. Váci út 1-3 (238 7777). M3 Nyugati pu./tram 4, 6. **Open** 10am-9pm Mon-Sat; 10am-6pm Sun. **Map** p246 C2.
This huge mall is the city's busiest and most comprehensive – everyone in retail and services is here.

Design & household services

Bazaar

V. Molnár utca 27 (318 5457). M3 Ferenciek tere/bus 7. **Open** 11am-6pm Mon-Fri; 10am-2pm Sat. **Credit** MC, V. **Map** p246 D3.
Candles of all colours, shapes, scents and origins make up this little shop of pyromania, complete with novelty candelabra. Seasonal specials.

Demko Feder

V. József Attila utca 20 (212 4408). M1, M2, M3 Deák tér. **Open** 10am-6pm Mon-Fri; 10am-1pm Sat. **Credit** AmEx, DC, MC, V. **Map** p246 C3.
This Hungarian bedding expert specialises in pure wool, non-allergenic comforters and pillows, in addition to back and neck-sparing 'bio-system' beds. **Branches**: Margit körút 29A (212 4108); MOM Park, Csörsz utca 45 (487 5650).

Hephaistos Háza

V. Molnár utca 27 (266 1550). M3 Ferenciek tere/bus 7. **Open** 11am-6pm Mon-Fri; 10am-2pm Sat. **Credit** MC, V. **Map** p246 D3.
Eszter Gál's light design defies the weight and austerity of wrought iron. Encompasses everything from beds to candelabras; made to order.

Holló Folkart Gallery

V. Vitkovics Mihály utca 12 (317 8103). M2 Astoria/tram 47, 49/bus 7. **Open** 10am-6pm Mon-Fri; 10am-1pm Sat. **Credit** AmEx, DC, MC, V. **Map** p249 C4.

As authentic as it gets, László Holló's traditional folk decoratives are matched in naive and simple beauty with original work from the countryside. Mostly wooden painted artefacts and pottery.

IKEA

XIV. Örs vezér tere (460 3100). M2 Örs vezér tere. **Open** 10am-8pm Mon-Sat; 10am-6pm Sun. **Credit** MC, V.
A recent extension scheme expanded the retail space into a hangar full of bare necessities.

Impresszió

V. Károly körút 10 (266 6700). M2 Astoria/tram 47, 49/bus 7. **Open** 10am-7pm Mon-Fri; 10am-2pm Sat. **No credit cards**. **Map** p249 D4.
Tiny shop in a courtyard with various other fashion outlets. The perfect antidote to urban beige minimalism, Impresszió seduces with its colourful, natural shapes.

Kátay

VI. Teréz körút 28 (311 0116). M1 Oktogon/tram 4, 6. **Open** 9.30am-6.30pm Mon-Fri; 9.30am-2pm Sat. **Credit** AmEx, DC, MC, V. **Map** p246 D3.
Excellent shop for things to put in the kitchen, fix up the bathroom, tidy the garden and set the table.

Magma

V. Petőfi Sándor utca 11 (235 0277/235 0278). M3 Ferenciek tere/bus 7. **Open** 10am-7pm Mon-Fri; 10am-3pm Sat. **Credit** DC, MC, V. **Map** p249 C4.
Exclusively shows and sells local handiwork by a collective of talented artisans, breaking the mould set by the more folksy merchants on nearby Váci. Fashion, glass and pottery. *See p129* **Smart art**.

Vasedény 1,000 Aprócikk

V. Bajcsy-Zsilinszky út 3 (269 6620). M1, M2, M3 Deák tér/tram 47, 49. **Open** 9am-6pm Mon-Fri; 9am-1pm Sat. **Credit** AmEx, DC, MC, V. **Map** p249 C4.
If you melt the gasket in your espresso-maker, this is where to get a new one, as well as 999 other household gadgets and spare parts.

Fashion

Accessories & jewellery

Bartha
*V. Károly körút 22 (317 6234). M3 Ferenciek tere/
M2 Astoria/tram 47, 49.* **Open** 10am-6pm Mon-Fri.
Credit MC, V. **Map** p249 C4.
This tiny shop designs and produces original gold
and silver jewellery, mostly in art deco style.

Craft Design
VI. Klauzál tér 1 (322 4006). Tram 4, 6. **Open**
10am-6pm Mon-Fri. **Credit** MC, V. **Map** p246 D3.
Ilona Ács's artistic vision dominates in this quiet
corner shop full of high-quality leather wallets,
handbags and accessories, all of which are handmade on the premises.

Ékes Kesztyű
V. Régiposta utca 14 (266 0986). M3 Ferenciek tere.
Open 10am-6pm Mon-Fri; 10am-1pm Sat. **Credit**
AmEx, DC, MC, V. **Map** p249 C4.
A family-run and nonchalantly operated artisan
store since 1883, Ékes makes gloves in various
leathers, including boarskin, by hand.

City Áruház
*V. Városház utca 1 (318 5191 ext 500). M3
Ferenciek tere/bus 7.* **Open** 10am-6pm Mon-Fri;
10am-2pm Sat. **Credit** AmEx, MC, V. **Map** p249 C4.
Also known as 'Manager Shop', City Áruház
stocks everything in the executive department:
cufflinks, ties, shirts, pens, calendars and diaries,
and very executive knickers. Best range of
Samsonite in town.
Branches: V. Váci utca 78-80 (267 6223);
Westend City Center, VI. Váci út 1-3 (238 7706).

Girardi Kalapház
XIII. Szent István körút 26 (340 4396). Tram 2, 4, 6.
Open *Winter* 10am-6pm Mon-Fri; 10am-1pm Sat.
Summer 10am-5.30pm Mon-Fri. **No credit cards.**
Map p246 C2.
Handmade hats have always enjoyed popularity in
the Hungarian haute bourgeoisie's wardrobe and
Girardi caters to the head held high.

M. Frey Wille
*V. Régiposta utca 19 (318 7665). M1, M2, M3 Deák
tér/tram 47, 49.* **Open** 10am-6pm Mon-Fri; 10am-
2pm Sat. **Credit** AmEx, DC, MC, V. **Map** p249 C4.
Gustav Klimt inspires this Austrian collection of fine
jewellery and accessories in enamelled gold.

Ómama Bizsuja
V. Szent István körút 1 (312 6812). Tram 2, 4, 6.
Open 10am-6pm Mon-Fri; 10am-2pm Sat. **No credit
cards.** **Map** p246 C2.
A treasure trove of nifty antique bijoux – display
cases of rhinestones, beads of all sorts, semi-precious
stones and silverwork – all at extremely reasonable
prices. This branch also features vintage clothes.
Branch: II. Frankel Leó utca 7 (312 0807).

Varga Design
V. Haris köz 1 (318 3221). M3 Ferenciek tere/bus 7.
Open 10am-6pm Mon-Fri; 10am-2pm Sat. **Credit**
AmEx, DC, MC, V. **Map** p249 C4.
Miklós Varga's pieces are made of platinum, Tahiti
pearl, gold and silver. Original design too.

Viktoria-R
V. Haris köz 6 (266 7638). M3 Ferenciek tere/bus 7.
Open 10am-6pm Mon-Fri; 10am-2pm Sat. **Credit**
AmEx, DC, MC, V. **Map** p249 C4.
From pens to bags, Montegrappa, Pininfarina, ST
Dupont and Cartier accessories lure the luxury lover
into this elegant store in the heart of local tag-land.
Especially strong on men's status quo essentials.

Violetta Kalapszalon
*V. Régiposta udvar 7-9 (266 0421). M1, M2, M3
Deák tér/tram 47, 49.* **Open** *Winter* 10am-6pm Mon-
Fri; 10am-1pm Sat. *Summer* noon-6pm Mon-Fri; Sat
by appointment. **No credit cards.** **Map** p249 C4.
Handmade hats in all styles, fabrics and colours,
plus repairs and dry-cleaning.

Clothing

Anda Emilia
*V. Váci utca 16B (06 30 933 9746). M3 Ferenciek
tere/bus 7.* **Open** noon-6pm Mon-Fri; 11am-2pm Sat.
Credit AmEx, MC, V. **Map** p249 C4.
One of the most revered couturiers in the industry,
Anda designs soft, structural women's collections.
Wladis jewellery also available.

Artista
*VIII. Puskin utca 19 (328 0290). M2 Astoria/tram
47, 49/bus 7.* **Open** by appointment. **No credit
cards.** **Map** p249 D4.
The label stands for six quirky designers on the cutting edge. The collections reflect inspirations and
impressions, cut out of lavish fabrics.

Christina Designer Shop
*V. Semmelweis utca 8 (266 8009). M2 Astoria/tram
47, 49/bus 7.* **Open** 10am-6pm Mon-Fri; 10am-1pm
Sat. **Credit** AmEx, DC, MC, V. **Map** p249 D4.
On one side, embroidered sheets, lace and tablecloths. On the other, things made from luxurious 100
per cent cotton terry, such as bathrobes and beach
wraps. Also beach bags, slippers and swimsuits, all
in bright summer colours and made in-house.

Classic Line
*VI. Andrássy út 28 (331 2837/243 1413). M1
Opera.* **Open** 10am-6pm Mon-Fri; 10am-1pm Sat.
Credit MC, V. **Map** p246 D3.
Suits, evening wear and accessories for men fill the
store to capacity with Italian and French couture.

Fidji Couture
*V. Haris köz 5 (318 2565). M3 Ferenciek tere/
bus 7.* **Open** 10am-6pm Mon-Wed, Fri; 10am-7pm
Thur; 10am-3pm Sat. **Credit** AmEx, DC, MC, V.
Map p249 C4.

Ostentatious outrage for women, somewhat sombre suits for men, as well as a rather colourful selection of must-have accessories.

Hampe Katalin

V. Váci utca 8 (318 9741). M1 Vörösmarty tér/tram 2. **Open** 10am-6pm Mon-Fri; 10am-1pm Sat. **Credit** AmEx, MC, V. **Map** p249 C4.
Katalin Hampe adapts historical Hungarian wear to today's standards and comfort. A small selection of original folklore also on sale.

Katti Zoób

V. Deák Ferenc tér 1 (486 0377). M1, M2, M3 Deák tér/tram 47, 49. **Open** 10am-8pm Mon-Fri; 10am-7pm Sat; 10am-3pm Sun. **Credit** AmEx, DC, MC, V. **Map** p249 C4.
Arguably the most business-oriented line, Zoób's design ranges from luxurious couture showpieces to her 'biznisz luk', a Donna Karan-esque take on women's suits and essentials.
Branch: MOM Park, XII. Alkotás utca 53 (487 5609).

Luan by Lucia

VI. Bajcsy Zsilinszky út 62 (331 6675). M1 Bajcsy-Zsilinszky út. **Open** by appointment. **Credit** AmEx, DC, MC, V. **Map** p246 C3.
Lucia S Hegyi's work screams bespoke tailoring in lavish fabrics – and a sartorial expression of the client's personality, elegant and haut bourgeois.

Manier

V. Nyáry Pál utca 4 (483 1140). M3 Ferenciek tere/bus 7. **Open** by appointment. **Credit** AmEx, MC, V. **Map** p249 C5.
Hardly street-smart, more theatrical couture, Anikó Németh creates eccentric women's gear to order in the atelier or buy off the peg in the store. Fine copper and silver clothing items and stunning accessories by Timea Balák.
Branch: V. Váci utca 68 (483 1141).

Náray Tamas

V. Károlyi Mihály utca 12 (266 2473). M3 Ferenciek tere/bus 7. **Open** noon-8pm Mon-Fri; 10am-2pm Sat. **Credit** AmEx, MC, V. **Map** p249 C4.
Náray dresses women caught in a Nina Ricci time warp – the collection is status design with a good selection of matching accessories.

Ninnillo

V. Galamb utca 7A (318 2462). M3 Ferenciek tere/bus 7. **Open** 10am-6pm Mon-Fri; 10am-2pm Sat. **Credit** MC, V. **Map** p249 C4.
Full of sex appeal, this smart little store should have your number in D&G, Ferrè, Cavalli and Moschino Jeans.

Vasseva

VI. Paulay Ede utca 67 (342 8159). M1 Opera. **Open** noon-8pm Mon-Fri; noon-3pm Sat. **Credit** AmEx, MC, V. **Map** p246 D3.
Éva Vass's minimalist store proffers her casual, clever design in everything from clothing to bedding and accessories.

Verri Sport Dodi's

V. Galamb utca 7B (06 30 234 1856). M3 Ferenciek tere/bus 7. **Open** 10am-6pm Mon-Fri; 10am-1pm Sat. **Credit** MC, V. **Map** p249 C4.
No better place to hunt for designer-label men's accessories, this Italophile store offers a variety of high-profile fashion items. Etro, Dolce & Gabbana and D&G, plus less sexy Ralph Lauren dominate.

White Spot

V. Galamb utca 9 (318 5043). M3 Ferenciek tere/bus 7. **Open** 10am-6pm Mon-Fri; 10am-1pm Sat. **Credit** MC, V. **Map** p249 C4.
Made-to-measure womenswear by Gizella Végső and Rózsa Márton, the collection mostly features sexy little dresses with an edge.

Costume hire

Revü Art

VI. Jókai tér 4 (331 2575). M1 Oktogon/tram 4, 6. **Open** 9am-3pm Mon-Thur; 9am-1.30pm Fri. **No credit cards.** **Map** p246 D3.
Mostly dancing gear and animal costumes to rent, with quasi-evening gowns thrown in.

Shoes & leather goods

La Boutique

VI. Andrássy út 16 (302 5646). M1 Opera. **Open** 10am-7pm Mon-Fri; 10am-6pm Sat. **Credit** AmEx, DC, V. **Map** p246 D3.
These shoes might not be made for walking, but they certainly impress. One of the best collections of fine imported designer styles, including Dolce & Gabbana. Very strong men's selection.
Branch: Le Meridien, V. Erzsébet tér 9-10 (267 4545).

Humanic

V. Váci utca 26 (266 3536). M3 Ferenciek tere/bus 7. **Open** 10am-6.30pm Mon-Fri; 10am-5pm Sat. **Credit** AmEx, MC, V. **Map** p249 C4.
The improved Humanic chain has emerged from the mass market as a trendy and at times elegant, affordable and convenient alternative to the more expensive boutiques.
Branch: II. Margit körút 49 (212 5736).

Kaláka Studio

V. Haris köz 2. M3 Ferenciek tere/bus 7. **Open** 10am-6pm Mon-Wed, Fri; 10am-7pm Thur; 10am-2pm Sat. **No credit cards.** **Map** p249 C4.
Simple shoes in soft, pastel suede are Ágnes Bodor's trademark. Match an outfit you already have, or pick something new from the small but solid selection of local designer frocks on the other side of the shop.

Mare

V. Aranykéz utca 1 (337 5442). M3 Ferenciek tere/bus 7. **Open** 10.30am-6.30pm Mon-Fri; 10am-2pm Sat. **Credit** MC, V. **Map** p249 C4.
Top-quality Italian shoes for men and women, for occasions when black and sex appeal are needed.

Eat, Drink, Shop

Anda Emilia couture. *See p131.*

Shoemakers & handmade shoes

Cipőkészítő GMK

*IX. Vámház körút 7 (218 7893). M3 Kálvin tér/
tram 47, 49.* **Open** 10am-5.30pm Mon-Fri; 10am-
12.30pm Sat. **No credit cards. Map** p249 D5.
Simple shoes and sandals all handmade by this local
cobbler. Samples copied and orthopaedic shoes sold.

Vass

V. Haris köz 2 (318 2375). M3 Ferenciek tere/bus 7.
Open 10am-6pm Mon-Fri; 10am-3pm Sat. **Credit**
AmEx, DC, MC, V. **Map** p249 C4.
Internationally renowned and boasting a faithful
clientele, the Manolo Blahnik of Hungary makes fine
men's shoes in excellent quality leather, also custom-
made to order. Prices are comparable to designer
labels. Limited women's collection.

Zábrák Shoes

*Kempinski Hotel, V. Erzsébet tér 7-8 (266 8175).
M1, M2, M3 Deák tér/tram 47, 49.* **Open** 9am-6pm
Mon-Fri; 9am-2pm Sat. **Credit** AmEx, DC, MC, V.
Map p249 C4.
Similar to Vass (*see above*), this family business
makes high-quality footwear, off the rack or to order.

Tailors

Eurotailors

*Hotel Inter-Continental, V. Apáczai Csere János utca
12-14 (327 6566). M1 Vörösmarty tér/tram 2.*
Open 10am-8pm Mon-Fri; 10am-1pm Sat; also by
appointment. **Credit** AmEx, MC, V. **Map** p249 C4.

This Hong Kong-based tailoring company, in the
Inter-Continental Budapest's shopping corner in the
lobby, offers made-to-measure suits and shirts for
men, and suits and dresses for women.

Ingkészítő

*VI. Nagymező utca 7 (267 4756; www.ingkeszito.hu).
M1 Opera.* **Open** 10am-6pm Mon-Fri; 10am-1pm Sat.
Credit MC, V. **Map** p246 D3.
Ms Schreiner's thriving small business has seen and
survived history, and her tiny corner shop is still
making the most exquisite shirts to order.

Merino-Szivárvány

*V. Petőfi Sándor utca 18 (318 7332). M1, M2, M3
Deák tér/tram 47, 49.* **Open** 10am-6pm Mon-Fri;
9.30am-1.30pm Sat. **Credit** AmEx, MC, V. **Map** p249
C4.
Founded at the turn of the century and preserving
the feel of an old-fashioned dry goods store, Merino-
Szivárvány has fine lace, velvet silks and woollens
stacked up on wide shelves lining wood-panelled
walls. You can pick out something to be specially
made up by a local designer here, or visit the shop's
tailor located below XIII. Pannónia utca 19 (320
5077). Women's fittings only.

Prinyi Zoltán

*V. Vitkovics Mihály utca 7 (338 4235). M3 Ferenciek
tere/bus 7.* **Open** 10am-7pm Mon-Fri; 10am-5pm Sat.
No credit cards. Map p249 C4.
Quintessentially Hungarian suits make up the
exquisite work of this specialist tailor's shop. All the
outfits here have been delicately handstitched to the
most minute detail.

Artista – one label, six cutting-edge designers. *See p131.*

Tangó Classic

V. Váci utca 8 (267 6647). M1, M2, M3 Deák tér/ tram 47, 49. **Open** 10am-6pm Mon-Fri; 10am-1pm Sat. **Credit** AmEx, MC, V. **Map** p249 C4.

Quick couture is at hand if you need something chic in a day at Tangó Classic, which integrates antique fabrics into new design – the style is very pre-war high society. Off the rack also available.

Taylor & Schneider

VI. Nagymező utca 29 (302 7951). M1 Opera. **Open** 7am-5pm Mon-Thur; 7am-2pm Fri. **No credit cards. Map** p246 D3.

You can have a complete suit made up – either bring your own material or choose from a selection of sober woollens.

Vintage & second-hand clothing

Ciánkáli

VII. Dohány utca 94 (215 9714). M2 Blaha Lujza tér/tram 4, 6. **Open** 10am-7pm Mon-Fri; 9am-1pm Sat. **No credit cards. Map** p249 D4.

Ciánkáli stocks the best collection of vintage clothes in the city. Loads of polyester, shoes, jewellery and leather jackets.

Gólya Áruház

VI. Király utca 52-54 (322 2058). M1 Opera. **Open** 9.30am-6pm Mon-Fri. **Credit** MC, V. **Map** p246 D3.

The legendary Gólya now features second-hand clothing cleaned to look like new.

Iguana

VIII. Krúdy Gyula utca 9 (317 1627). Tram 4, 6. **Open** 10am-7pm Mon-Fri; 10am-2pm Sat. **No credit cards. Map** p249 D5.

Scores of funky duds from the 1960s and 1970s and even some accessories: sunglasses, Indian jewellery, belts, bags and the like. Shop to old hip hop tunes under a flashy turquoise and orange ceiling mural – and let tack be your guide.

Branch: IX. Tompa utca 1 (215 3475).

Flea markets

Budapest's three main flea markets offer you the collected toot of eastern Europe. *See p137* **A load of old junk.**

Ecseri piac

XIX. Nagykőrösi út 156. Bus 52. **Open** 8am-4pm Mon-Fri; 7am-3pm Sat. **No credit cards.**

Budapest's biggest and most obscure.

Józsefvárosi piac

VII. Kőbányai út 21-23. Tram 28, 37. **Open** 6am-6pm daily. **No credit cards.**

Discount stalls have spread over the flea market in this Chinese empire of cheap, imported goods.

Városligeti Bolhapiac

Petőfi Csarnok, XIV. Zichy Mihály út (251 2485). M1 Széchenyi fürdő. **Open** 7am-2pm Sat, Sun. **No credit cards. Map** p247 F2.

Ecseri Jr, in a more central (and tranquil) location.

Folkart Centrum
V. Váci utca 58 (318 4697). M3 Ferenciek tere/bus 7.
Open 10am-7pm daily. **Credit** AmEx, DC, MC, V.
Map p249 C4.
The best bet for folk items on Váci; hundreds of local artists sell their wares here. Wooden knick-knacks, embroidery and clothing, plus rugs and pottery.

Judit Folklór
I. Országház utca 12 (375 1180). Várbusz from M2 Moszkva tér. **Open** 9.30am-6.30pm daily. **Credit** AmEx, MC, V. **Map** p245 A3.
Dyed fabrics, pottery, embroidery and accessories made in various folk styles are featured here.

Népművészeti Bolt
VII. Rákóczi út 32 (342 0753). M2 Blaha Lujza tér/tram 4, 6. **Open** 10am-6pm Mon-Fri; 10am-1pm Sat. **No credit cards.** **Map** p249 D4.
Off the central folk track, this quiet boutique stocks lovely woodwork, pottery and textiles.

Ceramics, glass & pottery

Ajka Kristály
V. József Attila utca 7 (317 8133). M1 Vörösmarty tér. **Open** 10am-6pm Mon-Fri; 10am-1pm Sat. **Credit** AmEx, MC, V. **Map** p249 C4.
The Fotex Group's takeover of the ailing crystal company catapulted it and its design back into the present tense, although some of the patterns are best explained away as retro. Still, the work is high quality and produces beautiful vases and glasses.
Branches: V. Kígyó utca 4 (318 3712); VI. Teréz körút 50 (332 4541).

Herend Porcelain
V. József Nádor tér 11 (318 9200). M1 Vörösmarty tér. **Open** 10am-6pm Mon-Fri; 9am-1pm Sat. **Credit** AmEx, DC, MC, V. **Map** p249 C4.
Herend has produced Hungary's finest porcelain since 1826; Queen Victoria picked out its delicate bird and butterfly pattern to put on her own table.
Branch: V. Kígyó utca 5 (318 3439).

Hollóházi Porcelán Márkabolt
Csillag Áruház, VII. Rákóczi út 20-22 (351 0463 ext 120). M2 Blaha Lujza tér/tram 4, 6. **Open** 10am-6pm Mon-Fri; 10am-1pm Sat. **Credit** AmEx, MC, V. **Map** p249 D4.
Another local household name, Hollóházi porcelain has long cheered up Hungarian homes with its hand-painted happy patterns. Tableware and gift items are also available.
Branches: Campona, XXII. Nagytétényi út 37-43 (424 3156); X. Ligeti út 11 (260 5976).

Majolika
V. Váci utca 46 (266 3165). M3 Ferenciek tere/bus 7. **Open** 10am-7pm Mon-Sat. **Credit** AmEx, DC, MC, V. **Map** p249 C4.
This small store showcases the very simplest folklore-inspired pottery – excellent value and tremendously functional in a colourful way.

Flowers

Interflora
XII. Ugocsa utca 6B (225 0328). Tram 59. **Open** 9am-5pm Mon-Fri; 9am-noon Sat. **No credit cards.**
Only catalogues at the above address. Interflora will deliver your order up until 4.30pm.

Sasplant
V. Irányi János utca 15 (317 7005). M3 Ferenciek tere/bus 7. **Open** 8am-7pm Mon-Fri; 8am-2pm Sat. **No credit cards.** **Map** p249 C4.
Excellent florist for beautiful bouquets and house plants. Decorative accessories made of dried plants, leaves, stems and the like are also available.

Yucca
V. Váci utca 54 (337 3307). M3 Ferenciek tere/bus 7. **Open** 9am-6pm Mon-Fri; 9am-2pm Sat. **No credit cards.** **Map** p249 C4.
Delightful speciality flowers from orchids to irises. Dried flowers and house plants too.

Folklore

Váci utca flogs the folklore theme to death. Embroidery on tablecloths and shirts, leather accessories from whips to pouches, and pottery for all purposes grace the numerous stores. The stands lining Deák Ferenc utca, the embankment on Vigadó tér and Kristóf tér all specialise in leather goods.

Eat, Drink, Shop

Zsolnay Porcelain

V. Kígyó utca 4 (318 3712). M3 Ferenciek tere/bus 7.
Open 10am-6pm Mon-Fri; 10am-1pm Sat. **Credit**
AmEx, MC, V. **Map** p249 C4.

Herend's heavyweight alternative, Zsolnay's
designs are more free-flowing and better suited to
the art nouveau patterns it commonly uses. Most
famous for a patented weatherproof glaze developed
around the late 19th century, which also graces the
mosaic roof tiles on Matthias Church, the Central
Market and the Applied Arts Museum. The firm
spent much of the Communist era producing power
line insulators, before happily returning to fine
porcelain. Bold new patterns of late.

Food & drink

For more information about Hungarian wines,
see p98 **Unknown pleasures**.

Drinks

1000 Teas

V. Váci utca 65 (337 8217). M3 Ferenciek tere/bus 7.
Open noon-9pm Mon-Fri; 11am-9pm Sat; 3-8pm Sun.
No credit cards. Map p249 C4.

The world's finest teas, with no artificial flavours.
Also doubles as a teahouse in the afternoons.

Borpatika

II. Margit utca 27 (326 4984). Tram 4, 6. **Open** 9am-
7.30pm Mon-Fri; 10am-3pm Sat. **No credit cards**.

This small new shop stocks about 300 types of
Hungarian wine and 20 imports.

Budapest Wine Society

I. Batthyány utca 59 (212 2569). M2 Batthyány tér.
Open 10am-8pm Mon-Fri; 10am-6pm Sat. **Credit**
AmEx, MC, V. **Map** p245 B2.

The best wines from all over Hungary presided over
by knowledgeable staff. Free tastings on Saturday
afternoons between 2pm and 5pm.

Coquan's Kávé

*IX. Ráday utca 15 (215 2444). M3 Kálvin tér/tram
47, 49.* **Open** 8am-8pm Mon-Fri; 9am-5pm Sat, Sun.
No credit cards. Map p249 D5.

Imported coffee beans roasted daily on the premises.
Very good tea selection. Also a café.
Branch: V. Nádor utca 5 (266 9936).

In Vino Veritas

*VII. Dohány utca 58-62 (341 3174/341 0646). M1,
M2, M3 Deák tér.* **Open** 9am-8pm Mon-Fri; 10am-
6pm Sat. **No credit cards. Map** p249 D4.

Excellent overview of local vintners' output. The
selection is top quality, the staff eager to help.

Hypermarkets & supermarkets

Kaiser's

VI. Nyugati tér (374 0294). M3 Nyugati/tram 4, 6.
Open 7am-8pm Mon-Fri; 7am-1pm Sat. **Credit**
AmEx, MC, V. **Map** p246 C2.

Supermarket entrance right ahead of you at underground level as you come out of Nyugati metro.
Branch: XI. Október 23 utca 6-10 (385 0189).

Rothschild

*VII. Károly körút 9 (342 9733). M1, M2, M3 Deák
tér/tram 47, 49.* **Open** 7am-10pm Mon-Fri; 7am-6pm
Sat; 9am-5pm Sun. **Credit** DC, MC, V. **Map** p249 C4.

Imported food and wine, plus kosher food. Free next-
day delivery for purchases over Ft5,000.
Branch: XIII. Szent István körút 4 (329 3566).

Tesco

XIV. Fogarasi út 15 (467 6800). **Open** 24hrs daily.
Credit AmEx, DC, MC, V.

The English retail chain's local branches, like the
rest, flog bulk and cheap. The old Brit treats section
is now reduced to a minimal selection.
Branch: XV. Szentmihályi út 131 (417 1991).

Markets & food halls

Hold utcai vásárcsarnok

V. Hold utca 13 (332 3976). M2 Kossuth tér. **Open**
6.30am-5pm Mon; 6.30am-6pm Tue-Fri; 6.30am-2pm
Sat. **No credit cards. Map** p246 C3.

Gem of a food hall with its lines of fresh farm produce and food counters, right by Parliament.

Vámház körúti vásárcsarnok

IX. Vámház körút 1-3 (217 6067). Tram 2.
Open 6am-5pm Mon; 6am-6pm Tue-Fri; 6am-2pm
Sat. **Map** p249 D5.

This popular food hall, renovated to its original
glory ten years ago, is in a prime spot at one end of
Váci utca – but has a reputation for rude service.

Speciality food

Ázsia

*IX. Vámház körút 1 (217 6067 ext 252). M3 Kálvin
tér.* **Open** 10am-5pm Mon; 7am-6pm Tue-Fri; 7am-
2pm Sat. **No credit cards. Map** p249 D5.

This is expat home-cooking central, reflected in the
prices. All the basics for Asian, Indian and Italian
cuisine, including fancy sauces, black beans, taco
shells, frozen squid and a glorious selection of spices.

Béres Egészségtár

VI. Bajcsy köz 1 (311 0009). M3 Arany János utca.
Open 9am-7pm Mon-Fri; 9am-1pm Sat. **Credit** DC,
MC, V. **Map** p246 C3.

Hungary's first alternative treatment specialist and
the product range he inspired, starting with Béres
drops to boost immunity. A wide range of natural
beauty products, vitamins, oils, teas and incense.

Bio-ABC

*V. Múzeum körút 19 (317 3043). M2 Astoria/tram
47, 49/bus 7.* **Open** 10am-7pm Mon-Fri; 10am-2pm
Sat. **Credit** MC, V. **Map** p249 D5.

Soy milk and sausages, carrot juice, organic produce,
wholegrains, natural cosmetics, herbal teas, oils,
medicinal herbs and jars of Marmite.

A load of old junk

A stroll around Budapest's flea markets confirms that the Carpathian Basin has been the black hole into which Europe's unwanted and unusable gifts and kitchen gadgets have drifted. But what is one man's junk is another's piece of history, and Budapest provides rich pickings for the curious traveller.

The mother of all flea markets (*bolha piac*) is **Ecseri** *(see p134)*, located in the middle of nowhere on the very western edge of town. The best time to go is on Saturday morning. The main market is a warren of antique dealers' shacks serving big buyers from the antique boutiques of Paris, Munich and Milan. Hot items are brass apothecary mortars, antique linen and old coal-fired clothes irons, but on Saturday the open areas are filled with weekend dealers spreading their wares on blankets and card tables. There are treasures to be found, but they are buried beneath the piles of Soviet-era cameras, East German toy cars, pottery, folk costumes, furniture and broken violins.

Nearer town is the weekend flea market at **Petőfi Csarnok** (pictured; *see p134*), located in the City Park and held each Saturday and Sunday morning. Junk outnumbers antiques but this is where you can find that wind-up Chinese Barbie to complete your collection, a set of old Polish Polaroid nudie pictures, Russian officers' pocket watches or prog rock 8-tracks. Transylvanian peasant women often line up here selling folk embroideries for a song.

For a truly unique trip, head out to the vast **Jozsefvárosi piac** *(see p134)*, also known as the Three Dragons Chinese Market, in the outlying district of Kőbánya. This is the main point of distribution for thousands of small family businesses from China that keep Eastern Europeans supplied with cheap underwear, running shoes, polyester jumpers and pink plastic hairclips. It enjoys a mysterious legal autonomy, run as a fiefdom by the private security force of a former Interior Minister and off-limits to city and district officials and inspectors. The guarded entrances forbidding guns, cameras and dogs guarantee your safety, however. The junk is not as interesting as the sellers, a mix of Chinese, Uzbeks, Vietnamese and various Balkanoids speaking a hybrid market language all their own. The snack stands on the north wall can provide some of the best Vietnamese spring rolls and Mandarin meat dumplings in town.

Eat, Drink, Shop

Dóczy Delicatessen

I. Országház utca 16 (212 3761).Várbusz from M2 Moszkva tér. **Open** 9am-6pm Tue-Fri; 10am-6pm Sat, Sun. **Credit** AmEx, MC, V. **Map** p245 A3.

This mouthwatering selection of foodstuffs gives you plenty of ideas for typically Magyar gastronomic gifts perfect for taking home and frightening your loved ones with: *pálinka* (strong fruit schnapps), Unicum (*see p113* **Kill or cure**), goose liver pâté, salami and sweet Tokaj wine.

Lekvárium

VII. Dohány utca 39 (321 6543). M2 Astoria/tram 47, 49/bus 7. **Open** 10am-6pm Mon-Fri. **No credit cards. Map** p249 D4.

The tradition of home-made preserves and jams is upheld in this quaint old boutique. Delicious nuts in honey are also available.

Pick

V. Kossuth Lajos tér 9 (331 7783). M2 Kossuth tér/ tram 2. **Open** 6am-7pm Mon-Fri. **No credit cards. Map** p246 C2.

Trademark Pick Salami's cold cuts, salami and meat products fill this store/buffet. Many of the products on offer are usefully packaged to keep for longer and will transport easily.

Rothschild Kóser Élelmiszer

VII. Dob utca 12 (267 5691). M1, M2, M3 Deák tér/tram 47, 49. **Open** 8.30am-6pm Mon-Thur; 8.30am-2.30pm Fri. **Credit** MC, V. **Map** p249 D4.

Israeli import shop filling the needs of the orthodox. Nifty tins, ramen noodles, sweets and exotic nuts.

Szamos Marcipán

V. Párizsi utca 3 (317 3643). M1, M2, M3 Deák tér/tram 47, 49. **Open** 10am-8pm daily. **No credit cards. Map** p249 C4.

The sweetest sweets in marzipan and chocolate, novelty figurines and hand-dipped treats, also boxed. In summer the store sells excellent ice-cream, most popular from its branch at the Zoo.

Branches: XII. Böszörményi út 44-46 (355 1728); Zoo, XIV. Állatkerti út 6-12 (no phone).

T Nagy Tamás Sajtüzlete

V. Gerlóczy utca 3 (317 4268). M1, M2, M3 Deák tér/tram 47, 49. **Open** 10am-6pm Mon-Fri; 9am-1pm Sat. **No credit cards. Map** p249 C4.

Some of the bigger supermarkets have now begun to stock imported cheeses, but this central store remains by far the best in Budapest with around 150 types always in stock.

Health & beauty

Azúr

V. Petőfi Sándor utca 11 (318 5394). M3 Ferenciek tere/bus 7. **Open** 8am-8pm Mon-Fri; 9am-2pm Sat. **Credit** AmEx, MC, V. **Map** p249 C4.

All essential and mainstream cosmetics, perfumes, shampoos, toiletries, washing powders and various house-cleaning products.

Ilcsi Néni

V. Apáczai Csere János utca 5 (267 0343). M1 Vörösmarty tér/tram 2. **Open** 8am-7pm Mon-Fri; 8am-2pm Sat. **No credit cards. Map** p249 C4.

Hungary's own preservative-free beauty product range has a keen local following. These popular products are only available via certain individual beauty salons dotted around town – call 200 5603 for your nearest location.

Lush

V. Szent István körút 1 (472 0530). Tram 2, 4, 6. **Open** 10am-7pm Mon-Fri; 10am-2pm Sat. **Credit** MC, V. **Map** p246 C2.

Offers an enticing range of natural, organic beauty products at its two main branches.
Branch: MOM Park, II. Alkotás út 53 (no phone).

Beauty salons

Báthoryné Gellért Katalin

XIII. Tátra utca 28. Bus 15. **Open** by appointment. **No credit cards. Map** p246 C1.

Treatments and therapies to de-stress and revitalise in the hands of this recommended cosmetician.

Estée Lauder

V. Váci utca 12 (266 7829). M1, M2, M3 Deák tér. **Open** 10am-6pm Mon-Fri; 10am-2pm Sat. **Credit** AmEx, DC, MC, V. **Map** p249 C4.

Hungarian-born Estée Lauder's business occupies a boutique here and provides beauty treatments in the back of the exclusive salon.

Lancôme

V. Váci utca 14 (486 1760). M1, M2, M3 Deák tér/tram 47, 49. **Open** 8am-8pm Mon-Fri; 10am-2pm Sat, by appointment. **Credit** AmEx, DC, MC, V. **Map** p249 C4.

Full-feature pampering treats for the face or body. Lancôme's own products are also available in this stylish downtown location.

Hair salons

Essensuals

V. Bajcsy-Zsilinszky út 12 (266 8388). M1 Bajcsy-Zsilinszky út. **Open** 9am-9pm Mon-Fri; 9am-2pm Sat. **Credit** AmEx, DC, MC, V. **Map** p246 C3.

Toni&Guy's diffusion salon where the cool-headed congregate for a crazy coiffe. A fresh atmosphere prevails in the spacious and airy shop, and the staff are young. Tigi products also available.

Hajas

V. Erzsébet tér 2 (485 0170). M1, M2, M3 Deák tér/tram 47, 49. **Open** 7am-7pm Mon; 7am-9pm Tue-Fri; 7am-3pm Sat. **Credit** AmEx, DC, MC, V. **Map** p249 C4.

Still very much at the forefront of fashion, Hungary's veteran star stylist operates this very successful business for the local upper classes. Wella products are also available here.

Zsidró

VI. Andrássy út 17 (342 7366). M1 Opera. **Open**
8am-9pm Mon-Fri; 9am-2pm Sat. **Credit** AmEx, DC,
MC, V. **Map** p246 D3.
In his stylish snipping suite, Zsidró challenges the
famous Hajas empire with a more avant-garde take
on current hair styling.

Laundry & dry-cleaning

Home Laundry

*V. Galamb utca 9 (266 7694). M1, M2, M3 Deák
tér/tram 47, 49.* **Open** 8am-7.30pm Mon-Fri; 9am-
1pm Sat. **No credit cards. Map** p249 C4.
Very good-quality cleaning services in a handful of
locations make this an expat fave. Home pick-up and
delivery also available (200 5305).
Branch: XI. Németvölgyi út 53B (214 2902).

Irisz Szalon

*V. Városház utca 3-5 (266 4857). M1, M2, M3 Deák
tér.* **Open** 10am-6pm Mon-Fri. **No credit cards.**
Map p249 C4.
Charmingly nonchalant service at affordable prices.
Laundry service is also available.

Marriott Dry Cleaning

*V. Apáczai Csere János út 4 (235 4874). M1
Vörösmarty tér/tram 2.* **Open** 10am-6pm Mon-Fri.
Credit AmEx, DC, MC, V. **Map** p249 C4.
The best dry-cleaning in town by far. It is more
expensive than most but worth every forint. Also
does alterations and problem stain removals.
Separate entrance by Vigadó tér.

Medical services

American Clinics International

I. Hattyú utca 14 (224 9090). M2 Moszkva tér.
Open 24 hrs daily. **Credit** AmEx, DC, MC, V.
Map p245 A2.
The first full-service clinic dedicated to expats.
Staffed by Hungarian and US doctors.

Conway Health Services – Chiropractic

XI. Györök utca 2 (385 2515). Bus 12. **Open** by
appointment. **No credit cards.**
Long-established, certified US chiropractors.

Keresztesi Tamás – Dentistry

V. Balassi Bálint utca 27 (311 6598). Tram 2, 4, 6.
Open by appointment. **No credit cards.**
Map p246 C2.
Not just a dentist, more of a dental sculptor,
Dr Keresztesi's practice is impeccable and reason-
ably priced. Highly recommended.

SOS Dental Service

*VII. Király utca 14 (269 6010). M1, M2, M3
Deák tér.* **Open** 24 hrs daily. **No credit cards.**
Map p249 C4.
Round-the-clock dental service at reasonable prices.
The small door is marked with a red cross.

Music

Concerto Records

VII. Dob utca 33 (268 9631). Tram 4, 6. **Open**
noon-7pm Mon-Fri; noon-4pm Sun. **Credit** AmEx,
DC, MC, V. **Map** p246 D3.
Charming shop offering an impressive collection of
new and second-hand vinyl and CDs. The stock is
mainly classical with a little bit of jazz and folk.

Fonó Budai Zeneház

XI. Sztregova utca 3 (206 5300). Tram 47. **Open**
3-10pm Wed-Fri; 6-10pm Sat. **No credit cards.**
Far from the centre, but an excellent selection of local
folk, jazz and world music, and the shopping tour
will reward with details of live concerts here.

MCD

*V. Deák Ferenc utca 19 (318 6691). M1, M2, M3
Deák tér/tram 47, 49.* **Open** 10am-7pm daily.
No credit cards. Map p249 C4.
A central place to pick out any CD in any musical
style. Divided between pop and classical, there's
always something good in the sales racks.

Rózsavölgyi Zeneműbolt

*V. Szervita tér 5 (318 3500). M1, M2, M3 Deák
tér/tram 47, 49.* **Open** 9.30am-7pm Mon-Fri; 10am-
5pm Sat. **Credit** AmEx, DC, MC, V. **Map** p249 C4.
An institution. In the back of this old store you'll find
an excellent selection of classical, ballet and opera.
Big collection of sheet music as well, with folk and
popular music downstairs. Lots of cheap old vinyl.

Trancewave

VI. Révay köz 2 (302 2927). M3 Arany János utca.
Open *Autumn-spring* 11am-7pm Mon-Fri; 11am-2pm
Sat. *Summer* 11am-8pm Mon-Fri; noon-4pm Sat. **No
credit cards. Map** p246 C3.
A solid choice of alternative music, with a firm
emphasis on electronica. Vinyl dominates.

Wave

VI. Révay utca 4 (331 0718). M3 Arany János utca.
Open 11am-7pm Mon-Fri; 11am-3pm Sat. **No credit
cards. Map** p246 C3.
Run by young music lovers, this store specialises in
the underground scene and world music.

Opticians

Fotex-Optika

*V. Károly körút 12 (317 6005). M2 Astoria/tram 47,
49/bus 7.* **Open** 9am-6.30pm Mon-Fri; 9am-2pm Sat.
Credit AmEx, DC, MC, V. **Map** p249 D4.
Grand selection of imported designer label frames
makes this omnipresent chain's optical store
unavoidably useful. It offers free computerised
examinations if you order your eyewear here.

Optinova

*VI. Andrássy út 1 (267 8883). M1 Bajcsy-Zsilinszky
út.* **Open** 10am-6pm Mon-Fri; 10am-1pm Sat. **Credit**
AmEx, DC, MC, V. **Map** p246 C3.

Eat, Drink, Shop

The computerised eye examination is free when you order frames and lenses here, otherwise your old pair can be measured and new pairs made. Contacts and lenses, all German, are less expensive than in the west, but the imported frames will cost the same.

Photography

Fotex

V. Váci utca 9 (317 1911). M1, M2, M3 Deák tér/tram 47, 49. **Open** 9am-8pm Mon-Fri; 10am-7pm Sat; 10am-8pm Sun. **Credit** AmEx, DC, MC, V. **Map** p249 C4.

The ubiquitous Fotex chain's developing branch offers generous opening hours, plus cameras and accessories. Ofotért stores provide the same services. **Branch**: Ofotért, V. Károly körút 14 (317 6313).

Photo Hall

V. Károly körút 21 (411 0070). M1, M2, M3 Deák tér/tram 47, 49. **Open** 10am-6pm Mon-Fri; 9am-1pm Sat. **Credit** MC, V. **Map** p249 C4.

Besides film development, cameras and accessories, the store also scans paper photographs or film to file.

Second-hand cameras

Soós Kereskedés

V. József Attila utca 84 (317 2341). M1, M2, M3 Deák tér. **Open** 10am-5pm Mon-Fri; 10am-1pm Sat. **No credit cards. Map** p246 C3.

One set of display windows holds tacky gifts, the other rows of old cameras. Inside, walk past the bins of cheap junk to the back counter and side room, which houses more cameras, used enlargers, a film processing service and miscellaneous parts.

Repairs

Szakmai Tudakozó

269 3333. **Open** 8am-8pm daily.

Part of the directory services, the operator will direct you to the nearest repair shop for your appliance.

Alterations

Ruhaszerviz

V. Szervita tér 5 (317 9232). M1, M2, M3 Deák tér. **Open** 10am-6pm Mon-Fri; 10am-2pm Sat. **No credit cards. Map** p249 C4.

Too small, too wide, taking up, letting out – the seamstresses here will fix your outfits in short order.

Computer repair

AT Design

II. Erőd utca 16 (201 1843). Tram 4, 6. **Open** 9.45am-5.30pm Mon-Fri. **No credit cards.**

Diagnosis here is only complete with a mandatory headshake, but rest assured your computer will be fixed by this enthusiastic team of specialists.

Intercas

I. Iskola utca 4 (214 6109). Bus 5. **Open** 8am-4pm Mon-Thur; 8am-2pm Fri. **No credit cards. Map** p245 B3.

Authorised sale and service of Apple computers.

Luggage repair

Flekk GMK

VI. Podmaniczky utca 19 (311 0316). M3 Nyugati pu./ tram 4, 6. **Open** 9.30am-5.30pm Mon-Fri; 9am-1pm Sat. **No credit cards. Map** p246 D3.

There's a shop like this in nearly every neighbourhood where you can copy keys, fix your shoes or pick up an assortment of DIY supplies.

Shoe repair

Mister Minit

Skála Metro, VI. Nyugati tér (312 2836). M3 Nyugati pu./tram 4, 6. **Open** 9am-6.30pm Mon-Fri; 9am-2pm Sat. **No credit cards. Map** p246 C2.

This chain has locations all over Budapest for shoe repair, key cutting and knife sharpening.

Watch & jewellery repair

Orex Óraszalon

V. Petőfi Sándor utca 6 (266 6304). M3 Ferenciek tere/bus 7. **Open** 10am-6pm Mon-Fri; 10am-1pm Sat. **Credit** AmEx, DC, MC, V. **Map** p249 C4.

Many little family-run shops will be happy to change a battery or make a repair; the reliable staff at this location speak English.

Sport

T-Short

V. Váci utca 25 (337 9296). M1, M2, M3 Deák tér/tram 47, 49. **Open** 10am-4pm Mon-Thur; 10am-6pm Fri; 10am-noon Sat. **No credit cards. Map** p249 C4.

Small courtyard store announced by a window full of football pictures from the black-and-white era. *The* place downtown to find a local football club strip, woolly hats or scarves. **Branch**: V. Petőfi Sándor utca 2 (318 7018).

Travel

Vista

VI. Paulay Ede utca 7 (429 9950/www.vista.hu). M1, M2, M3 Deák tér/tram 47, 49. **Open** 9am-6.30pm Mon-Fri; 10am-4pm Sat. **Credit** AmEx, DC, MC, V. **Map** p246 C3.

The largest private travel agency also offers a handy separate location just off the main office to cater to incoming tourists. Services include accommodation, reservations, money exchange and excursions, but individual requests are welcome too. **Branch**: MOM Park, XII. Alkotás utca 53 (201 4546).

Eat, Drink, Shop

Arts & Entertainment

Features

Festivals & Events

Magyar rites hark back to a bitter past.

Budapesti Búcsú. *See p143.*

Budapest is bitter in winter and blazing hot in summer, with a mood that changes accordingly. A palpable sense of euphoria takes over when things start to warm up: people shed winter blues, clothes and inhibitions. Spring and autumn offer the gentlest, most agreeable weather. In the wilting heat of August, the city shuts down and leaves for the countryside.

Hungarian traditions have survived two World Wars and 40 years of Communism. Although Western greeting card conglomerates push new traditions, such as St Valentine's Day, Hungarians prefer to celebrate name days, each László or Krisztina choosing one of several days allotted to them in the calendar. Christmas is a family affair; New Year is a street party.

INFORMATION AND TICKETS
Information is available in the weekly English-language *Budapest Sun*, or the Hungarian *Pesti Est*, available free around the city. The offices listed below have more detailed programme information and flyers, and offer tickets for concerts, sporting and cultural events.

Broadway Ticket Office
VI. Nagymező utca 19 (302 3841/http://jegyiroda. victorinet.hu). M1 Opera. **Open** 10am-7pm Mon-Fri; 10am-2pm Sat. **No credit cards. Map** p246 D3.

Ticket Express Booking Office
VI. Andrássy út 18 (312 0000/www.tex.hu/v2). M1 Opera. **Open** 9.30am-6pm daily. **No credit cards. Map** p246 D3.
Branch: Mammut Center, II. Lövőház utca 2-6 (345 8020).

Tourinform
V. Sütő utca 2 (438 8080). M1, M2, M3 Deák tér/ tram 47, 49. **Open** 8am-8pm daily. **No credit cards. Map** p249 C4.

Vigadó Ticket Service
VI. Vörösmarty tér 1 (327 4322). M1 Vörösmarty tér/tram 2. **Open** 9am-7pm Mon-Fri. **No credit cards. Map** p249 C4.

PUBLIC HOLIDAYS
New Year's Day (1 Jan); **Revolution Day** (15 Mar); **Easter Monday**; **Labour Day** (1 May); **Whit Monday**; **St Stephen's Day** (20 Aug); **Remembrance Day** (23 Oct); **Christmas Day, Boxing Day** (25, 26 Dec).

Spring

The **Budapest Spring Festival** ushers in modest counterparts nationwide and signals the official beginning of the tourist season.

Revolution Day
Public holiday. **Date** 15 Mar.
Revolution Day commemorates poet Sándor Petőfi reciting his *Nemzeti Dal* ('National Song') on the steps of the National Museum in 1848, an event commonly held to have launched the national revolution. Gatherings at Petőfi's statue were illegal until 1990. Current mayor Gábor Demszky received a serious biffing by police for going to the statue back in his dissident days. Now he stands with an ironic smile on his face in the official ceremony with prominent politicians outside the National Museum. The city gets decked out in red, white and green.

Budapest Spring Festival

Tickets & information: Budapesti Fesztiválközpont,
V. Egyetem tér 5 (486 3311/www.fesztivalvaros.hu).
M3 Kálvin tér. **Open** *box office* 10am-5pm Mon-Fri.
Date 2wks end Mar/early Apr.

The most prestigious event in the arts calendar. A
smattering of internationally renowned talent from
the world of classical music – and local orchestras
and classical music stars – provide a fortnight of
concerts. It's also a showcase for art and drama.
Book early for big-name shows. *See also p169.*

Easter Monday

Public holiday. **Date** 12 Apr 2004; 28 Mar 2005.

The most drunken occasion in a calendar soaked
with them, Easter Monday is when the menfolk
of Budapest go door to door indulging in the pagan
rite of *locsolkodás* – spraying women with cheap
perfume and receiving a large *pálinka* in return.

Labour Day

Public holiday. **Date** 1 May.

No longer a forced wave at medal-festooned leaders
along Dózsa György út, May Day still brings a lot
of people to various entertainments in the city's
parks. Open-air May Day (*Majális*) events from pre-
Communist days are organised in village squares, a
more recent tradition being the rock festival at the
open-air stage in the Tabán in Buda.

Summer

Budapesters strip to the bare essentials as the
temperature climbs into the 40s. At weekends
and for most of August, locals leave the city to
the tourist hordes and head for their country
cottage or Lake Balaton. Don't even think about
doing any kind of business in Budapest after
10am on a Friday.

World Music Day

Date nearest weekend to 21 June.

Although a French invention, Hungary takes World
Music Day to heart. Nearly every town of any size
has some kind of concert, usually in the main hall or
square. In Budapest, while leading venues open their
doors to jazz, folk and rock musicians, stages are set
up for an eclectic array of international talent in open
spaces such as Városliget, Népliget and Klauzál tér.

Budapesti Búcsú

Information: Budapesti Fesztivalközpont, V. Egyetem
tér 5. (486 3311/www.fesztivalvaros.hu). M3
Kálvin tér. **Open** 10am-5pm Mon-Fri. **Date** last
weekend June.

More than a decade after the event, Budapest still
celebrates the withdrawal of Soviet troops from
Hungary. Open-air music and theatre events are
organised in main squares and parks.

Hungary's pagan rites

Rio has Carnival, New Orleans has Mardi
Gras and Hungary has *farsang*, a pagan-style
ritual Christianised to be the season of
partying before the Lenten fast. Although few
seem to observe the fasting part, many locals
still indulge in parties or grand formal balls.

The first farsang celebrations in Hungary
were based on the pagan traditions of
Serbian and Croatian settlers who moved to
the southern town of Mohács in the 1400s to
escape the encroaching Turks. Revellers
blowing horns, ringing bells and wearing scary
masks and brightly coloured clothes would
march through town in a noisy parade. Known
as the *Busójárás*, it was intended to scare
away the spirits of winter and bring on the
spring, before a wild party. By the time the
tradition came to Mohács, folklore had
expanded the mandate, as it was also
supposed to scare away the spirits of the
invaders. It was pretty ineffective, as in 1526
the Turks captured Mohács and used it as a
stepping stone to occupy most of Hungary.

Like other pagan rituals, the Busójárás
was adapted to Christianity. It became a
way to mark the end of what is called the

farsang season, a six-week celebration
that stops with the beginning of Lent, the
40 days before Easter when Christians
traditionally fast.

In Mohács, they still hold the Busójárás,
and participants in the parade wear primitive,
pagan-couture masks, made of wood, fabric
and string. The celebration means a week
of drinking and sporting disguises in an
otherwise sleepy town, and brings out the
naughty beast in the locals.

In Budapest, the well-to-do put on their
own version of farsang fashion: monkey suits
and ballgowns, or fancy dress. This harks
back to the days when Hungary was ruled
by aristocrats, who made farsang their
season for parties.

These days a number of clubs and bars
hold their own farsang parties for regular folk,
though these don't often involve costumes.
On one weekend in January, some hearty
souls brave the cold to hold a costume
procession that mirrors Mohács. They
valiantly march across the Chain Bridge to
Vörösmarty tér, where there's a party, with
prizes going for best costume.

One-offs Harry Houdini

Escape artist, illusionist and father of the crass public event, Harry Houdini was born Eric Weissz on Dohány utca in 1874. The son of a Hungarian Jewish rabbi, Weissz moved to America in 1878 when his father was appointed rabbi at the Zion Reformed Jewish Congregation in Appleton, Wisconsin.

Inspired by the French illusionist Houdin, young Eric changed his name and developed an astounding repertoire of escape acts, which included being chained and dropped into rivers in a barrel, thrown over waterfalls in a straitjacket, and locked inside a safe and dropped to the bottom of New York harbour.

He was particularly talented in a most Hungarian art – self-promotion – and almost single-handedly founded the modern institution of the inane international superstar.

Houdini's performances drew thousands and commercial sponsorships made him a wealthy man. He died on Hallowe'en in 1926, in Dayton, Ohio, of peritonitis caused by a fan punching him to test his muscles. Although Houdini's final years were spent debunking occultists after a quack seer failed to find his beloved mother up there in the ether, magicians still celebrate Houdini by trying to contact him at seances every Hallowe'en.

Bridge Festival
Information: Budapest Tourism Office, VI. Liszt Ferenc tér 9-11 (322 4098/www.budapestinfo.hu). M1 Oktogon/tram 4, 6. **Open** 9am-5pm Mon-Fri. **Date** end June.
The Chain Bridge is closed for a day to celebrate its arrival in 1849 with fireworks and boat processions.

Bastille Day
Institut Français, I. Fő utca 17 (489 4200/ www.ins-francais.hu). M2 Batthyány tér/bus 86. **Date** 14 July, from 8pm.
This free open-air ball between the Danube and the French Institute celebrates Bastille Day by inviting leading accordion players from France, laying out a decent spread of French wines and snacks (though don't expect to get anywhere near them), and setting off loads of fireworks. Always attracts a big crowd.

Sziget Fesztival
Information: Sziget Csoport Kulturális Egyesület, XI. Orlay utca 5-7 (372 0650/www.sziget.hu). **Date** 1wk late July, early Aug.
Bringing thousands of music fans from all over Europe, the Sziget ('Island') Fesztival is a week-long open-air party on an island in the Danube. *See p172* **Let's spend the week together.**

Budafest
Information: VIP-Arts, VI. Hajós utca 13-15 (302 4290/opera 353 0170/www.viparts.hu). M1 Opera. **Date** 1wk mid Aug. (Tickets sold from end June.)
Budafest is a week of top-flight performances at a time when lesser classical music talent is wasted on busloads of Austrian tourists. Prices for the Opera House events are high, but so is the quality of acts.

Hungarian Formula One Grand Prix
Hungaroring, Mogyoród. Information: Ostermann Formula-1, V. Apáczai Csere János utca 11 (266 2040) or Hungaroring (06 28 444 444/ www.hungaroring.hu). **Open** 8am-4pm Mon-Thur; 8am-2pm Fri. **Date** 2nd or 3rd weekend Aug.

The biggest event in the sporting calendar sees the town fill up with Formula One fans, creating trade for the city's hotels, restaurants and sex clubs. The course is at Mogyorod, 20km from Budapest on the M3 motorway. *See p183.*

St Stephen's Day
Public holiday. **Date** 20 Aug.
Hungarians celebrate their founding father in style. The right hand of St Stephen, inside a reliquary, is taken in a religious procession in front of the Basilica. Cruise boats and river-view restaurants are booked up weeks in advance for the huge fireworks display set off from Gellért Hill at 9pm.

Budapest Parade
Information: Sziget Csoport Kulturális Egyesület, XI. Orlay utca 5-7. (372 0650/www.sziget.hu). **Date** end Aug.
This event tries to ape Berlin's Love Parade, though it's smaller and tamer. Still, it's a fun party as crowds estimated at close to 100,000 line Andrássy út to watch a parade of floats carrying DJs and dancers, before it ends near Hősök tere at Felvonulási tér. DJs keep spinning and outdoor dancing continues until 10pm. Most clubs host special after-parties.

Jewish Summer Festival
Information: Budapesti Zsidó Kulturális Központ VII. Síp utca 12 (344 5409/www.jewishfestival.hu). **Date** 1wk end Aug.
A week of Jewish theatre, art and concerts around town. Musical performances include classical, jazz and klezmer. *See also p76* **Jewish Budapest.**

Autumn

Autumn sees Budapest at its best, slowly emptying of tourists, its cultural life starting up again. Bars, clubs and concert halls reopen their doors to local audiences still bronzed from a summer down at the Balaton.

Arts & Entertainment

Budapest Wine Festival

Bacchus Arts Studio, V. Vörösmarty tér 1 (488 7092). M1 Vörösmarty tér/tram 2. **Date** 2wks Sept.
The most gregarious of the city's annual trade fairs sees leading wine producers descend on Budapest to woo international buyers with concerts in the Castle District and folk dancing in Vörösmarty tér.

Budapest Autumn Festival

Budapesti Fesztiválközpont, V. Egyetem tér 5 (486 3311/www.fesztivalvaros.hu). M3 Kálvin tér. **Open** *box office* 10am-5pm Mon-Fri. **Date** late Sept/Oct.
The leading annual contemporary arts festival, focusing on cinema, fine arts, dance and theatre.

Budapest Music Weeks

Information: Budapest Filharmónia, VI Jókai utca 6 (302 4961/www.deltasoft.hu/filharm). M1 Oktogon/ tram 4, 6. **Date** 2wks late Sept/early Oct.
The traditional opening of the classical season, often kicking off with a major concert as near to the anniversary of Bartók's death (25 Sept) as possible. Most performances take place at the Zeneakadémia or Vigadó (*see p166-9*).

Music of Our Time

Information: Budapest Filharmónia, VI Jókai utca 6 (302 4961/www.deltasoft.hu/filharm). M1 Oktogon/ tram 4, 6. **Date** ten days late Sept/early Oct.
Top-notch classical musicians let their hair down and enjoy the less stringent demands of Hungary's leading contemporary composers, many of whom compose pieces especially for this ten-day event.

Remembrance Day

Public holiday. **Date** 23 Oct.
The anniversary of the 1956 Uprising is a national day of mourning. Wreath-laying ceremonies take place at plot 301 of Újköz Cemetery, where rebellious 1956 leader Imre Nagy was secretly buried after his execution. There is also a flag-raising ceremony in Kossuth tér, an excuse for right-wing groups to gain media attention. Black-edged flags are flown around town. *See p18* **1956 and all that**.

All Saints' Day

Date 1 Nov.
While Hallowe'en is slow to catch on in Hungary, the traditional Christian holiday for remembering saints and dead children is marked by people from all religions. Large crowds wander the cemeteries all afternoon and into the evening to leave flowers and burning candles before 2 Nov, the 'Day of the Dead'.

Winter

Winter seems to go on forever, with below-zero temperatures and snow piled on the pavements. Shops slowly fill for Christmas, but without the hard sell of the West. Villagers gather for the annual *disznóvágás*, or pig-killing – a bloody, drunken ritual. February is carnival, or *farsang*, season. *See p143* **Hungary's pagan rites**.

Easter celebrations. *See p143.*

Mikulás

St Nicholas' Day. **Date** 6 Dec.
On the eve of 6 Dec, children put out their shoes on the window sill for Santa to fill with chocolates, fruit and little pressies. He is assisted by *krampusz*, the bogey-man, a threat to naughty children. Just to remind them, small *krampusz* puppets, hung on a gilded tree branch, *virgács*, are also left by Santa.

Karácsony

Christmas. Public holiday. **Date** 25, 26 Dec.
Trees and presents pepper the Nagykörút from mid-December. The traditional meal is carp, devoured on Christmas Eve, when present-giving takes place. The city closes for three days from noon on 24 Dec, when locals lock themselves away *en famille*.

Szilveszter

New Year's Eve. **Date** 31 Dec.
Szilveszter is when everyone takes to the streets in style, down the Nagykörút and around Blaha Lujza tér in particular. Buses and trams in Budapest run all night long. The national anthem booms out of radios at midnight. Then it's champers, kisses and fireworks. Merriment continues into the next day, a holiday, when *kocsonya*, a dish made from pork fat, is liable to wobble its way into your hangover.

Magyar Filmszemle

Hungarian Film Festival. *Filmunio Hungary, VI. Városligeti fasor 38 (351 7760).* **Date** early Feb.
A reasonably modest screening of the year's best Magyar films. Translations are provided for the main features. *See also p158.*

Baths

Authentically Ottoman or stylishly art nouveau, bathing in Budapest dates back more than two thousand years.

Budapest is the spa capital of Europe and the 120 thermal springs that gush up from Buda's limestone bedrock have long inspired a culture of bathing. Indeed, the mineral-rich waters seem to have been one of the reasons why there was a settlement here in the first place. Evidence suggests that neolithic peoples were drawn to Buda's warm springs, and later the Romans brought in bathing customs. From the ninth century, the Magyars continued the tradition, but it was under the Ottomans in the 16th and 17th centuries that bathing in Buda reached its golden age.

The natural and abundant supply, combined with the demands of Islam that its followers adhere to a strict set of rules for ablutions in running water before praying five times a day, inspired an aquatic and hedonistic culture that still thrives today. The Ottoman mosques, monasteries and schools that once filled the streets of Buda are all long gone (*see p54* **Turkish Budapest**), but centuries later it is still possible to bathe under an original Ottoman dome in the **Király**, **Rudas** or **Rác** – the only significant remains of the period.

With so much history involved, it's no wonder that Budapest's bathing regulars are holding their collective breaths now that extensive renovations have begun on both the Rudas and Rác. The more ambitious project involves the Rác. Not only will the historic building be completely refurbished, but a new 60-room luxury spa hotel will be built adjacent to it with private investors footing the bill. A funicular lift will also connect the site to the top of Gellért Hill. The project is sure to move slowly as historic protection laws require an archaeological survey when the hotel site is excavated (they're sure to find plenty in this area). The entire project is scheduled for completion by August 2004. Until then, the Rác will be closed. The Rudas will close down for part of 2003. Plans call for a total renovation of the exterior, pool area, changing rooms and reception. Renovation of the Turkish baths, including replacement of all the piping, is tentatively scheduled for 2004 and will proceed under the watchful eye of the Budapest Historical Society. Regulars are crossing their fingers that the special atmosphere of the Rudas won't be spoiled.

Newer facilities, yet still historic, can be found at the **Gellért** (*see p39* **Taking the waters**), connected to the art nouveau Gellért Hotel, and the 19th-century **Széchenyi** complex in the City Park. The Széchenyi has already undergone internal renovation and will soon see its neo-baroque façade renewed.

BARE ESSENTIALS

For anyone with little command of Hungarian, entering the baths for the first time can be a baffling experience. Lengthy menus offer such treats as ultra-sound or a pedicure, as well as massage. Signs in Hungarian, German and English (or Russian on some of the older signs) give various instructions, such as the 90-minute bathing limit, which is rarely enforced.

The routine is similar in all the Turkish baths, though it varies at the mixed facilities. After buying a ticket you enter a warren of passageways, the entrance to which is guarded by a white-clothed attendant (who is slowly being replaced by electronic turnstiles). Hand over your ticket and receive a white flap of cloth that is to be tied around your waist for modesty's sake. The ones for women have an apron-like addition that supposedly covers the breasts, but few women bother to wear them at all. Men tend to keep theirs on, though sometimes swivel them to cover their behinds, to prevent scorched buttocks on the wooden sauna seats. For the mixed facilities you'll need to take a swimming costume.

Once in the changing rooms, either the attendant will show you to a cubicle, or else you find one yourself, but each is locked twice and reliably secure. In some places the attendant has one key and you keep the other: tie it to the spare string on your flap.

The baths generally have one or two main pools and a series of smaller ones around the perimeter, all of different temperatures, ranging from dauntingly hot to icily cold. The precise drill depends on preference, but involves moving between different pools, taking in the dry heat of the sauna and the extreme humidity of the steam rooms, alternating temperatures and finally relaxing in gentle warm water.

An hour or two is usually sufficient. It's extremely relaxing and good for relieving aches and pains. The various minerals and mild radioactivity of the thermal waters supposedly help cure all sorts of ailments (Hungarians are still big on 19th-century quackery). Afterwards you shower (bring your own soap) and, in the Király and Rudas, are provided with a towel – take your own to the others. Most baths have a resting room where you can take a short nap before changing back into your street clothes. On the way out, tip the attendant Ft50-Ft100.

Apart from pools, saunas and steam rooms, most sites also offer massages. These come in two types: *vízi* (water) massage and *orvosi* (medical) massage – the latter is the gentler experience. Pay for the massage when you get your entrance ticket. When you get your flap, the attendant will also give you a small metal token with a number on it. Upon entering the baths area, go to the massage room and give your token to a masseur with a tip of Ft100 or

so. Also let him know you don't speak Hungarian (otherwise he'll just call out your number when it's your turn and get angry when you don't run over). Keep an eye out and he'll wave for you when your time has come.

A full visit to one of the baths demands a whole morning or afternoon. There's usually somewhere in the foyer to get a cold drink, coffee or snack, plus a stall selling soap and other toiletries. Don't expect to have the energy to do very much afterwards except settle down for a long lunch or stretch out for a nap, but do remember to drink lots of water to rehydrate.

Apart from the baths listed here, there are also limited thermal facilities at certain pools and lidos open from May to September such as the **Palatinus** (*see p187*).

Note that ticket offices always close an hour before listed closing times.

Take the waters at the
Szécheny Baths. *See p148.*

The baths

Gellért Gyógyfürdő

XI. Kelenhegyi út 4 (466 6166). Tram 18, 19, 47, 49/bus 7. **Open** 6am-7pm daily. **Admission** Ft2,700; Ft2,400 concs. Mixed. **Map** p249 C5.

The most expensive of all the baths, but you do get an art nouveau swimming pool chucked in. In the summer your Ft3,000 also allows access to the several outdoor pools and sunbathing areas, with a terrace restaurant. The separate thermal baths – one for men, one for women – lead off from the main swimming pool, which also has its own small warm water pool. The Secessionist theme continues in the maze of steam rooms and saunas that gives the Gellért a different atmosphere to the Turkish Rudas or Király. The clientele is also quite entertaining, composed of startled tourists and, in the male half, gay men on the prowl. The restroom is sometimes extremely active (*see p164*). The thermal water contains carbonic gases and is recommended for those with blood pressure problems and coronary disease.

Király Gyógyfürdő

II. Fő utca 84 (201 4392). M2 Batthyány tér. **Open** *Men* 9am-8pm Tue, Thur, Sat. *Women* 7am-6pm Mon, Wed, Fri. **Admission** Ft1,100. **Map** p245 B3.

The Király is one of the city's most significant Ottoman monuments, particularly the 16th-century pool. Originally called the Bath of the Cock Tower, it takes its name from the 19th-century owners, the König (King) family, who changed their name to its Hungarian equivalent: Király. Construction of the Turkish part was begun in 1566 and completed by Pasha Sokoli Mustafa in 1570. Located within the Víziváros town walls, it meant the Ottoman garrison could enjoy a good soak even during the siege. The classical bits were added in the 18th century. The Király follows the traditional pattern of a main pool surrounded by smaller ones of different temperatures, plus saunas and steam rooms. The bath's environs are light and airy, and three Turkish-style reliefs mark the entrance corridor. There is a big gay scene in the afternoons on men's days (*see p164*).

Lukács Gyógyfürdő és Strandfürdő

II. Frankel Leó utca 25-29 (326 1695). Tram 4, 6. **Open** *Men* 6am-7pm Tue, Thur, Sat. *Women* 6am-7pm Mon, Wed, Fri. **Admission** Ft1,100. **Map** p245 B1.

A complex of two outdoor swimming pools set in attractive grounds and thermal baths, in this case the Turkish-period Császár baths, although there aren't that many original features left and the layout is quite different from the other Turkish places. The baths are mixed, which also lends a different atmosphere to that at the Rudas or Király. There's something of an institutional feel to this warren-like facility, but the setting is verdant and restful. On the wall outside the entrance to the changing rooms, you'll find a selection of old stone plaques, testaments from satisfied customers – the waters are said to be efficacious for orthopaedic diseases.

Rác Gyógyfürdő

I. Hadnagy utca 8-10 (356 1322). Tram 18, 19, 47. **Map** p248 B5. **Closed until Aug 2004.**

Tucked under Gellért Hill, the Rác baths are named after the Hungarian word for the Serbs who once lived here. Though the exterior is 19th century (designed by Miklós Ybl), the octagonal pool and dome inside date back to the Turkish era, although they're drabber than those at the Rudas or Király. Massive renovation will include the addition of a small luxury hotel.

Rudas Gyógyfürdő

I. Döbrentei tér 9 (356 1322). Tram 18, 19/bus 7. **Open** 6am-8pm Mon-Fri; 6am-1pm Sat; 6am-midnight Sun. **Admission** *Baths* Ft1,100. *Pool* Ft750. **Map** p249 C5. **Closed for parts of 2003 & 2004.**

This is the finest and most atmospheric of Budapest's original Turkish baths (men only, mixed swimming pool), especially when rays of sunlight stab through windows in the dome's roof and fan out through the steam above the central pool. The intensity of the aesthetic experience is further enhanced by an extraordinary liquid ambience, as the sound of running water and the chatter of bathers echo from the shadowy corners and up into the dome. The first baths on this site date from the 14th century. The new site was constructed by the Pasha of Buda in the 16th century and his plaque still stands in the main chamber. The original cupola, vaulted corridor and main octagonal pool remain, although heavily restored. There are three saunas, two steam rooms as well as six pools of differing temperatures.

Széchenyi Gyógyfürdő és Strandfürdő

XIV. Állatkert körút 11 (321 0310). M1 Széchenyi fürdő. **Open** *Strand: May-Sept* 6am-7pm daily; *Oct-Apr* 6am-5pm daily. *Thermal baths* 6am-7pm : *men* Tue, Thur; *women* Mon, Wed; *mixed* Sat, Sun. **Admission** Ft1,700 (with locker); Ft2,000 (with changing room); Ft900 refund if you stay less than 2hrs. **Map** p247 F1.

In the middle of the City Park, an attractive complex of swimming pools and thermal baths, the Széchenyi is Europe's largest health spa, with an annual two million visitors. Its waters are used for treating arthritis, gout and respiratory diseases and, if you drink them, gall bladder disease. Outside is a statue of Zsigmond Vilmos, who discovered the thermal spring that fills the outdoor pool. The Széchenyi is probably the best choice for a day of relaxation as it offers outdoor thermal and swimming pools plus the usual indoor assortment of thermal baths and steam rooms. Guests can exercise, laze and sunbathe all on one site, lending an endearing holiday atmosphere. Outside, pools are beautifully laid out, with a swimming pool as well as a thermal one, open all year round, where bathers play chess with steam rising around them. Recent renovations have removed the ivy cladding from the façade, but have installed a whirlpool and ice machine.

Children

Puppet shows and prehistoric fairgrounds compete with mega malls and multiplexes for kiddies' entertainment.

New malls and entertainment centres have changed child-orientated entertainment in Budapest. Multiplexes, video arcades, internet cafés and indoor playgrounds have now been added to the appealingly old-fashioned attractions such as puppet theatres, folk dance clubs, eccentric conveyances and prehistoric fairground rides.

Not surprisingly, this modernisation has started to change people's way of life, including how and where they spend their free time with their children. Many spend Saturday or Sunday at the mall, window-shopping, eating at fast-food places and sending the kids to supervised play areas or video arcades. Others still prefer folk clubs, craft workshops and puppet shows in neighbourhood theatres or cultural centres.

Budapest can be fun to visit with kids, but it can be difficult too. You might enjoy finding an ancient tram or toy exhibition but then discover the pushchair doesn't fit through the door or that the show has closed an hour early.

The Hungarian family is still traditional in its approach to child-rearing. You don't see too many parents with small children in restaurants because children are supposed to stay at home with mum until they learn how to behave like little adults. But don't be surprised if people, especially old ladies, stop to stroke and praise your children – or to criticise their behaviour.

PRACTICALITIES AND DIFFICULTIES

Under-12s are not allowed to travel in the front seats of cars, and seat belts and baby-seats are compulsory in the back. Children under six travel free of charge on all public transport. If you're eating out, don't take highchairs and child-size meals for granted. On the other hand, disposable nappies, baby food and other essentials are available all over the city.

Heavy traffic and air pollution mean that long weekday walks along busy downtown streets aren't advisable. Instead, try the Danube embankment, the pedestrian streets around Váci utca, or one of the parks and playgrounds listed below. Only the narrowest pushchairs can get through the doors of some of the old buses and trams. Access can also be a problem when shopping, except in the new, spacious western-style shops downtown or the various new malls.

INFORMATION

Check the listings in the English-language weekly *Budapest Sun*, try *MaNcs* or *Pesti Műsor* under *Gyerekeknek ajánlott műsorok* ('shows recommended for children'), or call **Tourinform** (317 9800).

Babysitters

Young Hungarian parents tend to use the grandparents as babysitters. The agency listed below provides reliable and qualified child-minding services in Budapest. You might also be able to arrange babysitting through your workplace or hotel, but bear in mind that English-speaking minders cost more.

Minerva Family Helping Service
Minerva Családsegítő Szolgálat
VIII. Szerdahelyi utca 10 (313 6365). Tram 28, 29. **Open** 24hr answering machine. **No credit cards.** **Map** p250 F4.
English-, German-, French- and Spanish-speaking babysitters and full- or part-time nannies. Sitting is Ft600 and up per hour.

Children's activity centres

Activity centres offer a wide variety of programmes for kids during the school year and organise day camps and events during the school holidays. Check programmes and prices with the venues.

Almássy tér Recreation Centre
Almássy téri Szabadidő Központ
VII. Almássy tér 6 (352 1572). M2 Blaha Lujza tér/tram 4, 6. **Open** Sept-June. **Admission** varies. **No credit cards. Map** p247 E3.
Activities include craft workshops, chess, singing, dancing, swimming courses and puppet shows. Special events on offer can range from giant hands-on toy exhibits to performances by popular children's entertainers.

Capital City Cultural Centre
Fővárosi Művelődési Ház
XI. Fehérvári út 47 (203 3868). Tram 47, 49. **Admission** varies. **No credit cards.**
Children's theatre shows, folk dance club for kids with the famous Muzsikás ensemble, playgroups for three- to six-year-olds, dance, gymnastics and aerobics courses for little ones.

Kids' Park

Kölyökpark

IV. Fóti út 81B (399 2059/06 30 924 9126).
M3 Újpest-Városkapu, then bus 96. **Open**
10am-8pm daily. **Admission** Ft500 for 30mins.
No credit cards.

Five hundred square metres of indoor playgrounds
with monkey bars, slides, towers and tunnels for
children up to 12.

Marczibányi tér Culture House

Marczibányi téri Művelődési Ház

II. Marczibányi tér 5A (212 5660). M2 Moszkva
tér/tram 4, 6. **Admission** varies. **No credit cards.**
Map p245 A2.

Craft workshops, a folk dance club, drawing for four-
to seven-year-olds, a playgroup with music for six
months to six years, a magicians' school for nine- to
15-year-olds and an excellent playground for
younger kids. Special events include puppet shows,
pet fairs and concerts by popular performers.

Millenáris Park

II. Fény utca 20-22 (438 5335/
millenaris@millenaris.hu). M2 Moszkva tér/tram 4, 6.
Admission Ft200-Ft800. **No credit cards.**

Craft workshops, puppet shows, children's theatre
plays and playgroups in a new venue.

Children's theatres

Budapest Puppet Theatre

Budapest Bábszínház

VI. Andrássy út 69 (321 5200). M1 Vörösmarty
utca. **Shows** 3pm Mon-Thur; 10.30am, 4pm Fri-Sun.
Closed in summer. **Open** box office 9am-6pm daily.
Admission Ft300-Ft700. **No credit cards.**
Map p246 D2.

International fairy tales and Hungarian folk stories
in the repertoire. Language is usually not a problem
and the shows are highly original.

Circus

XIV. Állatkerti körút 7 (343 9630). M1 Széchenyi
fürdő. **Shows** 3pm, 7pm Wed-Fri; 10.30am, 3pm,
7pm Sat, Sun. **Admission** Ft700-Ft1,400. **No credit**
cards. Map p247 F1.

A permanent building with shows year-round,
although inside it looks just like an old-fashioned
travelling circus. International and Hungarian
performances with acrobats, magicians, jugglers,
clowns and animals.

Holdvilág Kamaraszínház

XVI. Ságvári utca 3 (405 8759). Bus 144 from M2
Örs Vezér tér to József utca. **Tickets** can be bought
at the door before the show or reserved by phone.
Admission Ft350-Ft500. **No credit cards.**

Children's plays staged by excellent young actors
and directors.

Kolibri Theatre

VI. Jókai tér 10 (353 4633). M1 Oktogon/tram 4, 6.
Shows 10am daily; 3pm Fri-Sun. **Open** box office

9am-6pm Mon-Fri. Closed in summer. **Admission**
Ft450-Ft900. **No credit cards. Map** p246 D3.

Small theatre presenting fairy tales.

Planetarium

Népliget, south-west corner (265 0725). M3 Népliget.
Open 5 shows per day 9am-4pm Tue-Sun. Laser
shows 7.30pm Mon-Sat. **Admission** Ft650. Laser
shows Ft1,690; Ft1,190 children. **No credit cards.**

Temporary exhibits as well as educational children's
shows. Popular with older kids. English-language
shows on request for groups of 30 or more.

Eating out

Although the number of restaurants with highchairs and children's menus is increasing, it's
best to call ahead and even reserve a highchair.

Films & TV

Several Budapest cinemas show cartoons and
children's films. Most, however, are dubbed into
Hungarian. Check film listings or look in the
local English-language press. Most hotels and
flats for rent have satellite and/or cable TV.

Health

In an emergency call 104 or 311 1666 and ask
for someone who speaks English. With sick
children you can also go to Heim Pál Children's
Hospital 24 hours a day.

Heim Pál Children's Hospital

Heim Pál Gyermekkórház

VIII. Üllői út 86 (264 3314/210 0720). M3
Nagyvárad tér. **Map** p250 F6.

International schools

American International School of Budapest

PO Box 53, Budapest 1525 (06 26 55 60 00/
www.aisb.hu).

International Kindergarten & School of Budapest

XII. Konkoly Thege utca 19B (395 9312/
isb@elender.hu). Bus 21, 90.

Magyar-British International Elementary School

II. Pasaréti út 82-84 (200 7571/www.mbis.hu). Bus 56.

Magyar-English Bilingual Elementary School

XIV. Hermina út 9-15 (343 8125). Bus 7.

Magyar-English Bilingual Secondary School

XVIII. Thököly út 7 (290 4316/www.karinthy.hu).
Bus 36, 93, 136.

Arts & Entertainment

Check out swingin' Budapest at **Károlyi Garden**. *See p153.*

Museums

Budapest has some excellent museums for children, but here more than anywhere kids are expected to behave. Attendants often scold visiting children for being too rumbustious. The **Transport Museum** can be fun with its life-size and model trains, cars and ships. You can climb the steps of an old train engine and peek into the wagons, and you can also turn a ship's wheel, but that's pretty much it for hands-on stuff. The aviation section next door has a nice collection of old aeroplanes. The **Natural History Museum** and the **Palace of Wonders** are the most interactive museums in town, with buttons to push and levers to pull. Other museums of possible interest include the ones for the **Underground**, **Military History**, and **Telephones**. For all details *see p43-88*.

Music

Classical

In the country of Bartók and Kodály, you're bound to find classical music performances adapted for children. Their nickname is *Kakaó koncert*, because children get hot chocolate at the end of the concert. The most popular is the one given by the **Budapest Fesztivál Zenekar** (*see also p167*) in Óbuda.

Budapest Fesztivál Zenekar

V. Vörösmarty tér 1 (317 9838). M1 Vörösmarty tér/tram 2. **Admission** Ft1,000. **Open** *Sept-Apr* 9.30am-4pm Mon-Fri. **No credit cards.** **Map** p249 C4.

Information and tickets for the Kakaó koncert series, as well as the rest of the orchestra's activities.

International Buda Stage

II. Tárogató út 2-4 (391 2525). Tram 56. **Tickets** Ft700 to children's shows. **Open** 15 Sept-15 June. **No credit cards.** English-language shows for adults and classical music concerts for kids.

Folk music

The folk music movement doesn't leave kids out of the fun. Venues (*see p173*) may be closed in July and August, but if you're ready for a week of intensive boot-slapping and craft workshops, you should call any of the dance houses (*táncházak*) and enquire about summer camps. **Muzsikás**, the best-known Hungarian folk band, offer a weekly *táncház* for kids at the Fővárosi Művelődési Ház (XI. Fehérvári út 47; 203 3868) with live folk music and the teaching of traditional dances, including folk tales and games. The **Kalamajka Dance House** turns into a wild *táncház* at night, after children's songs, dances and folk tales.

Outdoor activities

Zoo

Állatkert

XIV. Városligeti körút 6-12 (363 3797/ www.zoobudapest.com). M1 Széchenyi fürdő. **Open** *Winter* 9am-4pm daily . *Summer* 9am-7pm daily; daily. **Admission** Ft1,000 adults; Ft750 children; free under-2s; Ft3,100 family of 4. **No credit cards.** **Map** p247 E1.

Arts & Entertainment

The boating pond in **City Park** turns into an ice-skating rink in winter. *See p153.*

The zoo has developed tremendously in the last few years. There are new green areas, more animal-friendly cages and a great new playground. Animal names are written in English and Hungarian, and an English-language booklet with map is available for Ft500. You'll need a whole afternoon to see everything, including animal shows, a petting corner and a maze with questions on fauna and flora to help you find your way out. Apart from the usual animals there are stunning art nouveau buildings, pony carts, a beautiful exotic bird house, an indoor play area (Ft300 per hour, free for adults) and one of the few public nappy-changing rooms in town. Don't miss the renovated palm house and aquarium, the elephant house and the monkey islands.

Amusement park

Vidám Park
XIV. Városligeti körút 14-16 (363 3825). M1 Széchenyi fürdő. **Open** *Winter* 11am-sunset daily. *Summer* 10am-8pm daily. **Admission** Ft300 adults; free children under 120cm; Ft300-Ft600 a ride. **No credit cards. Map** p247 F1.
A big, tacky old place with a rickety wooden roller-coaster, big wheel, ancient merry-go-round and unfrightening ghost trains next to a few newer, scarier rides. Next door is the renovated funfair (Kis Vidám Park) for toddlers and pre-schoolers.

Parks & playgrounds

City Park
Városliget
M1 Hősök tere/Széchenyi fürdő. **Map** p247 E1.
Lots here apart from the zoo, amusement park and circus listed above. Behind Heroes' Square and the

boating pond is Vajdahunyad Castle, which houses the **Agriculture Museum** (*see p59* **Obscure Budapest**) with stuffed animals and tools. Safety standards are low on the slides and wooden castles in the south corner, but there's a new fenced playground with a treehouse, safe slides and monkey bars. The playground between the zoo and the pond is also in good shape and has a trampoline area where children can bounce up and down for Ft150 for five minutes. For other ball games check out the football fields, basketball and tennis courts behind Petőfi Csarnok on the east side of the park.

Honvéd tér
M3 Nyugati pu./tram 4, 6. **Open** 8am-sunset daily. **Admission** free. **Map** p246 C2.
Another centrally located fenced playground with lots of fun rides for all ages.

József Nádor tér
M1, M2, M3 Deák tér/tram 47, 49. **Open** 7am-sunset daily. **Admission** free. Dogs not allowed. **Map** p249 C4.
A great playground with wooden castles, a ship with slides, swings, ride-on toys, a sandpit and a stream with tiny dams for watery experiments.

Károlyi Garden
Károlyi kert
M2 Astoria, M3 Kálvin tér/tram 47, 49. **Open** 8am-sunset daily. **Admission** free. Dogs not allowed. **Map** p249 D4.
One of the cleanest fenced playgrounds in the downtown area. Includes sandpit, slide, ride-on toys and two ball areas.

Klauzál tér
M2 Blaha Lujza tér/tram 4, 6. **Open** 8am-sunset daily. **Admission** free. **Map** p246 D3.

Arts & Entertainment

Nice playground in the heart of busy and sometimes smelly District VII. Dogs have their own park (that is, toilet) next door.

Margaret Island

Margitsziget
Tram 4, 6 to Margaret Bridge/bus 26 from Nyugati station. **Map** p245 B1.
A huge recreational area with grassy spaces, old trees, swimming pools, playgrounds and a small zoo with domestic animals. You can rent bicycles, four-wheeled pedalos and tiny electric cars for children. Horse-drawn carts and open-topped minibuses leave on round trips every half hour. The best playground is near the Alfréd Hajós swimming pool on the south-west side and the best swimming is to be had at the Palatinus Strand, which also has an open-air thermal pool (*see p187*). Avoid summer weekends, when crowds snake from the ticket desk window.

Óbuda Island

Óbudai/Hajógyári sziget
HÉV to Filatorigát/bus 142/boat from Vigadó tér.
An island full of green areas and long slides north of Árpád Bridge. Ideal for picnickers, kite-flyers, skaters and bikers.

Rollerskating & skateboarding

Although Heroes' Square (Hősök tere) is teen Budapest's favourite rollerskating and skateboarding area, more fanatic skaters can go to **Görzenál Skatepark** (*see p185*) for hours of well-paved fun. In-line skates and skateboards can be rented on the spot.
The boating pond in the **City Park** turns into an ice-skating rink in winter (*see p186*). In summer you can go to the ice-skating rinks operated in the **Pólus Center** or **Duna Plaza Shopping Mall** (*see p129*).

Shopping

Classic, crafted wooden toys still outnumber Nintendo games in Budapest's toy shops. The city also has a good array of children's clothing stores (*see p126*) and sections in the malls and bigger department stores. If you need your children to be watched while you shop, Campona (XXII. Nagytétényi út 37-43; 424 3000), Duna Plaza (XIII. Váci út 178; 465 1666), Europark (IX. Üllői út 201-5; 269 6985), **IKEA** (see p130) and **Westend City Center** (*see p129*) have supervised playrooms.

Sports club

Meredek utcai sportpálya

XII. Meredek utca 1 (06 70 248 2379).
English-language sports club for four- to 14-year-olds on most weekday afternoons and Saturday mornings, with basketball, football and baseball.

Train & boat rides

You can go up to the Buda Hills (*see p60* **Green Budapest**) on the cogwheel train that departs across the street from the Budapest Hotel (M2 Moszkva tér, then two stops on trams Nos.18 or 56). If you ride all the way up to Széchenyi Hill, about 25 minutes, you can walk across the park to the **Children's Railway** – operated by children, except for the engine drivers. This doesn't run often in low season, so check the schedule by phone (395 5420) or you can spend waiting time in the neighbouring playground.

Chairlift

Libegő
(394 3764). M2 Moszkva tér, then bus 158.
Open *Winter* 10am-4pm Tue-Sun. *Summer* 10am-5pm Tue-Sun. **Tickets** Ft400; Ft200 children.
No credit cards.
This slow and gentle ski lift-style ride sweeps right up to the top of Jánoshegy, the highest hill within the city limits and equipped with a lookout tower.

Funicular

Sikló
I. Clark Ádám tér (201 9128). Tram 19. **Open** 7.30am-10pm Tue-Sun. **Tickets** Ft500 up; Ft400 down; Ft300 children. **Map** p248 B4.
The funicular goes from Clark Ádám tér up to the Castle District. It's a short ride, but the view and the carriages are cool.

Nostalgia Train

Nosztalgia vonat
Information & tickets *Nyugati station. VI. Nyugati tér (269 5242). M3 Nyugati pu./tram 4, 6.*
Tickets approx Ft1,000. **No credit cards**.
Map p246 D2.
The Hungarian Railway Company (MÁV) operates a steam engine with old-fashioned carriages, which leaves Nyugati at 9.40am and takes 90 minutes to puff its way up to Szob on the Danube on Saturdays from May to September. After time for lunch and a walk along the river, the train returns at 4.35pm, reaching Nyugati at 6pm. Tickets are priced as regular trains, but for an extra charge you can visit the driver and get a steam-engine driver's licence.

Boat trips

There are several boat rides down the Danube. The cheapest is the ferry that runs between the Pest end of Petőfi Bridge and Pünkösdfürdő in the north of Budapest, stopping at each of the bridges and Vigadó tér on the way. This is free for under-fours and about Ft400 for everyone else. A sightseeing cruise costs about Ft800-Ft2,400 (half price for under-14s) and offers a bigger boat, usually equipped with a bar and tour guide. Call **IBUSZ** or **Tourinform** for details (*see p214*).

Arts & Entertainment

Film

Keeping faith with proud local tradition, recently renovated classic cinemas now compete with mall multiplexes.

While the number of multiplexes increases, local art cinemas still offer a refreshing alternative to mainstream entertainment. Classic theatres in prime locations are part of Budapest's cinematic tradition; those recently renovated can compete with multiplexes for comfort and technology.

The most eye-catching is the **Uránia Nemzeti Filmszínház**, built in the 1890s and restored to its original form as the National Film Theatre. It was the location for the first ever Hungarian feature film and its main auditorium is unique. While older cinemas have closed, new ones such as the **Odeon-Lloyd**, dating back to the 1930s, now give style to cinema-going.

All the arthouse cinemas are near a metro stop or along the main 4/6 tramline. Many also function as late-opening cafés or clubs, like the **Toldi** and the **Kultiplex**. Others, such as the **Művész**, offer plentiful book and CD stalls.

Most cinemas screen a wide range of North American and European independent films both old and new. If you're after something classic, check out the programme in **Örökmozgó**, and for the latest developments in Hungarian film see what's on at the Uránia. Places like **Cirko-gejzir**, Tabán, Kultiplex and Toldi can also come up with weirder stuff, ranging from Polish cartoons from the 1970s to underground Hungarian documentaries.

Most films are in the original language with subtitles, but check beforehand: subtitled is *feliratos* ('fel.'), dubbed *szinkronizált* (or 'mb.'). Dubbing is reserved for cartoons, family-oriented movies and mainstream action films and comedies shown in multiplexes.

Tickets are cheap: prices run from about Ft200 to Ft950 and many theatres have matinée prices before 4pm or reductions from Monday to Wednesday. Seating is assigned by seat and row number: *szék* is seat, *sor* is row, *bal oldal* designates the left side, *jobb oldal* the right side, *közép* the middle and *erkély* the balcony.

PROGRAMME INFORMATION

The major English-language movie guide is featured in the weekly *Budapest Sun*, although it often misses out the more esoteric cinemas. Also useful are the Hungarian magazines *Pesti Műsor* and *Pesti Est*. The latter can be picked up free around town. *Pesti Est* includes a film guide in English. In Hungarian programmes,

'E' refers to the show times: n9 is 8.15pm, f9 is 8.30pm, h9 is 8.45pm. 'De' means morning, 'du' is afternoon, 'este' is evening and 'éjjel' refers to late screenings.

Cinemas

Kossuth

XIII. Váci út 14 (349 3771). M3 Nyugati/tram 4, 6. **Box office** *from* 9.30am, **last show** 10.30pm. **Tickets** Ft290-Ft690. **No credit cards.** 4 screens. **Map** p246 D2.

Decent seats and a first-rate sound system are the important elements here, as is the Kossuth's policy of featuring English-language first-runs that other cinemas will only show in dubbed versions.

Uránia Nemzeti Filmszínház

VII. Rákóczi út 21 (486 3400/486 3414/www.urania-nf.hu). Bus 7, 78. **Box office** *from* noon (Mon-Fri), 10.30am (Sat, Sun), **last show** 10pm. **Tickets** Ft390-Ft790. **No credit cards.** 3 screens. **Map** p249 D4.

If you're looking for a unique cinematic experience at an affordable price, treat yourself to one of the seven exclusive boxes: try *Kék Angyal* (Blue Angel), *Nagy Ábránd* (Grand Illusion) or *Díszterem* (Main Hall), where you are served from the café during the show if you order beforehand. The impressive Venetian/Moorish-style building has been restored to its original glory after more than a century. As Hungary's National Film Theatre, it features new local releases as well as international ones.

Art cinemas & second-run houses

Cirko-gejzir

V. Balassi Bálint utca 15-17 (269 0904). Tram 2. **Box office** *from* 4.30pm, **last show** 9pm. **Tickets** Ft300-Ft500. **No credit cards.** 1 screen. **Map** p246 C2.

Small cinema that showcases obscure independent movies from all over the world. Also presents new art exhibitions weekly.

Hunnia

VII. Erzsébet körút 26 (322 3471). M2 Blaha Lujza tér/tram 4, 6. **Box office** *from* 3.30pm, **last show** 10pm. **Tickets** Ft600. **No credit cards.** 1 screen. **Map** p247 E3.

The Hunnia specialises in showing cult classics such as *Clerks* or *Pulp Fiction*, peppering the schedule with the occasional money-maker. The café, open from 10am to midnight, is a popular meeting place whatever movie happens to be playing.

Arts & Entertainment

Tarred with a fine brush

New Hungarian cinema is considered way too depressing for Western tastes, and is often criticised for dealing with topics only Hungarians can understand. Yet recent works by Pécs-born Béla Tarr (pictured) have been received with enthusiasm – awards, even – the world over. His *Werckmeister Harmonies*, described by *Time Out* as 'wholly captivating' when on general release in London in the spring of 2003, is the latest in a line of slow-moving black-and-white creations. Where does his secret lie? Certainly not in making light and entertaining comedies.

Tarr, born in 1955, grew up with the work of filmmaker István Darday. At 22, he made his first piece, the prize-winning documentary-fiction piece *Family Nest*, then began his studies at the Hungarian Academy of Theatre and Film Art. He started to make features similar in feel to Italian neo-realism. Long, long features.

Satan's Tango (1991-1994) lasts for seven hours. *Damnation* (1987) and *Werckmeister Harmonies* also seem endless because of the lengthy, slow-pace takes Tarr likes to use. As for the script, he has found the ideal partner in writer László Krasznahorkai. *Satan's Tango* and *Werckmeister Harmonies*

are both based on Krasznahorkai's novels; *Satan's Tango* and *The Melancholy of Resistance* both concern the inhabitants of small, bleak towns in the Puszta, Hungary's Great Plain. In their world the sun never shines and life is desperate.

To emphasise the cheerless atmosphere, Tarr shoots his films on black-and-white stock. (Tarr himself prefers to dress mostly in black.) All this is accompanied by music from Mihály Víg, a charismatic figure from the underground music scene of the 1980s. As the leader of the bands Trabant and Balaton, Víg ('Happy') has composed some of the most truly depressing love songs in the history of the genre.

The whole creates a climate in Tarr's movies for people to change their minds about the way they look at going to the cinema. 'A horror born of a realisation of how low human souls may sink,' to quote *Time Out* again, on the essence of his work. He knows how to do something few other directors seem capable of, now that Russian Andrei Tarkovsky is no longer with us: to create a cinematic masterpiece with all these ingredients. All that is required is patience. Are you sitting comfortably?

Arts & Entertainment

Kultiplex

IX. Kinizsi utca 28 (476 0116/215 3388). M3 Ferenc körút/tram 4, 6. **Box office** *from* 1pm, **last show** 8pm. **Tickets** Ft200-Ft500. Some screenings free (*ingyenes* in the programme). **No credit cards**. 1 screen. **Map** p249 D5.

The Kultiplex screens anything from blockbusters to Hungarian documentaries. It doubles up as a nightclub (*see p179*) and the screening/concert hall is equipped with removable chairs, so don't expect the comfort and latest techniques of the multiplexes. The bar is a popular place at any time of the day, especially in summer when the garden opens.

Művész

VI. Teréz körút 30 (332 6726). M1 Oktogon/tram 4, 6. **Box office** *from* 2pm, **last show** 9.45pm.

Tickets Ft500-Ft850. **No credit cards**. 5 screens. **Map** p246 D3.

The most successful art cinema in the region. The Művész is usually plying a new independent release or two, with the remainder of its five halls featuring nightly changing programmes of the world's art films from the last decade. After a late show, there's music on offer at the Underground café below. Upstairs, soundtrack CDs and art books for sale.

Odeon-Lloyd

XIII. Hollán Ernő utca 7 (329 2065). Tram 2, 4, 6. **Box office** *from* 1hr before 1st show, **last show** 9pm. **Tickets** Ft750, Ft500 for 1st show Sat, Sun. **No credit cards**. 1 screen. **Map** p246 C2.

The excellent Odeon video rental service has taken over the Duna and transformed it into Odeon-Lloyd,

Moguls, ogres and misfits

Early Hungarian cinema developed around Sándor Korda and Mihály Kertész. A born organiser, Korda ran the high-quality Corvin Stúdió and by 1918 had made 19 films. Kertész directed Hungary's first feature, *Ma es holnap* ('Today and Tomorrow') in 1912. Hungary soon numbered 270 permanent cinemas. Silent stars included Arisztid Olt, born Béla Blaskó, and László Löwenstein, better known for his stage work. All four worked in the same environment, mixing at the New York Café (*see p111* **So good they built it twice**). In the chaos after 1918, all four would flee Hungary, never to return.

Anglophile Korda became Sir Alexander Korda, well-respected boss of London Films and Britain's first movie mogul. Kertész made it to Hollywood, where as the womanising workaholic Michael Curtiz he would direct nearly 100 films for the major studios, including *White Christmas*, *Yankee Doodle Dandy* and *King Creole*. His most famous, *Casablanca*, featured Löwenstein, by now known as Peter Lorre, an on-set prankster who would ruin a well-chosen career in a fug of drink and drugs, growing fat and collecting ex-wives. Lugos-born Olt became Bela Lugosi, typecast as Dracula, who ended his days stuck in the B-movie caricatures, earning barely enough to fuel his heroin habit.

Of the four, Curtiz spoke the worst English. Forever the butt of jokes for his cartoon malapropisms – David Niven's book title *Bring on the Empty Horses* stems from a classic Curtizism – he strutted around the *Casablanca* set in his riding boots, bedding

minor starlets whenever possible. A visual and technical genius, and expert at fast-moving drama, Curtiz spent his rare free time riding his horse around his orange groves and taking cold showers.

A pathological bully, Curtiz had little time for actors. Apart from Humphrey Bogart and Ingrid Bergman, the supporting cast was drawn from the flotsam and jetsam of central Europe, some refugees fleeing Hitler. Their anxiety could not be faked; Curtiz and his cast would all lose family in the concentration camps. It is said that for the scene in which *La Marseillaise* drowns out the Nazis in Rick's Café, half the set were in tears.

In real life the head Nazi, silent movie star Conrad Veidt, had fled Europe with his Jewish wife. Paul Henreid, who played the Hungarian-named Victor Laszlo, was a virulent anti-Nazi of aristocratic Austro-Hungarian stock. The headwaiter, Carl, was played by SZ Sakall, a Hungarian comedian from Curtiz's early days in film. Born Eugene Gero, Sakall would be visited on the set every day by his Magyar wife, who brought him goulash and watched him eat while she knitted.

No one knew how the film would end, certainly not Curtiz, who was barely able to contribute to the script. He would add visual gags, such as the bottle of Vichy water being thrown into the bin in the famous final scene at the airport, but would shout at Bogart for hours over lunch as to how the scene should be played. The finished product became the world's best loved film – Curtiz's jumbled acceptance speech for Best Director at that year's Oscars has never been reported.

Arts & Entertainment

The eyecatching **Corvin** is the best multiplex in Budapest. *See p158.*

showing cinema classics from *Psycho* to *Betty Blue*. The screening hall has the latest technology and comfortable seats, the decoration is stylishly simple, and there's a café. It's also the headquarters of the **Odeon** video rental service (*see p158*).

Örökmozgó Filmmúzeum

VII. Erzsébet körút 39 (342 2167). Tram 4, 6. **Box office** from 4.30pm, **last show** 8.30pm. **Tickets** Ft500-Ft600. **No credit cards**. 1 screen. **Map** p246 D3.

Best known for its proudly eclectic schedule of everything from silent classics to documentaries. Foreign-language films in this small house, subsidised by the Hungarian Film Archive, are often played in their original sound with simultaneous Hungarian translation via headsets. It's worth picking up a monthly guide at the cinema, as English-language coverage of this movie lovers' paradise is usually non-existent. There's a small coffee shop in the lobby and an adjoining bookshop with a handful of English titles.

Puskin

V. Kossuth Lajos utca 18 (429 6080). M2 Astoria/ tram 47, 49/bus 7. **Box office** *from* 10am, **last show** 10.30pm. **Tickets** Ft550-Ft800. **No credit cards**. 2 screens. **Map** p249 D4.

This 420-seat house features major Hollywood releases, while its second screen plays previously released movies, art films and Hungarian releases. The Puskin is connected to the Odeon café around the corner and has a branch of the Odeon video rental shop (*see p158*).

Szindbád

XII. Szent István körút 16 (349 2773). M3 Nyugati/ tram 4, 6. **Box office** *from* 30mins before 1st show, last show 8.30pm. **Tickets** Ft440-Ft690. **No credit cards**. 2 screens. **Map** p246 C2.

A decent two-screen art cinema with surly staff. Often the only place to see contemporary Hungarian releases with English subtitles. There's also a small video rental outlet and new art exhibitions weekly.

Tabán

I. Krisztina körút 87-89 (356 8162). Tram 18/bus 5, 78, 105. **Box office** *from* 30mins before 1st show, last show 8.45pm. **Tickets** Ft600. **No credit cards**. **Map** p245 A3.

Nestled in the old Serbian quarter of the city, this tiny theatre usually plays several English-language gems a week. German and French films also feature. Sound and picture quality are sometimes below par. There's also a video rental library and friendly café.

Toldi

V. Bajcsy-Zsilinszky út 36-38 (472 0397). M3 Arany János. **Box office** *from* 30mins before 1st show, last show 9.30pm. **Tickets** Ft620-Ft680, half price on Tue. **No credit cards**. 2 screens. **Map** p246 C3.

Large venue featuring modern independent releases and Hungarian features old and new. Hungarian, Czech and Polish children's animation films from the 1970s and 1980s are shown on Sunday afternoons. There's a gift shop (books, postcards, CDs) and small bar (*see p123*) open until late.

Multiplexes

With some multiplexes set in suburban malls, the Palace Westend (VI. Váci út 1-3; 238 7222/ www.palacecinemas.hu) behind Nyugati station is the most centrally located.

Arts & Entertainment

Corvin Budapest Filmpalota

VII. Corvin köz 1 (459 5050/www.corvin.hu). M3 Ferenc körút/tram 4, 6. **Box office** *from* 9am, **last show** 10.30pm. **Tickets** Ft650-Ft950. **Credit** AmEx, DC, MC, V. Free parking with cinema ticket. 6 screens. **Map** p250 E5.

The best multiplex in Budapest. The eye-catching building, one of the key resistance strongholds during the 1956 Uprising (*see p18* **1956 and all that**), now features the latest techniques in cinematic projection and sound, a branch of the Odeon video rental service (*see below*) and a café.

Mammut

II. Lövőház utca 2-6 (345 8140/www.mammutmozi.hu). M2 Moszkva tér/tram 4, 6. **Box office** *from* 9am, **last show** 11pm. **Tickets** Ft790-Ft1,090. **Credit** AmEx, DC, MC, V. Free parking with cinema ticket. 13 screens. **Map** p245 A2.

Mostly features Hollywood blockbusters and new Hungarian releases. Main venue for the **Magyar Filmszemle** (*see below*).

Film festivals

Magyar Filmszemle

c/o Filmúnió Hungary, VI. Városligeti fasor 38 (351 7760/351 7761/fax 351 7766). **Date** Feb.

The major event in the Hungarian cinema calendar. Each February, in several venues around town, the Magyar Filmszemle ('Hungarian Film Festival') shows all domestic features, documentaries and shorts produced within the previous calendar year. There's a prize for the best movie.

Mediawave

Festival Office H-9021 Győr, Kazinczy út 3-5 (06 96 517 666/fax 06 96 517 669). **Date** 1wk Apr.

Held at Győr, 125km west of Budapest, and characterised by productions from around the region, Mediawave runs for a week at the end of April, showing independent films and videos. Exhibitions, lectures, concerts and an 'à la carte' room, where any productions entered can be screened on request.

Titanic International Filmpresence Festival

Titanic Filmjelenlét Alapítvány, XI. Bartók Béla út 18 (06 30 971 0062/www.datanet.hu/titanic). **Date** Oct.

A showing of new arthouse and cult movies from Asia, Europe and North America, plus an excellent dual-language catalogue.

Video rental

Most English-language videos are dubbed into Hungarian but older releases are subtitled. All video shops will have titles in English.

British Council Library

VII. Benczúr utca 26 (478 4700). M1 Bajza utca. **Open** 11am-7pm Mon-Fri; 9am-1pm Sat. **Membership** Ft2,500. **Map** p247 E2.

Uránia – National Film Theatre. *See p154.*

Annual membership essential for access to this extensive video library. Superb selection of British TV shows, from documentaries to sitcoms.

English-Language Video Club & Shop

VI. Zichy Jenő utca 44 (302 0291). Tram 4, 6. **Open** 10am-10pm daily. **Membership** Ft2,000. **Rental** Ft300-Ft700 per video per night. **Map** p246 D3.

Wide range of Hollywood, independent and European arthouse movies. Over 4,000 films in English, or with English subtitles, so the best place to rent movies not yet shown in Hungary. Also possible to rent a VCR. **Branch**: XII. Hajnóczy József utca 11 (214 9499; noon-9pm daily).

Odeon

XIII. Hollán Ernő utca 7 (349 2776). Tram 4, 6. **Open** 10am-11pm daily. **Rental** Ft350-Ft450 per video per night (plus refundable Ft3,000 deposit). **Map** p246 C2.

Original soundtrack videos of US and UK features. Renowned for its large collection of Magyar classics subtitled in English (most of them in Puskin branch). **Branches**: Corvin Multiplex, VII. Corvin köz 1 (313 9896; open 10am-11pm daily). Puskin, V. Kossuth Lajos utca 18 (318 6464; open 10am-10pm daily). Tabán, I. Krisztina körút 87-89 (356 8162; open 4-10pm Mon-Fri; 3-9pm Sat, Sun).

Video Mania

VI. Andrássy út 33 (269 6812). M1 Opera. **Open** 10am-10pm Mon-Thur, Sun; 10am-midnight Fri, Sat. **Rental** Ft450-Ft750 per video per night, plus one-off Ft2,000 deposit. **Map** p246 D3.

This video outlet offers a large selection of movies in several European languages as well as in English.

Arts & Entertainment

Galleries

A refreshingly human art scene flourishes despite the pressures of the commercial mainstream gallery circuit.

The strength of the Hungarian art scene is that it still operates on a human level. Friendly and artistically open-minded, it's not celebrity or media driven, snobby or exclusive. It's also dynamic, with new galleries opening all the time, and has a strong tradition of artist-run projects and spaces. But commercial pressures are increasing, as a market for modern local art takes shape, posing a threat to the cosy ties linking artists, critics and curators in the first post-Communist decade.

The commercial side of Hungarian art is still predominantly oriented towards the future, with shrewd investors expecting membership of the EU to bring the price of contemporary art up to international levels. There are several major players in the collector-gallerist scene, who all seem to harbour secret ambitions of becoming the local Saatchi by discovering and buying the work of young stars before they become famous. 'New Painting' is still popular among collectors, with painters like Imre Bak and László Fehér commanding the best prices among living Hungarian artists, while younger stars, described as 'post-medial painters', include Attila Szücs and Ágnes Szépfalvi.

Fine art, which used to be a peripheral and non-commercial activity, is in danger of becoming trendy, and a new generation of image-conscious young artists eagerly awaits the breakthrough to celebrity status.

There are also a number of artist-run spaces and projects that deliberately position themselves outside the commercial circuit. Non-commercial artists tend to be interested in video art, installations and social art projects, rather than painting. Much happens outside the established gallery scene, in one-off venues, occupied buildings and artists' studios. Two successful artist-run projects seek to provide an alternative to the mainstream gallery scene: KMKK is a weekly low-budget studio event, announced via an electronic mailing list, and Kis Varsó, run by two young underground celebrities András Gálik and Bálint Havas, highlights guest artists.

All information on temporary exhibitions (*kiállítások*) around town can be found in *Index*, available at the larger venues listed below. It also has a useful website, with a section in English, at www.exindex.hu.

Public galleries & spaces

Artpool Art Research Centre

VI. Liszt Ferenc tér 10 (268 0114/www.artpool.hu). M1 Oktogon/tram 4, 6. **Open** 2-6pm Wed, Fri. Closed July, Aug. **Admission** free. **Map** p246 D3.
Founded in 1979 by dissident sculptor and mail artist György Galántai and his partner Júlia Klaniczay, Artpool has extensive archives of underground art, music, literature and videos from 1960 to 1989 – and probably the most extensive mail-art collection in the world. Their gallery, Artpool P60, round the corner at Paulay Ede utca 60, is used for shows of Fluxus, performance art and new media.

Budapest Gallery Exhibition House

Budapest Galéria Kiállítóháza
III. Lajos utca 158 (388 6771). Tram 1. **Open** 10am-6pm Tue-Sun. **Admission** Ft200; Ft150 concs. **No credit cards**.
Suburban branch of the Budapest Galéria is artistically more interesting than its downtown manifestation (*see below*). City funding supports eclectic, offbeat exhibitions of emerging local artists.

Budapest Gallery Exhibition Space

Budapest Galéria Kiállítóterem
V. Szabadsajtó út 5 (318 8097). M3 Ferenciek tere/ bus 7. **Open** 10am-6pm Tue-Sun. **Admission** Ft100; Ft50 concessions. **No credit cards**. **Map** p249 C4.
The headquarters of Budapest Galéria bears some responsibility for artistic affairs in the city. Its main gallery space is often wasted on an uninspired and conventional artistic programme.

Center for Culture & Communication

C3 Kulturális és Kommunikációs Központ
I. Országház utca 9 (214 6856/www.c3.hu). Várbusz from M2 Moszkva tér/bus 16. **Open** Library 10am-6pm Mon-Fri. *Labs* (by appointment) 9am-9pm Mon-Fri. **Admission** free. **Map** p245 D3.
Founded in 1996 by maverick philanthropist George Soros, C3 has attracted enough private sponsorship to thrive without his support. Most of the work is behind the scenes, in the world of virtual reality.

Centrális Galéria

V. Nádor utca 11 (327 3250/ www.osa.ceu.hu/ galeria). M2 Kossuth tér or M3 Arany János utca/ tram 2. **Open** 2-6pm Tue-Fri; 10am-6pm Sat. **Admission** free. **Map** p249 C5.
Analyses the Communist past from the extensive archives of Radio Free Europe/Radio Liberty. Via video, CD-Rom, sound and artefacts, it revives suppressed memories, often with offbeat humour.

Art attack

MEO stands for 'Quality Control Department' in Hungarian and is the bright and catchy name of a major new exhibition space on the industrial outskirts of Budapest.

The gallery (*pictured*) is housed in a converted 19th-century tannery, which has been carefully renovated and restored to provide a massive 2,600 square metres of exhibition space. A two-storey reception building takes the contrasting form of a minimalist white box covered with playful multicoloured lights that shine through plastic cladding at night. It's a Pop Art soapbox that stands out among the neighbouring Socialist-era flats and old factories.

MEO periodically hosts exciting international exhibitions, designed to complement and contextualise the gallery's core collection, and entice visitors out to the post-industrial wasteland of Újpest. You'll probably be most interested in its bang up-to-date stock of contemporary Hungarian art, the product of a decade of judicious private collecting by gallerist Lajos Kováts, self-confessed admirer of Brit art tycoon Charles Saatchi. Highlights include Antal Lakner, whose witty and physically interactive machines parody the notion of productive leisure at the heart of both the Communist and capitalist work ethic.

The so-called post-medial painters are well represented, including their standard-bearer Attila Szűcs, whose painterly, evocative dreamlike scenes are both instantly appealing and eventually disturbing. The collection is steadily being augmented and may soon rival that of the official Hungarian Museum of Contemporary Art.

Questions have arisen about the hybrid nature of the MEO, which also houses Kováts's commercial gallery, **Blitz Modern** (*see p162*). This will represent artists with works in the permanent collection. Supporters say this strategy is a sign of the long-awaited awakening of cultural interest among the nouveaux riches, which is a precondition for the development of the local contemporary art market. Critics say it gives one collector-curator the power to distort Hungary's art scene and interfere with sacrosanct artistic freedoms.

MEO – Contemporary Art Collection

MEO – Kortárs Mővészeti Gyűjtemény
IV. József Attila utca 4-6 (272 0876/
www.meo.org.hu). M3 Újpest-Városközpont.
Open 11am-6pm Tue-Sun. **Admission** Ft1,000;
Ft600 concessions. **No credit cards.**

Arts & Entertainment

Ernst Múzeum

VI. Nagymező utca 8 (341 4355/www.ernst muzeum.hu). M1 Opera. **Open** 10am-6pm Tue-Sun. **Admission** Ft100; Ft50 concessions. **No credit cards. Map** p246 D3.
This was an exhibition space in a block of artists' studios commissioned by collector Lajos Ernst in 1912. Organises exhibitions of contemporary local, and sometimes international, artists.

Goethe Institut

VI. Andrássy út 64 (374 4070/www.goethe.de/ms/ bud). M1 Opera. **Open** noon-7pm Tue-Fri; noon-4pm Sat. **Admission** *Exhibitions* free. **Map** p246 D3.
A regular fixture on the openings circuit, popular for its serious-minded exhibition programme, featuring both Hungarian and German artists.

Institut Français

I. Fő utca 17 (202 1133/www.inst-france.hu). M2 Batthyány tér/tram 19. **Open** 10am-7pm Mon-Fri. **Admission** *Exhibitions* free. **Map** p245 B3.
Within George Morriose's pastel pink-and-green cube along the Danube, the French Institute is the liveliest of the foreign cultural centres. Exhibitions feature modern art and photography.

Liget Galéria

XIV. Ajtósi Dürer sor 5 (351 4924/www.c3.hu). Trolleybus 74, 75. **Open** 2-6pm Mon, Wed-Sun. Openings on Fri. **Admission** free. **Map** p247 F2.
Tiny exhibition space in a peripheral location, run by respected artist Tibor Várnagy, consistently shows the most interesting and authentically underground Hungarian artists before their 'discovery'.

Ludwig Museum Budapest/ Museum of Contemporary Art

Wing A, Buda Palace, I. Dísz tér 17 (375 9175/ www.c3.hu/~ludwig). Várbusz from M2 Moszkva tér/bus 16. **Open** 10am-6pm Tue-Sun. **Admission** Ft200; Ft100 concessions. **No credit cards. Map** p248 B4.

One of many museums set up worldwide to show the modern collection of Peter and Irene Ludwig, it includes works by Picasso, Warhol and other stars. It's also Hungary's Museum of Contemporary Art, organising group and individual shows for Hungarian artists and major contests. A good place for an overview of Hungarian art since the 1960s, as well as contemporary art from all over Central Europe.

Mai Manó Fotógaléria

Magyar Fotográfusok Háza – Mai Manó Ház/Galéria
VI. Nagymező utca 20 (473 2666/www.maimano.hu). M1 Opera. **Open** 2-6pm Mon-Fri. **Map** p246 D3.
Housed in an appropriately photogenic fin-de-siècle gem, this gallery celebrates Budapest's rich photographic tradition (*see also p68* **Black-and-white Budapest**). It also hosts exhibitions straddling the fruitful boundary between fine art and photography. The biggest collection of Hungarian photography is at the Museum of Photography in Kecskemét.

Óbudai Társaskör Galéria

III. Kis Korona utca 7 (250 0288). Tram 1/bus 6, 60. **Open** 2-6pm Tue-Sun. Closed in summer. **Admission** Ft50. **No credit cards.**
For 20 years, this tiny vault in the cellar of the local community centre has displayed both 'forgotten' oeuvres and first shows. Often features globally acknowledged artists, or those who soon will be.

Palace of Exhibitions

Műcsarnok
XIV. Dózsa György út 37 (343 7401/ www.mucsarnok.hu). M1 Hősök tere. **Open** *Museum* 10am-6pm Tue-Sun. *Library & archive* 10am-6pm Mon-Fri. **Admission** Ft300; Ft100 concessions. **No credit cards. Map** p247 E1.
Established in 1896 as the exhibition hall of the Society of Artists, this is Hungary's largest exhibition space devoted to temporary exhibits of both Hungarian and international artists. Highlights include huge, single medium exhibitions, which give a true impression of the variety of Hungarian art.

Ateliers Pro Arts has a trendy gallery...

...and an arty restaurant. See p166.

Polish Contemporary Art Gallery

VI. Andrássy út 32 (331 1168/www.polinst.co.hu).
M1 Opera. **Open** 11am-7pm Tue-Fri; 10am-2pm Sat.
Admission *Exhibitions* free. **Map** p246 D3.
The gallery at the Polish Institute is becoming an
increasingly popular venue for contemporary art,
with a fresh, imaginative programme.

Stúdió Galéria

V. Képíró utca 6 (267 2033/www.c3.hu/fkse).
M3 Kálvin tér/tram 47, 49. **Open** 2-6pm Mon-Sat.
Closed Aug. **Admission** free. **Map** p249 D5.
The Studio of Young Artists limits full membership
to those under the age of 35 and provides its 300 or
so members with exposure and cheap studio space.

Trafó Galéria

IX. Liliom utca 41 (215 1600/www.c3.hu/trafo). M3
Ferenc körút/tram 4, 6. **Open** 4-7pm Mon-Sat; 2-8pm
Sun. Openings on Fri. **Admission** free. **Map** p250 E5.
The gallery element of this major cultural centre (*see*
p189 **Sparking a cultural revolution**).

Commercial galleries

Ateliers Pro Arts/A.P.A.!

VIII. Horánszky utca 5 (486 2370/www.ateliers.hu).
M3 Kalvin tér/tram 47, 49. **Open** 2-7pm Tue-Fri;
11am-6pm Sat. **No credit cards. Map** p249 D4.
New centre established by American John Warren
Gotsch shows well-known commercial painters.

Blitz Galéria

IV. József Attila utca 4-6 (272 0800/www.blitz.hu).
M3 Újpest-Városközpont. **Open** 11am-6pm Tue-Sun.
Admission varies. **No credit cards.**
Strategically located at the non-profit art museum
owned by Lajos Kováts, this is the commercial arm
of his art empire (*see p160* **Art attack**).

Deák Erika Galéria

VI. Jókai tér 1 (302 4927/deakgal@c3.hu). M1
Oktogon/tram 4, 6. **Open** noon-6pm Wed-Fri;
noon-3pm Sat. **No credit cards. Map** p246 D3.

The local art world's favourite private gallery showcases trendy figurative 'post-medial' painters, but
also includes less commercial art.

Dovin Galéria

V. Galamb utca 6 (318 3673/318 3659). M1
Vörösmarty tér/tram 2. **Open** noon-6pm Tue-Fri;
11am-2pm Sat. **No credit cards. Map** p249 C4.
Financially viable gallery shows Hungarian painters
and sculptors of the middle and younger generation,
notably El Kazovszkij and Andrea Huszár.

Knoll Galéria Budapest

VI. Liszt Ferenc tér 10 (267 3842/knollgaleria@
elender.hu). M1 *Oktogon/tram 4, 6.* **Open** 2-6.30pm
Tue-Fri; 11am-2pm Sat. Closed Aug. **No credit
cards. Map** p246 D3.
Hans Knoll's respected gallery shows Hungarian
artists like Ákos Birkas and János Sugár, rising
young stars like János Fodor and Tibor Horváth, and
artists from neighbouring countries.

MAMÜ Galéria

VII. Damjanich utca 39, entrance on Murányi utca
(306 1587/ma-mu@freemail.hu). Tram 70. **Open**
3-7pm Tue, Sat, Sun. **No credit cards. Map** p247 F2.
Small gallery in a cellar run by the association with
the same Dada-esque name that originally focused
on Hungarian artists in Romania.

Várfok 14 Galéria

I. Várfok utca 14 (213 5155/489 3920/www.varfok-
galeria.hu). M2 *Moszkva tér/tram 4, 6, 18.* **Open** 11am-
6pm Tue-Sat. **Credit** AmEx, MC, V. **Map** p245 A3.
Owned by collector Károly Szalóky, who's promoted
the careers of bankable artists like Imre Bukta,
István Nádler, László feLugossy and El Kazovszkij.

Vintage Galéria

V. Magyar utca 26 (337 0584/www.vintage.hu). M2
Astoria/tram 47, 49/bus 7. **Open** 2-7pm Tue-Fri.
Closed July, Aug. **No credit cards. Map** p249 D4.
Devoted exclusively to fine-art photography, espe-
cially Hungarian Modernists (1919-48) and younger
photo artists like Balázs Beöthy and Hajnal Németh.

Arts & Entertainment

Gay & Lesbian

Eastern Europe's emerging gay mecca provides cheap fun for Westerners.

Budapest has seen a pink revolution of late. Although not a big scene compared to the West, it offers some unique experiences for the gay traveller. A steam in one of the gay baths shouldn't be missed. Democracy has brought with it a new sexual freedom and although gay Hungarians remain closeted at work, their visibility in public is more pronounced. Sunset on the embankment between Erzsébet Bridge and Március 15 tér – the 'Danube Cruise' – gives you a good impression of gay society in Budapest. You'll find yourself in a very public (and very beautiful) gay cruising area, visited by locals, foreigners and hustlers alike.

Budapest's gay bars and clubs attract gays of every age and preference – you won't find anywhere that targets a particular audience, such as leather bars. Neither will you find a gay place open all day, apart from the odd gay café, and the commercial infrastructure still hasn't a great deal to offer lesbians.

Once Hungary joins the EU, locals can expect an influx of gay tourists keen to take advantage of one of the cheapest gay destinations on offer. This may alter the face of gay Budapest, but mass commercialism is a few years away and this vibrant city offers a refreshing alternative.

Many Magyar gays and lesbians have little experience of the gay liberation movement, and have difficulty acknowledging their gay identity. Gay and lesbian organisations still only attract a certain type of person today, and make little effort to be present at nightspots or get people involved in other ways. This could be why the Lesbian and Gay Pride event only attracts 1,000 people, although this represents a quadrupling over the last five years. There are two gay magazines: *Mások*, a monthly reaching a nationwide audience of over 15,000; and a free monthly *Na Végre!* with basic listings information in Hungarian and English. There are also two gay radio programmes: one on Tilos Rádió (98.0FM; every second Thursday 11pm-midnight); the other on state-run Petőfi Rádió (94.8FM; every fourth Monday 10-11pm). Both are presented by Balázs Pálfi, who interviews people and takes calls from listeners.

The age of consent for gay men has been lowered to 14, in line with heterosexuals. Gay marriage isn't possible, but gay couples can register themselves as 'partners living together' just like their straight counterparts. For a country whose gay scene is still in its infancy, this is a long-awaited radical move.

For local groups, information and helplines, *see p221 Gay & lesbian.*

Accommodation

The boom in gay-specific accommodation hasn't quite hit Budapest yet, but the following recommended places are gay-owned and regularly advertise in the gay press:

Holló Apartments

VII. Holló utca 4 (06 309 32 33 34/www.gaystay.net/hollo). M1, M2, M3 Deák tér/tram 47, 49. **Rates** €70 per room. **No credit cards. Map** p246 D3.
Near the Synagogue, these spacious apartments come with phone, fridge, bathroom and kitchenette. Cold breakfast available.

KM Saga Guest Residence

IX. Lónyai utca 17 (217 1934/www.gaystay.net/kmsaga). M3 Kálvin tér. **Rates** single €35-€63; double €43-€75. **No credit cards. Map** p250 F5.
This guesthouse near the Gellért and gay locations like the Action and Darling Bars is set in an antique-furnished art nouveau building. The gay owners speak English, German, French and Russian.

Eating out

Amstel River Café

V. Párizsi utca 6 (266 4334). M3 Ferenciek tere. **Open** noon-midnight daily. **Average** Ft1,500. **No credit cards. Map** p249 C4.
A café-restaurant by the Danube frequented by gays and the odd straight tourist. This tends to be a first-stop meeting place for gay people before going on to the bars. Outside tables in scenic surroundings.

Club 93 Pizzeria

VIII. Vas utca 2 (338 1119). M2 Blaha Lujza tér/tram 4, 6/bus 7, 78/night bus 78É. **Open** noon-1am daily. **Average** Ft1,000. **No credit cards. Map** p249 D4.
A popular place that's gay-owned, gay-staffed and frequented by local lesbians and gay men.

Events

For info on the annual Gay Pride Day and Gay & Lesbian Cultural Festival (June or July) and World AIDS Day (1 December), contact Háttér (*see below*) or visit www.gaypride.hu.

Arts & Entertainment

Gay

Cafés, bars & clubs

Action Bar
V. Magyar utca 42 (266 9148). M3 Kálvin tér/tram 47, 49/night bus 14É, 50É. **Open** 9pm-4am daily. **Admission** Ft1,000. **No credit cards. Map** p249 D4.
Popular cellar bar with videos and the busiest darkroom in town, especially around midnight. Drinks are purchased with a card and paid for later – don't lose it as you'll be charged a much higher flat fee. Drinks prices increase substantially after midnight.

Angyal Club
VII. Szövetség utca 33 (351 6490). M2 Blaha Lujza tér/tram 4, 6/night bus 6É, 78É. **Open** 10pm-midnight Thur; 10pm-dawn Fri, Sat. **Admission** Ft700-Ft800. **No credit cards. Map** p247 E3.
The city's most popular gay club, now in its 14th year. Downstairs is a well-lit basement bar, a crowded cave-like disco and darkroom. Upstairs there's a restaurant and a stage for weekend drag shows starting at 11.45pm. Friday is popular with lesbians, Saturday is men only.

Capella
V. Belgrád rakpart 23 (318 6231). M3 Ferenciek tere/tram 2/night bus 78É. **Open** 9pm-5am Tue-Sun. **Admission** Tue-Thur Ft1,000. Fri-Sun Ft1,500. Free varying nights of wk; free to all before 11pm Sun. **No credit cards. Map** p249 C5.
A labyrinth of bars and dancefloors. Wednesdays and Saturdays are the gay nights (but still quite mixed). Otherwise it's a trendy mixed crowd, and there are drag shows every Wednesday, Friday, Saturday and Sunday. Rarely gets going before midnight.

Chaos Music Pub
VII. Dohány utca 38 (344 4884). M2 Astoria/tram 47, 49/night bus 14É, 50É, 78É. **Open** 9pm-4am Mon-Sun; 8pm-5am Fri, Sat. **Admission** free. **No credit cards. Map** p249 D4.
Friendly gay pub with a small dancefloor. Popular with crowds going on to other clubs.

Darling Bar
V. Szép utca 1 (266 7564). M2 Astoria/tram 47, 49/night bus 14É, 50É, 78É. **Open** 7pm-2am daily. **Admission** free. **No credit cards. Map** p249 D4.
A small bar downstairs with a backroom behind the bar area. Upstairs is bench-lined walls for intimate video viewing, with a larger video behind the bar.

Gloryhole Video Mozi Centre & Fantasy Club
XIII. Radnóti Miklós utca 18 (490 3937/www.gloryhole.hu). **Open** 10am-midnight Mon-Thur; 10am-5am Fri; 2pm-5am Sat; 2pm-midnight Sun. **Admission** Day passes Ft1,500; Ft1,000 under-25s; Ft700 students. **No credit cards. Map** p246 C1.
By the Westend City Center mall, this bar, video emporium and sex cinema attracts a mixed crowd

for all-day and all-night cruising. Recommended for a younger clientele. Also semi-nude and erotic fetish and uniform disco. Check venue for times.

Mystery Bar
V. Nagysándor József utca 3 (312 1436). M3 Arany János utca/night bus 14É, 50É. **Open** 4pm-4am Mon-Fri; 6pm-4am Sat, Sun. **Admission** free. **No credit cards. Map** p246 C3.
This quiet sit-down bar doubles up as an internet café. Snacks served.

Baths & beaches

The most famous are at the **Gellért Hotel** (see p39 **Taking the waters** and pp146-8). A good time to go is weekdays between 4pm and 6.30pm, but recently gay men have shied away due to the high entrance fee and stuffy atmosphere. The most popular gay baths are at the **Király**; the best times to go are late afternoon on Tuesdays, Thursdays and Saturdays. Staff tend not to speak English. To the north of town is **Omszki Lake**, where the nudist area is recommended for swimming and cruising. Take the HÉV to Budakalász. The lake is about 30 minutes' walk.

Condoms & lubricant

Condoms for anal intercourse are available in pharmacy chains such as Azúr or Rossmann. Lubricants can only be purchased in sex shops and one or two of the bars with backrooms.

Cruising areas

The Danube Cruise, between Vigadó tér and the statue of Petőfi near Erzsébet Bridge, is busiest around sunset. Not everyone looking for action will be a hustler. Also known for night-time activity are the Germanus Gyula Park just north of the Buda foot of Margaret Bridge, and the Népliget around the Planetarium.

Sauna

Magnum Szauna
VIII. Csepreghy utca 2 (267 2532/www.magnum szauna.hu). M3 Ferenc körút/night bus 6É. **Open** 1pm-midnight Mon-Sun; 1pm-2am Fri; 1pm-4am Sat. **Admission** Ft1,500-Ft1,650. **Map** p250 F5.
New, clean and popular gay-only sauna with a steam room, video room, gym and massage services.

Sex shops

Apolló Szexshop és videomozi
VI. Teréz körút 3 (342 1911). M1 Oktogon/tram 4, 6. **Open** 10am-10pm Mon-Fri; 10am-2pm Sat. **No credit cards. Map** p246 D2.

Nights can really drag at **Capella**.
See p164.

Air-conditioned video screening room and shop with a gay clientele. Large video and DVD selection.

Connection Szex Shop
II. Bercsényi utca 3 (06 20 939 1651). Bus 57, 63. **Open** 10am-10pm Mon-Fri; 10am-2am Sat. **No credit cards.**
Well-stocked sex shop selling the usual adult fare.

Lesbian

Hungary's first registered lesbian organisation is now working to promote gay and lesbian education in schools, and an increasingly visible, supportive community is providing a safe space that makes it easier for women to come out. Though small, the lesbian community is an accessible one for foreigners to break into.

Cafés, bars & clubs

See also p164 **Angyal Club** *and* **Mystery Bar**.

Café Eklektika
V. Semmelweis utca 21 (266 3054). M2 Astoria/ tram 47, 49/night bus 14É, 50É, 78É. **Open** noon-1am Mon-Fri; 5pm-1am Sat, Sun. *Lesbian party* 10pm-dawn 2nd Sat of mth. **Admission** varies. **No credit cards. Map** p249 C4.
In a city without a lesbian bar, the monthly women's night in Eklektika is the one constant dykes in town can always count on, thanks to devoted manager and matron Gotti. Also offers gay and lesbian ballroom dancing, with instruction on Sundays from 7pm.

Kópia Café
VI. Zichy Jenő utca 4. M3 Arany János utca. **Open** 4-10pm Tue-Sat. **No credit cards. Map** p246 C3.
A friendly new cellar café/photo gallery with comfy armchairs and lesbian staff. Women's nights on Fridays from 4pm to 10pm.

Shokk Caffé Oestro-shock parties
VIII. Üllői út 66A, entrance at Nagytemplom utca. M3 Ferenc körút/night bus 6É. **Open** *Lesbian party* 9pm-dawn last Sat of mth. **Admission** Ft500. **No credit cards. Map** p250 E5.
The design marries Munch-style wall paintings to rococo metal furniture, the backdrop for renowned lesbian DJs Barbi-Q and Sissy to rock the house.

Information

You'll find English forums and chat rooms at www.pestidiva.hu and www.femfatal.hu.

Music

Distinguished in folk and classical, dire when it comes to rock.

Pesti Vigadó's faux-romantic interior
is an acoustic washout. *See p168.*

Classical & Opera

Magyars are raised with an elemental sense of
their rich musical history. After the two greatest
Hungarian composers of the 20th century, Béla
Bartók and Zoltán Kodály, had incorporated
traditional folk melodies into their work and
teachings, Hungarian music freed itself from the
influence of Germany and Vienna. The gradual
introduction of these harmonic structures
would be as important to Hungary's new-found
national identity as the works of any local
writer, architect or politician.

Bartók and Kodály had ventured out to the
remote regions of Greater Hungary to document
the vanishing folk heritage. Bartók assimilated
this ethnomusical research to become one of the
leading composers of the 1900s. By combining
the melodies and rugged dance rhythms of
Eastern European folk with the compositional
techniques of the Western avant-garde, Bartók
created a distinctly Magyar music style that
has proved an inspiration for successive
composers, György Ligeti and Péter Eötvös
included. Kodály created a method of music

training based on the folk songs they collected.
He would shape musical appreciation for every
Hungarian generation to follow.

Today, Budapest boasts seven symphony
orchestras, enjoyed by a knowledgeable concert-
going public. The season runs from September
to June, with anything from two to ten or more
concerts every night. Programming includes
plenty of Bartók, Kodály and the standards of
the classical tradition. There's also a thriving
scene for early and contemporary music.

In summer there are outdoor concerts at the
Vajdahunyad Castle in the **City Park**, the
Kiscelli Museum in Óbuda and **Matthias
Church** in the Castle District (*see pp43-88*).

A free monthly listing of classical and opera
events, *Koncert Kalendárium* (Hungarian only),
is available at ticket agencies and record shops.
Listings and concert recommendations in
English can be found in the *Budapest Sun*.

Orchestras & choirs

Although the city's seven orchestras maintain a
high standard – just a shade down from the
world's most famous names, in fact – local
musicians' salaries are still rather low by

Western standards. Many leading local musical figures are forced to head abroad to look for better paid work elsewhere.

The exception is the **Budapesti Fesztivál Zenekar**, winner of the Gramophone Award for best orchestral recording. Founded by its principal conductor Iván Fischer and pianist Zoltán Kocsis in 1983, the BFZ was originally an ad-hoc group of the country's best musicians, and only achieved permanent status in 1992. More financially secure than the other orchestras, the BFZ attracts the best musicians and is in a position to invite renowned soloists and conductors from abroad. As well as its orchestral concerts – most of which sell out – the players also give chamber music concerts.

The **Nemzeti Filharmonikusok** is also making a name for itself abroad. With artistic director Zoltán Kocsis and principal resident conductor Zsolt Hamar, the National Philharmonic received enthusiastic reviews of its US concert tour in 2003. Conductor Kocsis occasionally appears with the orchestra as piano soloist, but the ensemble also lures big names like Joshua Bell and Kim Kashkashian.

The latest big player on the orchestral scene is the **Matáv Szimfonikus Zenekar**. Its artistic director András Ligeti has developed the group from the humble Postal Orchestra to an eager-to-achieve dynamic young collective that excels in the music of Mahler, Strauss, Stravinsky and Bartók. With support from telecom giant Matáv, the MSzZ is competitive in getting young talent, and enviably has its own home for rehearsals and chamber concerts.

In 1993 pianist Tamás Vásáry came back from abroad to become the conductor of the **Magyar Rádió Szimfonikus Zenekar**. Both the charismatic Vásáry and the Radio Orchestra are very popular, and he often directs the orchestra from the piano in Mozart concertos.

Part of Kodály's legacy is that choirs here are second to none. The **Nemzeti Énekkar** (National Choir) and the **Magyar Rádió Énekkara** (Hungarian Radio Choir) perform both sacred and secular works, old and modern, either a cappella or with their orchestras. The **Magyar Rádió Gyermekkórusa** (Hungarian Radio Children's Choir) has no equal and joyously sings works from a broad repertoire, especially contemporary Hungarian works.

Soloists & smaller ensembles

There's no shortage of chamber music or solo recitals in Budapest. For piano music, try to catch recitals by Dezső Ránki and Gergely Bogányi. On occasion, Zoltán Kocsis gives or participates in a recital and András Schiff comes to the capital relatively regularly. Young violinist Barnabás Kelemen frequently appears in recital or as soloist with an orchestra, and you won't find a more sublime cellist than Miklós Perényi. Mezzo-soprano Andrea Meláth is the best singer of the younger generation. Any concerts by the **Forrás Chamber Group** and the **Keller Quartet** are a sure hit. Two young conductors to watch out for are Domonkos Héja and his **Danubia Ifjúsági Szimfonikus Zenekar**; and György Vashegyi and his early music groups, the **Purcell Kórus** and the **Orfeo Zenekar**, who perform baroque music on period instruments.

Concert venues

The most important concerts take place primarily in four or five halls, but smaller halls and churches are also called into service to accommodate the large number of performances.

Bartók Memorial House

Bartók Emlékház
II. Csalán út 29 (394 2100). Bus 5, 29. **Open** *no box office; museum* 10am-5pm Tue-Sun; *tickets* on sale 1hr before performance and during museum hours. Closed Aug. **No credit cards.**
Bartók's last Budapest residence, now a museum, hosts a series of Friday evening chamber concerts by Hungary's recitalists. The low ceiling can be somewhat claustrophobic, but the chairs here are the most comfortable of any venue in Budapest. Also used on other days of the week (*see p63*).

Budapest Congress Centre

Budapest Kongresszusi Központ
XII. Jagelló út 1-3 (372 5429). M2 Déli pu., then tram 61. **Open** *box office* 4-6.30pm Wed, Fri; 10am-2pm Sat. **No credit cards. Map** p248 A5.
An ugly convention centre with poor acoustics, this is where many of the world-famous stars perform, mainly during festivals, because of its large seating capacity of 1,750. Don't bother with famous smaller ensembles unless you can get seats up front.

Ceremonial Hall of the Hungarian Academy of Sciences

MTA Diszterme
V. Roosevelt tér 9 (411 6100). M1 Vörösmarty tér/ tram 2. **Tickets** on sale 1hr before performances. Closed July-Aug. **No credit cards. Map** p246 C3.
Count István Széchenyi (*see p11* **One-offs**) gave a year's income in 1825 to form the Hungarian Science Association, now the Hungarian Academy of Sciences. This decorated hall, by the Chain Bridge, is acoustically excellent for chamber music and smaller orchestras. Get here early because seating is on a first-come, first-served basis.

Matthias Church

Mátyás templom
I. Szentháromság tér 2 (355 5657). M2 Moszkva tér, then Várbusz/bus 16. **Tickets** on sale 1hr before

Arts & Entertainment

performances or 1-5.30pm Wed-Sun. **No credit cards. Map** p245 A3.

A top venue for organ recitals and concerts of sacred music for a cappella choir or choir and orchestra all year round. Arrive early and get a seat close to the front to avoid cavernous space acoustics.

Nádor Hall
Nádor terem

XIV. Ajtósi Dürer sor 39 (344 7072). Trolleybus 72, 74, 75. **Tickets** on sale 1hr before performance. Closed July-Aug. **No credit cards.**

A gorgeous little art nouveau concert hall in the Institute for the Blind, with excellent acoustics and a rich programme of song recitals, chamber music and baroque ensembles.

Óbuda Social Circle
Óbudai Társaskör

III. Kis Korona utca 7 (250 0288). HÉV to Árpád híd. **Open** *box office* 10am-6pm daily. **No credit cards.**

This charming little building is one of the few left from early 19th-century Óbuda. Intimate, it hosts excellent recitals and chamber music concerts.

Pesti Vigadó
V. Vigadó tér 2 (318 9903). M1 Vörösmarty tér/tram 2. **Tickets** on sale 1hr before performance. **No credit cards. Map** p249 C4.

Because of its riverside location, the Vigadó stages more touristically oriented concerts. But the kitschy Socialist-modern restoration of the faux-romantic interior (itself a scandal in 1864) makes it not only embarrassing to look at, but also an acoustic washout. Too bad, because the Vigadó also staged the première of Mahler's First Symphony.

Zeneakadémia
VI. Liszt Ferenc tér 8 (342 0179). M1 Oktogon/tram 4, 6. **Open** *box office* 10am-1pm, 2-8pm Mon-Fri; 2-8pm Sat, Sun. **No credit cards. Map** p246 D3.

A gem of Hungarian Secession architecture, the Zeneakadémia has been home to the Franz Liszt Academy of Music since 1907 – and is Budapest's primary concert hall. Nearly all of Hungary's top musicians learned their craft here, as did those who taught them. Recognised as one of the great acoustic masterpieces of the world, the 1,200-seat Nagy terem (Large Concert Hall) hosts concerts most nights. The lack of any air circulation system can make it quite stifling in the warmer months, but it's generally closed in July and August. The smaller Kisterem upstairs occasionally provides a space for chamber and contemporary music.

Opera

The Hungarian State Opera stages some 60 opera and ballet productions every year at two venues. The pride of all Hungarian theatres is the opulent **Opera House** on Andrássy út, where the bulk of the German repertoire and most prestigious Italian productions are given.

The more mainstream opera for the masses is performed at the starkly Socialist Erkel Színház, with acoustics as awful as its interior.

The Opera House has a rich history (Gustav Mahler and Otto Klemperer were intendants) and was the most modern building of its kind when finished in 1884. It has everything an opera house should have, except top-notch performers. Weak finances and mismanagement have sent the best talent abroad. Its principal conductors, Rico Saccani and János Kovács, know their business well, but the quality of the performances can be unpredictable. Familiar repertoire can be routine and lacklustre. At other times, everything clicks and performances are truly exhilarating. In spite of the lack of funds, new productions tend to be colourful and engaging through imaginative sets, costumes and direction, but older sets and productions can be shabby and low-budget. There are at least four opera and three ballet premieres a year. For two weeks in mid-August, an opera and ballet festival is held here (*see p144*). The Opera House also sometimes hosts symphonic concerts featuring its own orchestra.

The State Opera publishes a monthly schedule, available here and at ticket agencies. Performances are listed in the back of the *Koncert Kalendárium* and in the *Budapest Sun*.

Erkel Színház
VIII. Köztársaság tér 30 (333 0540). M2 Blaha Lujza tér/tram 4, 6. **Open** *box office* 10am-7pm Tue-Sat performance days; 10am-1pm, 4-7pm Sun performance days. **Credit** AmEx. **Map** p250 E4.

Opera House
Magyar Állami Operaház

VI. Andrássy út 22 (353 0170). M1 Opera. **Open** *box office* 11am-performance time on concert days; 11am-5pm daily otherwise. Closed July. **Credit** MC, V. **Map** p246 D3.

Ticket agencies

Few classical concerts in Budapest sell out. With the exception of the Festival Orchestra's subscription series, tickets are usually available and affordable unless a major international artist is involved. Tickets for most concerts can be bought at the **Vigadó Ticket Service**, the **Zeneakadémia**, the **Matáv Orchestra Ticket Office** and **Ticket Express**. What isn't available there can be bought at venues an hour or so before the performance. Tickets for the Opera House and Erkel Színház are only available at their respective box offices and at the State Opera Ticket Office a few doors down Andrássy út. Most places only accept cash, but prices aren't extortionate. *Koncert Kalendárium* notes where tickets are available for each event.

Arts & Entertainment

Zeneakadémia – the city's primary concert hall. *See p168.*

Matáv Orchestra Ticket Office

VI. Nagymező utca 19 (302 3841). M1 Opera. **Open** 10am-7pm Mon-Fri; 9am-2pm Sat. **No credit cards.** **Map** p246 D3.

Rózsavölgyi Music Shop

V. Szervita tér 5 (318 3500). M1 Vörösmarty *tér.* **Open** 10am-6pm Mon-Fri; 10am-3pm Sat. **Credit** AmEx, DC, MC, V. **Map** p249 C4.
Concert tickets for pop, classical and opera.

State Opera Ticket Office

VI. Andrássy út 20 (353 0170). M1 Opera. **Open** 10am-5.30pm Mon-Thur; 10am-4.30pm Fri. **Credit** AmEx. **Map** p246 D3.

Ticket Express

VI. Andrássy út 18 & 5 other locations (312 0000). M1 Opera. **Open** 9.30am-6.30pm Mon-Fri. Office at VI. Jókai utca 40 open 10am-7pm Sat. **No credit cards** unless ordered over the phone (06 03 303 0999) or online at *www.tex.hu.* **Map** p246 D3.
Branches (Open 9.30am-6.30pm Mon-Fri): IBUSZ, V. Ferenciek tere 10 (485 2700); V. Kecskeméti utca 8 (266 3025); V. Deák Ferenc utca 19 (266 7070); VIII. József körút 50 (334 0369).
Tickets for classical and pop concerts, opera and operetta, theatre, dance and TV shows.

Vigadó Ticket Service

V. Vörösmarty tér 1 (327 4322). M1 Vörösmarty *tér/tram 2.* **Open** 10am-6pm Mon-Fri; 10am-3pm Sat, Sun. **No credit cards.** **Map** p249 C4.
Centrally located office that has almost everything.

Festivals

The most important festival in Hungary is the Budapest Spring Festival, a cultural tour de force extravaganza over one fortnight in March. It attracts leading international soloists and orchestras, as well as the best local musicians. Its sister is the Budapest Autumn Festival in October, which focuses on contemporary Hungarian music and arts. The Music of Our Time festival in October is another week of new Hungarian music, and the Budapest Early Music Forum in the last week of May presents baroque and renaissance music in historical performances. Festival tickets are available at the regular outlets. *See also pp142-5.*

Budapest Festival Centre

V. Egyetem tér 5 (486 3311/www.fesztivalvaros.hu). M3 Kálvin tér/tram 47, 49. **Open** 10am-5pm Mon-Fri. **Map** p249 D5.

Rock, Roots & Jazz

Hungarian pop is trapped by circumstance. While Hungary's hit parade is often topped by local mainstream acts, pushing Eminem or Robbie Williams into third place, international acclaim is rare. Magyar artists, stuck with a language they can't export, struggle to release albums abroad, let alone sell them. The ever-decreasing number of sales required to notch a gold disc at home reflects this local stagnation.

Major foreign bands sometimes hit town, but the better ones are generally put off by the lack of decent mid-range venues; many would rather play Prague or Vienna. The one exception is the **Sziget Festival** (*see p172* **Let's spend the week together**), a major week-long bash near Budapest in summer. The **Petőfi Csarnok**, a large concrete hangar in the City Park, occasionally hosts known artists past their best; its open-air summer stage is a pleasant place to catch them, if neither audience nor band is too fussed about the sound quality.

A new, multipurpose arena was added in March 2003. The **Budapest Sports Arena** was built to replace the Sports Hall, burned down at a Christmas fair in 1999. It brought a rush of top acts – Paul McCartney, Bryan Adams and Moby – but little since. Ticket prices still need to suit the Magyar market.

At a lower level, as a network of alternative venues disappeared, so did its troubadours. While big local rock acts still fill stadiums with ceaseless reunion gigs (*see p174* **Never can say goodbye**), the Changes have killed a thriving underground scene. What was there to kick against? Soon came electronica and a revamp of traditional folklore in the name of world music. As Western winds brought in everything the rest of the world had already, Magyars copied it accordingly: reggae, hip hop, indie, Britpop – every genre found a local act happy to plagiarise it.

Rare originality today is provided by Belgä, who explicitly attack the influx of foreign music in homegrown rap numbers. Few of their tunes, however, are radio-friendly. Other acts worth catching are FreshFabrik, Superbutt, Nyers and Strong Deformity, whose latest album *Magic Syrup* is the current flavour of the month. No line-up of artists would be complete without indie band Kispál és a Borz, a veritable national treasure.

Anima Sound System is a collective of sample and scratch wizards who combine a compelling female singer with folk, dub and trance. They've been collaborating with London's Asian Dub Foundation in the last few years, to good effect. Korai Öröm and their various spin-off projects, including Korai Banditos, Korai Üősök and Korai Special Beats – with their fluctuating hordes of drummers and DJs – bridge world music, techno and psychedelia to unique effect. Other electronic acts include Yonderboi, who's aired on MTV and produces easy listening, downtempo music, and Amorf Ördögök, a mix of dub, world music and popular sounds from the 1960s.

Most clubs open until 3am, some until 6am. Admission fee varies from Ft300 to Ft1,000, bigger concerts nearer Ft5,000 to Ft15,000. Note that bouncers can be aggressive, so just smile and politely hand over the modest entrance fee.

Tickets & information

Concert details can be found in the *Budapest Sun*, *Pesti Est* and other assorted free listings magazines. Tickets are available at:

Publika

VII. Károly körút 9 (322 2010/www.publika.hu). M1, M2, M3 Deák tér/tram 47, 49. **Open** 10am-6pm Mon-Fri; 10am-1pm Sat. **No credit cards.** **Map** p249 C4.
Besides cultural and music events, Publika organises conferences, receptions and exhibitions.
Branches: EuroCenter, III. Bécsi út 154 (437 4604); XVII. Pesti út 34 (256 1886).

Ticket Express

VI. Jókai utca 40 (353 0692/ticketline 06 30 3030 999/www.tex.hu). M3 Nyugati pu./tram 4, 6. **Open** 10am-7pm daily. **No credit cards. Map** p246 C2.
Tickets to all the big rock concerts and various other cultural events.
Branches: IBUSZ, V. Ferenciek tere 10 (485 2700); V. Kecskeméti utca 8 (266 3025); VI. Andrássy út 18; VIII. József körút 50 (334 0362).

Concert venues

Budapest Sports Arena

Budapest Sportaréna
XIV. Stefánia út 2 (422 2600/tickets: 422 2682/ www.muco.hu). M2 Népstadion. **Open** *ticket office* 10am-6pm daily. **Admission** varies.
No credit cards.
The latest addition to the venue roster is a multi-purpose stadium with 12,500 seats and six bars. Its very functionality (ice rink transformed into rock venue in 30 minutes) takes away from any ambience it might offer, but it's very welcome all the same.

Millenáris Centre

II. Fény utca 20-22 (438 5335/www.millenaris.hu). Tram 4, 6. **Open** concerts 8pm. **Admission** from Ft500. **No credit cards.**
This culture complex of exhibition hall, theatre and concert hall is set amid greenery near the Mammut mall. Most concerts are held in the *fogadó* or tavern, a modest but satisfactory atmosphere for live music.

Petőfi Csarnok

XIV. Városliget, Zichy Mihály út 14 (363 3730/ www.petoficsarnok.hu). **M1 Széchenyi fürdő. Open** concerts 8pm. **Admission** varies. **No credit cards. Map** p247 F2.

Large events hall in City Park. The indoor arena is too large for most Hungarian bands, but Western acts will stop off here. The outdoor stage is ideal for summer. Both hold around 2,500 people.

Live music clubs

Fat Mo's

V. Nyári Pál utca 11 (267 3199). **M3 Ferenciek tere/bus 7/night bus 14É, 50É, 78É. Open** noon-2am Mon-Wed; noon-4am Thur, Fri; 6pm-4am Sat; 6pm-2am Sun. Concerts 9pm-midnight. **Admission** free. **Credit** DC, MC, V. **Map** p249 C5.

Prohibition-themed Fat Mo's features live blues and jazz acts, dance DJs, Tex-Mex kitchen and a dozen draught beers. Singles nights on Thursdays.

Gödör Klub

V. Erzsébet tér (06 20 943 5464). **M1, M2, M3 Deák tér/tram 47, 49. Admission** varies. **No credit cards. Map** p249 C4.

An occasional club venue under the glassy park of Erzsébet tér. Originally the construction site of the new National Theatre, this place is set in the bunker over which the artificial park was built. Surprisingly, this neon-lit hall with minimalist design has perhaps the best acoustics in town.

Kultiplex

IX. Kinizsi utca 28 (219 0706). **M3 Ferenc körút/ tram 4, 6. Open** 24hrs daily. Concerts start 10pm. **Admission** varies. **No credit cards. Map** p249 D5.

Formerly the Blue Box cinema and music venue, the two-storey Kultiplex still hosts bands, film and DJ nights (*see p156 and p179*), as well as the studio for former pirate station Tilos Rádió. The main concert hall is small and stuffy, its acoustics leave a lot to be desired, but who cares? The place is best in summer when the back garden is open. Cheap drinks and snacks and one or two foreign acts a week.

Old Man's Music Pub

VII. Akácfa utca 13 (322 7645/www.oldmans.hu). M2 Blaha Lujza tér/tram 4, 6/night bus 6É. **Open** 3pm-4am (or till dawn) daily; *restaurant* 3pm-3am daily. Concerts start 9pm. **Admission** varies. **No credit cards. Map** p248 A5.

Large and comfortably furnished, this is the place to catch local blues acts such as Muddy Shoes, György Ferenczi, Tamás Takács Dirty Blues Band and Dr Valter & The Lawbreakers, and stalwarts like Ádám Török, Tibor Tátrai and Hobo. Jazz also gets a look-in. Good acoustics, but book a table if you want a view of the small stage.

Wigwam Rock

XI. Fehérvári út 202 (208 5569/ www.wigwamrockklub.hu). Tram 47/night bus 3É. **Open** 8pm-5am Thur-Sun. **Admission** varies. **No credit cards.**

Belgä at the **Petőfi Csarnok** – hands up if you think the acoustics are rubbish.

Let's spend the week together

The largest music event in Central Europe, the one-week summer Sziget, 'Island' Festival (www.sziget.hu), is now in its second decade. It seems only its isolated location – on an abandoned boatbuilders' island (Hajógyári-sziget) on the Danube – can prevent further rapid expansion.

Visitors for 2002 reached almost 400,000, ten times more than its debut year of 1993. The event was the brainchild of minor music mogul Péter Müller, who wanted to revive two concepts that once forged local youth: the Communist Pioneer summer camps and the underground rock scene of the late 1980s, when bands hung out together free of musicbiz competition. Both concepts died with the Changes of 1989.

Müller and his team set up a few stages and filled them with non-commercial Magyar bands, along with a handful from the region. Camping and entrance fees were kept low, a principle that hasn't changed in ten years. In 1998, you could have seen Bowie for a fiver.

In order to attract such prestigious Western acts, the Sziget (first called Diáksziget, 'Student Island', then, embarrassingly, Eurowoodstock, and for a while – ye Gods – sponsored Pepsisziget) had to grow up fast. Along with attracting MTV Europe to cover the shows and check out the infrastructure (the event is a regular winner of MTV's annual 'Best Organised Festival' award), the Sziget introduced theatre, films, educational programmes, children's activities and fun parks. Today, it really is a cross between a holiday camp and a backstage pass for Glastonbury.

There are more than 50 types of venue on the island, the main stage and world music arena attracting the likes of Prodigy, Blur, Pulp, Oasis and Morcheeba. Confirmed names lined up for Sziget 2003 (30 July-6 Aug) include Massive Attack, the Asian Dub Foundation and Goran Bregovic.

Food and drink are both varied and cheap (one local beer company wins the rights to provide inexpensive ale), amusements plentiful and you can choose to camp or commute to the city by boat, night bus or suburban train. If the occasion arises, you can even get spliced in the wedding tent. In 1994 one fan married his beer.

Barn-sized venue with overdone Wild West theme, but one of Budapest's large stages for rock bands. Weekly rock 'n' roll parties and heavy metal acts. Three bars, dancefloor and games room. Far from the centre but right by the tram stop.

Jazz venues

Jazz has always had a cachet in Hungary, whose most accomplished musicians all made their living abroad. Now several key artists have returned, including saxophonist Tony Lakatos and guitarist Ferenc Snétberger.

Mihály Dresch, who recorded his latest album with Archie Shepp, is a world-class saxophonist who creates his own distinctive folk-jazz, spinning ancient Hungarian tunes into avant-garde experiments. Other ethno-jazzers worth seeking out include Tin Tin Quintet, Makám, violin virtuoso Félix Lajkó and Paris-based saxophonist Akosh S.

Mainstream concerts are also staged at the **Zeneakadémia** (*see p168*), **Institut Français** and **Műcsarnok** (*see p161*).

Jazz Garden

V. Veres Pálné utca 44A (266 7364). M3 Kálvin tér/night bus 6É, 14É, 50É. **Open** *bar* noon-1am Mon-Thur, Sun; noon-2am Fri, Sat; *restaurant* 6pm-1am daily; concerts start 8.30pm. **Admission** varies. **No credit cards. Map** p249 D5.
Cellar club decorated with plants and patio furnishings for a virtual outdoor effect. Beyond the bar/garden space is a rose-hued restaurant area where the live jazz is audible but unobtrusive. Perverse in warmer months, a welcome illusion in the winter.

New Orleans

VI. Lovag utca 5 (268 0802/www.neworleans.hu). M1 Oktogon/tram 4, 6/night bus 6É. **Open** 9pm-3am Thur-Sat. **Admission** varies. **No credit cards. Map** p246 D3.
Hidden in a little side street in the Theatre District, New Orleans is a spacious, lavishly ornamented club with a half-circular arrangement of comfy sofas and small coffee tables centred around the stage. Dinner tables line the balcony. Opened in 2001, New Orleans set itself up as Budapest's main jazz, blues and world music venue. International acts have included the likes of Al Di Meola, Robben Ford, John McLaughlin and Dewey Redman.

Folk & world music

Budapest is one of the few capitals with an active traditional music and dance scene, thanks to its revival by fiddler Béla Halmos and singer Ferenc Sebő in the 1970s. This new 'dance house' or *táncház* movement saw scores of young local musicians swap their electric guitars for fiddles and create a counterculture away from the meddling authorities.

The most well-known exponents were Muzsikás, whose singer, Márta Sebestyen, went on to global fame on albums like *Deep Forest* and film soundtracks like *The English Patient*. Halmos still holds the lead fiddler's chair at the **Kalamajka Dance House**. Beginners can learn the steps at 7pm before the participatory Saturday night session here. The archaic music of the **Csángó Dance House** combines long wooden flutes, koboz lutes, wild fiddling and drumming. Visiting Serbian bands have added a new dimension to the live scene here, with locals BeshoDrom crossing over from folk to dance grooves tied by wild Balkan brass.

The most reliable venue for folk is the **Fonó Budai Zenehz** for village bands, revivalists and the ethno-rave of BeshoDrom. The club also boasts the best folk, world music and jazz CD shop in Hungary, featuring the catalogue of the in-house Fonó record label.

Dance houses close down from June to mid-September, but festivals take place all summer in Budapest and beyond. For details the Dance House Workshop runs the English-language www.tanchaz.hu/thmain.htm.

The contemporary folk sounds of Budapest's Roma community are harder to find. Keep an eye out for Gypsy bands like Kalyi Jag, Ando Drom, Romano Drom or Kal, who all play Roma music in a style that Gypsies play for themselves (*see p85* **Roma Budapest**). You can still find Gypsy bands at restaurants like the Mátyás Pince (V. Március 15 tér 7; 266 8008), the Kulács (VII. Osvát utca 11; 322 3611) or the Margitkert (II. Margit utca 15; 326 0860). The Jewish Klezmer scene has grown in the last decade as well. Check the listings at the Fonó for monthly appearances of bands like Di Naye Kapelye or the Odessza Klezmer band.

Incoming world music acts are often featured at the Fonó and the **Millenáris** (*see p170*).

Csángó Dance House

Marczibányi téri Művelődési Ház, II. Marczibányi tér 5A (212 5660). M2 Moszkva tér/tram 4, 6. **Open** concerts 8pm-midnight Wed. **Admission** varies. **No credit cards. Map** p245 A2.
Best place to find Balkan folk that's all the rage these days. Also runs a folk dance club for kids.

Fonó Budai Zenehz

XI. Sztregova utca 3 (206 5300/www.fono.hu). Tram 41, 47. **Open** concerts from 8pm. **Admission** varies. **No credit cards.**
The Fonó ('Spinning House'), is the epicentre of folk, ethno-jazz and world music in Budapest and has something to offer everyone: traditional Transylvanian bands on a Wednesday night, weekend mini-festivals of Balkan music, plus Tibetan, Greek and Klezmer. Records released on the house label are on sale at the venue.

Arts & Entertainment

Never can say goodbye

To young Hungarians of the 1960s, rock 'n' roll was the sound of freedom, the audio lifeblood of that most desired of chimerae: the West. The repressive post-1956 period had passed and young Magyars put away their worries, picked up guitars, grew their hair as long as legally possible and rocked out – or as we say in Hungarian, *elrákolt*.

And thus was born some of the most bizarre, unmarketable and historically weird music in the history of rock. The Hungarian language – dense, agglutinative, lexically conservative and virtually unlearnable to an outsider – is uniquely unsuited to the singing of rock 'n' roll. Magyar has no sense of pop flow. The accent in Hungarian always falls on the first syllable, which kind of takes the shimmy-she-wobble out of a backbeat born in the American south. Of course, Magyars will take issue with that, but after hearing a group of students singing '*Mi mindannyian lakunk egy sárga tengerallatijáróben!*' you'll never feel quite the same about something as simple as *Yellow Submarine*.

Free to emulate Western music trends, young rockers eagerly snapped up every LP smuggled in from the bloc's rock paradise, Yugoslavia. The result was 'Magyar beat', an entire sound based on some of the worst white rockabilly to come out of the 1950s. Imagine Elvis with a sinus infection, singing with no pauses between words, doing battle with a dozen extra syllables.

In due course, the 1960s produced a slew of state-tolerated Magyar rock bands, such as Omega, LGT, Neoton and Illés. None ever broke outside of Hungary, apart from international releases such as *Live at the Uzbek SSR International Youth Festival*. But they did not quit. Like roadsweepers and registered nurses, rock stars had jobs for life.

As a band, these dinosaurs had their share of break-ups, tragedies and suicides. Post-1989, many became sharp dealers and are now businessmen and media moguls. And every summer these rockers get together for yet another final reunion concert, packing stadiums with denture-shaking power chords.

Geezer rock continues to overshadow the Hungarian pop market. The result has been stultifying for younger Magyar rock artists, who are now edged out by the proliferation of Hungarian-language video TV channels serving a steady diet of Hungarian knock-off rappers, boy and girl groups, and death metal – one of Hungary's more popular genres.

Arts & Entertainment

Kalamajka Dance House

Belvárosi Ifjúsági Művelődési Ház, V. Molnár utca 9 (317 5928). M3 Ferenciek tere/bus 7/night bus 14É, 50É, 78É. **Open** concerts 8pm-late Sat. **Admission** varies. **No credit cards. Map** p249 C5.
Legendary participatory Saturday folk nights.

Outdoor venues

From April to September, outdoor festivals and events take place in the City Park, in the Tabán and on Margaret Island.

Budai Parkszínpad

XI. Kosztolányi Dezső tér (466 9916). Tram 49/bus 7. **Open** from 7pm. **Admission** varies. **No credit cards. Map** p248 B6.
The main summer outdoor venue. Concerts tend to be mainstream pop, although also hosts folk events and the World Music Festival in June (*see p143*).

Specialist shops

Afrofilia Records

VI. Múzeum körút 7 (266 3080). M2 Astoria/tram 47, 49/bus 7. **Open** 11am-7pm Mon-Fri; 11am-4pm Sat. **No credit cards. Map** p249 D4.

Featuring loads of dub, reggae, Afro-Latin, house and drum 'n' bass.

Indie-Go

VIII. Krúdy Gyula utca 7 (486 1777). M3 Kálvin tér. **Open** 11am-8pm Mon-Sat. **No credit cards. Map** p249 D4.
Breakbeat, trip hop, hip hop, Goa and indie.

Tangó

VII. Klauzál utca 9 (352 1146). M2 Blaha Lujza tér/tram 4, 6. **Open** 11am-6pm Mon, Fri; 10am-1pm Sat. **No credit cards. Map** p249 D4.
Buys, sells and exchanges used CDs. Ever-changing collection. Perfect for bargain hunting.

Trancewave

VI. Révay köz 2 (302 2927). M3 Arany János utca. **Open** 11am-8pm Mon-Fri; noon-4pm Sat. **No credit cards. Map** p246 C3.
Hip hop, garage, house and trance feature heavily at Trance-Wave. *See p139 and p180.*

Underground Records

VI. Király utca 54 (343 2640). Tram 4, 6. **Open** 10am-7pm Mon-Fri; 10am-3pm Sat. **No credit cards. Map** p246 D3.
Techno, house, trance, breakbeat and trip hop.

Nightlife

Shake your booty on a boat, in a bath or down a metro underpass.

Budapest is a 24-hour city, albeit one that hides itself like a shy flower – but if you know where to look and are prepared to make a little effort, you can easily party till dawn most nights of the week. In terms of clientele, music and venue, the nightlife scene is varied. You could end up dancing in an isolated field or a glitzy club, but fans of everything from jazz to drum 'n' bass can find a crowd they feel at home with.

As with most things in Budapest, clubbing is still relatively cheap. Expect to pay between Ft1,500-Ft3,000 entry to a decent night, though one-off events with renowned DJs can be more.

Local DJs like Palotai and collectives like the Gimmeshot crew, Chi Recordings and the Tilos Rádió DJs know how to get things going (see p180 **Magyar mix masters**). And the parties they play at can be sublime – dancing in the pool at the **Cinetrip** (see p180) or watching the sun come up at **West Balkan** (see p178 **Summer night city**) could well turn out to be the best night all year. For those who don't need 180-bpm techno, there are still many little cellar clubs, where you can dance to more mainstream music or hear local live bands playing anything from blues to Serbian turbo folk.

The drug culture is not as open as the UK, and you're unlikely to bump into a dealer inside a club. Though penalties for possession are draconian, you can still smell skunk wafting over the city's outdoor clubs. Most people out after midnight are a friendly, befuddled bunch, but beware that bouncers in the commercial clubs can be aggressive and humourless.

As in any other vibrant city, Budapest's night scene is fluid; places open and close quickly, and the party crowd shifts with the current. Keep your eyes peeled, pick up the *Pesti Est*, check flyers at record shops and bars, talk to people and, most importantly, take part.

Music bars

These hybrid bar/dancefloor arrangements offer food, booze, dancing and mingling. Cover charges are rare (unless indicated below), music is patchy and crowds can be thin in the week.

Alcatraz

VII. Nyár utca 1 (478 6010/www.alcatraz.hu). M2 Blaha Lujza tér/tram 4, 6/night bus 6É. **Open** 4pm-midnight Mon-Wed; 4pm-4am Thur-Sat (kitchen closes at 1am). **No credit cards. Map** p249 D4.

Large prison-themed bar/restaurant. Enter a prison door, pay at the 'warden's booth', then descend for more jail buffoonery. Arrow-suited mannequins dig through a wall and Al Capone sits in his cell. The question 'why?' springs to mind, but it's popular with well-heeled twenty/thirtysomethings. Good live acts range from trad jazz to funk.

Bamboo Music Club

VI. Dessewffy utca 44 (312 3619/www.extra.hu/bamboo). M1 Oktogon/tram 4, 6/night bus 6É. **Open** 7pm-4am Tue-Sat. **Admission** free-Ft800. **No credit cards. Map** p246 D2.

Tropical-themed bar with a small cellar attracts a youngish, undiscerning crowd who drink, flirt and dance to mainstream jazzy house and funk. Occasional live bands and amateur talent nights.

ChaChaCha

V. Kálvin tér metro station (no phone). M3 Kálvin tér/tram 47, 49/night bus 14É, 50É. **Open** 11am-5am daily. **No credit cards. Map** p249 D5.

In a metro underpass, this crazy late-night dance bar with zebra-print furniture and pop-art fixtures is run and patronised by good-humoured nutters. Schizophrenic music ranges from dreadful Magyar disco to breakbeats and house by the town's best DJs. The party often overflows the glass-fronted one-room club, spilling into the underpass.

Nincs Pardon

VII. Almássy tér 11 (351 4351). M2 Blaha Lujza tér/tram 4, 6/night bus 6É. **Open** 8pm-4am daily. **Admission** free to Ft500. **No credit cards. Map** p247 E3.

A thirtysomething media crowd favours this cramped and friendly Gaudí-esque cellar. Enjoy well-mixed cocktails before hitting the oxygen-free dancefloor, which is packed, despite atrocious music: top 40 hits and Magyar party staples.

Pesti Est Café

VI. Liszt Ferenc tér 5 (344 4381). M1 Oktogon/tram 4, 6/night bus 6É. **Open** 11am-2am daily. **No credit cards. Map** p246 D3.

The Pesti Est, with its big terrace, is a fine place for daytime snacks and coffee, but, unlike other bars on this square, it also goes on late. The bright, bold design, with lots of metal and neon signs, is a bit shouty, but they can get interesting DJs and events.

Piaf

VI. Nagymező utca 25 (312 3823). M1 Oktogon/tram 4, 6/night bus 6É. **Open** 10pm-7am daily. **Admission** up to Ft1,000 incl a drink. **No credit cards. Map** p246 D3.

Arts & Entertainment

Crazy decor, crazy people
at **ChaChaCha**. *See p175.*

A marvellously depraved old Pest tradition that gets going in the wee hours. A century ago, the city was dotted with dimly-lit orpheums, a cross between a nightclub and a café chantant, louche and luring. In similar vein, the Piaf has an upstairs bar that is done in bordello red and comes with a piano player. The clientele leans towards showbiz/lounge lizard types, with the odd lady scooping up drunks. A dangerous staircase leads to a cellar with tiny dancefloor, where live bands or jazzy pop provide the soundtrack.

Roktogon Music Club

VI. Moszár utca 9 (353 0443). M1 Oktogon/ tram 4, 6/night bus 6É. **Open** 9pm-4am Wed-Sat. **Admission** *for bands* Ft400. **No credit cards.** **Map** p246 D3.

Fun, medium-sized cellar bar/disco specialising in local live bands, from Doors impersonators to hard-core acts. DJs play MTV hits between acts. Clientele is generally young, excitable and friendly.

Sakáltanya Club & Restaurant

V. Curia utca 2 (266 1165). M3 Ferenciek tere/bus 7/night bus 14É, 50É, 78É. **Open** *club* 8pm-2am Fri-Sat; *restaurant/bar* noon-midnight Mon-Sat. **No credit cards.** **Map** p249 C4.

Inspired by the film *Coyote Ugly*, Sakáltanya attempts to recreate the flick's crazy, tequila-fuelled madness, where waitresses are sexy-cool and completely in charge of the salivating male customers. It just about succeeds, and can be a good laugh – but only once.

Late-night clubs & bars

Alagút

I. Alagút utca (212 3754). Tram 18/night bus 49É. **Open** 24hrs daily. **No credit cards.** **Map** p248 A4.

A classic all-night bar, clouded by traffic fumes from the nearby *alagút* ('tunnel') and patronised by drinkers from all walks of life and all parts of Buda. Chess and cards are popular. Breakfast available.

Fészek Club

VII. Kertész utca 36 (342 6549). Tram 4, 6/night bus 6É. **Open** 8pm-5am daily. **Admission** free-Ft150. **No credit cards.** **Map** p246 D3.

In the basement of the actors' and artists' club, the Fészek has offered refuge and rum to performers and their friends for 50-plus years. The old codger on reception may not let you in – go with regulars or just be as polite as you can. Decorated in brothel style, with crushed velvet chaise longues and a natty piano keyboard bartop, depending on the mood you'll either encounter a heaving, glamorous crowd dancing till dawn to a superb live jazz-and-funk combo – or a handful of people sharing a last drink.

Múzeum Cukrászda

VIII. Múzeum körút 10 (338 4415). M2 Astoria/ tram 47, 49/bus 7/night bus 14 É, 50É, 78É. **Open** 24hrs daily. **No credit cards.** **Map** p249 D4.

This Budapest nightlife staple is basically a cake shop where you can get a pint or a shot with your coffee and sweets. Small terrace is a great place to

Kultiplex, run by Tilos Rádió. *See p179.*

have a breakfast beer and pity solid citizens as they scurry to work. Friendly, seen-it-all-before staff serve good-humoured late-night crowd. Recommended.

Noiret

VI Dessewffy utca 8-10 (331 6103). M3 Arany János utca/night bus 6É, 14É, 50É. **Open** 2pm-4am daily. **No credit cards.** **Map** p246 C3.

Billed as a pool and darts club – you can hire big, if worn, Brunswick tables for Ft300 per hour in the long cellar – the central location and late hours also make this a good bet for a last drink and natter. Old Bowie tunes on the jukebox add to the ambience. Bar snacks include hefty pizzas.

Stex Alfréd

VIII. József körút 55-57 (318 5716). Tram 4, 6/ night bus 6É. **Open** 8am-6am daily. **No credit cards.** **Map** p250 E5.

Large, idiosyncratic and recently renovated complex offering pool, gambling, large-screen footie and a bar and restaurant that serves decent Hungarian food until 4am. Nice terrace on the bustling ring road.

Arts & Entertainment

Tulipán Presszó

*V. Nádor utca 32 (269 5043). M2 Kossuth tér/
tram 2.* **Open** 24hrs daily. **No credit cards. Map**
p246 C3.
Friendly 24-hour bar, a haunt of insomniacs and taxi
drivers. The 1970s posters, long card games in the
back and the feeling that everybody knows each
other – they do – add to the charm. The outdoor
tables are quiet at night.

Nightclubs

Bed

*III. Reményi Ede utca (06 70 208 8389). HÉV to
Kaszásdülő.* **Open** 11pm-5am. **Admission** up to
Ft3,000. **No credit cards.**
Flashy new house/Goa trance club near the city's
northern edge is popular with those wishing to be
seen dancing. Glass VIP section overlooks the dancefloor; huge Buddha statue looks over the decks.
Occasional international 'name' DJs, stylish decor,
great sound system and (for Budapest) steep cover.

Capella

*V. Belgrád rakpart 23 (318 6231). M3 Ferenciek
tere/tram 2/night bus 14É, 50É, 78É.* **Open** 9pm-
4am Wed-Thur; 9pm-5am Fri-Sun. **Admission**
Ft1,000-Ft1,500. **No credit cards. Map** p249 C5.
Although invariably billed as a gay club (*see p163*),
straights are welcome to take in the midnight drag

show and get down to house and disco till dawn.
Cover charge will be included on your drinks bill.
Can be one of the best nights out in Budapest.

Citadella Club

XI. Citadella sétány 2 (209 3271). Bus 27. **Open**
10pm-5am on party nights. **Admission** varies.
No credit cards. Map p248 B5.
Indoor club and garden complex in the Citadella
affords unbeatable view of the city. It's now a venue
for one-off parties, which are pretty frequent. Scene
varies depending on the party, so check flyers.

Dokk Bistro & Club

*III. Hajógyári-sziget 122 (457 1023). HÉV to
Filatorigat/bus 86/night bus 42 É.* **Open** 8pm-4am
Mon-Sat. **Credit** AmEx, MC, V.
On an island in the Danube, this big, brassy
bar/club/terrace restaurant with strobe lights and a
car park resembling an Audi dealership is a bit far
away. On Friday nights, mainstream house and funk
are played on an excellent sound system for marketing execs, media moguls, porn stars, producers,
gold-diggers and central casting gangsters. If you
want to pull any of the above, saddle up.

E-Klub

*X. Népligeti, next to Planetarium (263 1614/
www.e-klub.hu). M3 Népliget/night bus 1É, 14É, 50É.*
Open 9pm-5am Fri; 10pm-5am Sat. **Admission**
Ft700-Ft900. **No credit cards.**

Arts & Entertainment

Summer night city

The best of Budapest nightlife takes place in
green spaces on balmy nights under clear
starry skies. From May to September, local
party-goers leave the regular venues and pack
the city's many outdoor clubs, where they can
revel with the abandon that comes from being
outside – and dawn arrives before they know
it. Most spots have concerts followed by DJs,
provide decent food and late closing times.
Admission varies. Clubs tend to be out of the
centre of town, far from pesky neighbours.
Many are clustered in South Buda, allowing
for an outdoor club crawl.

Three main venues sit on the Buda side of
Petőfi Bridge. The **Zöld Párdon** is the oldest.
The fenced-in complex has trees that create
private spaces, and a big deck for a
dancefloor. Great grilled foods too. The
nearby **Café Del Rio,** just north, is pretty
unimaginative. The newest, and perhaps
most interesting, club here is the big **A38
Boat**, a beautifully renovated Ukrainian barge.
Docked just south of the bridge, it's staffed
by some of Budapest's cooler night people.
The top deck offers a large open space for

dancing, small tables and a bar. There's a
glass-walled restaurant, and below decks a
windowless concert hall. Slightly higher door
prices mean a more mature crowd.

South of here, around Lágymányosi Bridge,
are two more outdoor venues. You might want
to take a taxi, but the trip to **West Balkan**
is worth it. This cool club gets known
international DJs and the better local ones.
Even if they're not much older than Zöld
Párdon's crew, the crowd is somehow much
mellower. There's decent food, tree-covered
grassy spaces and the free-flowing Danube
just past the fence.

A short stroll away is the **Partside**, a
tree-shaded club with a mini-wading pool,
grassy patches and its own sandy 'beach'
on the Danube, complete with beach chairs.
It could be sublime, but the meat-rack
atmosphere tends to drive up the
testosterone level on weekends.

Outside South Buda, the **Szimpla Kert** –
in the heart of Pest and close to many bars,
including sister venues the **Szimpla/Dupla**
(*see p123*) – is the most centrally-located

Communist-era rock disco reinvented as a mainstream house/techno nightclub with three dancefloors and a much-improved sound system. Popular with drunk and chemically altered suburban kids. Hosts regular foam parties and teeny discos.

Home Club Budapest

III. Hársany léjtő 6 (06 30 24 22 888/www.homeclub-budapest.com). Free party bus from Westend City Center every hour, M3 Nyugati pu.. Open 10pm-7am Thur-Sat. Admission up to Ft4,500
Huge, glitzy house/trance/techno club with great visuals and a top-notch sound system catering to beautiful people. Bit of a hike, but it's worth sharing a taxi. Events range from a 69 Party with lesbian shows to renowned DJs. Steep cover, but this is the place to catch the Ministry on tour.

Jailhouse

IX. Tüzoltó utca 22 (06 30 989 4905/ http://jailhouse.pardey.org). M3 Ferenc körút/ tram 4, 6/night bus 6É. Open 10pm-5am Wed-Sun. Admission free-Ft800. **No credit cards.** Map p250 E5.
Smoky two-level cellar where some of the better new DJs entertain a young, musically discerning crowd. Currently, Wednesday is African funk and jazz, Thursday chilled jazz and downtempo, Friday drum 'n' bass, Saturday breakbeats. Every second Sunday is progressive, industrial and ambient.

Közgaz Pince Klub

IX. Fővám tér 8 (215 4359). M3 Kalvin tér/tram 2, 47, 49/night bus 14É, 50E. Open 10pm-5am Tue-Sat. Admission Ft 600-Ft1,000. No credit cards. Map p249 C5.
Huge cellar club in the University for Economic Science, where students sink cheap booze, listen to loud Magyar pop, fall over and snog drunkenly. Fag makers BAT have turned the interior into one large cigarette advert. Fun if you like this sort of thing.

Kultiplex

IX. Kinizsi utca 28 (219 0706). M3 Ferenc körút/ tram 4, 6/night bus 6É. Open 24hrs daily. Admission free-Ft1,000. No credit cards. Map p249 D5.
Excellent arts cinema/club/bar complex run by Tilos Rádió and friends (*see p156 and p171*). Two dancefloors, three bars and table football draw a young, trendy, hedonistic crowd. Music often provided by reliable DJs from Tilos and the Gimmeshot Klub (*see p180* **Magyar mix masters**) with accent on drum 'n' bass and dancehall reggae. There are also live acts. Great beer garden with balcony and barbecue.

SOTE Klub

VIII. Nagyvárad tér 4 (210 2930 ext 6441). M3 Nagyvárad tér/night bus 14É. Open 9pm-4.30am Sat. Admission Ft700-Ft1,000. No credit cards. Map p250 F6.

---

outdoor club. It's still private, hidden in the 500sq m back courtyard of an abandoned building. Looking like an outdoor squat party, it has paper lanterns, picnic tables, a busy bar and a stereo that shuts off by midnight. Music or no, Szimpla Kert stays full until late, and will probably do so until it's lost to urban renewal – which may happen in 2004/5.

In the City Park the **Széchenyi Főúri Söröző** has been converted from a tacky, touristified beer garden catering to Bavarians to an outdoor party venue of far better taste catering to locals. DJs come from Juventus, a mainstream local radio station, and the place is handy for nearby one-off party venues Petőfi Csarnok (*see p171*) and Olaf Palme Ház.

A38 Boat

XI. Petőfi híd (217 4354/www.a38.hu). Tram 4, 6/night bus 6É. Open noon-late daily. No credit cards. Map p249 C6.

Café Del Rio

XI. Goldman György ter (no phone). Tram 4, 6/night bus 6É. Open May-Sept 2pm-5am daily. **No credit cards.** Map p249 C6.

Partside

XI. Vizpart utca 2 (463 0422/www.partside.hu). Bus 3, 10, 103/night bus 3É. Open May-Sept 2pm-late daily. No credit cards.

Széchenyi Főúri Söröző

XIV. Állatkerti körút 9-11 (363 8290/ www.szechenyietterem.hu). M1 Széchenyi fürdő/ night bus 1É. Open May-Sept 11am-late daily. **No credit cards.**

Szimpla Kert

VII. Kazinczy utca 55 (no phone). M1, M2, M3 Deák tér/tram 47, 49/night bus 14É, 50É. Open May-Sept noon-4am daily. No credit cards. Map p246 D3.

West Balkan

XI. Kopaszi-gát (371 1807). Bus 3, 10, 103 to Dombóvári út, then follow signs down the dirt road. Open May-Sept 2pm-late daily. **No credit cards.**

Zöld Pardon

XI. Goldman György ter (no phone/www.zp.hu). Tram 4, 6/night bus 6É. Open May-Sept 2pm-5am daily. No credit cards. Map p249 C6.

Magyar mix masters

With the spread of one-off events and special venues (see p178 **Summer night city**), the days of finding reliable resident DJs at a top-notch club in Budapest are fast disappearing. Anything run by Tilos Rádió – Hungary's original pirate radio (www.tilos.hu, 90.3FM) – will be a banker, although the music can vary from progressive house to reggae to hip hop and back again, so it's worth checking who's playing beforehand.

Mainstream house and techno fans will find plenty of entertainment at the more commercial venues – (see p178-9 **E-Klub, Home**) – plus at the annual **Budapest Parade** in August (see p144), where house and trance rule the roost.

For the eclectic end of things, DJ Palotai (pictured) is a sure thing. The daddy of dance music here, Palotai (www.palotai.hu) made his name in legendary underground club Tilos Az Á ten years ago. An obsessive record collector, the prolific Palotai has a large following. His excellent Rewind nights at the **Trafó** (see p180), often with sidekick Cadik, are worth checking out.

Dancehall, reggae and hip hop are well served by the excellent Gimmeshot Klub (DJs Bosi, Skunk and Mango) at the **Kultiplex** (see p179); For drum 'n' bass, the Bladerunnaz group put on a great night, currently Fridays at the **Citadella** (see p178) with DJs Ozon and Bal, plus the pick of the DJ talent from Airbag, DJs Longman and Bratwa. For breakbeats and

trippy dub check Kevin and Naga of Chi Recordings, currently holding court at the **St Tropez** (see p180) boat, and found all over town as well. They also put out some fine cuts on their own Chi label (www.chi-recordings.com). Minimalheadz (Tégla, Isu and Odin) pull a rocking electro/progressive party at the Kashmir Underground (IX. Üllői út 51; 06 20 393 7246).

For live dance acts, check Yonderboi for a mix of ephemera, visuals and breaks, Anima Sound System for Hungarian folk rhythms fused with beats and the Carbonfools for a mean bit of sitar playing. Titusz, the brains behind the Carbonfools, is also a fine DJ in his own right and a veteran of the local underground scene.

Big foreign names come to Hungary through the Global Underground label, which stages one-offs, usually in the Pacha Bar (V. Vígadó tér 2; no phone). If Nick Warren's playing, you'll find him here. The **Cinetrip** (www.cinetrip.hu) is an amazing night of water, visuals and music held in the **Rudas** Turkish baths (see p148), usually showcasing the best local DJs plus occasional Ninja Tune artists – these events are not to be missed. For further information check www.groove.hu or flyers at Trancewave records (VI. Révay köz 2; 269 3135/www.trancewave.hu, see p139). Shop owners TB-Gon and Marvin are also excellent DJs in their own right, regularly playing around town.

Every Saturday night, the University of Medicine is transformed into a seemingly endless complex of dancefloors, bars and stages for cheap student entertainment. If this is your thing too, bring your passport as ID to get in and watch young men in tight-fitting suits smooch young ladies in miniskirts. There's a gallery area to scan the strobe-lit disco, live local pop and Hollywood blockbusters shown on a grainy cinema screen.

St Tropez Állóhajó

V. Petőfi tér, 8. kikötő (dock 8) (266 7036). Tram 2. **Open** 9pm-5am party nights. **Admission** varies. **No credit cards. Map** p249 C4.
The home base of Chi Recordings (see p180 **Magyar mix masters**), this large, stationary boat moored to dock 8 along the Danube currently rocks every Thursday night to Chi's infectious mix of breakbeats, dub and trance. Also hosts one-off event nights featuring international DJs. A restaurant and longer opening hours are planned – check the usual places for flyers. Recommended.

Trafó Pince

IX. Liliom utca 41 (456 2040). M3 Ferenc körút/tram 4, 6/night bus 6É. **Open** Sept-May 6pm-4am daily, only for parties in summer. **Admission** free-Ft750. **No credit cards. Map** p250 6E.
Large basement in Budapest's alternative theatre (see p189 **Sparking a cultural revolution**) has comfortable booths and an ample dancefloor. Often taken over by, among others, DJs Palotai and Cadik (see above **Magyar mix masters**) for Rewind night, and DJ Naga for Dub till Dawn. Young, up-for-it crowd, great music, low prices.

Trocadero

V. Szent István körút 15 (311 4691). M3 Nyugati pu./tram 4, 6/night bus 6É, 14É, 50É. **Open** 9pm-3am Mon-Thur; 9pm-5am Fri-Sat. **Admission** varies. **No credit cards. Map** p246 C2.
The only Latin disco in town has sporadic live salsa and merengue acts, which pack the house. One of the few places in Budapest with a truly multinational crowd, it's quieter during the week, but still fun.

Arts & Entertainment

DJ Palotai, the daddy of dance music. *See p180.*

Sport & Fitness

Action for all – particularly skate rats, karate kids and bodybuilders.

Somewhat paradoxically for a nation addicted to fatty food, cigarettes and booze, Hungary has a proud and varied sporting tradition. No other country has won as many Olympic gold medals per head of population; Hungary boasts current champions in modern pentathlon, canoeing, weightlifting and swimming.

Another sport in which the country has traditionally excelled, football, is a sore point. Supporter apathy, corruption, underfunding and political meddling are given as excuses for Hungary's failure to qualify for any major championship since 1986. Go to a game and it becomes apparent that the real reason is more simple: the players are, on the whole, useless. Home matches are played at the rebuilt national stadium, the former Népstadion since renamed after local football legend Ferenc Puskás.

The biggest event of the sporting year is the **Hungarian Grand Prix** in August, when the city is flooded with red-faced, lager-swilling Scandinavians waving Ferrari flags and the city's sex bars do a roaring trade.

Even with limited Hungarian, you can find details of all sports events in *Nemzeti Sport*.

For the participatory amateur, Budapest, the Buda hills and the Danube offer plenty of sporting activity. Under the pre-1989 regime, sport was a cheap way of keeping the masses fit and entertained, and much of this low-cost infrastructure is still in place. The FIDESZ government of 1999-2002, under (football)-mad Prime Minister Viktor Orbán, poured a fortune into sport, for public good and political gain. Riding and fencing schools, new golf courses and a rash of private gyms and martial arts clubs (*see p184* **Under martial law**) complete a colourful active leisure industry.

Major stadia

Puskás Ferenc Stadion (Népstadion)

XIV. Istvánmezei út 3-5 (471 4100/fax 471 2236/ nsi@axelero.hu). M2 Népstadion.
The national stadium, built by and for the people (*nép*) in 1953, was falling to bits until major renovation for the 1998 European Athletics Championships. In 2002 it was renamed to honour Ferenc Puskás on his 75th birthday. An atmospheric venue, with Stalinist statues lining the approach, this 70,000-capacity bowl affords great views of the action below and the setting sun beyond.

Budapest Arena

XIV. Stefánia út 2 (422 2603). M2 Népstadion.
The old Budapest Sportcsarnok, rebuilt and renamed after a fire at a Christmas market gutted the place in 1999, the new Arena is a 12,500-capacity indoor sports venue adjacent to the Puskás Ferenc. It hosts basketball, boxing and rock concerts (*see p170*).

Spectator sports

Basketball

More and more kids are shooting hoops, and a handful of American NBA rejects are attracting bigger crowds to the domestic game, which runs from September to May. For fixtures see *Nemzeti Sport* or call the Hungarian Basketball Federation (252 3296/273 0470).

Danone Honvéd

XIV. Dózsa György út 53 (340 8916). M3 Dózsa György út.
The former Hungarian army club is now sponsored by Danone. The most successful of the men's teams.

Ferencváros

VIII. Ferencváros Népligeti Sportcsarnok, Kőbányai út (260 5859). M3 Népliget.
The most popular women's basketball team, which play its games in the city's finest small-scale sports hall. Rowdy supporters.

Football

Fifty years ago this November, the Hungarian national football team beat England 6-3 at Wembley. A year later, the same team came within a Welsh linesman's flag of winning the 1954 World Cup, key player Ferenc Puskás starring for the great Real Madrid side for years afterwards. Subsequent Magyar XIs presented stirring performances in the World Cups of 1966, 1978 and 1982. A 6-0 defeat to the USSR in 1986 – a game surrounded by rumour and controversy – marked Hungary's last entry on the world soccer stage.

The domestic game has since deteriorated to a shameful degree. After it was discovered that many key league games had been rigged – the phrase *bundameccs*, or fixed match, is still used whenever anything unusual happens on the pitch – local football soon lost all credibility and funding. Players left in droves, supporters likewise.

Puskás Ferenc Stadion – home turf for Hungary's national football team. *See p182.*

What's left is a shoestring championship played out before four-figure crowds. The two main clubs, Ferencváros and MTK, are owned by Gábor Várszegi, Fotex retail chain boss. The season runs August to November, and March to June, most games taking place on Saturdays. (*Nemzeti Sport* has details.) A ticket (*belépő*) is under Ft1,000; a *lelátó* offers a better view.

Ferencváros

IX. Üllői út 129 (215 3856). M3 Népliget.
Hungary's biggest club, Ferencváros (FTC or 'Fradi') has the star team, the best stadium and the largest following. Many of these people are bone-headed imbeciles, and FTC can be an intimidating place.

MTK

VIII. Salgótarjáni út 12-14 (333 8368/fax 303 0592). Tram 1/trolleybus 75/bus 9.
By tradition Budapest's Jewish club, MTK barely attracts 3,000 spectators to its improved Hungária körút ground, despite recent title wins. Fans of the cult war movie *Escape to Victory* may recognise the setting, as the football scenes were filmed here.

Ice hockey

Ice hockey is a popular spectator sport during the football break. Two of the four professional clubs in the capital, Ferencváros and Újpest, are in the Extra Liga, playing at the Budapest Arena (*see p182*) and the rink by Újpest football stadium (IV. Megyeri út 13; 390 6181).

Motor racing

A $4.3 million reconstruction of the Formula One Hungaroring circuit was to be ready by the summer of 2003, extending the track – and its

contract to host the money-spinning circus past 2006. Hungary's biggest sporting event of the year packs out city hotels and restaurants in the second weekend of August, and gives locals an opportunity for star-spotting.

Hungaroring

20km east of Budapest off M3 motorway at Mogyoród, H-2146 (Phone/fax 06 28 444 444/ 06 28 441 860. **Information** *Osztermen Forma 1 Kft, V. Apáczai Csere János utca 11 (ticket hotline 266 2040/fax 317 2963). M1, M2, M3 Deák tér/tram 47, 49.* **Open** *8am-4pm daily 1mth before event.* **Date** *2nd weekend in Aug.* **Advance ticket booking** *official agencies* www.gpticketshop.com or www.hungaroinfo.com.

Swimming & water polo

Hungary still produces Olympic champions in swimming, and enjoys a solid tradition in water polo, the nation's main summer sport.

Császár-Komjádi Sportuszoda

III. Árpád fejedelem útja 8 (212 2750). Bus 6, 60, 86. **Open** *6am-8pm daily.* **Tickets** *Ft680.* **No credit cards. Map** *p245 B1.*
Hungary's national swimming stadium, named after the coach who led Hungary to its first Olympic water polo gold in 1932, is packed for top matches and major swimming galas.

Activities

Cycling

Congested traffic, cobbled streets, tram lines and a lack of bike lanes mean that Budapest is hardly an ideal city to cycle around. Although

Under martial law

Among the thousands of flyers with tear-off phone numbers around town advertising apartments for rent or English lessons are a remarkably inordinate number of posters for *harcművészet*: martial arts. It's a modern phenomenon that has Hungary in its grip – and by martial arts, we're not just talking a little harmless grappling on the judo mat.

Every one of the main – and many of the obscure – martial arts are taught in the country, with an estimated 2,500 clubs being served by more than 50 different sports associations (*for club details see p186*). Karate has even made it on to the school sports curriculum in several Budapest primary schools. The *harcművészet* section in the local listings weekly *Pesti Est* is by far the longest sport entry. And it's not just in schools and gyms; many open green spaces become practice grounds in the summer. No, you're not hallucinating, there really are masked people wearing white robes whacking each other with sticks in the bushes on Margaret Island.

Of the many preferred explanations for the phenomenon, the idea that Hungarians are harking back to their Asiatic roots seems the most tenuous – although it is true that many Hungarians find solace in Eastern mysticism. Another reason is the disciplined school sports system of the late 1970s (when Hungary got a bad dose of Bruce Lee fever) coupled with the sheer bloody-mindedness of the Magyar psyche. The generation that studied martial arts in that era has gone on to be the teachers of the next, their Soviet-style discipline the perfect tool for a sport in which excellence requires an extremely high level of commitment and fitness.

Budapest boasts almost every martial art form you can think of, plus a few more to boot. Fancy learning Escrima, the hitherto little-known Filipino weapons-based martial art? Feel the need to wind down after a hard day with a bout of Capoiera, the Brazilian slave dance/fighting technique? How about kyokushinkai? Hungary is the biggest centre outside Japan for this brutal style of full-contact karate, tailor-made for headcases – the Stranglers' bass player is a Fifth Dan. It was founded by Masutatsu Oyama, whose favoured pastime was killing bulls with one punch between the eyes. Oyama also lived in Hungary for a time prior to his death in 1997, and is much revered by the lunatic fringe of Magyar martial arts. They've even put up a monument to him in some dark part of north-east Hungary. Oyama also invented 'hundred-man' kumite, a free sparring exercise in which the most initiated can fight the other 99 men in the room and still remain standing, a challenge still taken up in more obscure parts of Hungary.

If your personal quest is for peace and enlightenment rather than the ability to break roof tiles with your head, you can also enrol at the **Hungarian Shaolin Temple** (*see p186*), some ten kilometres outside Budapest at Kerepes. This quasi-cult group, with only a handful of bases scattered outside China, inducts people into a long-term study of how to be a fighting holy man. Close links with China mean that members really are learning from the masters.

Finally, although casual thuggery in Budapest is much rarer than in most UK cities, the streets are not as safe as they were ten years ago. The rush to learn self-defence may well be a product of a society witnessing a rise in street crime. The flip side is that many law enforcement officers, bodyguards and bouncers are also regular practitioners. While sporty young Magyars are getting fit and feisty, they can also enjoy the illicit thrill of whacking a copper in the sweaty confines of the dojo.

---

some 120 kilometres of cycle lanes have been created over the last ten years, many inner-city ones have simply been drawn on pavements. For a pleasant afternoon's ride away, Margaret Island has bike hire stalls situated near the main roundabout, or you can take the gentle road alongside the Danube up to Szentendre. Bikes can be taken on certain trains, but not on trams or the metro. The more adventurous can take the cog-wheel railway (*fogaskerekű*) to the top of Normafa and career around the

forest before launching themselves on an ear-popping descent back into town.

Friends of City Cycling Group

III. Miklós tér 1 (311 7855). Tram 1/bus 6, 86.
Produces a *Map for Budapest Cyclists*, detailing bike lanes, riding conditions and service shops.

Hungarian Cycling Association

XIV. Szabó József utca 3 (468 3511). Bus 7.
The Millenáris cycle track here is the only one of its kind in Hungary.

National Rail Office

VI. Andrássy út 35 (461 5400). M1 Opera. **Open** Oct-Mar 9am-5pm Mon-Fri. *Apr-Sept* 9am-6pm Mon-Fri. **Map** p246 D3.

The rail office (MÁV) has a list of cycle-friendly stations and surcharges for cycles (*kerékpárjegy*).

Extreme sports

Today's Magyar teenager is nobody without a skateboard and/or in-line skates. All major malls have a skate shop, complementing the specialist venue and store listed below:

Görzenál Skatepark

III. Árpád fejedelem útja 125 (250 4800). HÉV to Timár utca. **Open** 9am-7pm daily. **Admission** Ft600/Ft150 non-skating parents. **Rental** Ft500 for 3hrs. **No credit cards.**

Teenage paradise. Rollerskating track, skateboard park, BMX/cycle track and jumps, two basketball courts and several 'freestyle' areas with ramps and jumps for bike, skate or board.

ProCross

II. Margit körút 67 (315 1995). M2 Moszkva tér/ tram 4, 6. **Open** 10am-6pm Mon-Fri; 10am-1pm Sat. **No credit cards. Map** p245 A2.

Just before the Mammut 2 mall – boards, skates, BMX, accessories, clothing and protection gear.

Golf

Until the addition of the **Pólus Palace Country Club** at Göd, courses near Budapest were pretty naff and most serious hackers headed down to the Hencse by Lake Balaton, the Birdland by the Austrian border or the Old Lake Golf Club in Tata. For details on all facilities check www.golfhungary.hu.

Birdland Golf Country Club

240km from Budapest. M1 towards Győr, route 85 to Csorna, route 86 to Hegyfalug, through Tompaládony to Bükfürdő. Thermal körút 10 (06 94 358 060). **Open** 9am-8pm Mon-Thur; 8am-8pm Fri-Sun. **Fee** Ft8,000-Ft13,000. **Credit** AmEx, DC, MC, V.

Hungary's best course, championship-rated and sited in beautiful hills close to the Austrian border.

Hencse National Golf & Country Club

175km south-west of Budapest at Hencse. Kossuth Lajos utca 3 (82 481 245/fax 82 481 248). **Open** Feb-1 Dec dawn-dusk. **Fee** Ft11,000-Ft13,500. **Credit** AmEx, DC, MC, V.

Splendidly sited in a National Park.

Old Lake Golf & Country Club

64km from Budapest. H-2890 Tata, Remeteségpuszta Pf.127 (06 34 587 620/ old.lake.golf.club@axelero.hu). **Open** 15 Mar-16 Nov 8am-8pm Mon-Sun. **Fee** Ft8,000-Ft13,000. **Credit** AmEx, DC, MC, V.

An 18-hole championship course beautifully situated in a wooded park in the Gerecse foothills, near the Old Lake at Tata.

Pólus Palace Thermál Golf Club

H-2132 Göd, Kádár utca 49 (275 31141/06 30 400 5611/www.poluspalace.hu). **Fee** Ft9,000-Ft11,000. **Credit** AmEx, DC, MC, V.

The closest 18-hole championship course to Budapest, 20km north of town. Forms part of an extensive five-star thermal resort, built in 2002.

Hang-gliding, gliding and paragliding

The Buda hills offer plenty of opportunities to hang-glide. Traditional gliding, with or without an instructor, is also available. At weekends, spectators can take No. 11 bus from Batthyány ter to its terminus, then walk on through the forest to the clearing at Hármashatárhegy, following the noise of gliders humming and microlites buzzing overhead. The Airborne Club of Hungary (*www.airborneclub.hu*) offers courses in paragliding and trips out of town.

Hármashatárhegy Airfield

II. Arad utca 2 (376 5110/www.bme.hu/hhh). M2 Moszkva tér, then bus 56 to terminus at Hüvösvölgy, then bus 64 for 2 stops. **Open** 8am-8pm Sat, Sun. **Rates** vary.

Gliding, hang-gliding, microlites and paragliding, with instruction available for beginners.

Health & fitness

Modern gyms and solariums have sprung up all over town. Note that some backstreet gyms are unregulated and unprofessional. Better clubs, such as the ones listed here, meet standard regulations. Most of Budapest's major hotels also have fitness facilities.

Andi Studio

V. Hold utca 29 (311 0740). M2 Kossuth tér/M3 Arany János utca. **Open** 6am-9pm Mon-Fri; 7.30am-2pm Sat. **Rates** aerobics & sauna Ft800; gym & sauna Ft700; aerobics, gym & sauna Ft1,000. **No credit cards. Map** p246 C3.

Budapest's first Western-style fitness club, with on-site cosmetician, bar and café.

Astoria Fitness Centre

V. Károly körút 4 (317 0452). M2 Astoria. **Open** 6.30am-11pm Mon-Fri; 8.30am-9pm Sat, Sun. **Admission** Ft1,300. **No credit cards. Map** p249 D4.

Popular, well-appointed city-centre gym.

Marriott World Class Fitness Centre

V. Apáczai Csere János utca 4 (266 7000). M1 Vörösmarty tér/tram 2. **Open** 6am-10pm Mon-Fri; 8am-9pm Sat, Sun. **Rates** day ticket

Arts & Entertainment

Get airborne at **Hármashatárhegy Airfield.** *See p185.*

(gym & sauna) Ft5,600. **Credit** AmEx, DC, MC, V. **Map** p249 C4.
Personal trainers; rowing, cycling and running machines; Thai and Swedish massage.

Ice skating

Every winter locals dust off their skates and head to the open-air rink behind Hősök tere in the City Park. A rinkside bar is open for those happy just to watch. Skates can be rented out.

Városligeti Műjégpálya

XIV. Olof Palme sétány 5 (364 0013). M1 Hősök tere. **Open** *Nov-Mar* 9am-1pm, 4-8pm Mon-Fri; 10am-2pm Sat, Sun. **Rates** Ft600; Ft300 children. **No credit cards. Map** p291 E1.

Kayak & canoe

Although kayak and canoe hire places are few and far between around Budapest, Hungary remains one of the top nations in the sport.

Béke Üdülőtelep

III. Nánási út 97 (388 9303). Bus 34. **Open** *Apr-mid-Oct* 8am-6pm daily. **Rates** Ft800-Ft2,500. **No credit cards.**
Situated on the banks of the Danube, in the vicinity of the Hotel Lido.

Martial arts

Hungary is martial arts mad and offers ample opportunity to study every fighting technique imaginable (*see p184* **Under martial law**). Classes can change depending on gym space, so call ahead to check. The Székely-Budosport shop, VII. Wesselényi utca 47-49 (322 3906; 9am-1pm Mon-Fri; 9am-1pm Sat, Sun) will have a copy of quarterly *Magyar Budo* for details. The following have fixed classes:

Escrima: Állámi Artistaképző Intézet Bp

VII. Városligeti fasor 3 (342 5192). M1 Hősök tere. **Open** 6-8pm daily. **Rates** Ft700-Ft7,000. **No credit cards. Map** p247 E2.

Hungarian Shaolin Temple

H-2144, Kerepes, Szabadság utca 102 (06 28 492 310/www.shaolin.hu). **Open** 10am-6pm daily. **Rates** Ft700-Ft7,000. **No credit cards.**

Pit Bull Gym

IX. Telepi utca 17 (215 6247/www.pitbullgym.ini.hu). **M3** Nagyvárad tér. **Open** 11am-10pm daily. **Rates** vary. **No credit cards.**

Tae kwon do: ITF központi Edzőterem

II. Fillér utca 70-76 (326 6617). **Open** 6-8.30pm Mon-Fri. **Rates** Ft4,000 per mth. **No credit cards.** Also classes in karate, Thai boxing, jujitsu, akaido, nijitsu and Capoeira.

Riding

Hungarians are famed for their horsemanship and have a well-developed industry for riding holidays around the Puszta and Lake Balaton.

Hungarian Equestrian Tourism Association

V. Ferenciek tere 4 (317 1259/pegazus@pegazus.hu). **M3** Ferenciek tere/tram 2/bus 7. **Open** 9am-5pm Mon-Thur; 9am-4pm Fri. **Map** p249 C4.
Provides comprehensive information on riding holidays in Hungary.

Pegazus Tours

V. Ferenciek tere 5 (317 1644/pegazus@pegazus.hu). **M3** Ferenciek tere/tram 2/bus 7. **Open** 9am-5pm Mon-Thur; 9am-4pm Fri. **Map** p249 C4.
Tour company providing a range of riding holidays across the country.

Petneházy Riding School

II. Feketefej utca 2-4 (397 5048). Tram 56 from M2 Moszkva tér then bus 63. **Open** 9am-4pm Fri-Sun. **Rates** Ft2,500-Ft4,000 per hr. **No credit cards.**
Next door to the **Petneházy Club Hotel** (*see p35*), some 10km from the city centre. Offers riding lessons for children and beginners, plus some English-language tuition.

Arts & Entertainment

One-offs Lou Thesz

Pro wrestling has existed since the ancient Greeks, but as anybody who has ever seen a WWF match on cable, the modern version is crass, staged and, of course, wildly successful. How did this humble manly sport become gross TV entertainment? *Cherchez l'Hongrois!*

Lou Thesz was born in 1913 to Hungarian immigrant parents in Michigan. One of the real old-time grapplers, his career began at 17 and didn't end until he was 80, a six-time world wrestling champion whose reign from 1948 to 1967 stands unchallenged. Thesz brought wrestling to Hollywood, hanging with stars like Alan Ladd and Yvonne DeCarlo, and trading grips with boxing champ Joe Louis.

Thesz was instrumental in introducing pro wrestling to Japan, as well. Supported by the TV show *Mitsubishi Faitoman Awa* ('Mitsubishi Fightman Hour') pro wrestling became a symbol of post-war revival. Typically, a local champion, valiantly aiming to restore Japanese pride, would beat a huge masked American thug hired from a nearby army base. Crime boss Nick Zappetti contracted Thesz in 1961 to take part in a match against the top-rated Rikidozan. The fight became the most viewed programme in Japanese television history, boosting sales of privately owned TV sets overnight. The match was a tie, and today Thesz is still revered as Tesujin, or 'Iron Man', while poor Rikidozan never recovered from the scandalous revelation that he was, in fact, born in Korea.

Thesz died in 2002, a fierce champion of wrestling's credibility in and out of the ring.

Squash

City Squash Club

II. Marczibányi tér 1-3 (212 3110). Tram 4, 6/bus 11, 49. **Open** *7am-midnight Mon-Fri; 8am-10pm Sat, Sun.* **Rates** *off-peak Ft2,000. Peak Ft3,600 per hr.* Booking advised. **No credit cards**. **Map** p245 A2.
Four courts and a sauna.

Hotel Marriott

V. Apáczai Csere János utca 4 (266 7000). M1 Vörösmarty tér/tram 2. **Open** *6am-10pm Mon-Fri; 8am-9pm Sat, Sun.* **Rates** *Ft5,600 per day.* **Credit** AmEx, DC, MC, V. **Map** p249 C4.
Top-class squash facility and sauna.

Swimming

Swimming champion at the first modern Olympics in 1896, Alfréd Hajós designed the pool on Margaret Island where generations of medallists have since trained. In summer, other open-air pools are extremely popular all round Budapest. All require swimming hats to be worn by both sexes – the ones available for hire look ridiculous, so bring your own. Some pools, such as the Palatinus, double up as a *strand*, or lido, where locals laze the day away (*see also pp146-8 and pp25-42*).

Gellért Gyógyfürdő

XI. Kelenhegyi út (466 6166). Tram 18, 19, 47, 49/bus 7. **Open** *6am-6pm daily.* **Admission** Ft1,700-Ft2,000. **No credit cards**. **Map** p248 B5.
Grand, if expensive, setting for knocking out a few lengths. Warm indoor pool, relaxing outdoor pool, wave pool, children's pool, thermal pool and sauna.

Hajós Alfréd Nemzeti Sportuszoda

XIII. Margitsziget (450 4219). Bus 26. **Open** *6am-4pm Mon-Fri; 6am-6pm Sat, Sun.* **Admission** Ft430-Ft690. **No credit cards**. **Map** p245 B1.
Two outdoor pools, one indoor pool, sunbathing terrace and restaurant.

Palatinus Strand

XIII. Margitsziget (340 4505). Bus 26. **Open** *May-mid-Sept 8am-7pm daily.* **Admission** Ft1,200-Ft1,400. **No credit cards**.
This complex on Margaret Island has seven pools, including a thermal pool, two children's pools, slides and wave machines. Capacity of 10,000 and on a hot Saturday afternoon in July it's standing room only.

Tennis

There are some 40 clubs in Budapest, most with clay courts. Hotels also hire courts to non-guests.

Római Teniszakadémia

III. Királyok útja 105 (240 8616). Bus 34. **Open** 6am-10pm daily. **Rates** Ft900-Ft1,600 per hr. **No credit cards**.
Ten outdoor courts, ten indoor.

Városmajor Teniszakadémia

XII. Városmajor utca 63-69 (202 5337). Bus 21, 121. **Open** 7am-10pm Mon-Fri; 7am-7pm Sat; 8am-7pm Sun. **Rates** Ft1,300-Ft1,900 per hr. **No credit cards**.
Five outdoor courts, three indoor.

Vasas SC

II. Pasaréti út 11-13 (320 9457). Bus 5. **Open** 6am-8pm daily. **Rates** Ft1,300-Ft1,500 per hr (booking advised). **No credit cards**.
Nine outdoor courts, two indoor.

Theatre & Dance

Chaos reigns at the new National Theatre while Madhouse rules local English-language drama.

Visitors will enjoy the variety and quality of theatre on offer in Budapest, in English as well as Hungarian. The most important development has been the long-awaited opening of a new **National Theatre**. Set by the river where Pest loses its grandeur, the venue seems to compensate with a design evoking ancient Greece amid a modern façade. Its appeal is a matter of debate. Hampered by years of political bickering, it was built in a swift 15 months, perhaps accounting for the poor acoustics. The technical capabilities of the stage, though, are unparalleled anywhere in Europe.

If its artistic director Tamás Jordán's record at the **Merlin International Theatre** is anything to go by, the new National promises great things. He's always welcomed new writing and has housed a wealth of dance and movement pieces in repertory. The political pressure that comes with the job may shackle him somewhat, but EU membership and his own determination should free his hand.

Hungarian theatre is in a pretty healthy state with new writing making its way to the stage. This is most apparent at April's renowned Contemporary Drama Festival (www.dramafestival.hu), which includes productions from all over Europe.

Until the late 18th century, theatre here was a German affair. Ironically, it was Habsburg Emperor Josef II who first encouraged Magyar-language theatre and by doing so unwittingly set in motion an art form that would contribute to the national revival movement of the 19th century. Hungary built up a respectable tradition that looked west for inspiration. Naturalism was introduced in the early 20th century and although it took the Hungarians 400 years to translate Shakespeare, they were staging Wilde and Gorky within a few years of their appearance elsewhere. Stanislavsky also made a big impact on the local stage but his realist method holds less sway these days.

After the war, dull and didactic dross was the norm, but when Edmund Wilson visited in 1964 he professed his amazement at the sheer variety of theatre on offer. The change was down to the post-1956 leadership, who decided that more bread and (slightly censored) circuses were in order. Today, there's everything from Aristophanes to Arthur Miller. Strong visual effects help soften the gaping language barrier. Hungarian may be impenetrable, but seeing a play you're familiar with can still be enjoyable.

ENGLISH-LANGUAGE THEATRE

What was once a tiny outcrop has now become an impressive stronghold, with the Merlin well and truly at the helm. Its selection of first-rate English-language theatre grows with every season. Credit goes to László Magács, its artistic director, who combines in-house productions with visits from innovative foreign theatre companies. Recent guests include Derevo (Germany/Russia), KAOS, the Kosh, Kneehigh and the Right Size (all UK). Resident theatre group Madhouse (*see p190* **Sons of Shakespeare**) have become a local favourite with a diverse repertoire. Madhouse bring a level of professionalism hitherto missing in the English-language theatre scene.

The **Kolibri Cellar** is home to Scallabouche, a theatre group with shows as diverse as the popular *Scabaret*, a night of improv comedy, and *John Donne – A Scream Within*, a one-man show exploring the writer's life through his poems and sermons. The **International Buda Stage** has no resident company but it does host guest shows from Europe and the US. There's no regular slot for these visiting companies so check listings to see what's on.

Curtains usually rise at 7pm or 7.30pm. If they're not open all day, box offices begin selling tickets an hour prior to curtain. Ticket prices range from Ft600 to Ft2,000. Wheelchair access and hearing systems aren't available.

TICKETS AND INFORMATION

Productions run in repertory and can continue for ages. *Pesti Est* and *Pesti Műsor* cover most events. *Pesti Súgó* is a free monthly dedicated to theatre. The *Budapest Sun* also runs listings.

Broadway Ticket Office

VI. Nagymező utca 19 (302 3841/http://jegyiroda. victorinet.hu). M1 Opera. **Open** 10am-7pm Mon-Fri; 10am-2pm Sat. **No credit cards**. **Map** p246 D3.

Ticket Express Booking Office

VI. Andrássy út 18 (312 0000/www.tex.hu/v2). M1 Opera. **Open** 9.30am-6pm daily. **No credit cards**. **Map** p246 D3.
Branch: Mammut, II. Lövőház utca 2-6 (345 8020).

Theatre

English-language venues

International Buda Stage (IBS)

*II. Tárogató út 2-4 (391 2500). M2 Moszkva tér,
then tram 56.* **Open** *box office* 10am-noon, 1-6pm
Mon-Fri, until 7.30pm before shows. Closed mid
June-Sept. **No credit cards.**
English (guest shows) and Hungarian theatre as well
as movies, dance, concerts and cultural symposia.
English shows are all too rate, but often provides
simultaneous English-language translation for the
major Hungarian productions.

Kolibri Cellar Club

Kolibri Pince és Klub

*VI. Andrássy út 77 (351 3348/www.szinhaz.hu/kolibri).
Box office at VI. Jókai tér 10 (312 0622). M1
Vörösmarty utca.* **Open** *box office* 9am-5pm
Mon-Fri & 1hr before shows. Closed June-Sept.
No credit cards. Map p246 D2.
Small, intimate space showing a fair amount of
English-language theatre.

Merlin International Theatre

*V. Gerlóczy utca 4 (317 9338/318 9844/
www.szinhaz.hu/merlin). M1, M2, M3 Deák tér/
tram 47, 49.* **Open** *box office* 2-6.30pm daily.
Closed June-Aug. **No credit cards. Map** p249 C4.

Sparking a cultural revolution

The **Trafó** is quite simply unique. As the
city's only institution bringing together all
branches of contemporary art and culture
under one roof, its profile makes it the ideal
venue for experimental performances of
dance (*pictured*), theatre, fine arts, literature
and music – or often a chaotic fusion of
them all. Its mission is symbolised by the
history of the building itself.

Built in 1909, it was one of the first
electricity substations in the city, which by
the mid 1990s had been derelict for half a
century. Today, instead of the hum of the

trafó or 'transformer', there's a tangible buzz
of creativity. Part of the energy of the Trafó
comes from its location, on a side street in
the rapidly gentrifying District IX.

It arose from the ashes of the mythical
Young Artists' Club, or FMK. Set in a villa on
grand Andrassy út, the FMK became the key
venue for the decadent underground music
scene. The custom conversion of the Trafó
from a defunct electricity substation into a
hybrid cultural centre was made possible by
the sale of the dilapidated FMK villa to a
property developer.

Theatre and contemporary dance are at the
heart of the Trafó programme, and the main
interest of the director, György Szabó. Expect
performances by the best Hungarian theatre
and dance companies, such as Pál Frenák,
the Mozgó Ház Társulát and Yvette Bozsik.
Visiting groups have included celebrated
choreographer Akram Khan and the George
Piper Dance Company. Since opening in
1998, it has built a reputation for artistic
innovation both in Hungary itself and
internationally, thanks to close links with
the main foreign cultural institutes.

The subterranean gallery also divides its
programme between the work of young
Magyar artists and international shows.
Guest curators are invited from abroad,
resulting in novel and surprising exhibitions.
Always open an hour before theatre
performances, and set between the
auditorium and the cellar restaurant, the
gallery attracts more casual visitors than
most contemporary art spaces in town.

Meanwhile, the spirit of the FMK is kept
alive in the Trafó's cellar club, hosting
the best of Budapest's underground DJs
(*see p180* **Magyar mix masters**).

Arts & Entertainment

The most professional of the English-language venues. Despite these credentials, English is still an obstacle if you're booking tickets over the phone.

Nagymező utca

This attractive stretch, otherwise known as 'Budapest's Broadway', has been pedestrianised and allows for a pleasant stroll before a pre-show coffee at either the Operett Kavéház (see p121) or the Komédiás across the road.

Radnóti

VI. Nagymező utca 11 (321 0600/www.szinhaz.hu/radnoti). M1 Oktogon. **Open** *box office* 1-7pm daily. Closed June-Sept. **No credit cards**. **Map** p246 D3.
A highly regarded company performing a wide selection of highbrow classics and contemporary plays. Award-winning resident troupe.

Thália

VI. Nagymező utca 22-24 (312 1280/www.thalia.hu). M1 Oktogon. **Open** *box office* 10am-6pm daily. Closed June-Sept. **No credit cards**. **Map** p246 D3.
Elegant, air-conditioned venue for performances by established dance and theatre companies, as well as the occasional mainstream musical. *West Side Story*

sits comfortably alongside *21st Century Macbeth Ballet* on the programme. Also features Hungarian provincial and foreign companies.

Tivoli Színház

VI. Nagymező utca 8 (351 6812). M1 Oktogon. **Open** *box office* 2-7pm daily. Closed June-Sept. **No credit cards**. **Map** p246 D3.
Attractively art nouveau. Tends to show modern classics and comedies.

Establishment theatres

Katona József

V. Petőfi Sándor utca 6 (318 6599/www.szinhaz.hu/katona). M3 Ferenciek tere/bus 7. **Open** *box office* 10am-6pm Mon-Fri; 2-6pm Sat, Sun. Closed June-Sept. **No credit cards**. **Map** p249 C4.
The company with the highest reputation in Budapest and well received the world over. New mainstream and alternative plays are added to their repertory every year. Also houses ambitious big dance productions. The sister company performs equally exciting and dynamic productions at a smaller space around the corner.
Branch: Katona József Kamra, V. Ferenciek tere 3 (318 2487).

Sons of Shakespeare

Madhouse have changed the face of English-language theatre in Budapest. Five years ago, you would have been lucky to catch one good English show in a season. Today, this three-piece troupe of UK-trained actors have five plays running in repertory, with a host of other projects in the pipeline. Madhouse were also the first company to stage a play that continued beyond its standard one-week run – and still plays to full houses several years down the line: *The Complete Works of Shakespeare*.

Mike Kelly, Matt Devere and Jon Fenner met at the London Academy of Music and Dramatic Art (LAMDA). With encouragement from the Merlin's László Magács, Kelly, a former student of the School of Central and Eastern European Studies in London, had begun staging student plays in Budapest in the early 1990s. Soon cast in other Merlin productions, Kelly then invited Devere and Fenner over to set up Madhouse at the Merlin, the success of *Shakespeare* breaking the moribund state of English-language theatre in Hungary. The trio hasn't looked back since.

After *Shakespeare* came the tense Frank McGuinness's *Someone Who'll Watch Over*

Me, a gritty drama set in a Beirut prison cell. *Spinach'n'Chips* concerned an ambitious football referee and his two forlorn linesmen on the day of a big match. Written by Zoltán Egressy, its translation by Kelly played in Budapest and Hampstead's New End Theatre in April 2003. Madhouse then teamed up with the Atlantis theatre group to do an English-language version of its hit *Two Blind Mice*, devised by mercurial young director Ádám Horgas. Recently, Magács directed Madhouse in Marie Jones's *Stones in His Pockets*, in which two actors played all 15 characters in an Irish village.

Local recognition has allowed the Madhouse members to grab various cameo roles with the likes of John Cusack, Glenn Close and Eddie Murphy, all filming in the region. Their own tours have also taken their shows to Kraków, Zagreb and Mitrovica in war-torn Kosovo, for which local young Serb and Albanian spectators gathered in the same venue for the first time since the war. Further such events are being planned at the moment.

Madhouse plays can be seen at the **Merlin** (*see p189*) from late September through to May and at the occasional summer festival.

Arts & Entertainment

National Theatre

Nemzeti Színház

*IX. Bajor Gizi park 1 (476 6800/476 6801/
www.nemzetiszinhaz.hu). Tram 2.* **Open** *box
office* 10am-6pm Mon-Fri; 2-6pm Sat, Sun.
Closed June-Sept. **No credit cards.**
Count István Széchenyi first built a National Theatre
in the 1830s. The new version, opened in 2002, has
been beset by controversy. Architect Mária Siklós
and artistic director Tamás Jordán have been at odds
over the poor acoustics and other issues; the main
auditorium seats an odd 619 and the interior is
decked out in shocking blue carpet. On the plus side,
the stage can be raised or lowered at 72 different
points, the lifts offer a panoramic view of the city,
and the façade of the old building lies half-sub-
merged in a pool by the main entrance. Expect more
heavyweight Hungarian drama on and off the stage.

Vígszínház Comedy Theatre

*XIII. Szent István körút 14 (329 2340/www.vig-
szinhaz.hu). M3 Nyugati pu./tram 2, 4, 6.* **Open** *box
office* 1-6.30pm Mon-Fri & 1hr before shows Sat, Sun.
Closed June-Sept. **No credit cards. Map** p246 C2.
A splendid baroque venue for large-scale musicals
and grand productions of Shakespeare. The name
betrays the focus but productions run the whole
gamut. The same company performs less mainstream stuff at the Pesti Színház. Recent successes
include *Stones in His Pockets* and *Waiting for Godot.*
Branch: Pesti Színház, V. Váci utca 9 (266 5245).

Alternative theatres

Bárka Theatre

*VIII. Üllői út 82 (303 6505/www.barka.hu). M3
Klinikák.* **Open** 9am-7pm Mon-Fri & 2hrs before
shows. Closed June-Aug. **No credit cards.**
Resident company of some 15 actors with a diverse
repertoire from Pinter to Pirandello.

Mu Színház

*XI. Kőrösy utca 17 (466 4627/www.mu.mentha.hu).
Tram 4, 47, 49.* **Open** box office 1hr before shows.
Closed June-Sept. **No credit cards.**
Space for small alternative companies, musicians
and dancers, but no resident company. Worth a visit
to check out what the cutting edge is up to.

Szkéné

*XI. Műegyetem rakpart 3 (463 2451/www.szkene.hu).
Tram 18, 19, 47, 49.* **Open** 10am-3pm Mon-Thur;
10am-1pm Fri & 1hr before shows. Closed June-Sept.
No credit cards. Map p246 C5.
A theatre that sponsors the International Meeting of
Moving Theatres every other October, at which
obscure dance groups gather at this small black box,
and the Alternative Theatre Festival in April. Look
out for Béla Pinter's acclaimed theatre group.

Trafó House of Contemporary Arts

*IX. Liliom utca 41 (215 1600/www.trafo.hu). M3
Ferenc körút/tram 4, 6.* **Open** box office 5-8pm daily.
Closed July-Aug. **No credit cards. Map** p249 D6.

On the rise: talented dancer **Éva Duda**

Centre with an imaginative mix of arts events (*see
p189* **Sparking a cultural revolution**).

Új Színház

*VI. Paulay Ede utca 35 (269 6021/269 6024/
www.szinhaz.hu). M1 Opera.* **Open** 10am-7pm &
until 1st interval of evening show. Closed June-Aug.
No credit cards. Map p246 D3.
The 'New Theatre', designed by Béla Lajta as the
Parisiana nightclub, stages a range of new and established plays. *See p72* **Art nouveau Budapest.**

Dance

The ballet scene consists mainly of competently
executed traditional pieces drawing on Russian
and Hungarian traditions. New work includes
Giselle directed by Mihail Lavrovszky and *The
Taming of the Shrew* by László Seregi.
There's much innovative local work too.
Experimental groups abound, often thanks to
the **Trafó House of Contemporary Arts**
(*see p189* **Sparking a cultural revolution**).
One exciting young talent to have performed
her work here is the acclaimed Éva Duda, a

One-offs Ferenc Molnár

Hungary's most famous modern playwright was a suicidal maniac born in Budapest in 1878: Ferenc Molnár.

A regular at the New York Café (see p111 **So good they built it twice**), and a cultural heavyweight of the Golden Age, Molnár had his first play, *The Lawyer*, produced in 1902. Others, such as *The Devil* and *The Play's the Thing*, were staged in Europe and America, and adapted for film.

His most famous work was *Liliom*. Made into a musical by Rodgers and Hammerstein under the title *Carousel*, and rendered into English by PG Wodehouse, *Liliom* was set in the circus tent of the City Park, and told the cheery story of a former fairground barker allowed to spend one day back on Earth with his loved ones. The musical spawned the communal anthem *You'll Never Walk Alone*.

Molnár himself most surely walked alone. Despite his huge success – he also wrote the children's classic *The Paul Street Boys*, set in

Budapest's IX. District and translated into countless languages – Molnár attempted suicide many times. Once he even tried it with a revolver, but only succeeded in shooting himself in the leg. When he appeared the next day at his usual table at the New York Café, his mentor, writer Sándor Bródy, suggested that he shouldn't wave the gun around but instead hold it firmly to his temple and shoot. 'I will only take such advice from someone previously successful in this matter,' came back Molnár's ready wit.

His sharp theatrical dialogue also reflected a lifetime of stormy relationships.

Like Bartók and many of his artistic peers, Molnár sailed from Hitler's Europe to America in 1940. But despite enough royalties coming in from Broadway and Hollywood – and compatriots to call on – Molnár lived out a lonely existence at New York's Plaza Hotel until his death in 1952, surrounded by his scribblings in bitter private diaries.

---

dancer and choreographer whose rise has been meteoric. The most internationally recognised figure is Yvette Bozsik. Her vigorous style leans strongly towards grotesque comedy – as evidenced in her recent adaptation of Orwell's *Animal Farm* at the **Katona József Theatre**.

Pál Frenák has been sending shockwaves through the Budapest dance scene for some years now. This notorious maverick splits his time between Hungary and France, where he has created his own company of contemporary dancers. The shock quotient is always pretty high in Frenák's productions – but anything goes at the Trafó.

Iván Markó was a solo dancer with none other than Maurice Bejart in Paris so he had a considerable headstart when he returned to pursue his career in Hungary. Now in his mid-fifties, Markó is past anything too athletic but compensates for this with experience, grace and good ideas. His troupe of modern ballet dancers is based in Győr, an hour west of Budapest, but his productions frequently make their way to the capital. See him at the new **National**, the **Thália** and the **Várszínház**.

Éva Magyar's impressive Sámán Theatre Company mixes dance with theatre to great effect and Magyar is steadily gaining no little international kudos with regular visits to the Edinburgh Festival. You can catch her company at the **Merlin** and **Bárka** theatres.

Contemporary Dance Theatre Society

Kortárs Táncszínházi Egyesület
XI. Kőrösy József utca 17 (209 4016). Tram 47, 49. **Open** 4-7pm Tue-Thur. Closed June-Sept.
Represents most of the modern Hungarian dance groups in the city.

Hungarian National Ballet

Magyar Nemzeti Balett
The Hungarian National Ballet perform both at the **Opera House** and at its rather ugly sister, the **Erkel Színház** (see pp166-9).

Várszínház – The National Dance Theatre

I. Színház utca 1-3 (375 8649/ www.nemzeti-tancszinhaz.hu). Várbusz from M2 Moszkva tér/ bus 16. **Open** 1-6pm daily. **Map** p248 B4.
The Ministry of National Cultural Heritage brought about this badly needed venue in the beautiful surroundings of the Castle District. Dance productions of the highest quality.

Festivals

Further information from **Ticket Express Booking Office** (see p188) or the National Philharmonic Ticket Office. The Budapest Spring and Autumn Festivals, though primarily classical music events, also often feature top local and international dance companies.
See pp142-5 and pp166-9.

Arts & Entertainment

Trips Out of Town

Getting Started

Exploring Hungary is cheap, easy and fun.

The Hungarian countryside is dotted with quiet, friendly, lazy towns easily accessible from Budapest. No journey from the capital – ten times the size of the next biggest town – will take more than three or four hours by car or train. The most popular destinations from the city are **Lake Balaton** and the **Danube Bend**. A boat service in summer leaves the capital for spots further up the Danube and hops between Balaton resorts.

In the provinces, the most interesting towns to visit are **Eger** and **Pécs**, both boasting historic monuments and thriving cultural scenes. The countryside is equally attractive, its key features being healing waters (*see p202* **Hungary's healthy breaks**) and wine-growing (*see p205* **Touring the vineyards**).

Although EU membership may redress the balance, only the west of Hungary near the border with Austria has reaped the rewards of the Changes. Other regions, once powerhouses of heavy industry, are stuck in economic decline, although recent cultural developments (*see p208* **Rustbelt renaissance**) may attract the more curious traveller.

For further details about travelling in Hungary, contact:

Ibusz

V. Ferenciek tere 10 (485 2700/www.ibusz.hu).
M3 Ferenciek tere/bus 7. **Open** 8.30am-4.30pm Mon-Fri. **Credit** MC, V. **Map** p249 C4.

Tourinform

V. Vigadó utca 6 (317 9800/helpline 438 8080).
M1 Vörösmarty tér/tram 2. **Open** 24hrs daily. **No credit cards. Map** p249 C4.

By train

Trains are cheap and reliable, with tickets priced by the kilometre and no discount for returns. The fastest trains, Intercity, require a seat reservation (Ft440). Leave reasonable time to buy your ticket as queues can be maddening. You can also buy tickets from the conductor on the train, though you have to pay a small fine.

No one speaks English at stations. Yellow departure timetables are posted at all of them. At ticket offices, it's easiest to write down what you want on a piece of paper: destination, number of tickets and the time of the train you want to catch.

Oda-vissza means return. 'R' means you must reserve a seat. Budapest's three main stations are Keleti, Nyugati and Déli, all of which have their own metro station. Avoid *személy* trains, which stop at all stations. *Gyors* ('fast') trains are one class down from Intercity.

MÁV Information

Information: 461 5400/international 461 5500.
VI. Andrássy út 35 (322 8082/342 5151/ www.elvira.hu). M1 Opera. **Open** *1 Oct-31 Mar* 9am-5pm Mon-Fri; *1 Apr-30 Sept* 9am-6pm Mon-Fri. **Credit** MC, V. **Map** p246 D3.
The easiest place to buy tickets or find information from English-speaking staff. The phone lines are manned until 8pm.

To Balatonfüred: *Déli.* Journey time 2hrs 20mins. Price Ft1,160. 17 trains daily. Last Intercity returns 7.42pm.
To Eger: *Keleti.* Journey time 2hrs. Price Ft1,330. 15 trains daily. Last Intercity returns 7.10pm.
To Esztergom: *Nyugati.* Journey time 90 mins. Price Ft440. 22 trains daily. Last return 10.10pm.
To Keszthely: *Déli.* Journey time 3hrs 15mins. Price Ft1,660. 2 fast trains daily. Last Intercity returns 3.07pm. Last return 8.13pm. (Note: train often divides).
To Pécs: *Déli.* Journey time 3hrs 30mins. Price Ft2,300. 5 fast trains daily. Last Intercity returns 6.05pm.
To Siófok: *Déli.* Journey time 90mins. Price Ft1,490. 15 trains daily. Last Intercity returns 4.40pm. Last return 9.20pm.

By car

Many roads in Hungary are still single carriageway and everybody seems to be in a hurry, but there has been renovation of the main motorways. Major routes are now easier to travel, but you have to buy a *matrica*, a sticker for your windscreen. These are available at most petrol stations leading up to the motorways. Look for the word *matrica* on blue signs. The rates vary, but a *matrica* lasting one week to one month can range from Ft1,000 to Ft3,000.

Getting out of Budapest is easy and the routes are well signposted. From Buda, follow M7 for destinations to the Balaton region and M6/E73 for Pécs. From Pest, follow M3/E71 signs for Eger. From Árpád Bridge, take the 10 for Esztergom and the 11 for Szentendre and Visegrád, following the west bank of the Danube.

By boat

In the summer months, leisurely boats cruise up the Danube to Szentendre, Visegrád and Esztergom. Nippy jetfoils go to Visegrád and Esztergom on weekends and holidays.

All boats to and from Esztergom stop at Visegrád. Most Szentendre boats continue to Visegrád, making a total of five boats to Visegrád every day. It's easy to visit Visegrád plus either Esztergom or Szentendre in a day trip by boat. Taking in all three by boat on one day is theoretically possible, but pushing it.

Boats run daily from 1 April to 23 September, and you can usually get tickets at the dock.

You can get jetfoils to Visegrád/Esztergom, from June to August. Book tickets in advance.

MAHART Tours

Phone 484 4000 or 486 1765 for information about boats mentioned below.

Boats at Vigadó tér terminal

V. Vigadó tér (318 1223). M1 Vörösmarty tér/ tram 2. **No credit cards**. **Map p249 C4.**

Boat to Esztergom: Ft1,200 one way; Ft1,920 return. 3 boats daily in summer. First boat leaves Vigadó tér 7.30am. Last boat leaves Esztergom 4pm.
Boat to Szentendre: Ft950 one way; Ft1,520 return. Several boats daily in summer. First boat leaves Vigadó tér 9am. Last boat leaves Szentendre 5.15pm.
Boat to Visegrád: Ft1,050 one way; Ft1,680 return. 5 boats daily in summer. First boat leaves Vigadó tér 7.30am. Last boat from Visegrád 5.30pm.

Hydrofoils

Hydrofoil to Visegrád: Ft1,990 one way; Ft3,290 return. 1 trip daily on summer weekends. Leaves Budapest 9.30am. Leaves Visegrád at 3.55pm.
Hydrofoil to Esztergom: Ft2,190 one way; Ft3,700 return. 1 trip daily on summer weekends. Leaves Budapest 9.30am. Leaves Esztergom at 3.30pm.

Telephone numbers

Provincial numbers all start with 06, which is how you dial them from Budapest or anywhere in Hungary that's not in the local area code. From abroad, ring +36, drop the 06 and dial the rest of the number. Once you reach the town itself, drop the 06 and two-digit area code and dial the six-digit number.

All aboard – every summer boats take day-trippers up the Danube.

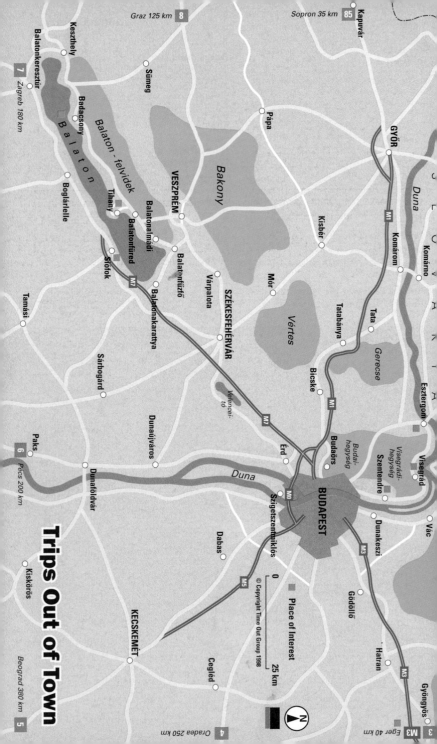

Trips Out of Town

The Danube Bend

Castles, old churches and modern art liven up a lazy bend in the river.

The kink in the Danube about 40 kilometres north of Budapest is one of the most scenic stretches in the river's 3,000 kilometre course. Here the Danube widens and turns sharply south, into a narrow valley between the tree-covered Börzsöny and Pilis Hills, before flowing onwards to Budapest.

The two main settlements on the west bank of the Danube Bend, Visegrád and Esztergom, were respectively a Hungarian medieval capital with a hilltop citadel and a royal seat with the nation's largest cathedral. Both are easily accessible as day trips by train, bus or regular summer boats from Budapest.

Although both places can be fitted into one long day, they lend themselves more to an overnight stay. Most day-trippers aim for Szentendre instead, a quaint old Serbian village and artists' colony at the end of the regular HÉV train line from downtown Batthyány tér.

Life is sweet on the Danube Bend.

Szentendre

Szentendre is a settlement of 20,000 people 20 kilometres north of the capital, offering shady walks along the Danube, glimpses of Serbian history and a sizeable collection of art galleries.

The HÉV takes a pleasant 45 minutes to pass gentle suburbs and grazing horses. The summer boat service from Vigadó tér is only an extra hour and the evening journey back to Budapest can be equally delightful.

Long an artists' colony (*see p199* **Where the art is**), today Szentendre is mainly a tourist destination, with daft museums (marzipan, wine), overpriced crafts and folklore, and horse-drawn carriages clip-clopping along cobbled streets. But don't let the tack put you off, as there's history aplenty to be seen.

Serbian refugees reached Szentendre centuries before souvenir-sellers. Their legacy is a small immigrant community and a handful of Orthodox churches, some still in operation. The Serbs came here in several waves, escaping war and persecution to enjoy religious freedom under Habsburg rule and prosper in the wine and leather trades. Although the exteriors are baroque, their church interiors preserve Orthodox traditions, in which all sanctuaries face east, irrespective of dimension or streetscape. The resulting disjointed layout gives the town a distinctly Balkan atmosphere.

The first church you come to is Pozarevacka, in Vuk Karadzics tér, open to visitors at weekends. Inside is Szentendre's oldest iconostasis, small iconic representations of saints that are joined together in a screen, which partially obscures the altar of the church. In the main square, Fő tér, Blagovestenska Church provides a heady mix of deep music, incense and a glorious iconostasis. Szentendre's most stunning place of worship is the Belgrade Cathedral, seat of the Serbian Orthodox bishop, with its entrance in Pátriáka utca (open 10am-4pm Tue-Sun). The entryway is decorated with oak wings carved in rococo style. The inside features a pulpit adorned with carvings and paintings, and an ornate bishops' throne. On the same grounds is a museum of Serbian church art, containing bishop's garments, icons and lavish religious trappings made of gold and other precious metals (open Oct-Apr 10am-4pm Tue-Sun; May-Sept 10am-6pm Tue-Sun).

After a series of floods and epidemics, a group of artists moved into Szentendre in the 1920s, delighted to find a living museum of Serbian houses and churches. Later generations set up galleries, with varying degrees of merit. While some 'galleries' are really more like shops, others are worth a look. Cultural activity is not limited to art; there has long been a flourishing local music scene, centred on the Dalmát Pince, Malom utca 5, a cellar with regular live music, or the Dunaparti Művelődési Ház (DMH) at

Trips Out of Town

The citadel and Visegrád Palace were built in the 13th and 14th centuries. The latter was the setting for the Visegrád Congress of 1335, when the Kings of Hungary, Czechoslovakia and Poland quaffed 10,000 litres of wine while discussing trade strategy. Representatives of the so-called 'Visegrád Group' of Hungary, Poland, the Czech Republic and Slovakia still meet here to discuss joint concerns.

In the 15th century King Mátyás Corvinus overhauled the palace in splendid renaissance style, where he held court. All this fell into ruin after a Turkish invasion and mudslides buried the palace, and it wasn't rediscovered until extensive excavations in 1934.

What you'll see today is ruins or modern recreations. Several restored rooms house small displays about everyday life here in medieval times. Some original pieces uncovered during excavations can be found at the Mátyás Museum, in the Salamon Tower, halfway up the hill to the citadel.

You can reach the citadel via a strenuous, literally breathtaking 25-minute walk up the stony Path of Calvary, by one of the thrice-daily buses from the village or by taking a taxi (call 06 30 949 0972) or car up Panoráma út.

Before taking the boat back, a beer with a view can be had at the terrace bar above the kitschy Renaissanz restaurant opposite the landing. For lunch, try the Fekete Holló, Rév utca 12 (06 26 397 584), with its open fire.

Visegrád Tours
Rév utca 15 (06 26 398 160). **Open** 9am-5.45pm daily.

Esztergom

Although Esztergom is Hungary's most sacred city, home of the Archbishop and the nation's biggest church, it has a real-life edge that makes it worth a night's stopover. Not all of its 30,000 inhabitants are pious; there's a Suzuki factory on the outskirts and, in town, a string of bars full of drunken fishermen.

But it's the past that brings visitors here. Esztergom was Hungary's first real capital. The nation's first Christian King, Szent István, was crowned here on Christmas Day 1000. He built a royal palace, unearthed in 1934, parts of which can be seen in the Castle Museum south of the cathedral. For nearly three centuries Esztergom was the royal seat, until the Mongol invasion all but destroyed the city. It suffered more damage under the Turks, but most of what's worth seeing was rebuilt in baroque style some 250 years ago: the Víziváros Parish Church on Mindszenty tere, the Christian Museum on Berényi Zsigmond utca and the Balassi Bálint Museum in Pázmány Péter utca.

Szentendre – history and tack aplenty.

Dunakorzó 11A (06 26 312 657), a cultural centre with eclectic music. Trendy bars always seem to be closing and opening on Fő tér.

There are good restaurants at Fő tér and by the river. The Görög Kancsó, Görög utca 1 (06 26 301 729), offers a diverse menu at fair prices. You'll find finer at Chez Nicolas, Kígyó utca 10 (06 26 311 288). Locals prefer the fish at Rab Ráby, Péter-Pál utca 1A (06 26 310 819).

Tourinform Szentendre
Dumtsa Jenő utca 22 (06 26 317 965). **Open** *Oct-Apr* 8.30am-4.30pm Mon-Fri. *May-Sept* 8am-5pm Mon-Fri; 10am-2pm Sat, Sun.

Visegrád

From the citadel in Visegrád, you can get spectacular views of a beautiful stretch of the Danube, but the sleepy village below is only worth visiting for the ruins of the palace.

Where the art is

Don't be fooled by Szentendre's picturesque ambience. There's a quiet tension between the iconoclastic artistic community, the 'official' aesthetics of the state-funded exhibition spaces and the hordes that descend to coo over the naive ceramics of Margit Kovács. This is still an interesting place to spot innovative Magyar art.

The link between Szentendre and art was forged in the balmy summers of the 1920s, but it wasn't until the 1960s that a permanent base for artists was established with the setting-up of the Vajda Lajos Stúdió. Named after a pre-war Hungarian surrealist, the VLS was ostensibly dedicated to 'Edwinism', a psychedelic version of Dadaism. The group's peripheral position enabled them to resist the conformist pressures of the Communist era and achieve cult status within the cultural underground of the 1980s.

Today, the automatic association of Szentendre with the ageing hippies of the VLS has become a cliché, but a profitable one for the many private galleries in town. Despite, or perhaps because of, its kitsch, picture-book appearance, there's something surreal about Szentendre. To escape the hordes, dive into one of the following galleries:

Art'éria

Városház tér 1 (06 26 310 111). HÉV to Szentendre. **Open** 10am-1pm, 2-5pm Wed-Sun. **Admission** free. **Credit** AmEx, DC, MC, V.
Hungary's first private, post-Communist gallery exhibits and sells works by István ef Zámbó, László fe Lugossy, Imre Bukta, András Wahorn, István Nádler, Pál Deim and others of the Vajda Lajos Stúdió.

Erdész Galéria

Fő tér 20 (06 26 310 139). HÉV to Szentendre. **Open** 10am-6pm Tue-Sun. **Admission** free. **Credit** AmEx, DC, MC, V.
Commercial gallery includes a permanent collection of 20th-century masters Sándor Bortnyik, Lajos Kassák, József Rippl-Rónai, László Moholy-Nagy and Lajos Vajda. **Branch:** Bercsényi utca 4 (06 26 317 925).

Kovács Margit Múzeum

Vastagh György utca 1 (06 26 310 790). HÉV to Szentendre. **Open** 10am-6pm daily. **Admission** Ft250; Ft150 children. **No credit cards.**
Margit Kovács (1902-77) was a popular Hungarian sculptor – really a ceramicist – and queen of the easy aesthetics encouraged during the Communist era. To be fair, it's not all kitsch. Her work has certain votive aspects more reminiscent of Etruscan or Persian religious mythology than Hungarian folktales. Hungarians do expect you to be interested.

Vajda Lajos Múzeum

Hunyadi utca 1 (no phone). HÉV Szentendre. **Open** 10am-4pm Fri-Sun. **Admission** Ft150; Ft100 children. **No credit cards.**
The montages and surrealist paintings of Lajos Vajda (1908-41), a member of the Kassák circle, are a powerful commentary on looming disaster as World War II approached.

Vajda Lajos Stúdió Pinceműhelye

Péter Pál utca 6 (06 26 310 593). HÉV to Szentendre. **Open** 10am-6pm Tue-Sat. **Admission** free. **No credit cards.**
Cellar gallery exhibiting the works of VLS artists since 1972 and, more recently, those by foreign visitors.

It's the cathedral that dominates, though. What strikes most is the size of the thing. When the Catholic Church moved its base back to Esztergom in 1820, Archbishop Sándor Rudnay wanted a vast monument on the ruins of a 12th-century church destroyed by the Turks. It took 40-odd years and three architects to create this bleak structure. A bright spot is the Bakócz Chapel, built in red marble by Florentine craftsmen, dismantled during the occupation of the Ottomans and reassembled in 1823. In town you'll find a dozen reasonable restaurants; the Csülök Csárda, Batthyány utca 9 (06 33 412 420), is as good as any.

The Pension Ria, nearby at Batthyány utca 11-13 (06 33 313 115), is a charming, inexpensive place to stay and has bright, modern bathrooms. The Alabardos Panzió, Bajcsy-Zsilinszky utca 49 (06 33 312 640), can also provide you with a cheapish double room. The Hotel Esztergom, Primas Sziget, Nagy Duna sétány (06 33 412 555), is a more expensive and modern option, with a nice river terrace and sports centre.

GranTours

Széchenyi tér 25 (06 33 417 052). **Open** 8am-6pm Mon-Fri; 9am-noon Sat.
Private company more reliable than the state office.

The Balaton

An easy lay, but no cheap date.

The Balaton is one of Europe's largest lakes, a huge area of water for such a small, landlocked country. No wonder Hungarians have flocked here for generations. Even those on modest salaries have access to a weekend house on the shores of this shallow lake.

As a foreigner, unless you get invited too, your trip here might be different: high-rise hotels, concrete beaches, white plastic chairs, advertising umbrellas and a string of over-priced resorts. Although there are quieter parts, a trip to this lake is first and foremost an excursion into deepest naff – which doesn't mean to say that it can't also be a lot of fun.

Its lure goes way back, attracting Celts, Romans, Huns and Slavs, whose word for swamp, *blatna*, probably gave the lake its name. The Magyars brought fishing and farming, and built a lot of churches, before the Mongols came in 1242. The Turks occupied the south shore and scuffled with Austrians on the other side in the 16th and 17th centuries. Once they were driven out, the Habsburgs came along and blew up any remaining Hungarian castles.

Most of the best sights, therefore, date from the 18th century, when viticulture flourished and baroque was in vogue. Landmarks include the Abbey Church in Tihany and the huge Festetics Mansion in Keszthely.

Although Balatonfüred was declared a spa in 1785, it wasn't until the 19th century that bathing and the therapeutic properties of the area's thermal springs began to draw the wealthy in large numbers. In 1836 Baron Miklós Wesselényi, leading reformer of the period, was the first to swim from Tihany to Balatonfüred. Lajos Kossuth suggested steamships, and Count István Széchenyi rustled some up. Passenger boat services still link most of the major resorts and are an appealing way to get around, though the ferry from the southern tip of the Tihany peninsula to Szántód – a ten-minute journey spanning the lake's narrowest point – is the only one that takes cars.

The southern shore – now an 80-kilometre stretch of tacky resorts – was developed after the 1861 opening of the railway. The line along the hillier and marginally more tasteful north shore wasn't completed until 1910. Despite the easy transit, the Balaton mainly remained a playground for the well-to-do until after World War II, when the Communists reconstructed the area with an eye to mass recreation. Before the Berlin Wall fell, Hungary was one of the few places where East Germans could travel and the Balaton became the place where West Germans would meet up with their poor relations. Tourism is still heavily geared towards the needs of Germans, and in some shops and restaurants German is the first language and Hungarian the second.

The lake itself is weird. A 77 kilometre-long rectangle, 14 kilometres at its widest, it covers an area of about 600 square kilometres but is shallow throughout. Lake Geneva contains 20 times as much water. At its deepest, the 'Tihany Well' near the peninsula that almost chops the lake in half, the Balaton reaches only 12-13 metres down. At Siófok and other south shore resorts, you can paddle out nearly 1,000 metres before the water gets up to your waist – which means it's very safe for children.

But it's not ideal swimming water. It's silty and milkily opaque, and can feel oily on the skin. Motor boats are strictly forbidden here but you can sail or windsurf on the lake. Fishing's popular too. Balaton is home to around 40 varieties of fish, many of which are served in local restaurants. The *fogas*, a pike-perch, is unique to the lake and makes a fine accompaniment for one of the very drinkable local wines.

Because Balaton is traditionally the place where Hungarians make money off Western tourists, prices are high here. Affordable hotels and restaurants exist, but nothing's very cheap.

Despite its drawbacks, the Balaton can make for an interesting trip. Most destinations can be reached by train in about two or three hours. Siófok and the other resorts at the western end of the lake are manageable in a day.

Balatonfüred

The north shore's major resort is also the Balaton's oldest and has long been famed for the curative properties of its waters.

The State Hospital of Cardiology and the Sanitorium dominate the baroque and, these days, somewhat dilapidated Gyógy tér in the old town centre. The neo-classical Kossuth Well in the square dispenses warm, healing, mineral-rich water, which is the closest you'll get to the thermal springs without having to check into the hospital.

Balatonfüred has a busy harbour with a pier, a shipyard, promenade, six major beaches and an assortment of uninspiring things to see. Romantic writer Mór Jókai cranked out many of his 200 novels here, and his summer villa (at the corner of Jókai Mór utca and Honvéd utca) is now a memorial museum that includes a coffeehouse, the Jokai Kávézó. Across the road is the neoclassical Kerék templom (Round Church), built in 1846. The Lóczy Cave (*barlang*), off Öreghegy utca on the northern outskirts of town, is the largest hole in the ground hereabouts. You can catch ferry boats from Balatonfüred to Tihány and Siófok.

The Hotel Flamingo at Széchenyi utca 16 (06 87 340 392) is par for the tacky course, with a private beach. Modest but comfortable is Hotel Thetis, Vörösmarty utca 7 (06 87 341 606).

After dinner at one of the many restaurants all along Tagore sétány and up Jókai Mór utca – the ones by the end of the pier all specialise in fish dishes – the disco in the Wagner Galéria and Club complex offers pop techno, go-go dancers and lots of teenagers on the dancefloor.

The Füredi Feszek Kávézó on Kisfaludy utca offers both pizzas and house music until the wee hours. From the end of the pier, with the lights of Siófok in the distance and the Tihany peninsula looming darkly to the west, the lake looks delightful by moonlight.

Balatontourist Balatonfüred

Blaha Lujza utca 5 (06 87 342 823). **Open** *Oct-May* 9am-4pm Mon-Fri. *June-Sept* 9am-5pm Mon-Sat.

Tihany

Declared a national park in 1952, the Tihany peninsula is one of the quietest and most unspoilt places in the whole Balaton region – although even in this picturesque, historic spot, summertime means the blooming of Coca-Cola umbrellas.

The 12 square kilometres of the peninsula jut five kilometres into the lake, almost cutting it in half. Tihany village lies by the Inner Lake, separated from the Balaton by a steep hill. Atop this hill stands the twin-spired Abbey Church, completed in 1754. This is one of Hungary's most important baroque monuments, and not just because of its outstanding woodcarvings – though there are certainly plenty of those. King

Lake Balaton – the closest landlocked Hungary gets to a day at the seaside.

Trips Out of Town

Hungary's healthy breaks

With most of its land sat on thermal waters, Hungary is looking to revive the spa culture that saw high society soak away its woes in Central Europe a century or more ago. In its programme oddly entitled 'Wellness', the Hungarian tourist board has named 2003 the Year of Health Tourism. At its disposal are over 1,000 thermal springs and 40 medicinal baths across Hungary, some in magnificent mansions. The image of luxuriating in a country castle, resting in thermal waters, being massaged and fed wine on doctor's orders, is not far from the truth.

A plethora of restored castles now offer spa treatments and rooms for as little as €20 a night. Treatments improve circulation, boost metabolism, relax the muscles and enhance equilibrium. Guests can enjoy general pampering or prescribed therapies, including interesting alternative health programmes such as the wine treatment at the **Szidónia Castle**.

Along with therapy, the following places generally offer other outdoor activities, such as horse-riding or extreme sports. Unless otherwise noted, these places are all in restored castles:

Cívis Grand Hotel Aranybika

Debrecen, Piac utca 11-15 (06 52 508 600/ www.civishotels.hu). **Rates** single €70; double €90; suite €150; apartment €150-€200; extra bed €16. **Credit** DC, MC, V.
Debrecen's most famous hotel has 205 reasonably spartan rooms with full health services.

Danubius Thermal Hotel Hévíz

Hévíz, Kossuth Lajos utca 9-11 (06 83 500 750/www.danubiusgroup.com/heviz). **Rates** single €70-€92; double €114-€136; suite €190; extra bed €44. **Credit** AmEx, DC, MC, V.
Located next to the largest thermal lake in Europe. The water is rich in mineral content and its mud is also used for therapies.

Gróf Apponyi Kastélyszálló

Hőgyész, Ady Endre utca 2 (06 74 588 800/ www.apponyi.hu). **Rates** single €58-€96; double €77-€128; suite €123-€191.
Credit AmEx, DC, MC, V.
This 18th-century baroque castle set in parkland south of Siófok has mineral-rich water from 800m below ground.

Kolping Családi Hotel

Alsópáhok, Fő utca 120 (06 83 344 143/ www.kolping.hotel.hu). **Rates** €40 per person.
Credit AmEx, DC, MC, V.
This 8.5-hectare complex close to Hévíz and Keszthely caters particularly to families. Horse-riding, children's pool and babysitting are all readily available.

Maróthy Kúria – Sárvári Gyógyfürdő

Zsédeny, Rákóczi utca 31 (06 95 343 031/ www.hotels.hu/marothy). **Rates** €20 per person. **Credit** MC, V.
Health services in this 19th-century mansion include hot water rich in saline for rheumatic conditions, plus a salt cave for respiratory illnesses.

Puchner Kastély Bikal

Bikal, Rákóczi utca 22 (06 72 459 546/ www.hotels.hu/puchner). **Rates** double €60-€100; apartment €106-€154.
Credit AmEx, MC, V.
Set in the Mecsek Hills, and restored in Habsburg yellow and white, the Puchner offers history, thermal pools and more.

Szidónia Kastélyszálloda

Röjtökmuzsaj, Röjtöki út 37 (06 99 544 810/ www.szidonia.hu). **Rates** double €82-€170; suite €112-€257; extra bed €30. **Credit** AmEx, DC, MC, V.
This newly renovated neo-classical castle offers a range of standard therapies and an unusual treatment based on the curative powers of local wine.

Andrew I's 1055 deed of foundation for the church originally on this site was the first written document to contain any Hungarian – a few score place names in a mainly Latin text (it's now in Pannonhalma Abbey near Győr). The Abbey Museum in the former monastery next door has exhibits about Lake Balaton and a small collection of Roman statues.

Perhaps the most stunning sight on this hilltop is the view. The church is on a sheer cliff, which affords splendid vistas of the Balaton and the countryside around it. There's beautiful nature around here, and **Tourinform Tihany** can provide information about walks in the area, which has a bird sanctuary, two small lakes, some geyser cones and Echo Hill.

The Kakas, in a rambling old house below the Erika hotel, is an agreeable spot for lunch or dinner and, unusually, open all year round. Otherwise there's an assortment of bars and restaurants around the main square and along Kossuth utca. Places to stay are limited, although the Hotel Park by the lake on Fürdőtelepi utca (06 87 448 611), formerly a Habsburg summer mansion, offers a modicum of elegance and its own private beach. Just say no if staff try to stick you in the ugly 1970s annexe on the same grounds. Alternatively, private rooms in Tihany village can be arranged through Balatontourist.

It may be best to stay in Balatonfüred, just 11 kilometres distant, and do Tihany as a side trip.

Tourinform Tihany

Kossuth utca 20 (06 87 438 016). **Open** 9am-5pm Mon-Fri; 9am-3pm Sat.

Keszthely

The only town on the Balaton that isn't totally dependent on tourism, Keszthely has a mellow feel quite different from other lakeside resorts. The two busy lidos seem to swallow up all the tourists, while the agricultural university means a bit of life off-season as well as some variety at night.

The main tourist attraction is the Festetics Palace, a 100-room baroque pile in pleasant grounds at the north end of the town centre. The Festetics family owned this whole area and Count György (1755-1819) was the epitome of an enlightened aristocrat. He not only built the palace but made ships, hosted a salon of leading literary lights and founded both the Helikon library – in the southern part of the mansion and containing more than 80,000 volumes – and the original agricultural college, these days the Georgikon Museum at Bercsényi utca 67. There's also the Balaton Museum, dedicated to the history of the region, with artifacts dating back to the first century AD.

The Gothic Parish Church on Fő tér has a longer history than most Balaton buildings. Originally built in the 1380s, it was fortified in 1550 in the face of the Ottoman advance. When the rest of the town was sacked, it managed to hold out against the Turks. In 1747 the church was rebuilt in baroque style.

The Hotel Bacchus at Erzsébet királyné útja 18 (06 83 314 096) is a small and friendly modern hotel, ideally located between the town centre and the lido, with a terrace restaurant that's one of the best in town. If you'd prefer a place by the lake, try the Hotel Hullám at Balatonpart 1 (06 83 312 644), a 1930s joint with airy, high-ceilinged rooms.

There are many bars and restaurants on and around Kossuth Lajos utca, the main street, catering to the town's student population.

Keszthely is a good base for venturing up the lake towards Badacsony, a scenic village with wine cellars and volcanic hills, or the cute little village of Szigliget with its 14th-century castle ruins. Hévíz, eight kilometres inland (15-minute bus ride from stop No.4 in Fő tér) has the largest thermal lake in Europe. Bathing is possible all year round (in winter the lake steams dramatically). The deep blue, slightly radioactive warm water is full of Indian water lilies and middle-aged Germans floating around with rubber rings.

Tourinform Keszthely

Kossuth Lajos utca 28 (06 83 314 144). **Open** *June-Sept* 9am-6pm Mon-Fri; 9am-1pm Sat, Sun. *Oct-May* 9am-5pm Mon-Fri; 9am-1pm Sat.

Siófok

Siófok, the first big lakeside town you'll hit by car or rail from Budapest, is Balaton's sin city: big, loud, brash and packed in high season. Although it's the lake's largest resort – Greater Siófok stretches for 15 kilometres along the shore – there isn't much in the way of sightseeing.

Siófok is mindless fun. Its Petőfi sétány strip runs for about two kilometres. Here you'll find big Communist-era hotels, bars with oom-pah bands, amusement arcades, Western-style steakhouses, topless places, portrait painters, video game arcades, parked cars blasting pop techno, naff T-shirt stalls, a reptile house full of scary snakes and an endless procession of Hungarian, German and Austrian tourists.

The Roxy at Szabadság tér 4 is a decent brasserie where the drinks are well made. Flört at Sió utca 4 (06 20 333 3303/www.flort.hu) is one of Hungary's best nightclubs: two dancefloors (one techno, one tacky), some occasionally excellent DJs, a succession of bars on different levels of the barn-like main room, and a roof terrace overlooking the Sió Canal. Its main rival is the Palace (06 84 350 698), just out of town. Both clubs occasionally host big-name house and techno DJs.

By the strip are tacky diners and food stalls. The Diana Hotel at Szent László utca 41-43 (06 84 315 296) has a fine restaurant with excellent *fogas*. The Janus at Fő utca 85-93 (06 84 312 546) is a good hotel, though pricey. On the strip, the Hotel Napfény, Mártírok utca 8 (06 84 311 408) is cheaper, with big rooms and balconies.

Tourinform Siófok

Fő tér 41 (06 84 310 117). **Open** *June-Sept* 8am-8pm Mon-Fri; 9am-noon Sat, Sun. *Oct-May* 9am-4pm Mon-Fri; 9am-noon Sat, Sun.

Trips Out of Town

Overnighters

Wine country or rustbelt, there's plenty for the curious traveller to explore.

Eger Castle – home to the original Magyar myth.

Trips Out of Town

Eger

With a castle that was the scene of a historic victory, a quaint downtown designed for walking and a rich tradition of making and drinking wine, Eger has plenty to offer visitors.

Located 128 kilometres north-east of Budapest, the town is at the foot of the low, rolling Bükk Hills, ideal for fishing, hunting and camping. They also produce the grapes that make wines like Egri Bikavér (Bull's Blood), Hungary's best known – along with sweet, white Tokaj. Bikavér is a hearty, dry red blend of local wines (*see p205* **Touring the vineyards**).

Inside Hungary, Eger is best known as the place where a small, outnumbered group of Magyars held off 10,000 invading Ottomans during a month-long seige in 1552. The Turks came back and finished the job 44 years later, but the earlier siege of Eger has been fixed in the nation's imagination by Géza Gárdonyi's 1901 adventure novel *Egri csillagok, '*Eclipse of the Crescent Moon'. Gárdonyi's version, which has the brave women of Eger dumping hot soup on the Turks, is required school reading, and his fiction seems almost to have replaced the actual history. There's a statue of the author within the castle, and a Panoptikum featuring wax versions of his characters. Copies of the novel are on sale all over town, and there's a Gárdonyi Géza Memorial Museum.

The castle was later dynamited by the Habsburgs in 1702. What remains is big, but there's not too much to see. Still, it's a nice place for a stroll and it affords a fine view over Eger's baroque and flatblock-free skyscape. Tours, available in English on site, offer a recap of the battle's history and a chance to see the interior of the battlements. You can just walk around, or visit the castle's various exhibits, most of which are closed on Monday.

Another place for a great view is atop the one minaret left since the Turkish occupation, though the ascent of the stairs inside is rather long and claustrophobic. Located at the corner of Knézich utca and Markó Ferenc utca, this is one of the northernmost minarets in Europe. The mosque that was once attached is gone.

Eger's baroque buildings are splendid, most notably the 1771 Minorite church, centrepiece of Dobó tér. The Basilica on Eszterházy tér is an imposing neo-classical monolith, crowned with crucifix-brandishing statues of Faith, Hope and Charity by Italian sculptor Marco Casagrande. Designed by József Hild, who also designed the one in Budapest, this cathedral has a similarly imposing façade that looks all the larger due to the long flight of steps from the square below. The statues of Hungarian kings and apostles along these steps were also made by Casagrande. The Lyceum opposite, now a teachers' college, has a 19th-century camera obscura in its east tower observatory that projects a view of the entire town.

Small and with a pedestrianised centre, Eger is ideal for strolling. You could easily do the town in a day, but it's a relaxing and rewarding overnighter. The Senátorház at Dobó tér 11 (06 36 320 466) is comfortable and well situated. The Minaret Hotel at Knezich Károly utca 4 (06 36 410 233) is cheaper.

Although you can find commercial wine cellars downtown, the local vintages are most entertainingly sampled just out of town – at

Szépasszonyvölgy, the Valley of Beautiful Women, a horseshoe-shaped area of dozens of wine cellars, many with tables outside. The offerings here, from small, private cellars, are not necessarily Eger's best, but the wine is very cheap. Gypsy fiddlers entertain drinkers, and parties come to eat, dance and make excessively merry. Get there by the afternoon, as places close by early evening. Out of high season, it's quiet on Sundays and Mondays. The valley bustles during a two-week harvest festival in September. It's a 25-minute walk from Dobó tér or a short cab ride. It can be hard to find a cab back – try calling City Taxi (06 80 412 111).

In town the Dobos Cukraszda at István utca 6 is a historic old coffeehouse and restaurant that's open early enough for breakfast.

Tourinform Eger

Dobó tér 2 (06 36 517 715). **Open** *May-Oct* 9am-5pm Mon-Fri; 9am-1pm Sat. *June-Sept* 9am-8pm Mon-Fri, 9am-5pm Sat, Sun.

Pécs

Though the sea is far away, there's something Mediterranean about Pécs. Hungary's fourth-largest town is southerly enough to have a climate warmer than Budapest's, and the pace of life is more relaxed. The effect is enhanced by the fig trees and Turkish monuments.

The historic sites of Pécs's attractive old town, the curious architecture, the clutch of interesting art museums and the nightlife, fuelled by a large student population, all recommend Pécs as the main contender if you're only making one foray out of Budapest.

Romans settled here and called their town Sopianae – a name that lives on as a Hungarian cigarette brand. The town prospered on the trade route between Byzantium and Regensburg, King Stephen established the Pécs diocese in 1009, and Hungary's first university was founded here in 1367. Then came the Turks

Touring the vineyards

The dual attractions of rustic getaway and robust wine provide the perfect excuse to visit Hungary's two top wine-growing spots of Villány and Tokaj.

Villány is a village of 3,000 people a 45-minute train ride from Pécs, in the heart of the region to which it gave its name – Hungary's best red wine country and home to several robust vintages (*see p98* **Unknown pleasures**). The main street is full of cellars, where you can sample the local grape per glass. Bottles are equally cheap – as is a five-litre jug of the stuff. There's even a wine museum in an old cellar on Bem József utca.

Accommodation is plentiful in Villány, but the best option is probably the *pánziók* of the winemakers themselves. The Gere Cellar Pension, at Diófás tér 4 (06 72 492 195), is run by Attila Gere – who, along with his brother Tamás, makes some of Hungary's best wines. For less than Ft10,000, a couple can get a room, breakfast and a corkscrew. The manager offers you some wine samples, then you plop down in the garden, choose the bottles you like and pay as you open them. You'll enjoy top-quality wines at very low prices. Bock, another excellent vintner, has a similarly priced wine cellar and pension at Batthyány utca 15 (06 72 492 919).

Beyond are activities like horse-riding and hiking and even a short stroll will take you to the surreal sculpture park on Nagyharsány

Hill, where art students from around the country practise carving on the huge rocks strewn about an unused quarry. The beautiful, often comical statues seem to have dropped here from nowhere – looking like the stone heads of Easter Island or a weird American roadside attraction.

Friday nights in summer are festive, as the main street of Baross utca is taken over by wine stalls and music shows. There are a few good restaurants here, too, meals complemented by local reds. The main tourist information office in Pécs (*see p207*) can provide more details.

Probably the most famous wine from Hungary is Tokaji Aszu, the sweet dessert wine made from a blend of grapes, including some that have nearly turned into raisins. While the wines of this region are outstanding, the village of Tokaj has limited charm – and limited public transport from nearby Eger. Once you've seen a few local cellars, you've done the town. Perhaps a bigger problem is that, unlike the heavy reds of Villány, it's hard to spend hours necking the finer sweet whites of Tokaj. Enjoy a glass or two before stocking up on a cheap bottle or two.

Tourinform Tokaj

Serház út 1 (06 47 352 259/www.tokaj.hu). **Open** *June-Sept* 9am-6pm Mon-Fri; 9am-5pm Sat, Sun. *Oct-May* 9am-4pm Mon-Fri.

Trips Out of Town

in 1543, pushing the locals outside the walls that still define the city centre and flattening the place. Thus, as in the rest of Hungary, little pre-Turkish stuff survives. But after staying 143 years, longer than in most of Hungary, the Turks definitely left their mark on the city.

Signs of the historical struggle between Magyars and Muslims are evident in the Belvárosi Plébániatemplom (Inner City Parish Church), which dominates the town's main square, Széchenyi tér. Under the Ottomans, an ancient Gothic church that once stood on the square was torn down and the stones were used to make the mosque of Pasha Gazi Kassim. After the Turks left, Jesuits converted the mosque to its present state, which is decidedly un-churchlike: the ogee windows, domed and facing Mecca, are at variance with the square's north-south orientation. The minaret was demolished in 1753 but inside, on the back wall, are recently uncovered Arabic texts. As if to counter this influence, the main interior decor features a grand mural depicting Hungarian battles with the Turks. Outside, the statue of János Hunyadi, the Hungarian leader who successfully thwarted an earlier Turkish invasion, sits on horseback in the square.

The mosque of Pasha Hassan Jokovali, complete with minaret, is at Rákóczi utca 2. The most intact Ottoman-era structure in Hungary, this was also converted into a church, but in the 1950s the original mosque was restored. Excerpts from the Koran on the plaster mosque's dome have been recovered, and the building next to the mosque is a museum of Turkish artifacts. Hungary's only active mosque, built more recently, is located about 30 kilometres south of Pécs, in the small town of Siklós, which is also home to a restored castle.

On Dóm tér stands the symmetrical four-towered, mostly neo-Romanesque Basilica of St Peter. The choir, the crypt, the west side of the nave and the two western towers were built in the 11th century, and the two eastern towers were added about a century later. Highlights include stunning wall frescoes, the red marble altar of the Corpus Christi Chapel and the incredible wall carvings on the stairs leading to the crypt. Nearby Szent István tér has Roman ruins and a small park with cafés and a market.

Káptalan utca, a small street running east off Dóm tér, is packed with museums and galleries. At No.2, in a building built in 1324, is the museum of Zsolnay tiles, the colourful ceramics

One-offs Tony Curtis

Sometime between divorces and treatments for alcohol and drug abuse, Hollywood movie star Tony Curtis went in search of his Hungarian roots. He found them in darkest Mátészalka, a poor and shabby village on the edge of the drab, flat miles of the endless plain of the Nagyalföld, squeezed right up to the Romanian and Ukrainian borders.

'We were able to walk the streets and visit the house where my grandfather was born,' was how his daughter and travelling companion Kelly described it in Curtis's autobiography.

Other accounts relate Curtis being ferried around the dusty streets in a carriage.

In any case, to his credit, Curtis, whose first language was Hungarian, has contributed a considerable amount to the restoration of Hungary's synagogues, and is honorary chairman of the Emanuel Schwartz Foundation for Hungarian Culture – a fund-raising organisation named after his father.

Manny and Helen Schwartz left Hungary for America, married in New York in 1924, and had their first son, Bernard, a year later. They always spoke Hungarian at home. Curtis, as he came to be, was raised in the Bronx while

his father ran a series of tailor's shops. When he began to make it in the movies, the whole family shipped out to Hollywood, his mother spending her free time there with the Hungarian film community. She would teach Curtis's daughters Magyar folk tales and cooking.

As his movies became more successful – Houdini, The Sweet Smell of Success, Some Like It Hot – Curtis's private life slowly spiralled out of control. Perhaps his involvement with the Emanuel Foundation was one way to redress the equilibrium.

In 1988, he and Kelly went to Budapest for the official dedication of the Victims and Heroes' Memorial at Budapest's Central Synagogue (see p76 Jewish Budapest). Then they went to Mátészalka, where the main synagogue on Kossuth út, regularly used by Manny Schwartz, had been closed since 1956: 'One old guy had the key and opened it for us,' describes Curtis. 'There were holes in the ceiling and birds flying around, a beautiful old place. On the wall were the names of some of our relatives who didn't survive the Holocaust. It was a very moving experience.'

you see on top of Budapest's more extravagant buildings from the turn of the century (*see p72* **Art nouveau Budapest**) and in Pécs on top of new buildings too. The Zsolnay factory is in Pécs, and this building houses some unusual Zsolnay pieces, though the best of the collection is probably what's visible from the courtyard. Across the street, at No.3, is a museum dedicated to Magyar op-artist Victor Vasarely, in the house where he was born. Underneath this house is the mining museum. Nearby, at Janus Pannonius utca 11, is an interesting museum of works by Tivadar Csontváry. Hungary's answer to Van Gogh, Csontváry made haunting paintings with vivid colours.

The Santa Maria at Klimó György utca 12, built into the old city walls with nice outdoor seating, is a good spot for lunch. The slightly fancier and more expensive Aranykacsa

Étterem, at Teréz utca 4 (06 72 518 860), makes fantastic duck – its speciality – and other standard Hungarian fare.

Király utca, the pedestrianised street off Széchenyi tér, is an excellent stretch for a bar crawl, and there are some clubs here too. Other clubs in town, like Tabacco Labirintus (Megyeri utca 53) and Boccaccio (Bajcsy-Zsilinszky utca 45), can host good DJs. Grab a copy of *Pesti Est*, free in many bars, for entertainment listings.

The best hotel in Pécs, the art nouveau and elegant Palatinus, at Király utca 5 (06 72 233 022), has double rooms for around Ft20,000. The friendly Hotel Főnix at Hunyadi út 2 (06 72 311 680), just north of Széchenyi tér, is just as central and cheap, with doubles at Ft9,000.

Tourinform Pécs
Széchenyi tér 9 (06 72 212 632). **Open** 8am-4pm Mon-Fri; 9am-2pm Sat.

Faith, Hope and Charity top Eger's **Minorite Church**. *See p204.*

Rustbelt renaissance

Once called Sztalinváros, after the Soviet dictator, Dunaújváros was built in the 1950s as a showcase for heavy industry and Socialist urbanism. By the 1980s the city was known as a rusting enclave for metal-heads and heroin addicts, but it's changing its image again, building a reputation as an enclave for the arts.

A visit to this alternative destination, 90 minutes from Budapest, offers a glimpse of recent Hungarian history and an antidote to the stereotypical view of provincial life in Central Europe as just one baroque market town after another. Along with unusual architecture, the town hosts the **Institute of Contemporary Art** (*pictured*), trying to revive the area as an innovative cultural centre.

Local history began on May Day 1950 with the festive start of a communal effort to build a Socialist steel town from scratch at the geographical centre of the country. Open-topped trucks packed with volunteers drove down from Budapest to chip in. The chief architect was Tibor Weiner, who was forced to tone down the Bauhaus modernism he'd been reared on in Dessau, and build neo-classical people's palaces. The boulevards and green squares surrounded by mansion flats preserve a sense of ornamental grandeur that has outlived the demise of the Socialist utopia.

The **Intercisa Museum**, named after the ancient Roman town discovered on the site of the Duna steel works, is itself a particularly good example of Socialist realist architecture.

Along with local archaeological artifacts, the museum presents the history of the town's development from the early 1950s.

The Institute of Contemporary Art opened its doors in 1997 to put Dunaújváros at the cutting edge of high culture, with exhibitions of modern Hungarian and international art. It has a strong presence in the art scene, partly due to the reputation of curator Zsolt Petrányi, selector of the 2003 Hungarian Pavilion at the Venice Biennale. Openings are usually fun occasions and treated as a free outing by the Budapest art crowd, who take the courtesy bus from Buda's Technical University. To make the trip worthwhile, the ICA usually throws a party after the opening. Check local listings for details (*see p159*).

Between the city and the Danube is a sprawling park, home to more than 50 enormous metal sculptures created for the annual International Steel Sculptors' Colony.

Buses leave for Dunaújváros every hour from Budapest's Etele tér station, at the terminus of the red No.7 city bus route.

Institute of Contemporary Art

Kortárs Művészeti Intézet
Vasmű út 12 (06 25 412 220/www.ica-d.hu).
Open Tue-Sun 10am-6pm. **No credit cards.**

Intercisa Museum

Városháza tér 4 (06 25 411 315). **Open** *even weeks* 10am-2pm Tue-Fri; *odd weeks* 2-6pm Tue-Fri, Sat, Sun. **No credit cards.**

Travel Insurance

An annual policy
for the price
of a fortnight's

Our annual policy gives you 120 days cover for less than the cost of a two week policy from some travel agents. We even do a backpacker policy for longer trips.

0845 246 8971
call or buy online
DIRECT LINE® **directline.com**

Annual cover available to travellers under the age of 65 only. Each trip can be up to 42 days long. Subject to our normal underwriting criteria. Call 8am - 8pm Monday to Friday, 9am - 5pm Saturday, 11am - 5pm Sunday. Calls may be monitored or recorded. Direct Line Insurance plc is a member of the General Standards Insurance Council.

TimeOut
City Guides

If you've enjoyed this guide or have any useful comments, don't forget to fill in the questionnaire at the back of the book.

www.timeout.com

GATEWAY TO SUPERB INDIAN CUISINE

Bombay Palace®

INDIA'S CULINARY AMBASSADOR

London • Toronto • Montreal

Beverley Hills • Washington • Houston

BUDAPEST

Budapest's finest Indian restaurant. Now serving lunch specials at HUF 2000 and dinner specials at HUF 3000.

Andrássy út. 44
Open 12:00-14:45, 18:00-23:00 daily
Tel: **332 8363**
bombayp@axelero.hu, www.oisz.hu

Directory

Features

Directory

Getting Around

Arriving & leaving

By air

Ferihegy airport is 20 kilometres south-east of Budapest on the E60. There are two modern terminals next to each other: Ferihegy 2A & 2B. Terminal 2A is for Malév flights; 2B is for all other airlines. For information call: Ferihegy 2A arrivals 296 8000/departures 296 7000; Ferihegy 2B arrivals 269 5052/departures 269 5883. For any other information call 296 9696. English spoken.

Ferihegy 1 (269 9696), the old terminal, is currently under reconstruction to be the host airport for budget flights. Although several airlines have expressed their intention to fly to Budapest, negotiations are still going on.

Airport Minibus Shuttle

296 8555. **Open** 5am-10pm or until last flight. English spoken. The best way into town: for Ft2,100 (Ft3,600 return) this will take you to any address within the Budapest city limits. Buy a ticket at the counter in the arrivals hall, tell staff where you're going, then wait for a driver to call your destination after they've planned their route. To be picked up from town and taken to either terminal, call a day in advance. Accessible for wheelchair users.

Public transport

Take the Reptérbusz (Airport bus) or the 93 bus to Kőbánya-Kispest metro station and the blue M3 metro from there for the cost of one public transport (BKV) ticket for each (Ft125 from the airport newsagent). Last buses from the airport are at 11.45pm. Last metro leaves at 11.10pm, or there's the 50É night bus from the station.

Taxis from the airport

Fixed taxi prices from Ferihegy to each district in town are indicated on a board in the arrivals area. A taxi to the centre should cost Ft3,500-Ft5,000. Avoid the rogue taxi drivers who'll pester you around the arrivals hall – you'll be fleeced. Call any of the firms recommended (*see p215* **Taxis**) to arrange one for the journey back – most can quote you a fixed price.

Airlines

Air France

V. Kristóf tér 6 (483 8800/airport 296 8415/www.airfrance.com/hu). M1, M2, M3 Deák tér/tram 47, 49. **Open** 9am-5pm Mon-Fri. **Credit** AmEx, DC, MC, V. **Map** p249 C4.

American Airlines

V. Aranykéz utca 4-8 (266 6222). M1 Vörösmarty tér. **Open** 9am-5pm Mon-Fri. **Credit** AmEx, DC, MC, V. **Map** p249 C4.

Austrian Airlines

V. Régiposta utca 5 (327 9080/airport 296 0660). M1, M2, M3 Deák tér/tram 47, 49. **Open** 9am-5pm Mon-Fri. **Credit** AmEx, DC, MC, V. **Map** p249 C4.

British Airways

VIII. Rákóczi út 1-3 (411 5555/airport 296 6970/www.british airways.hu). M2 Astoria. **Open** 8am-5pm Mon-Fri. **Credit** AmEx, DC, MC, V. **Map** p249 D4.

KLM

VIII. Rákóczi út 1-3 (373 7737/airport 296 5747/www.klm.hu). M2 Astoria. **Open** 8.30am-4.30pm Mon-Fri. **Credit** AmEx, DC, MC, V. **Map** p249 D4.

Lufthansa

V. Váci utca 19-21 (266 4511/airport 292 1970/www.lufthansa. hu). M1, M2, M3 Deák tér/tram 47, 49. **Open** 8.30am-5pm Mon-Fri. **Credit** AmEx, DC, MC, V. **Map** p249 C4.

Malév

V. Dorottya utca 2 (235 3565/airport 296 9696/www.malev.hu). M1 Vörösmarty tér. **Open** 8.30am-5pm Mon-Fri. **Credit** AmEx, DC, MC, V. **Map** p249 C4. Malév's 24-hour information service for both terminals is on 296 7554. Ticket reservations can be made on 235 3888/06 40 212 121/www.malev.hu.

By bus

If arriving by bus, you'll be dropped at **Népliget bus terminal** (IX. Üllői út 131; 219 8020; 6am-6pm Mon-Fri; 6am-4pm Sat, Sun. No English spoken). M3 Népliget. There are left luggage facilities here (*see p224* **Left luggage**).

Volánbusz/Eurolines

XIII. Szabolcs utca 17 (219 8080/www.volanbusz.hu). The main international carrier with connections to all major European cities. **Ticket offices**: Népliget bus terminal (IX. Üllői út 131; 219 8020), M3 Népliget; Volánbusz Travel Agency (V. Erzsébet tér 1; 318 2122), M1, M2, M3 Deák tér/tram 47, 49. **Open** 8am-4pm Mon-Fri. **Credit** AmEx, DC, MC, V.

By train

Budapest has three main train stations: **Déli** (south), **Keleti** (east) and **Nyugati** (west), all with metro stops of the same name. The Hungarian for a main station is *pályaudvar*, often written as *pu*. Keleti station serves most trains to Vienna, Bucharest, Warsaw, Bulgaria, Turkey and north-western Hungary. Déli station also serves Vienna and Austria, as well as Croatia, Slovenia and south-eastern Hungary. Nyugati station is

Directory

the main point of departure for Transylvania and Bratislava. Services can get moved around according to season, so always double-check your departure station before you travel.

MÁV Information

VI. Andrássy út 35 (322 8082/ www.mav.hu/www.elvira.hu). M1 Opera. **Open** *Oct-Mar* 9am-5pm Mon-Fri. *Apr-Sept* 9am-6pm Mon-Fri. **Credit** MC, V. **Map** p246 D3. Often the easiest place to buy tickets in advance. Phone lines are open 6am-8pm daily. After that, call the 24-hour infolines (national enquiries 461 5400/international enquiries 461 5500) or one of the stations listed below.

Déli station

I. Alkotás út (355 8657/375 6593). M2 Déli pu./tram 18, 59, 61. **Open** 24hrs daily. **Map** p245 A3.

Keleti station

VIII. Baross tér (313 6835/333 6342). M2 Keleti pu./bus 7. **Open** 24hrs daily. **Map** p247 F3.

Nyugati station

VI. Nyugati tér (331 5346/333 6342). M3 Nyugati pu./tram 4, 6. **Open** 24hrs daily. **Map** p246 D2.

MÁV Railbus

VI. Kmety György utca 3 (353 2187).
MÁV runs a minibus service that will take you anywhere in the city for Ft1,500; between railway stations Ft900. Reservations should be made in advance on the phone.

Public transport

The Budapest transport company (BKV) is cheap and efficient, and gets you close to any destination. (*See p45* **Transport connections**.) The network consists of three metro lines, trams, buses, trolleybuses and local trains. In summer there are also BKV Danube ferries. Maps of the system can be bought at main metro stations. Street atlases also mark the routes.

Public transport starts around 4.30am and finishes around 11pm, although there's

a limited night bus network along major routes. Tickets can be bought at all metro stations, and at some tram stops and newsstands. A single ticket (*vonaljegy*) is valid for one journey on one piece of transport (except for ferries, which have a separate system, and buses that go beyond the administrative boundary of Budapest). So if you change from metro to tram, or even from metro line to metro line, you have to punch a new ticket, unless you use a transfer ticket (*átszállójegy*) or a metro transfer ticket (*metro átszállójegy*).

One-day, three-day, weekly, fortnightly and monthly passes are also available from metro stations, although you'll need a photograph to obtain anything except a one-day or three-day pass. Take your photo to a main metro station to be issued with a photopass. Ask for *napijegy* (one-day), *turistajegy* (three-day), *hetijegy* (weekly), *kétheti bérlet* (fortnightly) or *havibérlet* (monthly). All these tickets run from the day of purchase, apart from the monthly, which is valid per calendar month. There is also a 30-day pass (*harmincnapos bérlet*) valid from the day of purchase. It's possible to ride without a ticket, but plain-clothes inspectors are common and can levy on-the-spot fines of Ft1,500. Playing the dumb foreigner doesn't usually work.

Prices

Single ticket – Ft125
Transfer ticket – Ft220
Metro ticket for 3 stops – Ft90
Metro ticket for 5 stops – Ft140
Metro transfer ticket – Ft205
10 tickets – Ft1,100
20 tickets – Ft2,150
Day – Ft975
3-day – Ft1,950
Passes (with photo)
Week – Ft2,350
2-week – Ft3,000
Month – Ft4,670
30-day – Ft4,670

Budapest card

Two- and three-day cards work as BKV passes for an adult and a child under 14, as well as providing free admission to 60 museums, half-price sightseeing tours and discounts in certain restaurants, baths and shops. Ask for a free brochure at the main metro stations or at tourist information offices.
Budapest card for 2 days – Ft3,950
Budapest card for 3 days – Ft4,950

BKV Information

Free infoline: 06 80 406 611.

Metro

The Budapest metro is safe, clean, regular and simple. There are three lines: yellow M1, red M2 and blue M3. These connect the main stations and intersect at Deák tér. The renovated M1 line, originally constructed for the 1896 Exhibition, was the first underground railway in continental Europe. The other lines, constructed post-war with Soviet assistance, still have Russian trains.

Trains run every two to three minutes (the length of time since the last train is shown on a clock on the platform). Single tickets, three-stop, five-stop and metro transfer tickets can be purchased from either the ticket machines or ticket office in the stations. Ticket offices close at 8pm. After that, knock on the station's office door to get a ticket. Reluctant clerks are often more reliable than ticket machines. Validate tickets in the machines at the top of the escalators and in Deák tér passageways when changing lines. The first trains run from 4.30am and the last ones leave around 11pm.

Buses & trolleybuses

There's a comprehensive bus and trolleybus network, the main lines being line 1 from

Budapest online

www.access-hungary.hu
Daily excerpts from the
email/fax news service
Hungary Around the Clock.
www.budapest.hu
A portal concentrating on the
capital maintained by the
mayor's office.
www.fsz.bme.hu
Maintained by the Budapest
Technical University. General
info, maps, plus directory of
regional and local websites.
www.hudir.hu
Easy-to-follow directory of
websites set out according
to main categories.

www.hungary.org
News and info on a variety of
subjects. Free email service.
www.index.hu
Directory, forums, email,
online services and a
complete search engine of
the Hungarian web.
www.origo.hu
Full portal with news,
directory, forums, email,
online services and search
engine of the Magyar web.
www.startlap.com
A comprehensive list of what
you can find out where on
the web in Hungarian.

Kelenföld station to the centre
and then following the M1
metro, and line 7 connecting
Bosnyák tér, Keleti station,
Blaha Lujza tér, Astoria,
Ferenciek tere, Móricz
Zsigmond körtér and
Kelenföld. The Castle bus
(Várbusz) goes from Moszkva
tér round the Castle District
and back. Buses with red
numbers are expresses that
miss certain stops.

Night buses & trams

Night buses are marked with
'É'. A reduced but reliable
service works at night
following the main routes and
is usually full of drunks on
weeknights and teenagers at
weekends. Handiest services
are the 6É following the
Nagykörút, the 50É following
the blue M3 metro line, and
the 78É from Döbrentei tér on
the Buda side of Elizabeth
Bridge to Örs Vezér tere,
followingthe M2 route.
On these routes buses run
every 15 minutes.

Trams

Budapest has retained and
expanded its tram network.
The most important routes are

lines 4 and 6, which follow the
Nagykörút from Moszkva tér
to Fehérvári út and Móricz
Zsigmond körtér respectively;
line 2, which runs up the Pest
side of the Danube; and lines 47
and 49, which run from Deák
tér to Móricz Zsigmond körtér
and beyond into wildest Buda.

Suburban trains (HÉV)

There are four HÉV lines.
You'll probably only need the
one from Batthyány tér via
Margaret Bridge to Szentendre,
price Ft195 (a normal BKV
ticket valid as far as the border
at Békásmegyer, an extra Ft70
thereafter). First and last trains
from Batthyány tér are at
3.50am and 11.40pm, and from
Szentendre at 3.30am and
10.30pm. Other lines run from
Örs vezér tere to Gödöllő,
Vágóhíd to Ráckeve, and
Boráros tér to Csepel.

Danube ferries

Undoubtedly the most civilised
method of travelling within
Budapest, the BKV Danube
ferries also offer a river ride
that's exceedingly cheap when
compared with the various
organised tours. The local

service runs from May to the
beginning of September,
between Pünkösdfürdő north
of the city and Boráros tér at
the Pest foot of Petőfi Bridge,
stopping at most of the
bridges, Vigadó tér and either
end of Margaret Island. Fares
vary between Ft200 and Ft500
for adults and Ft120 and Ft250
for children. Boats only run
once every couple of hours,
with extra services laid on at
weekends. Timetables are
posted at all stops. Boats to
Szentendre, Visegrád and
Esztergom on the Danube
Bend leave from Vigadó tér
(*see pp193-209*).

Ferry information

Jászai Mari tér terminal
(Margaret Bridge, Pest side)
(369 1359/www.ship-bp.hu).
Or try the BKV information line
as listed above.

Eccentric conveyances

Budapest has a bizarre
assortment of one-off public
transports. *See p60* **Green
Budapest**. For the price of a
BKV ticket the **cog-wheel
railway** runs up Széchenyi-
hegy. It runs from the Hotel
Budapest, two stops from
Moszkva tér on tram 56 or 18.
Last train down is at 11.30pm.

Across the park from the
cog-wheel railway is the
terminal of the narrow-gauge
Children's Railway
(*gyermekvasút*; 395 5420),
which wends its way through
the wooded Buda Hills.
Formerly the Pioneer Railway,
run by the Communist youth
organisation, many of the
jobs are done by children.
Trains leave hourly between
9am and 5pm and tickets
cost Ft200 (return Ft400) for
adults and Ft65 (return Ft130)
for children.

Another way up into the
hills is the **chairlift** (*libegő*;
394 3764) up to Jánoshegy –
at 520 metres the highest point

in Budapest. Take the 158 bus from Moszkva tér to the terminus at Zugligeti út. It costs Ft400 one-way (Ft500 return), Ft250 for students and Ft150 for children, and runs 9am-5pm May- September, 9.30am-4pm October-April (closed every second Monday). There are cafés and bars at the top, and you can walk to Erzsébet lookout tower or the Jánoshegy stop on the Children's Railway.

Tamer but more central, the **funicular** (*sikló*) takes a minute to run up from Clark Ádám tér to the Castle District. It's a vertiginous ride but the view's good. This runs from 7.30am to 10pm (closed every second Monday morning) and a one-way ticket costs Ft450 adults; Ft250 children.

There's also the **Nostalgia Train** – a steam engine with old-fashioned carriages that puffs its way from Nyugati up to the Danube Bend every Saturday.

Taxis

Taxis in Budapest have yellow numberplates and yellow taxi signs on them. Rates vary from relatively cheap to outrageous. Stick to cabs displaying the logo of one of the companies mentioned below. Others often have tampered meters or will take you by the scenic route. Avoid cars hanging around outside hotels and tourist spots. They're usually crooks. The reliable Fôtaxi has yellow cabs, yellow-black checked patterns on their doors and can be spotted from a distance. Calling a taxi is the safest and easiest method. Most dispatchers can speak English and the cab will be there in five to ten minutes. Even though taxi companies have different tariffs, which comprise a basic fee, a fee per kilometre and a waiting fee, there's a price ceiling for all.

To give you an idea, the highest chargeable tariffs go like this (the companies listed below offer more competitive prices). Daytime tariff (6am-10pm): basic fee Ft300; fee per km Ft240; waiting fee Ft60 per min. Night-time tariff (10pm-6am): basic fee Ft336; waiting fee Ft84 per min. A receipt should be available on request. Say '*számlát kérek*'. A small tip of around 10 per cent is usual but not compulsory.

The most reliable companies are the following:

Budataxi (233 3333)
City Taxi (211 1111)
Fôtaxi (222 2222)
Rádió Taxi (377 7777)
Tele5 (355 5555)

Driving

Budapest has all the traffic problems of most modern European cities with a few extra ones thrown in. Hungarian driving is not good. Hungarians have constant urges to overtake in the most impossible places, they lack concentration and jump traffic lights. Many vehicles are of poor quality. Roads are even worse. There's been a huge influx of Western cars in recent years, increasing traffic levels and daytime parking problems. Practically all the bridges and central streets are jammed from 7am to 7pm on weekdays due to roadworks.

This is the beginning of the long process of replacing cobblestones and old tram tracks, and making pavements inaccessible for parking cars. Talk of restricting traffic hasn't yet amounted to much.

If you can't find your car where you left it, it doesn't necessarily mean it's been stolen. It may have been towed for illegal parking (*see p216* **Parking**).

● Seatbelts must be worn at all times by everyone in the car.
● Children under eight must be in a child safety seat. If a child can't be fitted into a safety seat, special cushions (*ülésmagasító*) should be used, so the child is lifted up enough to fasten the seatbelt. Children under 12 or under 150cm can't travel in the front seat without a safety seat.
● Always carry your passport, driving licence, vehicle registration document, motor insurance, and *zöldkártya* (exhaust emissions certificate) for cars that are registered in Hungary. Don't leave anything of value in the car.
● Headlights are compulsory by day when driving outside town. It's also recommended to use them in the city at all times.
● Priority is from the right unless you're on a priority road, signified by a yellow diamond on a white background.
● Watch out for trams, particularly in places where the passengers alight in the middle of the road.

Useful numbers

Ambulance: 104 (*English-language helpline*: 311 1666).
Central Emergency Number: 112 (*English-language hotline*: 4388 8080).
Customs: 470 4122.
Emergency breakdown: 188
Fire: 105.
Police: 107.

Directory (*national*): 198.
Directory (*international*): 199.
Tourist information: 438 8080 (*24hr hotline*: 06 80 660 044).
Up-to-date traffic information: 322 2238.
Up-to-date border information: 456 7101.

- Speed limit on motorways is 130kph, on highways 110kph, on all other roads 90kph unless otherwise indicated, and 50kph in built-up areas. Speed traps abound, with spot fines that vary greatly.
- The alcohol limit is 0.08 per cent and there are many spot checks, with severe penalties. Take a taxi if you're drinking.
- You're not allowed to speak on a mobile phone while driving unless you're using a speakerphone or hands-free set.

Breakdowns

A 24-hour breakdown service is provided by the Magyar Autóklub, which has reciprocal agreements with many European associations. English and German are usually spoken, but if not they'll ask you for the model (*típus*), colour (*szín*), numberplate (*rendszám*) of the vehicle and also the location.

Magyar Autóklub
(345 1800/24hr hotline 345 1755/emergency 188). **Open** 24hrs daily. **No credit cards** but they will accept a credit letter from affiliated organisations.

City Segély
(342 4564/06 20 933 1330). **Open** 24hrs daily. **No credit cards.**

Hungária Autómentő
(307 9308/06 30 948 3572). **Open** 24hrs daily. **No credit cards.**

Car hire

It's advisable to arrange car hire in advance. When asking for a quote, check whether the price includes *ÁFA* (VAT). You have to be over 21 with at least a year's driving experience. A valid driver's licence is required and a credit card is usually necessary for the deposit. There's an insurance charge and varying rates of mileage. The main companies have desks at both airport terminals.

Avis
V. Szervita tér 8 (318 4158/Ferihegy 296 6421/www.avis.hu). M1, M2, M3 Deák tér/tram 47, 49. **Open** 7am-6pm Mon-Sat; 8am-noon Sun. **Credit** AmEx, DC, MC, V. **Map** p249 C4.

Budget
I. Krisztina körút 41-43 (214 0420/Ferihegy 296 8197/www.budget.hu). M2 Déli. **Open** 8am-8pm Mon-Fri; 8am-6pm Sat, Sun. **Credit** AmEx, DC, MC, V. **Branch:** Hotel Mercure Buda, I. Krisztina körút 41-3 (488 8100).

Europcar
V. Deák Ferenc tér 3 (328 6464/Ferihegy 421 8370/hotline 421 8333/www.eurent.hu). M1, M2, M3 Deák tér. **Open** 8am-6pm daily. **Credit** AmEx, DC, MC, V. **Map** p250 E5.

Hertz
Vecsés, Hertz utca 2 (296 0997/Ferihegy 296 0988/www.hertz.hu). **Open** 8am-5pm Mon-Fri. **Credit** AmEx, DC, MC, V. **Branch:** Hotel Marriott, V. Apáczai Csere János utca 4 (266 4344).

Parking

More and more areas have parking meters, so look for the signs that show you've entered a zone where you have to pay. Little red bags (popularly known as Santa bags) behind the wipers of other cars might suggest the same. Check signs for hours (usually 8am-6pm weekdays, 8am-midday Sat). After that parking is free. Tickets are valid for one to three hours. Tickets can be purchased at the meters but you'll need to have change, or a parking card that can be bought in advance in amounts of Ft5,000, Ft10,000 and Ft30,000. The disadvantage of using a card is certain cards are only accepted in certain areas. Parking can also be paid for over the phone – you need a parktel-card, from Budapesti Önkormányzati Parkolási Kft (XIII. Hegedűs Gyula utca 20B, 478 5000/www.parktel.hu).

If you forget to buy a ticket or it exceeds the time covered, you might find a red bag under your wiper. In this case you need to pay the bill you find in the bag. The fine increases if you don't pay it within three or six days. You can pay it at the parking meters. Find 'extra fee' and 'paying the demanded amount' in the menu and you'll get a receipt. If you pay at the meter, you must forward the copy of the receipt via fax or post to the customer service office (V. Gerlóczy utca 2, open 9am-5pm Mon-Fri; 327 1390/fax 318 3460). Alternatively, you can pay the fine at any post office. In more serious cases you might find your car clamped or towed away. For wheel-clamping release, about Ft10,000, call the number displayed on a parking meter nearby. Cars that have been towed away can be traced by phone (307 5208/383 0700/383 0770).

In the city use the parking attendant controlled areas (V. Március 15 tér; under Nyugati station flyover) or car parks:

Car parks
V. Szervita tér 8. V. Aranykéz utca 4-6. VII. Nyár utca 20. VII. Osvát utca 5. VIII. Üllői út/Baross utca corner. VIII. Futó utca 52.

Petrol

Most filling stations are open 24 hours. Unleaded is *ólommentes*. Stay away from fuel marked with a 'K' as this is for lawnmowers and Trabants. Nearly all petrol stations accept credit cards and sell tobacco and basic groceries.

Cycling

Budapest isn't bike-friendly. Pollution is high and drivers unwary. Bike use is on the increase and there are some cycle lanes. Bikes can be hired on Margaret Island or at Charles Apartment House, I. Hegyalja út 23 (201 1796).

Resources A-Z

Addresses

When addressing an envelope in Hungarian, write the name of the street first followed by the house number. Hungarian street names can be confusing. The most common is *utca* (street), often abbreviated to *u* on street plates, envelopes and maps. This shouldn't be mixed up with *út* (*útja* in the genitive), which is road or avenue – unless it's a *körút*, which means ring road. *Tér* (genitive *tere*) is a square, *körtér* is a roundabout. Other Hungarian thoroughfares include *köz* (lane), *fasor* (alley), *sétány* (parade), *udvar* (passage or courtyard) and *rakpart* (embankment).

Letters require four-figure postcodes, in which the middle numbers stand for the district; for flats, the floor number is given in Roman numerals, followed by the flat number. On street plates, the district is written in Roman numerals, with the building numbers within the block underneath.

Age restrictions

In Hungary, the age of consent is 14 and people officially come of age at 18. Until then you're not allowed to buy cigarettes and alcoholic drinks or get a driving licence without parental consent.

Business

Hungary will join the European Union on 1 May 2004. So business will change radically, right? Wrong. Hungary has done all the tough work of preparing for EU membership over the course of the last ten years.

With only a few modest exceptions, the markets were liberalised and open to foreign competition years ago. State-owned companies have nearly all been privatised.

Foreign-owned companies and individuals have long been able to buy property – although only a private Hungarian citizen is permitted to own farmland.

EU membership for Hungary will be more like getting the diploma for an education already earned.

Some areas of reform do remain, mainly related to the execution and enforcement of laws already passed. For businesses, that means that cheating on taxes and hiring employees off the books will become increasingly difficult. It will also become easier, over time, to enforce contracts, as the company court system gets more effective.

But don't expect old ways of doing business to die out completely. Even more so than in the West, Hungarian business revolves around personal contacts. Western investors will also continue to find their Hungarian counterparts maddeningly fixated on bleeding short-term benefit out of long-term business ventures.

Maybe history has taught Hungarians to distrust the future, or maybe they're just born cynical. Either way Westerners, especially those involved in small and medium-sized business, should be extremely wary of entering deals that require far-sighted local partners.

Accounting & consulting firms

Deloitte & Touche
V. Nádor utca 21 (428 6800/ fax 428 6801). Bus 15, 105. **Open** 8.30am-5.30pm Mon-Fri. **Map** p246 C3.

Ernst & Young
XIII. Váci út 20 (451 8100/ fax 451 8199). M3 Lehel tér. **Open** 8.30am-5.30pm Mon-Fri.

KPMG
XIII. Váci út 99 (270 7100/fax 270 7101). M3 Forgács utca. **Open** 8am-7pm Mon-Fri.

Price Waterhouse Coopers
VII. Wesselényi utca 16 (461 9100/fax 461 9101). M2 Astoria/ tram 4, 6. **Open** 8.30am-5.30pm Mon-Fri. **Map** p249 D4.

Commercial banks

Central-European International Bank (CIB)
II. Medve utca 4-14 (212 1330/fax 212 4200). M2 Batthyány tér. **Open** 8.30am-4pm Mon, Tue, Thur; 8.30am-6pm Wed; 8.30am-2.30pm Fri. **Map** p245 B2.

Citibank
V. Vörösmarty tér 4 (288 2351/fax 288 2360). M1 Vörösmarty tér/tram 2, 2A. **Open** 9am-5pm Mon-Thur; 9am-4pm Fri. **Map** p249 C4.

K&H Bank
V. Vigadó tér 1 (328 9000/ fax 328 9696). Tram 2. **Open** 8am-5pm Mon; 8am-4pm Tue-Thur; 8am-3pm Fri. **Map** p249 C4.

OTP Bank
V. Nádor utca 16 (353 1444/ fax 312 6858). Bus 15, 105. **Open** 8am-4pm Mon; 8am-3pm Tue-Fri. **Map** p246 C3.

Conventions & conferences

All major hotels also offer comprehensive conference facilities (*see pp25-42*).

Budapest Convention Centre
Budapest Kongresszusi Központ *XII. Jagelló utca 1-3 (372 5700/ fax 461 9101). Tram 61/bus 8, 12, 112.* **Open** 8am-7pm Mon-Fri. **Map** p248 A5.

Directory

European Serviced Offices (ESO)

VI. Révay utca 10 (269 1100/ fax 269 1030). M1 Bajcsy-Zsilinszky út. **Open** 24hrs daily. **Map** p246 C3.

ESO also rents out offices on a short-term basis and offers multilingual secretarial services.

Regus Business Centre

VII. Emke Building, Rákóczi út 42 (267 9111/fax 267 9100). M2 Blaha Lujza tér/tram 4, 6. **Open** 8.30am-5.30pm Mon-Fri. **Map** p250 E4.

Short-term leases and various multilingual secretarial services also available.

Couriers & shippers

DHL Hungary

XI. Kocsis utca 3 (382 3499/ fax 204 6666). Tram 19, 47, 49. **Open** 8am-6pm Mon-Fri. **Credit** AmEx, MC, V.

Hajtás Pajtás Bicycle Messenger

VIII. Mária utca 54 (327 9000). M3 Kalvin tér. **Open** 8am-8pm Mon-Fri. **No credit cards.**

Royal Express/ Federal Express

IX. Nádasdy utca 2-4 (216 3606/fax 218 3808). Tram 23, 24, 30. **Open** 8am-6pm Mon-Fri; 9am-1pm Sat. **Credit** AmEx, V.

TNT Express Hungary

IX. Ecseri út 14-16 (431 3000/ fax 431 3096). M3 Ecseri út. **Open** 7.30am-6pm Mon-Fri. **No credit cards.**

Lawyers

Allen & Overy/ Déry & Co

VII. Madách Imre utca 13-14 (483 2200/fax 268 1515). M1, M2, M3 Deák tér. **Open** 9am-6pm Mon-Fri. **Map** p249 C4.

Baker & McKenzie/ Martonyi & Kajtár

VI. Andrássy út 102 (302 3330/ fax 302 3331). M1 Hősök tere. **Open** 8am-8pm Mon-Fri. **Map** p247 E2.

CMS Cameron McKenna/ Ormai & Partners

3rd Floor, V. Károlyi Mihály utca 12 (483 4800/fax 483 4801). M3 Ferenciek tere. **Open** 8am-8pm Mon-Fri. **Map** p249 C4.

Köves Clifford Chance Pünder

VII. Madách Imre utca 13-14 (429 1300/fax 429 1390). M1, M2, M3 Deák tér. **Open** 8am-8pm Mon-Fri. **Map** p249 C4.

Money

Hungary's currency is the forint. It's fully convertible. In June 2003 the exchange rate was Ft245/¤1. Hungary isn't expected to adopt the euro until at least 2007.

Because of policies aimed at bringing Hungary into the eurozone, you should expect the forint to appreciate slightly against the euro over the next couple of years. In other words, your euros may actually buy fewer forints in the future – although there is inflation.

Credit and debit cards connected to any of half-a-dozen international clearance systems can be used to receive forints at thousands of ATMs around Hungary. Wire transfers are quickly and easily arranged – but expect a one-day delay.

Cheques (except travellers' cheques) are practically non-existent in Hungary, can't be cashed in less than three weeks, and only then at grievous personal expense. Foreigners are free to open a bank account in any currency with minimal hassle.

Office hire & business centres

Taking prices from mid 2003, top-quality office space in Budapest cost ¤10-¤15 per square metre, per month.

The following offices have English-speaking staff:

Biggeorge's International

I. Logodi utca 44C (487 3300/ fax 487 3333). M2 Mószkva tér/tram 4, 6. **Open** 8.30am-5pm Mon-Fri.

Colliers International

II. Mammut Shopping Centre, Margit körút 87-9 (336 4200/ fax 336 4201). M2 Mószkva tér/tram 4, 6. **Open** 8am-7pm Mon-Fri.

Cushman & Wakefield, Healey & Baker

Emke Building, VII. Rákóczi út 42 (268 1288/fax 268 1289). M2 Blaha Lujza tér. **Open** 8.30am-6pm Mon-Fri. **Map** p250 E4.

Jones Lang LaSalle

V. Váci utca 81 (489 0202/fax 489 0203). M1 Vörösmarty tér. **Open** 8am-6pm Mon-Fri. **Map** p249 C4.

Recruitment agencies

Antal International

VII. Emke Building, Rákóczi út 42 (267 9103/fax 267 9104). M2 Blaha Lujza tér. **Open** 8.30am-6pm Mon-Fri. **Map** p249 D4.

Grafton Recruitment

V. Szent István körút 11 (474 3222/fax 474 3221). Tram 4, 6. **Open** 8.30am-5pm Mon-Fri. **Map** p246 C2.

TMP Worldwide

III. Lajos utca 74-6 (430 5400/ fax 430 5401). Bus 6, 84, 86. **Open** 8.30am-5pm Mon-Fri.

Relocation services

The following companies help deal with residence and work permits to save you queuing time – for various fees.

Business Umbrella

VI. Andrássy út 2 (312 3552/ fax 312 3556). M1 Bajcsy-Zsilinszky út. **Open** 9am-5pm Mon-Thur; 9am-4pm Fri. **Map** p249 C4. Also arranges translation, interpreting, customs clearance.

Settlers Hungary

II. Ady Endre utca 19 (212 5017/fax 212 5146). Bus 11.

Open 8.30am-4.30pm Mon-Thur;
8.30am-4pm Fri.
Will also help with all aspects of
moving to Budapest as a foreigner:
nearest international schools, car
registration, bureaucracy and
customs clearance.

Useful organisations

American Chamber of Commerce

*V. Deák Ferenc utca 10 (266
9880). M1, M2, M3 Deák
tér/tram 47, 49.* **Open** 9am-5pm
Mon-Fri. Consultations by
appointment only. **Map** p246 C3.

British Chamber of Commerce

*V. Bank utca 6 (302 5200).
M3 Arany János utca.* **Open**
9am-noon, 2-5pm Mon-Fri.
Consultations by appointment only.
Map p245 B3.

British Embassy Commercial Section

*V. Harmincad utca 6 (266 2888).
M1 Vörösmarty tér.* **Open** 9am-
5pm Mon-Fri. **Map** p249 C4.

Budapest Stock Exchange

Budapesti Értéktőzsde
*V. Deák Ferenc utca 5 (429 6636).
M1 Vörösmarty tér.* **Open** 10am-
4.30pm Mon-Fri. **Map** p249 C4.

Hungarian Chamber of Commerce

Magyar Kereskedelmi és
Ipari Kamara
*V. Kossuth Lajos tér 6-8 (474
5101). M2 Kossuth tér/tram 2.*
Open 8.30am-4pm Mon-Fri.
Map p246 C2.

Hungarian Investment & Trade Development Agency

Magyar Befektetési és
Kereskedelem Fejlesztési Rt.
*VI. Andrássy út 12 (472 8100).
M1 Bajcsy-Zsilinszky út.* **Open**
9am-4.30pm Mon-Thur; 9am-2pm
Fri. **Map** p246 D3.

Hungarian National Bank

Magyar Nemzeti Bank
*V. Szabadság tér 8-9 (302 3000).
M2 Kossuth tér/tram 2, 2A.*
Open 8am-1pm Mon-Fri. **Map**
p246 C3.

Ministry of Economics, Transport & Informatics

Gazdasági, Közlekedési és
Informatikai Minisztérium
*V. Honvéd utca 13-15 (374 2700).
M2 Kossuth tér/tram 2.* **Open**
8am-4.30pm Mon-Thur; 8am-2pm
Fri. **Map** p246 C2.

US Embassy Commercial Service

*Bank Center Building, V.
Szabadság tér 7 (475 4090). M2
Kossuth tér/tram 2.* **Open** 9am-
4.30pm Mon-Fri. **Map** p246 C3.
The Information USA office also
organises a regular commercial
database for interested parties,
open 11am-5pm Tue, Thur.

Customs

Coming into Hungary, any
items of clothing or objects
that could be deemed to be for
personal use are exempt from
any duties.

Individuals over 16 years
old are also allowed to bring in
250 cigarettes, 50 cigars, 100
cigarillos or 250 grams of
tobacco, as well as one litre of
wine, one litre of spirits and
five litres of beer and 100ml of
perfumes. Merchandise up to a
value of Ft29,500 is allowed in
duty free, after which a 15 per
cent duty and two per cent
customs tax are payable in
addition to 25 per cent ÁFA
(VAT). In practice, foreigners
are rarely checked. There's no
limit to the amount of foreign
currency you can bring in.
It's forbidden to bring in
drugs or arms.

On exit the following
limits apply:
● wine – 1 litre
● spirits – 1 litre
● 250 cigarettes, 100 cigars
or 250 grams tobacco
● Ft29,500 worth of gifts
When leaving the country,
visitors are able to reclaim
the sum of the value added
tax on most items (except, for
example, antiques, works of
art and services) bought in
Hungary. The total value of

the items should exceed
Ft50,000 and the goods should
be taken out of the country
within three months of
purchase. For VAT refunds
keep the receipt you get when
purchasing an item (ask for
an '*ÁFAs számla*') and get it
stamped by the customs
officers at the border or the
airport. At the airport you
have to show the item to the
officer, so make sure you keep
it in your hand luggage. Get an
ÁFA visszaigénylő lap (VAT
refund form), which will
contain all the necessary
information. A claim has to
be made within six months.

Customs information: 470 4122,
vam.info@vpop.hu.

Disabled

Despite being home to the
world-famous Pető Institute,
which treats children with
cerebral palsy, Budapest
doesn't have much access for
the disabled. Public transport
is basically inaccessible, apart
from the M1 yellow metro line
and certain buses. The airport
minibus is similarly accessible.

There is a special BKV bus,
use of which can be arranged
through the **Hungarian
Disabled Association**
(MEOSZ), which also has its
own minibus and can provide
a helper. The Museum of Fine
Arts, Museum of Applied Arts
and others (*see pp43-88*) are all
now accessible, as is the
National Foreign Language
Library (*see p224* **Libraries**).

Wherever new stretches of
street are built, there are
almost always ramps for
wheelchairs, and all new
buildings, such as shopping
malls (*see pp124-140*) and the
numerous new office blocks,
are now designed with the
disabled in mind.

There are also a limited
number of special trips
available, such as the one to
Lake Balaton by train once a
week. For more details call:

Directory

Hungarian Disabled Association

MEOSZ
III. San Marco utca 76 (368 1758/ 388 8951). Tram 1. **Open** 8am-4pm Mon-Fri.

Drugs

After the heavy-handed problem-solving policy of the former FIDESZ government, there's a call to decriminalise light drugs in Hungary. The issue of handling light drugs with a more liberal mind, regularly brought up by the Free Democrats, causes heated debates in the Parliament, but nothing else so far.

Even though the law doesn't explicitly prohibit the 'use' of drugs, everything else – from producing and growing to selling, buying, offering and obtaining – is illegal. If caught with a small amount of drugs, you can be sentenced from two to nine years' imprisonment. If it's a first-time offence and you're not dealing, especially not to minors, you might get away with a fine, compulsory rehabilitation treatment or a warning. For a large amount of drugs, the punishment can be anything from five years' imprisonment to a life sentence, depending if the drugs were for personal use or for peddling. Small amounts of drugs are defined as follows:
Amphetamines 1-10 grams
Cocaine 3-8 grams
Ecstasy 10-20 tablets
Grass 10-100 grams
Hashish 10-100 grams
Heroin 1-6 grams
LSD 5-15 pieces
Methadone 200 pieces

Large amounts are defined as 20 times the small amounts.

If the police consider you suspicious, they have the right to stop and search, and if you are driving, they can give you a compulsory urine and blood test. In all these cases you have the right to ask for a lawyer or call your own. In a drug-related emergency call 104. Doctors must observe strict laws of confidentiality.

CAT

AIDS Prevention Needle Change Programme
XIII. Hollán Ernő utca 40 (320 2866). Tram 2, 4, 6. **Open** 4-10pm Mon-Fri; 4-8pm Sat, Sun. **Map** p246 C2.
CAT's risk-decreasing programme provides clean needles, as well as counselling and information on medication and rehabilitation.

Drog Stop Hotline

06 80 50 56 78/272 0383. **Open** 24hrs daily.

Kék Pont Drug Consultation Center

215 7833/215 0734. **Open** *telephone enquiries* 10am-6pm Mon-Fri.

Electricity

The current used in Hungary is 220V, which works fine with British 240V appliances. If you have US 110V gadgets, it's best to bring the appropriate transformers with you. Plugs have two round pins, so bring an adaptor for any other plug.

Embassies & consulates

For a full list of embassies and consulates look in the phone book or Yellow Pages under *Külképviseletek.*

American Embassy

V. Szabadság tér 12 (475 4400/ after office hours 475 4703/ www.usis.hu). M3 Arany János utca/tram 2. **Open** 1-4pm Mon-Thur; 9am-noon Fri. **Map** p246 C3.

Australian Embassy

XII. Királyhágó tér 8-9 (457 9777). M2 Déli pu. **Open** 8.30am-12.30pm, 1.30-4.30pm Mon-Fri.

British Embassy

V. Harmincad utca 6 (266 2888/ 266 0907). M1 Vörösmarty tér/ tram 2. **Open** 9.30am-12.30pm, 2.30-4.30pm Mon-Fri. **Map** p249 C4.

Canadian Embassy

XII. Budakeszi út 32 (392 3360/ 392 3390). Bus 22. **Open** 8am-noon Mon-Fri.

Irish Embassy

V. Szabadság tér 7-9 (302 9600). M2 Kossuth tér/tram 2. **Open** 9.30am-12.30pm, 2.30-4pm Mon-Fri. **Map** p246 C3.

New Zealand Consulate

VI. Teréz körút 38 (428 2208). M1 Oktogon/tram 4, 6. **Open** by appointment only. **Map** p245 A3.

Romanian Embassy

XIV. Thököly út 72 (352 0271). Bus 7. **Open** 8.30am-noon Mon-Wed; 8.30-11.30am Fri.

South African Embassy

II. Gárdonyi Géza utca 17 (200 7277). Bus 11. **Open** 9am-12.30pm Mon-Fri. **Map** p249 D4.

Gay & lesbian

Information

GayGuide.Net Budapest

06 30 932 3334/www.gayguide. net/europe/hungary/budapest/ Budapest@gayguide.net. **Open** *phoneline* 4-8pm daily.
Founded by a group of expats, the site offers an up-to-date gay guide with accommodation, a gay tour and general city information. It operates a year-round hotline and replies to every email within 48hrs. You can subscribe to its mailing list or insert a classified ad into the web page to make contacts before going to Budapest.

Ki-más

www.fikszradio.hu
Fiksz Rádió 98 FM.

Mások

1461 Budapest, PO Box 388 (266 9959/www.masok.hu).
Hungary's main gay magazine, available in gay venues around the city and at central newsstands. The current issue is now also available online.

Paradiátor

www.pararadio.hu/radiator
Para Radio's popular online show.

Other groups & organisations

The Budapest Lesbian Film Committee

Information: Katrin Kremmler (www.geocities.com/budapest lesbianfilms/K.Kremmler@ gmx.net).
A non-profit community project, whose latest feature, *The Godmother Strikes Back,* is due for release in 2003.

CEU Gay Group

The gay group of the Central European University initiates public discussions and organises debates and lectures. Film club every week, usually Thursdays. Its stated goals are to encourage people to openly talk to each other and to promote and encourage gay-related academic activities. Email gayceu@justice.com for further information.

Habeas Corpus Jogsegély

1364 Budapest, PO Box 31 (06 30 996 5666/ www.habeascorpus.hu).
A group addressing the legal issues of sexuality in Hungary.

Háttér Support Society for Gays & Lesbians

Háttér Baráti Társaság a Melegekért
1554 Budapest, PO Box 50 (office 350 9650/329 3380/helpline 06 40 200 358/www.hatter.hu).
Open 6-11pm daily.
Formed in 1995, Háttér ('background') is the largest gay and lesbian organisation in Hungary. It runs several projects, including a hotline offering information and counselling, an HIV/AIDS prevention project and a self-help group. It's also one of the main organisers of the Gay and Lesbian Film and Cultural Festival and the Budapest Gay Pride March (*see pp163-165*).

Labrisz Lesbian Society

1395 Budapest, PO Box 408 (329 3380/www.labrisz.hu). **Open** *phoneline* 6-11pm daily.
The group, formed in 1999, organises meetings and educational programmes and takes part in organising the summer Gay and Lesbian

Festival. Among its chief goals are to call attention to the discrimination women have to face and to destroy prejudices and stereotypes. Monthly discussions are held on the first Friday of each month between 7pm and 9pm (V. Sas utca 6, ground-floor entrance).

Öt Kenyér

1461 Budapest, PO Box 25 (www.otkenyer.hu).
This Catholic gay group meets Thursdays at 7pm. For details, email otkenyer@otkenyer.hu.

Rainbow Mission Foundation

Szivárvány Misszió Alapítvány
VIII. Bezerédi utca 5 (323 1125/ www.szivarvany-misszio.hu).
Chief organiser of the annual Gay and Lesbian Festival and the Gay Pride March.

Szimpozion Society of Friends

Postal address: 1553 Budapest, Pf. 50 (http://szimpozion.freeweb.hu).
Szimpozion, founded in March 2002, aims to provide an organisational background for the gay, lesbian, bisexual and transgender youth community in order to advance their personal development, self-confidence and social mobilisation through educational projects, consultation opportunities, leisure and sports.

Vándor Mások

1360 Budapest, PO Box 2 (06 30 210 2329).
Gay and lesbian hiking group. Dates of regular events and excursions are published monthly in *Mások* magazine.

Health

Despite severe cutbacks and restrictions, the Hungarian health service is considered to be one of the best in Eastern Europe. The service provided is adequate, although a lot of queuing may be involved. Most doctors will speak some kind of English.

Emergency care is provided free to citizens of the UK, Finland, Norway, Sweden and former Socialist countries, although it's probably wise for

you to take out medical insurance as well.

Those working here should get a TB (social security) card through their employer to obtain free state health treatment and register with a local GP. Private clinics now offer the opportunity to avoid the queues and discuss problems in English.

See also p139 **Medical services**.

Accident & emergency

In an emergency the best thing to do is to go to the casualty department of the nearest hospital. *See p215* **Useful numbers**. Make sure you take a Hungarian speaker and some form of identification with you.

Ambulances

The normal emergency number is 104 but this will generally be Hungarian-speaking only. If you call 311 1666, you should find an English- or German-speaker. Companies listed below offer private ambulance services:

American Clinics International

I. Hattyú utca 14 (224 9090). M2 Moszkva tér. **Open** 8.30am-7pm Mon-Thur; 8.30am-6pm Fri; 8.30am-noon Sat. **Credit** AmEx, MC, V. **Map** p245 A2.
24hr emergency service.

Fönix SOS Ambulance

II. Kapy utca 49B (200 0100).
Open 24hr emergency service.
No credit cards.

IMS

XIII. Váci út 202 (329 8423).
M3 Újpest-Városkapu. **Open** 7.30am-8pm Mon-Fri. **Credit** AmEx, MC, V. **Map** p246 D2.
24hr emergency service.
Branch: III. Vihar utca 29 (250 3829). Tram 1/bus 86. Open 8am-8pm Mon-Fri.

Complementary medicine

Complementary medicine in Hungary is still in its infancy. There are now several Chinese doctors who offer acupuncture and massage therapies. Pick up a copy of the magazine *Harmadik Szem* for full listings of homeopaths and Oriental practitioners. Or try the following:

Dr Funian Yu
VII. Damjanich utca 58 (342 2772). Trolleybus 75/79. **Open** 1-6pm Mon-Fri (by appointment). **No credit cards.** **Map** p245 A3.
Chinese acupuncture at a fraction of Western prices.

Homeopathic Doctors' Association
XI. Ratkóc köz 4 (246 2132). Bus 40, 139. **Open** 2-7pm Mon, Wed, Fri; 9am-1pm Tue, Thur. **No credit cards.**

Contraception & abortion

Condoms are available at chemists, supermarkets and many 24-hour corner shops. Abortion is legal and widely used. Birth control pills can be bought at pharmacies with a doctor's prescription. Refer to a local doctor or gynaecologist. To avoid undesired pregnancies, a medicinal treatment is available within 72 hours after conception. For information on the nearest clinic, call 06 30 30 30 456. You'll need a Hungarian-speaker to get through.

Dentists

Although there's state dental care, most people go private if they can. Prices are reasonable compared to the West, as evidenced by the amount of Austrians who come here for treatment. German and/or English spoken in the clinics below. *See also p139.*

Dental Co-op
XII. Zugligeti út 58-60 (275 1444). Bus 158. **Open** 9am-6pm Mon-Fri. **Credit** AmEx, MC, V.

SOS Dental Clinic
VI. Király utca 14 (267 9602/ 269 6010). M1, M2, M3 Deák tér/tram 47, 49. **Open** 24hrs daily. **Credit** AmEx, DC, MC, V. **Map** p249 C4.

Super Dent
XIII. Dózsa György út 65 (451 0506). M3 Dózsa György út. **Open** 8am-2pm Mon, Wed, Fri; 2-7pm Tue, Thur. **Credit** AmEx.

Doctors

See also p139.

American Clinics International
I. Hattyú utca 14 (224 9090). M2 Moszkva tér. **Open** 8.30am-7pm Mon-Thur; 8.30am-6pm Fri; 8.30am-noon Sat. **Credit** AmEx, MC, V. **Map** p245 A2.
24hr emergency service.

IMS
XIII. Váci út 202 (329 8423). M3 Újpest-Városkapu. **Open** 7.30am-8pm Mon-Fri. **Credit** AmEx, MC. Cardiology, paediatrics, gynaecology, urology, radiology and 24hr emergency service. **Branch:** III. Vihar utca 29 (250 3829). Tram 1/bus 86. Open 8am-8pm Mon-Fri.

Professional Orvosi Kft
V. Múzeum körút 35, 3rd floor, No.6 (317 0631). M3 Kálvin tér/tram 47, 49. **Open** 8am-8pm Mon-Fri. **No credit cards.** **Map** p249 D4.

Westend Klinika
Westend Business Center, V. Váci út 22-4 (465 3100). M3 Nyugati pu./tram 4, 6. **Open** 7am-7pm Mon-Fri. **Hotline** 06 80 329 677). **Credit** AmEx, MC, V. **Map** p246 C2.
24hr emergency service for Medicover members.

Opticians

If in urgent need, the easiest way to get a new pair of contact lenses, have your glasses repaired or your sight tested is to drop in at any of the Ofotért or Optirex chain stores, where you can get a full-scale ophthalmological service. Eye tests can also be performed here by qualified doctors or optometrists. *See also p139.*

Ofotért
V. Károly körút 14 (317 6313). M1, M2, M3 Deák tér/tram 47, 49. **Open** 10am-6pm Mon-Fri; 10am-1pm Sat. **Credit** DC, MC, V. **Map** p249 C4.
Branches: II. Margit körút 4 (212 2980); V. Szent István körút 19 (473 0150); VIII. Rákóczi út 28 (268 1139).

Optirex
Campona Bevásárlóközpont, XXII. Nagytétényi út 27-47 (424 3210). Tram 47 to terminus, then bus 3, 14 or 114. **Open** 10am-8pm Mon-Sat; 10am-6pm Sun. **Credit** MC, V.
Branches: III. Lajos utca 48-66 (250 8327); V. Szent István körút 11 (312 6676); XI. Bartók Béla út 22 (466 5966).

Pharmacies

Pharmacies (*patika* or *gyógyszertár*) are always marked with a green cross outside. lit up after hours. Opening hours are generally 8am-6pm or 8am-8pm Mon-Fri, with some also open on Saturday mornings. Some English will be spoken in all of these pharmacies.

The following are all open 24 hours every day:

Fagyöngy Patika
IX. Boráros tér 3 (217 5997). Tram 2, 4, 6. **Map** p249 D6.

Déli Gyógyszertár
XII. Alkotás utca 1B (355 4691). M2 Déli/tram 61. **Map** p248 A4.

Mária Gyógyszertár
XIII. Béke tér 11 (320 8006). Bus 4, 32.

Óbuda Gyógyszertár
III. Vörösvári út 86 (368 6430). Tram 17. **Map** p248 A4.

Szent Margit Gyógyszertár

II. Frankel Leó út 22 (212 4311/ 212 4406). HÉV to Margit-híd/ tram 4, 6, 17. **Map** p245 B2.

Teréz Gyógyszertár

VI. Teréz körút 41 (311 4439). Tram 4, 6. **Map** p246 D2.

STDs, HIV & AIDS

AIDS still remains at a relatively low level in Hungary, although this may soon be on the increase with the influx of foreigners, general lack of public awareness and high promiscuity levels.

Since January 1998 the Hungarian government has insisted that HIV-positive people be centrally registered. As a result, only a first HIV test can be done without showing a passport. If the result is positive and a second test is required, you can go to Vienna for an anonymous free test. With admission to the European Union, this law will be repealed; in the meantime, it's wise to exercise caution and seek advice to check the status of the law. The mainly Hungarian website www. anonimaids.hu provides up-to-date information.

AIDS hotline

338 2419. **Open** 8am-4pm Mon-Thur; 8am-1pm Fri.

Aids-Hilfe Wien

Mariahilfer Gürtel 4, Vienna 6 (00 43 1 59937/wien@aidshilfe.or.at). **Open** 4-7pm Mon, Wed; 9am-noon Thur; 2-5pm Fri.
Test results one week later, but must be collected in person.

Anonymous AIDS Advisory Service

Anonim AIDS Tanácsadó Szolgálat
XI. Karolina út 35B (466 9283). Tram 61. **Open** *hotline* 9am-8pm Mon-Sat; *in person* 5-8pm Mon, Wed, Thur; 9am-noon Tue, Fri. **Map** p248 A6.
Free anonymous AIDS tests.

PLUSS

1570 Budapest, PO Box 184 (455 8193/www.pluss-hiv.hu). Support group for people with HIV and AIDS.

Skin & Genital Clinic

Bőr és Nemikórtani Klinika
VIII. Mária utca 41 (266 0465). M3 Ferenc körút. **Open** 8am-12pm Mon-Fri. **Map** p249 D5. The place to go if you have STD problems. An AIDS test here costs Ft4,000.

Helplines

Alcoholism

Alcoholics Anonymous
352 1947.

Domestic violence

NaNE – Women United Against Violence
06 80 505 101.

Drugs

Drog Stop Hotline
06 80 505 678/272 0383.

Poisoning

Erzsébet Kórház
322 3450/321 5215 (adults).

Heim Pál Kórház
210 0720/333 5079 (children).

Toxicology information service
215 3733/476 1120.

ID

Hungarian law requires you to carry photographic ID or passport with you at all times and, although in practice you'll rarely be checked, it might happen. If you lose your passport, you should report it immediately to the police station nearest you, then go to the embassy or consulate of the country that issued it and they'll provide you with an emergency one. *See p228* **Police stations**.

Insurance

Britain, Norway, Finland, Sweden and the former Warsaw Pact countries all have reciprocal agreements for free emergency treatment for their citizens. Non-emergency treatment isn't covered. Taking out travel insurance, covering this and lost or stolen valuables, is wise.

Internet

The best places for internet access are the cybercafés and Matáv Pont branches in malls (*see pp124-140*).

Internet cafés

Budapest Net

V. Kecskeméti utca 5 (328 0292/ www.budapestnet.hu). M3 Kálvin tér. **Open** 10am-10pm daily. **Rates** Ft700 per hr. **No credit cards.** **Map** p249 D5. This is a large, functional downtown spot with 32 computers. Tutorials and games are also available. Atmosphere is more workshop than café. Lower rates for longer time blocks.

Matáv Pont

V. Petőfi Sándor utca 17-19 (485 6612/www.matav.hu). M1, M2, M3 Deák tér. **Open** 9am-8pm Mon-Fri; 10am-3pm Sat. **Rates** Ft300 for 30mins, Ft500 for 1hr. **Credit** DC, MC, V. **Map** p249 C4.
Chain of shops run by Matáv, Hungary's national telephone company, can be found in almost every mall. Eight to ten computers and speedy access. Expect some queues.
Branches: Duna Plaza, XIII. Váci út 178 (237 8031); Mammut Center, II. Lövőház utca 2-6 (345 7451); Westend City Center, V. Váci út 1-3 (8238 7616).

Teleport Netc@fé

VIII. Vas utca 7 (267 6361). M2 Astoria/bus 7. **Open** 2-10pm Mon-Fri; 2-8pm Sat. **Rates** Ft350 per hr. **No credit cards.** **Map** p249 D4.
An adolescent underground, complete with role-playing games, pet scorpions, ice-creams and

Directory

Flat hunting

It has happened all too often. People come here, they fall in love with Budapest, and they want to stay. Yippee!

Then comes the problem of where they are going to live. Finding a flat in a city that is a magnet for foreigners and Hungarians from the countryside is no easy task.

Flats are often offered in the listings of local English-language newspapers (see p225), but most of these are either wildly overpriced or are clearly intended for the diplomatic and business communities – villas perched in the airy Buda Hills, with swimming pools and international schools nearby. Prices in Pest are much lower, and the options vary from mansions to Communist-style tract housing (panelház).

The most common source for flat listings is newspapers, such as Expressz, Újpressz and Hirdetes. Holdings are often grouped by district, so have a good map handy. Look for the category 'lakás' (flat, apartment) and then 'kiadó' (to let) or 'albérlet' (sub-let).

University bulletin boards are also a good place to hunt for a room or flat, and the lounge outside the library of the French Institute (I. Fő utca 17, see p161) has a good board for listings directed at foreigners. Many people manage to obtain their digs simply by personal contacts, and asking around at an expat pub (see pp108-123) is often the easiest way to do this.

Renters should remember that they've moved to Hungary to experience something very different from what they're used to at home – and that is exactly what Hungarian landlords have in mind.

The Magyar landlord is a quirky character, a staple of expatriate folklore. The landlord may barge in on you unannounced at six in the morning just to fix the plumbing. He/she may ask you to evacuate for a weekend while relatives come to visit, or request to raise the rent 250 per cent because they need to buy a new car. You will probably be asked to tutor a cousin in English, or perhaps marry a widowed in-law needing a work visa.

One day you may come home to find that grandmother has died and they needed to store her furniture in your space. Or worse, that grandmother has not died and you have a new flatmate.

---

fantasy coffees. A dimly lit teen hacker's paradise devoted to networked games.

Left luggage

24-hour left-luggage facilities are available at Nyugati and Keleti stations: Ft240 or Ft480 for large items. Prices run from midnight to midnight. Lockers are also available.

Legal help

If in need of legal assistance contact your embassy, which will provide you with a list of English-speaking lawyers (see p218 Business).

Libraries

British Council Library

VI. Benczúr utca 26 (478 4760). M1 Bajza utca. Open 11am-7pm Mon-Fri; 9am-1pm Sat. Map p247 E2.

Excellent magazine and periodicals section and English-teaching section, plus a huge video library. Membership open to anyone over 16 for a one-off fee of Ft2,500.

National Foreign Language Library

V. Molnár utca 11 (318 3688). M3 Ferenciek tere. Open 10am-8pm Mon, Tue, Thur, Fri; noon-8pm Wed. Closes 4pm during summer. Map p249 C5. Open to anyone. Membership for yr Ft2,000; day ticket Ft200. Good periodicals section and helpful staff.

National Széchényi Library

I. Buda Palace Wing F (224 3848). Várbusz from M2 Moszkva tér. Open 9am-9pm Tue-Sat during academic year. Map p248 B4.

Hungary's biggest public library – it claims to have every book written in Hungarian, and about Hungary and Hungarian issues published in any foreign language. Also stocks academic papers, periodicals, microfilms and inter-library services. Useful for research but you can't check books out. Take your passport or some form of ID for entry.

Lost property

If you lose something, enquire at the police station in the area where you lost it. Take along a Hungarian-speaker, especially if you need a statement for insurance purposes. In case your passport is lost or stolen you should also report it to the police first (see p223 ID and p228 Police stations).

Airport

Ferihegy airport 2A: 296 8108/ 296 7217. Ferihegy 2B: 296 7690/295 3480. You can try tracing your luggage at: www.worldtracer.com/filedsp/ma.

Public transport

BKV Lost Property Office
Talált Tárgyak Osztálya
VII. Akácfa utca 18 (267 5299).
M2 Blaha Lujza tér. **Open**
7.30am-3pm Mon-Thur; 7.30am-
7pm Wed; 7.30am-2pm Fri.
Map p250 E4.

Rail

For items left on trains go back
to the station, find the office
'ügyelet' and be persistent but
pleasant; it can get results.
Also try calling: Nyugati (349
0115), Déli (375 6269) and
Keleti (314 5010).

Taxi

For taxis, phone the company
you rode with. Főtaxi claims to
hold on to items left in its
vehicles for five years.

Media

Daily newspapers

Népszabadság
The closest thing that Hungary
has to a paper of record.
Népszabadság, once the
mouthpiece of the Communists
and still closely aligned with
the Hungarian Socialist Party,
now ranks second behind the
number one tabloid in terms of
overall readership. Owners
include France's Ringier and
Germany's Bertelsmann.

Magyar Hírlap
Hírlap has been going since
1968. Aligned with dissident
intellectuals and now with the
liberal Free Democrats, it has a
liberal attitude and a sharp focus
on economy and finance. Also
controlled by Ringier.

Mai Blikk
Top-selling daily with more than
700,000 readers. Usual tabloid fare
of crime, page three girls and
sports, but less malicious in
political and celebrity coverage
than its British counterparts.
Owned by Ringier.

Népszava
Old organ of the Communist
trade unions, *Népszava* remains
close to the left but survives
only through the largesse of
mysterious sponsors.

Magyar Nemzet
Last bastion of the non-extreme
right among daily newspapers.
Takes its marching orders directly
from the centre-right party
FIDESZ. Allegedly propped up by
politically sympathetic backers.

Világgazdaság
The green newspaper. A truly
professional publication
covering business, economic
and financial news. Owned by
Germany's Axel-Springer.

Nemzeti Sport
Hungary's leading daily sports
paper, with a news and results
coverage second to none in
Europe. Owned by Ringier.

Expressz
Daily classifieds newspaper. An
absolute must if you're looking to
rent or rent out a flat. *See p224*
Flat hunting.

English language

International newspapers and
magazines are available
downtown at A Világsajtó
Háza, *see p126.* Free copies of
the *Budapest Sun* and other
listings rags can be found in
major hotels and at the airport.

Budapest Sun
Owned by Britain's Associated
Newspapers, the *Sun* transplants
provincial British tabloid
style to Budapest. It features
decidedly unambitious news
coverage, naive and insular
coverage of the expat community,
poor film listings and lots of
'escort service' ads.

Budapest Business Journal
Formula-driven coverage of
Hungarian corporate and
economic news. The *BBJ*, which
used to break news but now
seems to have become lazy or
tired, is part of a chain that
includes editions in Warsaw
and Prague.

Hungary Around the Clock
*Subscription rates 351 7142/fax
351 7141/info@kingfish.hu*
An English-language digest of
each day's news covering politics,
economics, business and finance.
Compiled from Hungarian press
and faxed or emailed to subscribers
by 9am each business day.

The Hungarian Quarterly
Academic journal in English with
essays on Hungarian history,
politics and culture, plus book,
film and music reviews. Usually
available in downtown bookstores.

Listings

Pesti Est, Open
These two useful pocket-sized
weekly freebies are available from
venues around Budapest every
Thursday. *Pesti Est* offers the
more comprehensive service,
including separate listings for
English-language films – although
the reviews are in Hungarian.
Open is sharper about nightlife.

Pesti Műsor
What's on weekly (Ft119)
available every Thursday with
comprehensive listings, also
featuring events outside Budapest.

Magazines

Heti Világgazdaság (HVG)
Hungary's answer to the
Economist. The most influential
weekly for more than two decades,
HVG is owned by its employees
and is largely politically
independent. One of the few
publications in Hungary that
aspires to non-partisan, hard-
hitting journalism. Online version
has English section. www.hvg.hu

168 Óra
Weekly, consisting mostly of
interviews. Maintains a liberal
slant, yet has managed to enrage
every government since its
founding in the 1980s.

MaNcs
Hungary's only alternative
newspaper has survived
numerous attempts to close it

Directory

One-offs Paul Erdős

Paul Erdős first learned to butter his own bread at the age of 21. He never had a permanent address and carried his worldly goods in a battered suitcase and an orange plastic bag. He died a virgin. He is generally considered one of the greatest mathematical minds of the 20th century.

If you were a promising mathematician, you might be honoured by a surprise visit from Erdős. He would arrive and announce: 'My brain is open.' That was his invitation to do maths, an occupation he pursued 19 hours a day, often with the assistance of a little bag of benzedrine pills he carried with him at all times. Your job was to keep pace with Paul's thoughts, provide him with food and shelter, and generally keep him out of trouble.

His was not a solitary genius. In his lifetime, Erdős co-authored 41,475 academic papers, a monumental achievement not only in quantity, but also in the quality of his impact on the mathematical world. One badge of status in the maths world is your Erdős number. If you wrote a paper with Paul Erdős, you have an Erdős number of one. If you wrote a paper with somebody who wrote a paper with Erdős, then your number is two. Bill Gates reportedly takes no small pride in his Erdős number: four.

Erdős's speciality was number theory, a field that dazzles mathematicians with elegant questions and impossible answers. Many have little practical application, but number theory has provided breakthroughs in fields such as cryptography and nuclear physics. Erdős may well have been the model for Count Count on TV's *Sesame Street*.

One of Erdős's most colourful discoveries took place in 1974, when baseball player Hank Aaron hit his 715th home run, eclipsing Babe Ruth's record of 714. A young mathematician named Carl Pomerance noticed that the product of 714 and 715 equalled the product of the first seven primes (numbers that can only be divided by one and themselves). Such numbers, now known as Ruth-Aaron pairs, are extremely rare, and Erdős and Pomerance developed a theorem to predict them. In 1995 Erdős and Pomerance were awarded honorary doctorates by Emory University, and at the official ceremony Pomerance persuaded Aaron and Erdős to sign a baseball together, which means that Hank Aaron now has an Erdős number of one.

Numbers were Paul Erdős's foremost, but not exclusive, passion. He especially loved children, whom he referred to as epsilons (the mathematical symbol for a small quantity). He gave his money to strangers and spent his last four decades on the road with the most brilliant mathematical minds of his day.

This was no easy life, when you consider that he carried a Hungarian passport throughout the Cold War. To Erdős, America was 'Sam' and Russia was 'Joe'. Their squabble, which caused him no end of trouble (he was denied entry to the United States in 1954 and couldn't return for another decade), was merely the 'Sam and Joe show'. In 1955, at the urging of well-connected friends who argued that Erdős was a singular asset to world culture, the Hungarian government granted Erdős a special passport stating that he was a Hungarian citizen, but resident in Israel. This unique document allowed Erdős to enter and leave Hungary at will.

When he died in 1996, at the age of 71, 500 notables attended his quasi-state ceremony in Budapest.

---

down. Fresh and liberal, with extensive coverage of minority issues, in-depth news features and extensive listings.

Radio

There are three state-run stations. **Kóssuth Radio** (540 MW) is the national station, offering a gabby yet informative mix of talk and music. **Petőfi Radio** (98.4 FM) provides the regular inane background of Hungaropop music, sport and occasional political discussion. **Bartók Radio** (105.3 FM) plays the highbrow card, with classical music, poetry and dramas.

Apart from broadcasts propped up by the state, almost every music station plays commercial pop. The one alternative station is **Tilós Rádió** (90.3 FM). Tilós began as an anti-regime pirate broadcast under Communism. Today, it's still non-profit with no ads, surviving on state support and listener donations. There is also one all-news station, **Infó Rádió** (95.8 FM).

BBC World Service

BBC frequencies change every six months. For up-to-date frequencies see www.bbc.co.uk/worldservice/schedules

Television

TV2

Majority-owned by Scandinavian Broadcast System with a local group holding a minority interest. Airs a predictable mix of news, mostly dismal foreign films and locally produced trash, including the latest wave of game shows and voyeur TV.

RTL Klub

Majority-owned by Luxembourg/Germany-based CLT-UFA, Europe's largest broadcasting group. Same programming mix as TV2 but with higher local production quality. News broadcasts, however, rely more on the tabloid approach.

MTV1

The flagship of state-owned broadcasting. That sucking sound is public money going down the toilet in order to spread propaganda for whatever party is in government. The quality of its news division has recently been substantially improved, but don't expect it to be impartial.

MTV2

Second state-owned channel. Offers more documentary, cultural and public service programming, but often simply broadcasts what MTV1 is airing.

Duna TV

Satellite channel aimed at serving the substantial ethnic Hungarian minorities in neighbouring countries. Heavy on cultural and documentary programming.

Cable TV

Each district in Budapest – and each municipality outside the capital – has a separate arrangement for cable TV. The Netherlands' UPC dominates the Hungarian market. Cable packages tend to include some English-language channels, such as CNN, BBC World, SkyNews, CNBC, Eurosport and Cartoon Network/TCM.

Money

The Hungarian unit of currency is the forint, usually abbreviated as HUF or Ft – the convention we've used in this guide. Forint coins come in denominations of Ft1, Ft2, Ft5, Ft10, Ft20, Ft50 and Ft100. Notes come in denominations of Ft200, Ft500, Ft1,000, Ft2,000, Ft5,000, Ft10,000 and Ft20,000. Please note that although Hungary joins the EU in May 2004, the Euro will not be introduced until at least 2007. *See p3* **Money matters**.

ATMs

There are cash machines all over town. Apart from those on the Cirrus and Plus systems, allowing you to draw on a foreign bank account or credit card, there are also exchange machines, forints for foreign banknotes. American Express has a 24-hour machine and both Nyugati and Keleti stations have round-the-clock exchange facilities.

Banks & foreign exchange

Most banks open at 8am and close at 3pm, 4pm or 5pm Monday to Friday, some are open on Saturday morning. Apart from cash and travellers' cheques, banks can advance money on a credit card. ATM and exchange machines are available 24 hours at most banks.

Banks might give better rates than change kiosks, but shop around as rates can vary quite dramatically. Travellers' cheques are exchangeable at banks and change kiosks, although sometimes at a worse rate than the cash equivalent.

Bureaux de change

Usual opening hours from 9am to 6pm daily:

American Express

V. Deák Ferenc utca 10 (235 4340). M1, M2, M3 Deák tér/tram 47, 49. **Open** 9am-5.30pm Mon-Fri; 9am-2pm Sat. **Map** p249 C4.
Currency exchange and cash advances, moneygrams, mail and fax delivery for card- and travellers' cheque-holders, hotel and airline reservations. Various fees.

IBB/Intergold

VI. Teréz körút 62 (331 8361). M3 Nyugati pu./tram 4, 6. **Open** 10am-6pm Mon-Fri; 10am-1pm Sat. **Credit** AmEx, DC, MC, V. **Map** p246 D2.

IBUSZ Bank

V. Ferenciek tere 10 (485 2700). M3 Ferenciek tere/bus 7. **Open** 9am-5.30pm Mon-Fri; 9am-12pm Sat. **Map** p249 C4.

Interchange

V. Deák Ferenc utca 17 (317 2673). M1, M2, M3 Deák tér/tram 47, 49. **Open** 7.30am-10.15pm daily. **Credit** AmEx, MC, V. **Map** p249 C4.
Branches: Keleti station (open 24hrs daily; 342 7913); Nyugati station (302 8485).

M&M Exclusiv Tours

V. Váci utca 12 (267 4368). M1, M2, M3 Deák tér/tram 47, 49. **Open** 9am-6pm daily. **No credit cards. Map** p249 C4.
Branch: V. Nyugati tér 6 (311 1610).

Credit cards

Credit cards are accepted in thousands of outlets. The most widely accepted cards are AmEx, Diners Club, Euro/Mastercard and Visa.

Lost/stolen credit cards

American Express 484 2639/484 2638
Visa Global 06 80 011 272

Opening hours

Opening hours vary according to the type of shop. Most shops are open from 10am to 6pm Monday-Friday, and 10am to 1pm on Saturday. Shopping malls usually open at 10am and close at 9pm daily. Supermarkets, greengrocers and bakeries usually open at

Directory

6-7am and close between 6pm and -8pm Monday-Friday, and 1pm and 3pm on Saturdays. '*Rögtön jövök*' means that the owner will be back in five minutes – maybe. Many shops stay open later on Saturdays and on Thursday evenings. There are many non-stops – small 24-hour corner shops where you can buy basics and booze. Most restaurants close by 11pm or midnight.

Police stations

Unless you commit a crime, you shouldn't have much contact with the police, but they can stop and ask for ID. If you're robbed or lose something, report it to the police station nearest the incident. Take a Hungarian-speaker and bank on filling in forms with little chance of success. It's only worth the bother if the item was valuable, or your insurance company needs the forms.

You can report a crime on the Central Emergency Number (112) or to the police (107). In case you can't get through to an English-speaking dispatcher, try the English-language hotline (4388 8080).

Police headquarters
XIII. Teve utca 4-6 (443 5500).

Police stations
V. Szalay utca 11-13 (373 1000/373 1012).
VII. Dózsa György út 18-22 (461 8100/461 8112).
VIII. Vig utca 36 (477 3700/477 3712).

Postal services

The Hungarian postal service is reasonably efficient. Letters from the UK take about four working days to arrive. Post boxes are square and red with post horn and envelope symbols. It's more usual to take your letters to the post office, where staff will affix the stamp and post it for you. Expect to queue, especially at Christmas. Most post offices are open from 8am to 7pm on weekdays. There are no late-night post offices, but the one at Keleti (VIII. Baross tér 11C) is open 7am to 9pm Monday to Friday and the one at Nyugati (VI. Teréz körút 51) is open 7am to 9pm Monday to Saturday, 7am-8pm Sunday.

Letters weighing up to 20g cost Ft31 within Budapest and Ft35 to the rest of Hungary. A letter weighing up to 20g to neighbouring countries costs Ft140, to other European countries Ft150 and anywhere else in the world Ft160. Up to 100g it's Ft260, Ft270 and Ft290 respectively. To send them airmail (*légiposta*) is an extra fee depending on the weight of the letter. Postcards to bordering countries are Ft40, Ft100 to elsewhere in Europe and Ft110 overseas.

To send something registered (*ajánlott*) is an extra Ft370 and express is an extra Ft250.

Poste Restante letters go to the office at Nyugati station. For courier services and express mail, *see p217* **Business**.

Sending packages

The Hungarian post has a complicated system for sending packages, depending on what you're sending, where and how. You can send a package up to 2kg as a normal letter, which costs slightly less than if you send it as a package. Otherwise, a 2kg package costs Ft3,930 to neighbouring countries, Ft4,700 to anywhere else in Europe and Ft7,200 overseas. A 5kg package is Ft5,000 to neighbouring countries, Ft6,280 to anywhere else in Europe and Ft10,070 overseas. Tie packages with string and fill out a blue customs declaration form (*vámáru nyilatkozat*) from the post office. Sending anything worth over Ft10,000 is so complicated that it's hardly worth the bother. Special boxes can be purchased at the post office. Most post offices can supply a booklet in English detailing charges.

Religion

According to the latest Hungarian census carried out in 2001, out of the 1.7 million people living in Budapest 45.5 per cent are Roman Catholic, 12.6 per cent are Protestant, 2.6 per cent are Lutheran, 1.6 per cent are Greek Catholic and 0.5 per cent are Jewish.

The rest belong to minor churches or none. Many churches around town have services in English.

Catholic services

International Church of Budapest
III. Kiskorona utca 7 (376 4518). M3 Árpád-híd.
Multi-denominational worship in English and children's ministry on Sundays at 10.30am.

International Baptist Church
Móricz Zsigmond Gimnázium, II. Törökvész út 48-54. Bus 11.
Services on Sundays from 10.30am.

Jesuit Church of the Sacred
Jézus Szive templom
VIII. Mária utca 25 (318 3479). M3 Ferenc körút. **Map** p250 E4.
Catholic mass in English on Sundays at 5pm.

Anglican services

St Columbia Church of Scotland, Presbyterian & St Margaret's Anglican/Episcopal Chaplaincy
VI. Vörösmarty utca 51. M1 Vörösmarty utca. **Map** p246 D2.
Anglican Eucharist on 1st and 3rd Sun at 11am. Anglican Holy Communion 2nd, 4th and 5th Sun

at 9am. Presbyterian services 2nd and 4th Sun at 11am. Joint Presbyterian/Anglican service 5th Sun at 11am. Sunday school at 11am Sept-May.

Jewish services

Central Synagogue

VII. Dohány utca 2. M2 Astoria/ tram 47, 49. **Map** p249 D4. Services take place at 9am Sat; 6pm Mon-Fri, Sun.

Jewish Community Centre

VII. Síp utca 12 (342 1335). M2 Astoria/tram 47, 49. **Open** 8am-noon Mon-Fri. **Map** p249 D4. Summer services in Hebrew.

Safety & security

Budapest is a relatively safe city. But, as anywhere, a little common sense goes a long way. Do keep a watch out for pickpockets and purse-snatchers around the tourist spots of Váci utca, the Castle District, Heroes' Square and at stations. Don't exchange

money on the street. Be careful on trams 2, 4 and 6, where gangs sometimes operate. Be careful if walking alone at night around the ill-lit outlying areas of town or District VIII around Rákóczi tér, and consider taking a taxi if alone or if you happen to be in a dodgy-looking neighbourhood.

As a rule, the police tend not to be of much assistance. You are obliged by law to carry some kind of identification on you at all times and the police make spot checks, especially in places where expatriates tend to congregate. In most other places, it is pretty unlikely that you'll be checked.

Smoking

Hungarians are among the heaviest smokers in Europe. It is quite normal for people to ask strangers for a cigarette or a light on the street. Smoking is banned on public transport, on certain trains, in theatres and cinemas, but allowed in almost

all restaurants and cafés, most of which now have smoking and non-smoking areas.

Study

Language classes

Arany János Nyelviskola

VI. Csengery utca 68 (472 0620/ 311 8870). M1 Oktogon/tram 4, 6. **Open** 10am-5pm Mon-Thur; noon-3pm Fri. **Map** p246 D2. One of the largest language schools, offering courses in most European tongues. Four-, ten- or 15-week courses of 30, 40 or 60 lessons are available for Ft790 per lesson. International student ID nets a 10% discount.

Centre for Advanced Language Learning

Idegennyelvi Továbbképző Központ *VIII. Rigó utca 16 (459 9666/ www.itk.hu). Tram 4, 6.* **Map** p250 E5. The Centre for Advanced Language Learning is an independent non-profit institution under the auspices of Eötvös

One-offs La Cicciolina

While thin young Hungarian women have been undressing in public since Eve, few have changed the face of feminism in Italy.

Spunky, funky, outspoken and uninhibited, La Cicciolina, aka Ilona Staller, made waves by encouraging the use of prophylactics, supporting the right to abortion – while also opposing nuclear energy and battling world hunger. Better known as a porn star and self-proclaimed nymphomaniac, La Cicciolina entered Italian politics in 1987.

Born on 12 December 1951 in Budapest, the daughter of a government bureaucrat, the platinum blonde with unlikely eyebrows moved to Italy in 1976. She began a radio programme that same year and earned her nickname, which is based on a racy slang double entendre. She went on to achieve success in porn videos by taking the limits to the limits.

When the Radical Party nominated La Cicciolina for the parliamentary elections of 1987, they were taking a jab at fickle and

uninformed voters and the ineffectively monitored candidate requirements. Never in their wildest dreams did they expect her to win the seat – and keep hold of it until 1992, longer than any parliamentarian at the time. She put other deputies to shame with her steady presence and dedication to reforms.

Films made while she was in parliament, such as *The Rise of the Roman Empress*, co-starring porn legend John Holmes, soon became bestsellers and built her fame. La Cicciolina's speeches always include a glimpse of her left breast, just to remind audiences which side she's on.

Now over 50, the retired porn diva is the divorced mother of a young son conceived with contemporary artist Jeff Koons.

But La Cicciolina is still active and outspoken in politics. Her latest move was to offer sex with Saddam Hussein to stop the second Gulf War, after a similar offer for the first one – when she was never granted the decency of a response.

Directory

Lóránd University (ELTE). One of the important tasks of the institution is the standardised assessment of knowledge of the Hungarian language and culture within the framework of a modern system of examinations.

European Language School

Tandem Studio
V. Múzeum körút 39 (317 1302).
M3 Kálvin tér/tram 47, 49.
Map p249 D4.
European Language School offers a wide range of Hungarian courses all year round. The school, founded in 1982, was one of the first to be recognised and accredited by the Association of Language Schools. Beginner, elementary, intermediate, upper-intermediate, advanced levels. Individual tuition is structured according to the student's personal interest, level and timetable; ¤5 per lesson. For company groups ¤17 per lesson.

Hungarian Language School

VI. Rippl-Rónai utca 4 (351 1191).
M1 Hősök tere. **Open** *office* 9am-4pm Mon, Tue, Thur, Fri; 9am-7pm Wed. **Map** p247 E2.
Normal groups (6-12 students): ¤4-¤6 per lesson; organised groups (3-6 students): ¤5-¤8 per lesson; private lessons: ¤12-¤20 per lesson; company and outreach groups (maximum of 12 students): ¤18-¤25 per lesson per group.

Katedra Language School

VII. Madách tér 4 (327 8383).
M1, M2, M3 Deák tér/tram 47, 49 . **Open** *office* 8am-8pm Mon-Fri; 9am-12pm Sat. **Credit** DC, MC, V. **Map** p249 C4.
Intensive and less intensive courses available. **Rates** *standard courses* Ft24,990 for 36 lessons; *intensive courses* Ft44,990 for 72 lessons, Ft69,990 for 120 lessons.

Universities

Budapest Technical & Economic Sciences University

Budapesti Muszaki és Gazdasági Egyetem (BME)
XI. Muegyetem rakpart 3 (463 1111). Bus 86/tram 4, 6, 47, 49.

Open 9am-4pm Mon-Thur; 9am-2pm Fri. **Map** p249 C6.
Established in 1782, the BME has over 9,000 students studying at seven faculties that include Architecture and Chemical, Electrical and Civil Engineering. The education is highly practical, and BME is among the few Hungarian institutions whose diplomas are accepted worldwide.

Budapest University of Economic Sciences & Administration

Budapesti Közgazdaságtudományi és Államigazgatási Egyetem
IX. Fővám tér 8 (218 6855).
Tram 2, 47, 49. **Open** 8am-noon, 1-4.30pm Mon-Thur; 8am-2pm Fri. **Map** p249 D5.
An independent institution since 1948, the BKE issues diplomas in International Economics and Business, and Political Studies.

Central European University (CEU)

V. Nádor utca 9 (327 3000/fax 327 3001/www.ceu.hu). M2 Kossuth tér. **Open** 9am-5pm Mon-Thur; 9am-3pm Fri. **Map** p246 C3.
Founded in 1991 by George Soros, CEU offers postgraduate courses for students from Central and Eastern Europe and the former USSR. Departments include History, Legal Studies, Gender Studies, and Political and Environmental Sciences.

Eötvös Loránd University

Eötvös Loránd Tudományegyetem (ELTE) International Secretariat
V. Piarista köz 1 (postal address 1364 Budapest, PO Box 107) (266 9100 ext 5171/266 3521). M3 Ferenciek tere. **Open** 10am-2pm Mon-Thur; 10am-noon Fri. **Map** p249 C4.
The largest and oldest Hungarian university, this was founded in 1635 in Nagyszombat (now Trnava, Slovakia), moved to Buda in 1777, and to Pest in 1784. Today, there are 12,000 students at the Faculty of Humanities, Sciences, Law and the Institute of Sociology.

Semmelweis University of Medicine

Semmelweis Orvostudományi Egyetem (SOTE)

VIII. Üllői út 26 (266 0452/ www.sote.hu). M3 Klinikák. **Open** 1-4pm Mon; 10am-3pm Tue, Thur; 9am-1pm Fri. **Map** p250 E5.
Over 200 years old, and in its current form since 1955, when the faculties of Pharmacy and Dentistry were incorporated. Ignác Semmelweis, who discovered the cause of puerperal fever, taught here in the 1800s.

Telephones

The old phone system has been largely modernised and phoning home is easy, but remember that there are no cheap hours for making international calls.

Dialling & codes

For an international call dial 00, wait for the second purring dial tone, then dial the country code and number: Australia 61, Canada 1, Eire 353, New Zealand 64, UK 44, USA 1.

To call other places around Hungary from Budapest, or to call Budapest from the rest of the country, you have to dial 06 first, wait for the second tone, and then follow with code and number. You also have to dial 06 before calling mobile phones, which are commonplace in Hungary.

To call Hungary from abroad dial 36 and then 1 for Budapest. For a provincial Hungarian town from abroad, dial 36 then the town code – you don't need to dial the 06 code beforehand.

Public phones

Most are card phones, costing Ft800 for 50 units or Ft1,800 for 120, on sale at post offices and newsagents. Coin phones still exist, but are much more rare. They take Ft10, Ft20, Ft50 and Ft100 coins; a quick local call should cost no more than Ft20-Ft40.

To get a cheap international rate you might consider using a Neo Phone card, which is available at most post offices, fuel stations and newsstands.

Mobile phones & pagers

If you need a phone but your flat doesn't have one – not an uncommon occurrence – mobile phones or pagers are your best bet. GSM companies currently operating in Hungary:

Eurohívó
XIII. Klapka utca 4 (467 5555/ www.eurohivo.hu). M3 Dózsa György út. **Open** 8.30am-6.30pm Mon-Thur; 8.30am-3pm Fri. **No credit cards.**
The only pager company in Hungary that has English-language services.

Pannon GSM
XI. Budafoki út 64 (464 6020/ 464 1210/www.pannongsm.hu). Tram 6. **Open** 9am-7pm Mon-Fri; 9am-2pm Sat. **Credit** DC, MC, V.

Vodafone
Westend City Center, VI. Váci út 1/3 (288 1270/www.vodafone.hu). M3 Nyugati pu./tram 4, 6. **Open** 10am-9pm Mon-Sat; 10am-6pm Sun. **Credit** DC, MC, V. **Map** p246 C2.

Westel
XI. Karinthy utca 21 (265 8262/ www.westel.hu). M3 Ferenciek tere. **Open** 8.30am-5pm Mon-Fri. **Credit** AmEx, MC, V. **Map** p249 C4.
Branch: V. Deák Ferenc utca (06 30 900 0000). Open 9am-9pm daily.

Faxes

Some post offices have a fax service but this involves a lot of form-filling and waiting around. Most major hotels also have fax services. Otherwise, try the following phone, fax and telex centre.

MATÁV Pont Telepont
V. Petőfi Sándor utca 17-19 (485 6612/www.matav.hu). M3 Ferenciek tere. **Open** 9am-8pm Mon-Fri; 10am-3pm Sat. **Credit** DC, MC, V. **Map** p249 C4.
Branches: Duna Plaza, XIII. Váci út 178 (237 8031); Mammut Center,

II. Lövőház utca 2-6 (345 7451); Westend City Center, V. Váci út 1-3 (8238 7616).

Time

Hungary is on Central European Time, which means that it's one hour ahead of GMT, six hours ahead of US Eastern Standard Time and nine hours ahead of US Pacific Standard Time.

Tipping & VAT

There are no fixed rules about tipping in Hungary but it's usual to leave about ten to 15 per cent for waiters in restaurants and bars.

Some restaurants add a ten per cent service charge, in which case don't feel obliged to give any tip or just round up the bill. As you pay, tell the waiter either how much your rounded-up amount comes to or how much change you'd like back. Saying *köszönöm* (thank you) as you hand over a note means you are expecting them to keep all the change. The same rule applies to taxi drivers. It's also customary to tip hairdressers, beauticians, cloakroom attendants, repairmen, changing room attendants at baths and swimming pools, and even doctors and dentists.

Value added tax (*ÁFA*) is normally included in the price of goods and services and ranges between 12.5 and 25 per cent. For VAT refunds *see p219* **Customs.**

Toilets

There are public toilets at various locations, for which you'll have to pay a small fee (usually Ft50-Ft100) to an attendant. Look for WC or Toilette signs: *Hölgyek* (Ladies) and *Urák* (Gents). The quality of toilets in the more down-market bars leaves a lot to be desired. It's often easier to pop

into a smarter bar or a fast-food restaurant, although they might also charge a fee if you are not a customer.

Tourist information

The best place is Tourinform. Other national tourist agencies can also help, though not necessarily with a smile. Services are often duplicated. IBUSZ is the best agency for accommodation. Express is essentially a student travel agency. In addition to its offices, Tourinform has set up 11 'info-touch' terminals at different points around town.

Cooptourist
VI. Nyugati tér 1-2 (312 3621/ www.cooptourist.hu). M3 Nyugati pu./tram 4, 6. **Open** 9am-4pm Mon-Fri. **No credit cards. Map** p246 D2.
Money exchange, information, tours, holidays, flights.
Branches: V. Kossuth Lajos tér 13-15 (332 6387); VI. Bajcsy-Zsilinszki út 17 (311 7034).

Express
V. Semmelweis utca 1-3 (266 6188). M1, M2, M3 Deák tér. **Open** 8.30am-4.30pm Mon-Fri. **No credit cards. Map** p246 C3.
Friendly staff, flights, student cards, youth hostel cards.

IBUSZ
V. Ferenciek tere 10 (485 2700). M3 Ferenciek tere. **Open** 9am-5.30pm Mon-Fri; 9am-noon Sat. **Credit** AmEx, MC, V. **Map** p249 C4
Hungary's oldest tourist agency can book rooms, organise tours and provide information as well as the usual travel agency services.
Branches: II. Margit körút 5 (212 4825); V. Roosevelt tér 2 (485 0933).

Tourinform
V. Sütő utca 2 (438 8080/ 24hr hotline 06 80 660 044/ www.hungarytourism.hu). M1, M2, M3 Deák tér/tram 47, 49. **Open** 8am-8pm daily. **Map** p249 C4.
Staff are helpful and multilingual, and can provide you with information on travel, sightseeing and entertainment.

Directory

One-offs The Gabor sisters

Of all the scientists, film stars and musicians, the most famous Hungarians are two stunning Budapest sisters who early on recognised that fame is its own best reward. The Gabor sisters, Zsa Zsa and Eva, were famous for being famous.

Zsa Zsa, Eva and their sister Magdi (whose claim to fame is that she was the third Gabor sister) were all born in Budapest. Nobody will ever know exactly when, given that the Gabor sisters absolutely never revealed their ages – a routine that dovetailed nicely with an early Magyar attraction to advanced plastic surgery. Brought to the United States on the eve of World War II, the girls were taught by their mother, Jolie Gabor, that the road to fame and success was lined with the diamond necklaces of very rich husbands.

Zsa Zsa left for Hollywood, appearing in minor European femme fatale roles. In 1943 she married hotel magnate Conrad Hilton, the first in a winning streak of eight high-profile marriages that would make her the most wealthy of the sisters. Her film career, however, floundered except for parts in the classic *Queen of Outer Space* and appearing as the villainess Minerva in the final episode of the 1960s TV series *Batman*. But in matrimony Zsa Zsa found her true talent, immortalised in comments such as: 'I want a man who is kind and understanding. Is that too much to ask of a millionaire?' and: 'I am a great housekeeper. Every time I leave a man I keep his house.'

Eva was the younger sister, and also the one with real talent. Her first marriage, to Greta Garbo's physician, ended after only a few years but did establish her as a Hollywood presence. Overshadowed by Zsa Zsa through the 1940s, Eva married millionaire Charles Isaacs and bided her time before truly blossoming in the 1950s in films like *The Last Time I Saw Paris* and *Gigi*. She even found time to publish her 1954 autobiography, *Orchids and Salami*, the title referring to the only two items always found in her house. Eva did possess a sharp sense of humour, however, and this was revealed when she accepted the role of Lisa Douglas in the 1960s TV comedy *Green Acres*. Eva played a rich Hungarian war bride taken by husband Eddie Arnold to live on a small rural farm. Cloaked in feather boas and designer chiffon while wielding a pitchfork, she parlayed her thick Hungarian accent into an American television cliché. American-Hungarians wildly embraced Eva as the only Magyar voice in television, since she always spoke Hungarian to her cute barnyard co-star, Arnold the Pig.

Both Zsa Zsa and Eva became regulars on the early television talk and gameshow circuit – they were masters of the rich divorcee one-liner, strong and empowered women in a decidedly pre-feminist age. Eva went on to maintain her comedic career, working for charities, developing a wig company and taking a deep interest in the welfare of her fans, whom she treated like family. Time was not so graceful to Zsa Zsa, however, who developed a nasty serial tendency towards traffic policemen, reserving a snarling contempt for judges and court officers trying to process her case(s). Stories hit the press of her spending time in overnight detention near her Florida home.

Eva passed away after a brief illness in 1998. In his eulogy, co-star Eddie Arnold told of asking her to refrain from wearing feather boas, since so many birds had to die to make one. Eva replied: 'Dahlink, feathers don't come from birds! They come from pillows!'

Branches: V. Vörösmarty tér 6 (24hrs daily; 235 4480); VII. Király utca 93 (352 1433); VI. Liszt Ferenc tér 11 (322 4098); VI. Nyugati station, main hall (302 8580).

Visas & immigration

Although laws will change completely after Hungary has become a member state of the EU in May 2004, the regulations enacted in 2002 are in force till then. Citizens of the United States, Canada and almost every European country (apart from Turkey and Albania) can stay in Hungary for up to 90 days without a visa; only a passport is required. Citizens of Australia and South Africa still need visas, which are valid for up to 30 days. Anyone who wishes to stay longer than 90 days must have a residence visa (except UK citizens who can stay for six months without it) for the first year of their residence. Residence visas must be obtained from the Hungarian consulate in your country (except UK citizens who can get it in Hungary). Please note that the process of issuing it might take two months. Residence visas are valid for one year and must be renewed prior to their expiration dates. For a second year you'll have to apply for a separate residence permit, which is valid for another year. Then you may be eligible to obtain a residence permit for a longer period of time.

Requirements for a residence permit include a work permit, a legal permanent residence, an AIDS test, a chest X-ray, numerous value stamps that you buy at post offices, countless application forms and passport photos, your passport and official translations of every foreign language document with stamps on them.

If you're not working in Hungary, but would like to live here, then you should apply for the residence visa based on your financial status, which means that you'll need to prove, with the assistance of a recent bank account statement, that you have enough wherewithal to reside in Hungary without having recourse to work.

For foreign citizens who have no Hungarian spouse or parents, the process of obtaining Hungarian citizenship takes about eight years. First, you must have a residence visa for one year and a separate residence permit for two years. Then you can apply for an immigration certificate, which takes about a year to get. After four years with the certificate, you can apply for a Hungarian passport.

If you have Hungarian parents, you can apply for a local passport after one year of legal residence in Hungary. If you're married to a Hungarian, you can apply for an immigration certificate after you've lived in Hungary with a residence permit or visa for a year, but you need to have been married to the Hungarian person for two years before applying for the immigration

certificate. The certificate takes about a year to get, and then you must wait another three years before applying for a local passport. *See also p235* **Working in Budapest**.

Water

The water in Hungary is clean and safe to drink. In some old houses there are still lead pipes, so you should run the tap for a few minutes before drinking.

Weights & measures

Hungary has its own unique system for measuring out solids and liquids. A *deka* is ten grams; a *deci* is ten centilitres. In a bar, for example, you might be asked whether you want *két deci* or *három deci* (0.2 or 0.3 litres) of whatever drink you've just ordered. Wine in bars (but not in restaurants) is priced by the *deci*. At a fruit stall, if you want 300 grams of tomatoes, you'd ask for 30 dekas – *harminc (30) deka paradicsomot*.

When to go

Although Budapest can be icy cold in winter and infernally hot in summer, the climate is basically agreeable.

Spring

Average temperature 2°C-10°C in March; 11°C-22°C in May. May is probably the most pleasant month in the city, before the influx of tourists begins. Winter attire gets discarded, though rain showers can sometimes dampen spirits.

Summer

Average temperature 16°C-32°C. Most Hungarians leave

Budapest for the Balaton or their weekend house. It can get very hot, especially during July. If there's a breeze off the Danube it's pleasant – if not, you can expect a pall of pollution.

Autumn

Average temperature 7°C-23°C. The weather is lovely in September, but it starts to get cold in October when everything moves inside and the heating gets turned on.

Winter

Average temperature -4°C-4°C. Winters are cold and quite long, but not unbearably so: the air is very dry and the central heating is good. Snow usually falls a few times, giving Budapest a different light. Smog can descend if there's no breeze to blow away the fumes from the coal used for heating.

Public holidays

New Year's Day; 15 March, national holiday; Easter Monday; 1 May, Labour Day; Whit Monday; 20 August, St Stephen's Day; 23 October, Remembrance Day; 25, 26 December.

There's usually something open on most holidays apart from the evening of 24 December when even the non-stops stop. New Year's Eve is very lively, as is St Stephen's Day on 20 August, with fireworks launched from Gellért Hill (*see pp142-145*).

Women

Although men and women are equal by law in Hungary, there are countless problems – from wage differentials to sexual harassment at work, unfair division of labour and domestic violence. Women's organisations have been set up

Directory

since 1989 to help solve these problems, but the 'feminist' is still an ugly word in Hungary. Feminists are seen as a bunch of militant, man-hating masculine women who fight for something that most Hungarian women think they already have: equality. The 'new' values which were imposed upon the traditional division of labour by the Communist regime meant that women kept their traditional roles, but were also suddenly expected to work eight hours a day outside the home. Thus were the problems of 'emancipation' solved in Hungary in the 1950s.

Meanwhile, women were made to believe that driving tractors meant that they'd achieved equality with the stronger sex. By 1967, when it had become obvious that many women were exhausted with the double shift, the three-year childcare allowance system came in. As fathers were not expected, and until 1982 were not allowed, to stay at home with their children as primary carers, women's careers suffered. Women also did all the housework, teaching children traditional roles.

With the women's movement this has started to change. Abortion is legal and accessible, women's wages are slowly rising, sexual harassment and wife beating are more often reported and punished by law, and more men do the housework. But the old values still surface, such as sexist jibes, gentlemanly courtesy, odd looks if you enter a bar alone and macho attitudes.

Association of Hungarian Women

Magyar Nők Szövetsége
VI. Andrássy út 124 (331 9734). M1 Hősök tere. **Open** 10am-3pm Mon-Fri. President Judit Thorma. **Map** p247 E2.
Now independent, this was the original Communist-era association, so not particularly radical. It has 40 member organisations and 500 members striving for equal opportunity and participation.

Feminist Network

Feminista Hálózat
Budapest 1399, PO Box 701/1092. The first real grass-roots campaign group for women in Hungary, the Network organises meetings, training and campaigning sessions and publishes a quarterly magazine, *Nőszemély* (The Female Person), focusing on the social and political situation of women in contemporary Hungary.

A tale of two cities

Arthur Phillips's bestselling novel, *Prague*, is a semi-autobiographical exploration of expat life in the Budapest of the early 1990s. Many of its peers still live and work in the city – without having written a successful novel.

Few expat journalists admit to reading the book, let alone liking it, but every local writer has been talking about it – on email lists and weblogs, at the trendy cafés on Liszt Ferenc tér and at the Turkish baths. And nobody could remember even meeting the author.

For them it was irritating enough that Phillips named his novel *Prague*. The two cities are rivals – at least in the minds of expatriates. Prague got all the glory, despite its boho buskers and avant-garde readings by third-rate Hemingways.

Even more galling was the book's quite inexplicable success. Within less than a month of publication, in the summer of 2002, *Prague* was one of the 5,000 top-selling books on Amazon.

In a roundabout way, it was the fulfilment of a fairy tale that the expat media tribe had helped create. Prague (or Budapest?) was supposed to be the 'Paris of the 1990s', the citadel of a new Lost Generation of expatriate artists, writers and thinkers. It was all myth.

For one, a post-Communist capital lacked the sheer gravitas of the City of Lights. It was a different age, and a budding writer in Budapest would simply find it easier to make his name as a foreign correspondent here. Many did. But many more secretly nursed a desire to write that One Great Novel. How could it be that it was Arthur Phillips – someone whom nobody had heard of?

Envy aside, *Prague* is a damn good read. From the opening pages, Phillips captures the cynicism, opportunism and naive enthusiasm of the day. You had to be there, but if you weren't this is the book. Those who know the Magyars will catch a few obvious gaffes (a Hungarian crowd would never applaud a parody of their national anthem). But that's missing the point. Phillips is writing about the transient, superficial world of early 1990s expat Budapest – and in this he most certainly succeeds.

When he was eventually tracked down, it came to light that Arthur Phillips was in Budapest at the time. He never even tried to learn the language, and wrote his book in Paris. His original title was *Budapest* – but he couldn't attract a publisher until he changed its name to *Prague*.

MONA Hungarian Women's Foundation

Magyarországi Női Alapítvány
1357 Budapest, PO Box 453/277;
XIII. Tátra utca 46 (329 8755).
Tram 4, 6. **Open** 9am-5pm
Mon-Fri. Contact Violetta Zentai.
Map p246 C2.
Draws together women from other
campaign organisations with
meetings for mayors, journalists
and businesswomen.

NaNE – Women United Against Violence

NaNE – Nők a Nőkért Együtt az
Erőszak Ellen
IX. Vámház körút 7. Postal
address: 1447 Budapest, PO Box
502 (337 2865/helpline 06 80 505
101). M3 Kálvin tér/tram 47, 49.
Open *office* 9am-5pm, *helpline*
6-10pm daily. Contact Antonia
Burrow. **Map** p249 D5.
Rape and domestic violence are
low-profile issues in Hungary.
There's no law against marital
rape and little sympathy for
rape victims. NaNE gives
information and support to
battered and raped women and
children, campaigns for changes
in law, and challenges social
attitudes to violence.

Ombudswoman

Ombudsnő
VIII. Múzeum körút 4C (266 9833
ext 2308/hotline 06 80 505 303).
M2 Astoria/tram 47, 49. **Open**
2-6pm Thur. *Hotline* 4-7pm Mon,
Wed, Fri. Contact Maria Adarnik.
Map D4.
Helps put women in touch with
psychiatrists, lawyers and social
workers. Hotline and gender
studies centre, including a library.

International Women's Associations

British Women's Association of Budapest

The charity group provides
services to children's and women's
organisations in Budapest. It also
helps British women adapt to life
in Hungary, meet other women
with similar interests or with
children of similar ages, and find a
range of social activities. Meetings
are held at the Marriott Hotel on

the last Friday of every month
from 10am to noon. Membership
required, but guests are welcome
at the meetings. Contact Alison
Lambert on 387 7868 or Mandy
Morris on 200 2500.

International Women's Club Foundation of Budapest

I. Krisztina körút 59B (225 3078/
www.iwcf.org.hu).
This group aims to promote good
relations with the international
community and the host country.
It also supports charity activities
and foundations. Meetings are
held monthly. Membership
required. Contact Dagmar Ohl,
hospitality chair, on 424 0200.

North American Women's Association of Budapest (NAWA)

II. Kuruclesi út 13B
(www.awa.org.hu).
Meetings are held at the American
Club. Membership required.
Contact Dayle Holleger (274 4733/
rholleger@hotmail.com),
Tammy Hodges (355 1450/
thodgeshu@yahoo.com) or
the NAWA Chair Sharlene
Helfgott (200 6499/
shar.helfgott@axelero.hu).

Professional Women's Association of Budapest (PWA)

Meetings are held on the second
Monday of every month. The
meetings are open to any
professional women. For more
information contact Erika
Clements at pwa@nextra.hu.

Working in Budapest

According to the law, anyone
entering Hungary for the
purpose of working in the
country must already have a
work permit and a residence
visa, except managing
directors and board directors,
who must obtain the
Hungarian corporate
documents and residence visa.

It's necessary to start the
whole process in your home
country, because you will

need to obtain a residence visa
from the Hungarian embassy
there. The work permit is
normally your employer's
responsibility. You'll need to
provide such documents as
translated educational
certificates (usually a
university diploma) and a
translated medical certificate.
Please note that they only
accept documents translated
by the Országos Fordító Iroda.
The medical certificate
includes having your lungs
and blood pressure checked.
The employee submits the
work permit to the Hungarian
embassy in his or her home
country. The terms of your
work permit require you to
have a medical examination
every year.

In addition, a more
thorough medical examination
is also required when you're
applying for your residence
permit for the second year of
residence in Hungary. This
exam will include X-rays and
blood tests, as well as a stool
sample and skin examination.

Capital City Labour Centre

Fővárosi Munkaügyi Központ
VIII. Kisfaludy utca 11 (303 0720).
Tram 4, 6. **Open** 8.30am-3pm
Mon-Thur; 8.30am-1pm Fri.
Map p250 E5.

Országos Fordító Iroda

VI. Bajza utca 52 (269 5730).
M1 Bajza utca. **Open** 9am-4pm
Mon-Thur; 9am-12.30pm Fri.
Map p247 E2.

Settlers Hungary

II. Ady Endre utca 19 (212
5989/212 8146). **Open** 8am-5pm
Mon-Fri. **No credit cards.**
Can arrange work permits and
residence permits.

State Public Health & Medical Administration

Állami Népegészségügyi és Tiszti
Orvosi Szolgálat (ÁNTSZ)
XIII. Váci út 174 (329 0490).
M3 Újpest-Városkapu. **Open**
8am-noon Mon-Fri; 1-3pm
Mon-Thur.

Directory

Hungarian Vocabulary

Nowhere else in Europe will the traveller be confronted with as great a linguistic barrier as in Hungary. Basic words bear no resemblance to any major European language.

The good news is that pronunciation of common words is easy – and the long ones, such as *viszontlátásra*, ('goodbye') can be shortened (*viszlat*). *Köszönöm*, thank you, can be rendered as *köszi*. *Szervusz* is an all-purpose greeting, more formal than *szia*, both hello and goodbye.

For menu terms, *see p96*.

Pronunciation

The stress is always on the first syllable. Accents denote a longer vowel. Double consonants are pronounced longer (*kettő, szebb*). Add 't' to nouns if they are the object of the sentence: 'I would like a beer' is *egy sört kérek,* (*sör* + t).

a – like 'o' in hot
á – like 'a' in father
é – like 'a' in day
í – like 'ee' in feet
ö – like 'ur' in pleasure
ü – like 'u' in French tu
ő, ű – similar to ö and ü but longer
sz – like 's' in sat
cs – like 'ch' in such
zs – like 's' in casual
gy – like 'd' in dew
ly – like 'y' in yellow
ny – like 'n' in new
ty – like 't' in tube
c – like 'ts' in roots
s – like 'sh' in wash

Useful expressions

Yes *Igen*
No *Nem*
Maybe *Talán*
(I wish you) good day *Jó napot (kívánok)* (formal)
Hello *Szervusz* (informal); *szia* (familiar)
Goodbye *Viszontlátásra*
How are you? *Hogy van?* (formal); *hogy vagy?* (familiar)
I'm fine *Jól vagyok*
Please *Kérem*

Thank you *Köszönöm*
Excuse me *Bocsánat*
I would like *Kérek...* (an object)
I would like (to do something) *Szeretnék...* (add infinitive)
Where is...? *Hol van...?*
Where is the toilet? *Hol van a wc?* (wc vay tzay)
Where is a good/not too expensive restaurant? *Hol van egy jó/nem túl drága étterem?*
When? *Mikor?* Who? *Ki?*
Why? *Miért?* How? *Hogyan?*
Is there...? *Van...?*
There is none *Nincs*
How much is it? *Mennyibe kerül?*
We're paying separately *Külön-külön fizetünk*
Open *Nyitva;* closed *zárva*
Entrance *Bejárat;* exit *kijárat*
Push *Tolni;* pull *húzni*
Men's *Férfi;* women's *női*
Good *Jó;* bad *rossz*
I like it *Ez tetszik*
I don't like it *Ez nem tetszik*
I don't speak Hungarian *Nem beszélek Magyarul*
Do you speak English? *Beszél angolul?*
What is your name? *Mi a neve?*
My name is... *A nevem...*
I am (English/American) *(angol/amerikai) vagyok*
I feel ill *Rosszul vagyok*
Doctor *Orvos*
Pharmacy *Patika/gyógyszertár*
Hospital *Kórház*
Ambulance *Mentőautó*
Police *rendőrség*

Getting around

Railway station *Pályaudvar*
Airport *repülőtér*
Arrival *Érkezés*
Departure *Indulás*
Inland *Belföldi*
International *Külföldi*
Ticket office *Pénztár*
I would like two tickets *Két jegyet kérek*
When is the train to Vienna? *Mikor indul a bécsi vonat?*
Here *Itt*
There *Ott*
Towards *Felé*
From here *Innen*
From there *Onnan*
To the right *Jobbra*
To the left *Balra*
Straight ahead *Egyenesen*
Near *Közel/far Messze*

Accommodation

Hotel *Szalloda*
A single room *Egyágyas szoba*
A double room *Kétágyas szoba*
Per night *Egy éjszakára*
Shower *Zuhany*
Bath *Fürdőkád*
Breakfast *Reggeli*
Do you have anything cheaper? *Van valami olcsóbb?*
Air-conditioning *Légkondicionálás*

Time

Now *Most*
Later *Később*
Today *Ma*
Tomorrow *Holnap*
Morning *Reggel*
Late morning *Délelőtt*
Early afternoon *Délután*
Evening *Este*
Night *Éjszaka*
(At) one o'clock *Egy óra (kor)*

Numbers

Zero *Nulla*
One *Egy*
Two *Kettő* (note *két*, used with an object: *két kávét* two coffees)
Three *Három*
Four *Négy*
Five *Öt*
Six *Hat*
Seven *Hét*
Eight *Nyolc*
Nine *Kilenc*
Ten *Tíz*
Eleven *Tizenegy*
Twenty *Húsz*
Thirty *Harminc*
Forty *Negyven*
Fifty *Ötven*
Sixty *Hetven*
Eighty *Nyolcvan*
Ninety *Kilencven*
One hundred *Száz*
One thousand *Ezer*

Days of the week

Monday *Hétfő*
Tuesday *Kedd*
Wednesday *Szerda*
Thursday *Csütörtök*
Friday *Péntek*
Saturday *Szombat*
Sunday *Vasárnap*

Directory

Further Reference

Books

Biography, memoir & travel

Fermor, Patrick Leigh: *Between the Woods and the Water/A Time of Gifts* In the 1930s Fermor hiked from Holland to Istanbul, stopping off in Hungary along the way. These evocative memoirs are the result.
Márai, Sándor: *Memoir of Hungary 1944-48* Insightful memoir by exiled Magyar author.
Pressburger, Giorgio & Nicola: *Homage to the Eighth District* Authentic and touching recollections of Jewish society before and during World War II.

Children

Dent, Bob *Budapest for Children* Slim volume full of suggestions for keeping the little ones entertained.
Gárdonyi, Géza *Eclipse of the Crescent Moon* Boys' own adventure about the 1552 Turkish siege of Eger.
Molnar, Ferenc *The Paul Street Boys* Turn-of-the-century juvenile classic of boys' gang warfare over a derelict District VIII building site.

Food & drink

Gundel, Károly: *Gundel's Hungarian Cookbook* The best Hungarian recipe book by the man who invented Hungarian cuisine.
Lang, George: *The Cuisine of Hungary* Detailed study of the development of Magyar cuisine.
Liddell, Alex: *The Wines of Hungary* A useful introduction to the art of Hungarian viticulture.

History, architecture, art & culture

A Golden Age: Art & Society in Hungary 1896-1914 Colourful compendium, with works by all the Hungarian greats. Drab essays, all the same.
Búza, Péter: *Bridges of the Danube* Everything you could ever want to know about Budapest's famous bridges, with occasional absurd asides.
Crankshaw, Edward: *The Fall of the House of Habsburg* Solid, and solidly anti-Hungarian, account of the dynasty's demise.
Garton Ash, Timothy: *We the People: The Revolution of 1989 Witnessed in Warsaw, Budapest, Berlin and Prague* Instant history by this on-the-spot Oxford academic.
Gerő, András: *Modern Hungarian Society in the Making* Collection of essays on the last 150 years of Hungarian political, social and cultural history. Excellent piece on Széchenyi.
Hanak, Peter & Schorske, Carl E: *The Garden and the Workshop: Essays on the cultural history of Vienna and Budapest* Comparative cultural history of the Golden Age in the two capitals of the Austro-Hungarian Empire.
Heathcote, Edwin: *Budapest: A Guide to 20th Century Architecture* Portable, clear and concise guide.
Kontler, László: *Millennium in Central Europe: A History of Hungary* The most thorough account in English of the Magyars.
Lendvai, Paul: *The Hungarians: A Thousand Years of Victory in Defeat* Not as comprehensive as Kontler, but a great read.
Litván, György: *The Hungarian Revolution of 1956: Reform, Revolt and Repression 1953-1963* Five Hungarian members of the Institute for the History of the Hungarian Revolution offer blow-by-blow accounts of the uprising.
Lukács, John: *Budapest 1900* Extremely readable and erudite literary and historical snapshot of Budapest at its height. The best book about the city's history and culture currently in print.
Taylor, AJP: *The Habsburg Monarchy 1809-1918* Terse history of the twilight of the Habsburg era.

Language

Payne, Jerry: *Colloquial Hungarian* More entertaining than most language books, drawing on interesting dialogues. Grammar introduced rapidly early on.

Literature

Ady, Endre: *Neighbours of the Night: Selected Short Stories* Prose pieces somewhat stiffly rendered in English, but at least they translate – unlike his gloomy but stirring poetry.
Bánffy, Miklós: *They Were Counted/They Were Found Wanting/They Were Divided* Acclaimed Transylvanian trilogy recalls the lost world of Hungarian aristocracy as it falls apart.
Eszterházy, Péter: *A Little Hungarian Pornography/Helping Verbs of the Heart/The Glance of Countess Hahn-Hahn/She Loves Me/Celestial Harmonies* One of Hungary's most popular contemporary writers, Eszterházy's postmodern style represents a radical break with Hungarian literary tradition.
Fischer, Tibor: *Under the Frog* Seriously funny and impeccably researched Booker-nominated romp through Hungarian basketball, Stalinism and the 1956 revolution.
Kertész, Imre: *Fateless/Kaddish for a Child Not Born* Accounts of the Holocaust and its effects by the 2002 Nobel Laureate for Literature.
Konrád, George: *Stonedial* Covering the period of the Soviet occupation into the 1990s.
A Feast in the Garden Highly autobiographical novel leads from village to Holocaust to Communist tyranny.
Kosztolányi, Dezső: *Skylark/Anna Édes/Darker Muses, The Poet Nero* Kosztolányi, who wrote these novels in the 1920s, was probably the best Magyar prose writer of the last century. Hungarians claim his translations of Winnie-the-Pooh are even better than the original. But they would.
Krasznahorkai, László: *The Melancholy of Resistance* A tale of events in a tiny village is the basis for the film *Werckmeister Harmonies*. See p155 **Tarred with a fine brush**.
Örkény, István: *One Minute Stories* Vignettes of contemporary Budapest: absurd, ironic, hilarious.
Phillips, Arthur: *Prague* Story of expats in 1990s Budapest. *See p234* **A tale of two cities**.

Directory

Advertisers' Index

Please refer to relevant sections for full details

Maps

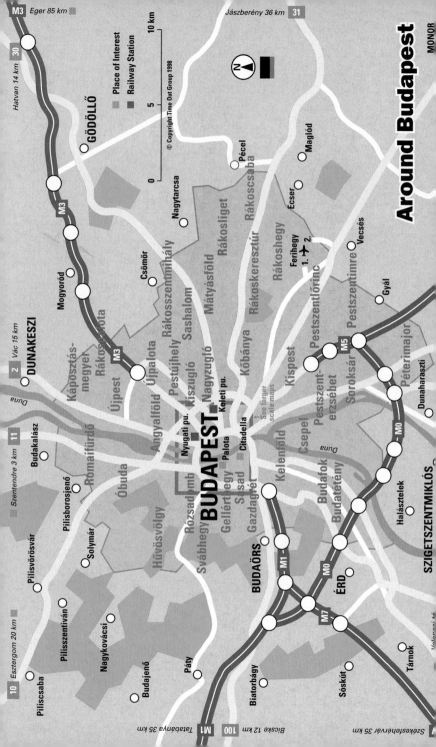

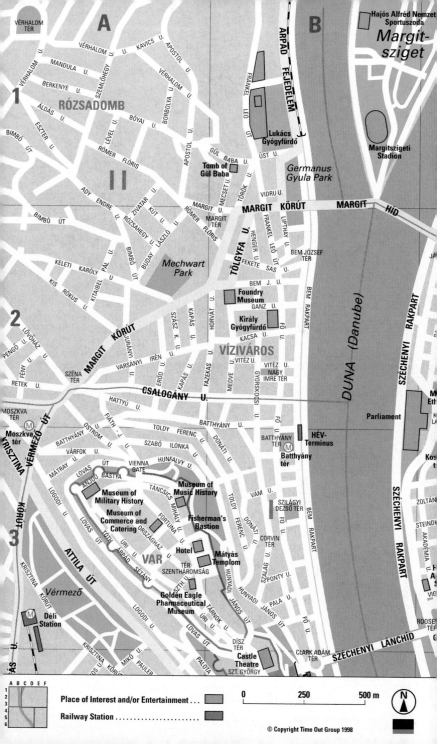

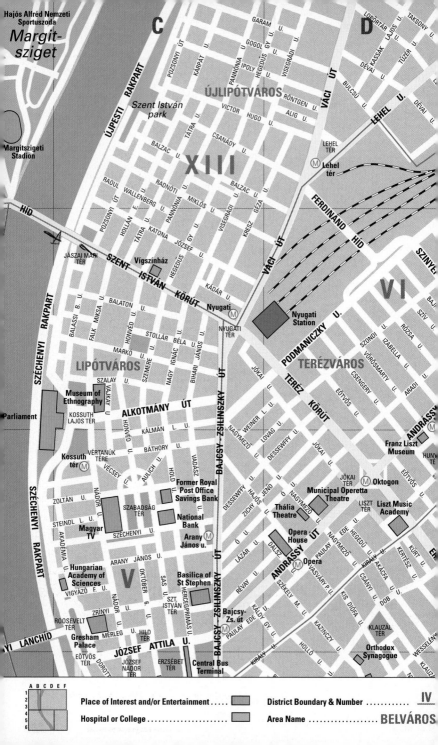

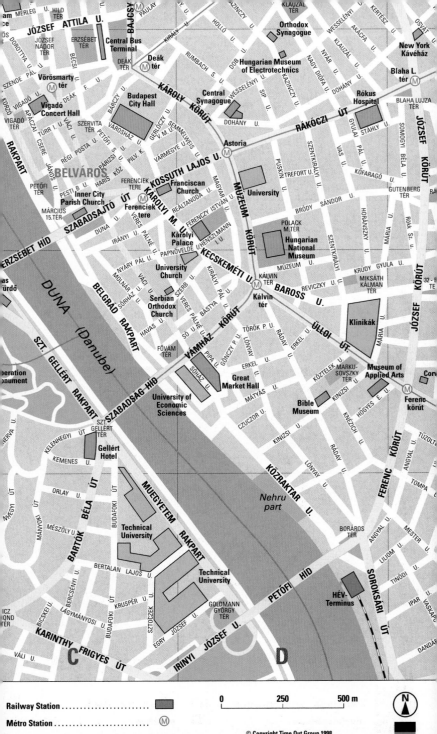

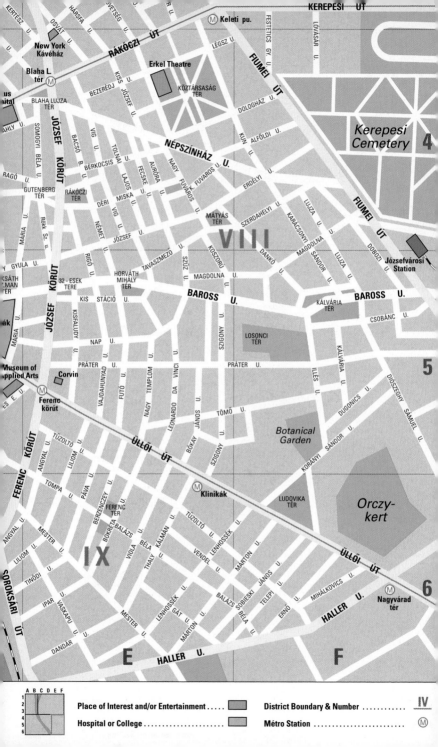

Street Index

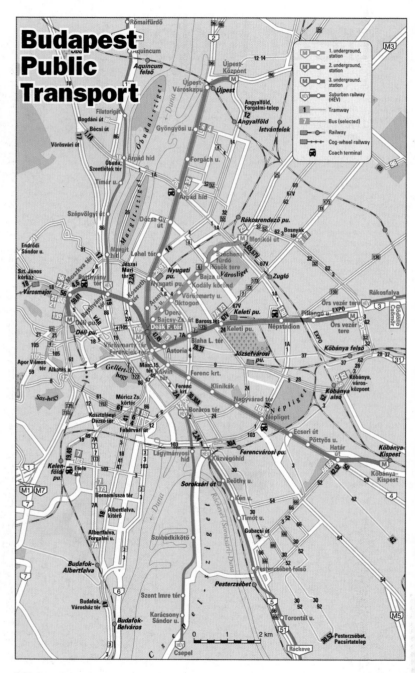

Budapest Public Transport